# BIRDS IN THE
# AUSTRALIAN
# HIGH COUNTRY

To
Harry Temple Watts

# BIRDS IN THE AUSTRALIAN HIGH COUNTRY

Fully Revised Edition

Edited by H. J. Frith

Division of Wildlife and Rangelands
Research, CSIRO

Illustrated by Betty Temple Watts

ANGUS & ROBERTSON PUBLISHERS

ANGUS & ROBERTSON PUBLISHERS
London · Sydney · Melbourne

First published in Australia by A. H. & A. W. Reed, 1969
Revised 1976
This revised edition published by
Angus & Robertson Publishers in 1984

Copyright © 1969, 1976 Betty Temple Watts and
estate of H. J. Frith

National Library of Australia
Cataloguing-in-publication data.
Birds in the Australian high country.

   Rev. ed.
   Previous ed.: Terrey Hills, N.S.W.: Reed, 1976.
   Bibliography.
   Includes index.
   ISBN 0 207 14464 8.

   1. Birds — Australia. I. Frith, H. J. (Harold James),
   1921-1982. (Series: Australian natural science library).

598.2994

Typeset in 11pt Baskerville by Setrite Typesetters Limited
Printed in Hong Kong

# FOREWORD

*Birds in the Australian High Country* covers the south-eastern highlands of the Commonwealth, a region that extends from Goulburn, New South Wales to Melbourne, Victoria and which encompasses the Australian Capital Territory, the Snowy Mountains, and other ranges in the Southern Alps. Canberra is the main centre of population in the region covered by this book. The Australian national capital started to grow at a phenomenal rate shortly after World War II, and many of the people who came to live in Canberra already had an interest in birds. Some merely wanted help in identifying the species they saw in their gardens and the country around, but others brought with them valuable knowledge and field experience. A few came as professionals, to research posts.

In addition to the indefatigable Mr Stephen Wilson, the amateurs who brought knowledge and experience from which local bird studies immediately benefited included two senior members of the staff of the US Embassy. Canberra ornithologists have not forgotten their considerable debt to Mr William Belton and Mr Donald Lamm; and I have little doubt that those friendly and energetic Americans, wherever they are to-day, remember our hills and forests with a touch of nostalgia.

Foremost among those who came here as professionals were Dr H. J. Frith, fresh from his Riverina duck investigations, who was to succeed me as leader of the CSIRO Wildlife Research team, and Dr Robert Carrick, knowledgeable on banding, bird lore in general, and starlings in particular.

Ornithological activity in and around Canberra built up quickly after 1950, with interest stimulating interest and a growing number of skilled observers in the field. Inevitably the idea was conceived of a handbook on the local birds; and inevitably the conception grew in scope until it was to include the birds of the whole south-eastern highland region.

The book really got under way when Robert Carrick persuaded Mrs Temple Watts to come to Canberra and work on the plates. From then on the problem was to produce a text worthy of her illustrations, for Betty Temple Watts can surely claim rank among the great bird portraitists.

I have several times encountered her in Harry Frith's domain, with sketchbook in hand, ready to spend an hour or two patiently watching and sketching a new bird that has been brought in to one of the aviaries or enclosures. Her sketches always show her intense preoccupation with birds as living things; and only those who have seen her at work can appreciate the trouble she takes to make her portraits true to life, in the precise meaning of that rather hackneyed phrase.

Knowing the way she set about preparing the illustrations for this book, I was surprised to learn how Betty Temple Watts started her bird portraiture. She tells me she always had an urge to put names to the creatures she encountered in the bush. She was dissatisifed with the figures in the bird books available and so, armed with lists of species she was likely to see on fishing expeditions with her husband, she set about making her own album of bird paintings, working at first entirely from museum skins and photographs. It was not long, however, before the skins went back to their cabinets, and her books began to be filled with sketches of birds going about their daily business—preening, flying, perching, feeding. She had learned that silhouette and pose, which can crystallise a bird's individuality, are just as important for identification in the field as colour pattern; and if they are wrongly drawn a portrait can be positively misleading, apart from appearing slightly ridiculous to the knowing eye.

Through this book, many people will be able to appreciate and benefit by Betty Temple Watts's careful and devoted artistry. The text, a co-operative effort in which Dr Frith acted as inspirer and pace-setter, has the quality called for in a work of scientific reference. The combination of text and illustrations will, I am convinced, ensure for *Birds in the Australian High Country* a very important place in Australian ornithological literature.

*Francis Ratcliffe*
*Canberra*

# CONTENTS

CONTENTS

# ILLUSTRATIONS

*Other plates appear between pages 16 and 17*

*Figures and maps*

# PREFACE

When the first edition of this book was published in 1969 systematic research on the birds of the south-eastern tablelands had been established only recently but since then it has increased greatly in volume. In addition, up-to-date checklists of Australian birds now have been published and there are several excellent, illustrated accounts of the birds of the whole continent and of separate families. The time is now ripe for this revised and updated edition.

SCOPE: This book brings together information that has accumulated in the notebooks of the contributors and, in this way, is, mostly, "first hand". The book deals with the birds that an observer might be expected to encounter in a day's outing in the highland region between Goulburn, New South Wales, and Melbourne, Victoria. We have all lived in Canberra and our normal home range finishes at about Kosciusko, so the Australian Capital Territory and its neighbourhood can be referred to as "local". The birds described, however, cover those that are normally found in the south-eastern highlands generally and most of those in the Tasmanian high country also.

In earlier editions we defined the region in terms of altitude and attempted to describe every species that had been recorded, even the rare vagrants. Increasing knowledge has shown this aim to be unrealistic and has made some modification essential. The region dealt with is generally that above 500 m but, on the eastern escarpments, habitats that are more typical of the lowlands creep up to higher altitudes in places and typically low country species are often seen there. In the west, vagrants from the inland come into the area, particularly in drought, and the number of potential visitors is very great.

Because of this the list of birds can never be really complete. We have therefore omitted the intrusion of coastal birds and their habitats, in the east, and some of the vagrants from the west. As this policy has evolved gradually, some of both groups of birds are treated in full and a few are discussed but not illustrated.

NOMENCLATURE: The scientific names of species are those that appear in the *Checklist of the Birds of Australia, Part 1, Non-passerines* by H. T. Condon 1975 and the *Interim List of Australian Songbirds, Passerines* by R. Schodde 1975, as modified and combined in the journal *Emu*, Volume 77, Supplement May 1978.

The English names for birds that we have used are those adopted by CSIRO as those that seem to be the most commonly and widely used name for each species. These differ sometimes from those preferred by the Royal Australasian Ornithologists' Union.

COLOUR PLATES: The plate on which each bird appears is given at the head of its description in the text. Where there is no such reference, that bird has not been illustrated. The keys opposite the colour plates give the approximate length of each bird, its status in summarised form, and the page on which its life history is begun.

July 1980                                                                H. J. Frith


To our great regret Dr Frith suffered a severe heart attack in October 1980, and died on 28 June 1982.

At the time of his illness it was intended that the text of this new edition be updated with a minimum of resetting of lines, and the inclusion of a section containing descriptions of those species recorded in the region since the publication of the first edition in 1969. Fortunately, in late 1982 the publishers decided to reset the entire edition. This has enabled a complete revision of the text, and the placing of all species in a systematic sequence. We believe that the information contained in the book is up-to-date to July 1983.

This fully revised edition covers 281 species, and includes accounts of nine recorded in the region since the previous edition was published in 1976. One species (Yellow-throated Miner) included in earlier editions has been dropped. The supposed occurrence was based on eggs collected by school boys in 1957; the eggs are not now available for checking and we believe that the record was an unlikely one. In previous editions three species of striped-crowned pardalotes were recognized. These are now known to be forms of a single species, the Striated Pardalote, and are treated accordingly.

This edition contains three new plates by Betty Temple Watts. Two illustrate a total of fifteen species recently recorded from the region or not illustrated in previous editions. The other replaces Plate XII, and includes two species of wader not figured previously.

I am grateful to Peter Fullagar and Chris Davey for revising the accounts of waterfowl, and especially Mark Clayton for much assistance with details of the text. Members of the Canberra Ornithologists Group who recorded their observations in *Canberra Bird Notes* made a valuable contribution.

The National Library of Australia, which owns all of the original drawings but the three new ones, through its Director-General Mr Harrison Bryan, generously allowed the use of the drawings for reproduction in this new edition and waived the reproduction fees.

August 1983                                                            John Calaby

# CONTRIBUTORS

The book is the result of the collaboration of many Canberra ornithologists, selected for their knowledge of different birds. Their contributions are identified by initials as listed below:

| | |
|---|---|
| J.H.C. | Dr J. H. Calaby |
| R.C. | Dr R. Carrick |
| G.S.C. | Mr G. S. Chapman |
| M.C. | Mr M. Clayton |
| J.M.F. | Mr J. M. Forshaw |
| H.J.F. | Dr H. J. Frith |
| W.B.H. | Mr W. B. Hitchcock |
| J.L.McK. | Mr J. L. McKean |
| M.G.R. | Dr M. G. Ridpath |
| F.N.R. | Mr F. N. Robinson |
| I.C.R.R. | Mr I. C. R. Rowley |
| K.G.S. | Mr K. G. Simpson |
| E.S. | Mr E. Slater |
| G.F.vT. | Dr G. F. van Tets |
| S.J.W. | Mr S. J. Wilson |

With the exception of Mr S. J. Wilson, a well known Canberra ornithologist who collaborates with the Division in many ways and has done extensive and valuable work with birds on his own account, all are or were officers of the CSIRO Division of Wildlife and Rangelands Research.

The line drawings are by Mr F. Knight and the photographs are from Mr E. Slater, both of the Division of Wildlife and Rangelands Research. Dr D. L. Serventy has advised on distribution matters. The Museum of Victoria has made skins available and we have had access to the Nest Record Scheme of the Royal Australasian Ornithologists' Union. The idea of this handbook was conceived, and the first stages of its preparation supervised, by Dr R. Carrick a former member of the Division.

We have used our friends' data, and also information in some standard reference books without special acknowledgement. These include: *Birds of Western Australia*, by D. L. Serventy and H. M. Whittell; *What Bird is That*, by N. W. Cayley; *Nests and Eggs of Australian Birds*, by A. J. North; *A Handlist of the Birds of Victoria*, by W. R. Wheeler. Mr Mark Clayton has provided valuable editorial assistance at all stages of this edition.

# THE PLATES

1.  Emu *Dromaius novaehollandiae,* 200 cm, adult male, a very rare
    resident, formerly common. Page 22.
2.  Emu, female.
3.  Emu, chick.

Betty Temple Watts 1963

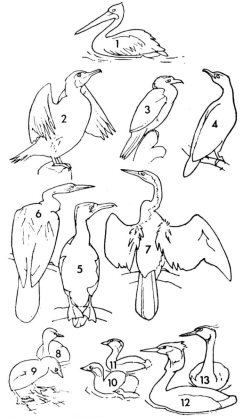

1. Pelican *Pelecanus conspicillatus*, 163 cm, a common resident. Page 28.
2. Black Cormorant *Phalacrocorax carbo*, 79 cm, a common resident. Page 31.
3. Little Pied Cormorant *Phalacrocorax melanoleucos*, 58 cm, a common resident. Page 34.
4. Little Black Cormorant *Phalacrocorax sulcirostris*, 62 cm, a common resident. Page 33.
5. Pied Cormorant *Phalacrocorax varius*, 76 cm, an uncommon visitor. Page 32.
6. Darter *Anhinga melanogaster*, 90 cm, adult male, an uncommon resident. Page 30.
7. Darter, immature.
8. Hoary-headed Grebe *Poliocephalus poliocephalus*, 30 cm, non-breeding plumage, a common resident. Page 25.
9. Hoary-headed Grebe, breeding plumage.
10. Little Grebe *Tachybaptus novaehollandiae*, 28 cm, breeding plumage, a common resident. Page 24.
11. Little Grebe, non-breeding plumage.
12. Great Crested Grebe *Podiceps cristatus*, 50 cm, breeding plumage, an uncommon resident. Page 26.
13. Great Crested Grebe, non-breeding plumage.

B.T.W. 1960

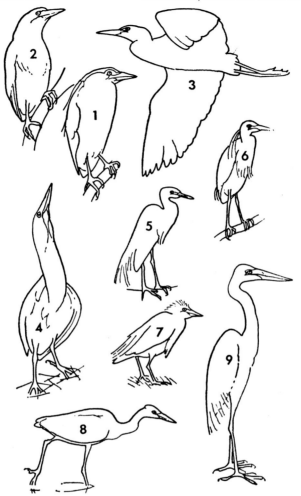

1. Nankeen Night Heron *Nycticorax caledonicus,* 59 cm, adult, a common visitor. Page 41.
2. Nankeen Night Heron, immature.
3. White-necked Heron *Ardea pacifica,* 91 cm, a common visitor. Page 36.
4. Brown Bittern *Botaurus poiciloptilus,* 71 cm, a rare vagrant. Page 42.
5. Plumed Egret *Egretta intermedia,* 62 cm, breeding plumage, an uncommon visitor. Page 39.
6. Little Egret *Egretta garzetta,* 56 cm, breeding plumage, an uncommon visitor. Page 39.
7. Cattle Egret *Ardeola ibis,* 53 cm, breeding plumage, an uncommon visitor. Page 40.
8. White-faced Heron *Ardea novaehollandiae,* 67 cm, a common breeding resident. Page 37.
9. White Egret *Egretta alba,* 83 cm, breeding plumage, a common vagrant. Page 38.

B.T.W. 1960-67

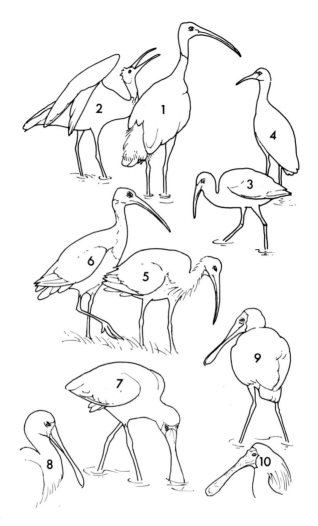

1.   White Ibis *Threskiornis aethiopica*, 71 cm, adult, a common visitor. Page 46.
2.   White Ibis, immature.
3.   Glossy Ibis *Plegadis falcinellus*, 52 cm, adult, an uncommon visitor. Page 47.
4.   Glossy Ibis, immature.
5.   Straw-necked Ibis *Threskiornis spinicollis*, 72 cm, adult, a common visitor. Page 45.
6.   Straw-necked Ibis, immature.
7.   Yellow-billed Spoonbill *Platalea flavipes*, 89 cm, non-breeding plumage, a common visitor. Page 48.
8.   Yellow-billed Spoonbill, breeding plumage.
9.   Royal Spoonbill *Platalea regia*, 76 cm, non-breeding plumage, a common visitor. Page 48.
10.   Royal Spoonbill, breeding plumage.

B.T.W. 1958

1.  Black Duck *Anas superciliosa*, 57 cm, a common breeding resident. Page 54.
2.  Freckled Duck *Stictonetta naevosa*, 56 cm, an uncommon visitor. Page 52.
3.  Hardhead *Aythya australis*, 49 cm, a common visitor, occasionally breeding around Canberra. Page 60.
4.  Grass Whistle-duck *Dendrocygna eytoni*, 50 cm, a rare vagrant. Page 50.
5.  Shoveler *Anas rhynchotis*, 50 cm, adult male, an uncommon breeding resident. Page 57.
6.  Shoveler, adult female.
7.  Grey Teal *Anas gibberifrons*, 45 cm, a very common breeding resident. Page 55.
8.  Chestnut Teal *Anas castanea*, 45 cm, adult male, an uncommon breeding resident. Page 56.
9.  Chestnut Teal, adult female.
10. Pink-eared Duck *Malacorhynchus membranaceus*, 42 cm, a common visitor. Page 58.
11. Blue-billed Duck *Oxyura australis*, 41 cm, adult male, a rare vagrant. Page 63.
12. Blue-billed Duck, adult female.
13. Musk Duck *Biziura lobata*, 66 cm, adult male, a common breeding resident. Page 62.
14. Wood Duck *Chenonetta jubata*, 48 cm, adult male, a very common breeding resident. Page 61.
15. Wood Duck, adult female.
16. Mountain Duck *Tadorna tadornoides*, 67 cm, adult male, a common breeding resident. Page 53.
17. Mountain Duck, adult female.

B.T.W.1967

1. Swamp Harrier *Circus aeruginosus,* 50 cm, an uncommon resident. Page 83.
2. Spotted Harrier *Circus assimilis,* 53 cm, an uncommon vagrant. Page 82.
3. Brown Goshawk *Accipiter fasciatus,* 40-43 cm, adult male, a common resident. Page 75.
4. Brown Goshawk, 46-56 cm, immature female.
5. White-breasted Sea-eagle *Haliacetus leucogaster,* 76 cm, an uncommon resident. Page 80.
6. Sparrowhawk *Accipiter cirrocephalus,* 28-33 cm, an uncommon resident. Page 76.
7. Grey Goshawk *Accipiter novaehollandiae,* 42 cm, a rare resident. Page 74.
8. Wedge-tailed Eagle *Aquila audax,* 90 cm, a common resident. Page 79.
9. Little Eagle *Hieraaetus morphnoides,* 48 cm, an uncommon resident. Page 77.

B.T.W. 1960

1. Whistling Eagle *Haliastur sphenurus,* 53 cm, an uncommon resident. Page 71.
2. Fork-tailed Kite *Milvus migrans,* 52 cm, an uncommon visitor. Page 70.
3. Black-shouldered Kite *Elanus notatus,* 36 cm, adult, a common resident. Page 67.
4,5. Black-shouldered Kite, immature.
6. Peregrine Falcon, *Falco peregrinus,* 38 cm, adult male, an uncommon resident. Page 84.
7. Peregrine Falcon, immature female.
8. Little Falcon *Falco longipennis,* 30 cm, a common resident. Page 85.
9. Kestrel *Falco cenchroides,* 31 cm, adult male, a common resident. Page 90.
10. Kestrel, adult female.
11. Brown Hawk *Falco berigora,* 43 cm, light phase, a common resident. Page 88.
12. Black Falcon *Falco subniger,* 54 cm, adult male, an uncommon visitor. Page 87.

B.T.W. 1960

1. Masked owl *Tyto novaehollandiae,* 38 cm, status unknown, apparently rare. Page 97.
2. Barn Owl *Tyto alba,* 32 cm, an uncommon resident of variable status. Page 95.
3. Tawny Frogmouth *Podargus strigoides,* 46 cm, a common resident. Page 187.
4. Boobook Owl *Ninox novaeseelandiae,* 35 cm, a common resident. Page 94.
5. Owlet-Nightjar *Aegotheles cristatus,* 22 cm, a common resident, but rarely seen. Page 189.
6. Barking Owl *Ninox connivens,* 38-43 cm, resident species, apparently rare. Page 93.
7. White-throated Nightjar *Caprimulgus mystacalis,* 33 cm, rarely recorded around Canberra. Page 190.

B.T.W. 1960

1. King Quail *Coturnix chinensis,* 14 cm, adult male, a rare vagrant. Page 102.
2. King Quail, adult female.
3. Plain Wanderer *Pedionomus torquatus,* 15 cm, adult female, a rare vagrant. Page 106.
4. Plain Wanderer, adult male.
5. Brown Quail *Coturnix australis,* 18 cm, an uncommon visitor. Page 101.
6. Little Quail *Turnix velox,* 14 cm, female, a rare vagrant. Page 104.
7. Painted Quail *Turnix varia,* 20 cm, a common resident. Page 103.
8. Stubble Quail *Coturnix novaezelandiae,* 18 cm, adult male, a common resident. Page 99.
9. Stubble Quail, adult female.

B.T.W
1963-7

1. Brolga *Grus rubicundus,* 116 cm, a rare vagrant, but formerly abundant. Page 109.
2. Australian Bustard *Ardeotis australis,* 114 cm, extinct in the region, but formerly common. Page 107.
3. Black Swan *Cygnus atratus,* 129 cm, a very common resident. Page 51.

B.T.W.
1967

1. Lewin Water Rail *Rallus pectoralis*, 20 cm, adult, status uncertain, probably a rare vagrant. Page 111.
2. Lewin Water Rail, immature.
3. Marsh Crake *Porzana pusilla*, 17 cm, adult, an uncommon visitor. Page 114.
4. Marsh Crake, immature.
5. Spotless Crake *Porzana tabuensis*, 20 cm, an uncommon visitor. Page 114.
6. Spotted Crake *Porzana fluminea*, 17 cm, adult, an uncommon visitor. Page 113.
7. Spotted Crake, immature.
8. Banded Landrail *Rallus philippensis*, 31 cm, an uncommon visitor. Page 112.
9. Coot *Fulica atra*, 38 cm, adult, a common resident. Page 117.
10. Coot, immature.
11. Eastern Swamphen *Porphyrio porphyrio*, 44 cm, a common resident. Page 116.
12. Dusky Moorhen *Gallinula tenebrosa*, 38 cm, adult, common resident. Page 115.
13. Dusky Moorhen, immature.

1. Red-capped Dotterel *Charadrius ruficapillus,* 15 cm, adult male, a common resident. Page 125.
2. Red-capped Dotterel, adult female.
3. Black-fronted Dotterel *Charadrius melanops,* 16 cm, a common breeding resident. Page 127.
4. Red-kneed Dotterel *Erythrogonys cinctus,* 18 cm, immature, a common visitor. Page 128.
5. Red-kneed Dotterel, adult.
6. Wood Sandpiper *Tringa glareola,* 23 cm, a rare summer visitor. Page 133.
7. Curlew Sandpiper *Calidris ferruginea,* 20 cm, breeding plumage, an uncommon summer visitor. Page 137.
8. Curlew Sandpiper, non-breeding plumage.
9. Japanese Snipe *Gallinago hardwickii,* 24 cm, a regular summer visitor. Page 134.
10. Sharp-tailed Sandpiper *Calidris acuminata,* 21 cm, non-breeding plumage, an uncommon summer visitor. Page 136.
11. Pectoral Sandpiper *Calidris melanotos,* 23 cm, non-breeding plumage, very rare vagrant. Page 136.
12. Broad-billed Sandpiper *Limicola falcinellus,* 18 cm, non-breeding plumage, very rare vagrant. Page 138.
13. Red-necked Stint *Calidris ruficollis,* 15 cm, partial breeding plumage, an uncommon summer visitor. Page 135.
14. Red-necked Stint, non-breeding plumage.

1.  Bar-tailed Godwit *Limosa lapponica,* 38 cm, a very rare vagrant.
    Page 131.
2.  Australian Painted Snipe *Rostratula benghalensis,* 25 cm, female, a
    very rare vagrant. Page 119.
3.  Australian Painted Snipe, male.
4.  Double-banded Dotterel *Charadrius bicinctus,* 18 cm, breeding
    plumage, a regular visitor from New Zealand. Page 126.
5.  Double-banded Dotterel, non-breeding plumage.
6.  Greenshank *Tringa nebularia,* 32 cm, an uncommon migrant.
    Page 132.
7.  Marsh Sandpiper *Tringa stagnatilis,* 22 cm, a very rare migrant.
    Page 132.
8.  Pacific Golden Plover *Pluvialis dominica,* 25 cm, a rare migrant.
    Page 124.
9.  Common Sandpiper *Tringa hypoleucos,* 20 cm, a very rare migrant.
    Page 134.

B.T.W. 1967

1.  Marsh Tern *Chlidonias hybrida,* 26 cm, breeding plumage, an uncommon summer visitor. Page 147.
2.  Marsh Tern, non-breeding plumage.
3.  Caspian Tern *Hydroprogne caspia,* 56 cm, a rare visitor. Page 148.
4.  White-winged Black Tern, non-breeding plumage.
5.  White-winged Black Tern *Chlidonias leucoptera,* 24 cm, breeding plumage, a very rare vagrant. Page 146.
6.  Silver Gull *Larus novaehollandiae,* 41 cm, adult, a common resident. Page 144.
7.  Silver Gull, first year plumage.
8.  Silver Gull, immature.
9.  White-headed Stilt *Himantopus himantopus,* 38 cm, a regular summer visitor. Page 139.
10. Red-necked Avocet *Recurvirostra novaehollandiae,* 43 cm, a rare visitor. Page 141.
11. Banded Plover *Vanellus tricolor,* 26 cm, a fairly common resident. Page 123.
12. Southern Stone-curlew *Burhinus magnirostris,* 55 cm, a very rare breeding resident. Page 142.
13. Masked Plover *Vanellus miles,* 34 cm, a very common resident. Page 121.

B.T.W. 1961-7

1. Wonga Pigeon *Leucosarcia melanoleuca,* 39 cm, a common resident. Page 155.
2. Spotted Turtle-dove *Streptopelia chinensis,* 25 cm, a very rare resident. Page 156.
3. Domestic Pigeon *Columba livia,* 34 cm, a common resident. Page 157.
4. Peaceful Dove *Geopelia striata,* 20 cm, an uncommon visitor. Page 150.
5. Crested Pigeon *Ocyphaps lophotes,* 33 cm, a rare visitor. Page 154.
6. Diamond Dove *Geopelia cuneata,* 20 cm, a rare vagrant. Page 151.
7. Forest Bronzewing *Phaps chalcoptera,* 33 cm, a common resident. Page 152.
8. Brush Bronzewing *Phaps elegans,* 30 cm, a rare visitor. Page 153.

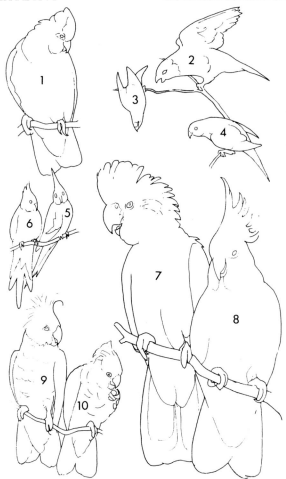

1.  Galah *Cacatua roseicapilla,* 36 cm, a very common resident.
    Page 165.
2.  Rainbow Lorikeet *Trichoglossus haematodus,* 29 cm, a rare non-
    breeding visitor. Page 159.
3.  Little Lorikeet *Glossopsitta pusilla,* 16 cm, an uncommon visitor.
    Page 161.
4.  Swift Parrot *Lathamus discolor,* 25 cm, an occasional winter visitor.
    Page 176.
5.  Cockatiel *Nymphicus hollandicus,* 30 cm, adult male, a rare vagrant.
    Page 168.
6.  Cockatiel, adult female.
7.  Yellow-tailed Black Cockatoo *Calyptorhynchus funereus,* 65 cm,
    adult female, an uncommon resident. Page 162.
8.  Sulphur-crested Cockatoo *Cacatua galerita,* 51 cm, a common
    resident. Page 166.
9.  Gang-gang Cockatoo *Callocephalon fimbriatum,* 35 cm, adult male,
    a common resident. Page 164.
10. Gang-gang Cockatoo, adult female.

B.T.W
1958

1. Superb Parrot *Polytelis swainsoni,* 40 cm, adult male, an uncommon breeding visitor. Page 170.
2. Superb Parrot, adult female.
3. King Parrot *Alisterus scapularis,* 41 cm, adult male, a common breeding resident. Page 169.
4. King Parrot, adult female.
5. King Parrot, immature male.
6. Crimson Rosella *Platycercus elegans,* 36 cm, adult, a common breeding resident. Page 171.
7. Crimson Rosella, immature.
8. Budgerigar *Melopsittacus undulatus,* 10 cm, a very rare vagrant. Page 177.
9. Eastern Rosella *Platycercus eximius,* 32 cm, a common breeding resident. Page 172.
10. Red-rumped Parrot *Psephotus haematonotus,* 25 cm, adult male, a common breeding resident. Page 173.
11. Red-rumped Parrot, immature.
12. Red-rumped Parrot, adult female.

1.  Brush Cuckoo *Cuculus variolosus*, 24 cm, a rather rare breeding
    migrant. Page 180.
2.  Koel *Eudynamys scolopacea*, 42 cm, adult male, a rare vagrant.
    Page 185.
3.  Koel, adult female.
4.  Black-eared Cuckoo *Chrysococcyx osculans*, 19 cm, a very rare
    migrant. Page 181.
5.  Pallid Cuckoo *Cuculus pallidus*, 33 cm, adult male, a common
    breeding migrant. Page 178.
6.  Pallid Cuckoo, immature.
7.  Horsfield Bronze Cuckoo *Chrysococcyx basalis*, 17 cm, a common
    breeding migrant. Page 182.
8.  Fan-tailed Cuckoo *Cuculus pyrrhophanus*, 27 cm, immature, a
    common resident. Page 180.
9.  Fan-tailed Cuckoo, adult.
10. Golden Bronze Cuckoo *Chrysococcyx lucidus*, 16 cm, a common
    breeding migrant. Page 183.

B.T.W. 1963

1.  White-backed Swallow *Cheramoeca leucosternum,* 14 cm, a rare but regular visitor. Page 209.
2.  Welcome Swallow *Hirundo neoxena,* 12 cm, a common resident. Page 210.
3.  Fairy Martin *Cecropis ariel,* 12 cm, a common breeding migrant. Page 213.
4.  Tree Martin *Cecropis nigricans,* 13 cm, a common breeding migrant. Page 212.
5.  Fork-tailed Swift *Apus pacificus,* 17 cm, a rare summer visitor. Page 193.
6.  Spine-tailed Swift *Hirundapus caudacutus,* 20 cm, a common summer visitor. Page 191.

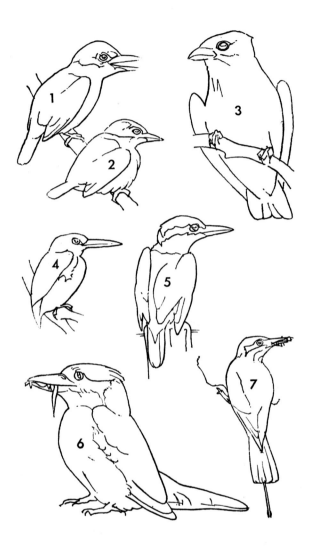

1. Sacred Kingfisher *Halcyon sancta,* 22 cm, adult, a common migrant. Page 198.
2. Sacred Kingfisher, juvenile.
3. Dollar Bird *Eurystomus orientalis,* 27 cm, a common migrant. Page 201.
4. Azure Kingfisher *Ceyx azurea,* 18 cm, a rare vagrant. Page 194.
5. Red-backed Kingfisher *Halcyon pyrrhopygia,* 22 cm, a very rare vagrant. Page 197.
6. Kookaburra *Dacelo novaeguineae,* 46 cm, a very common resident. Page 195.
7. Rainbow-bird *Merops ornatus,* 23 cm, a common migrant. Page 199.

B.T.W 1962

1.  Satin Bower-bird *Ptilonorhynchus violaceus,* 32 cm, adult male, a common resident. Page 365.
2.  Satin Bower-bird, adult female.
3.  Superb Lyrebird *Menura novaehollandiae,* 97 cm, adult male, a common resident. Page 202.
4.  Superb Lyrebird, adult female, 82 cm.

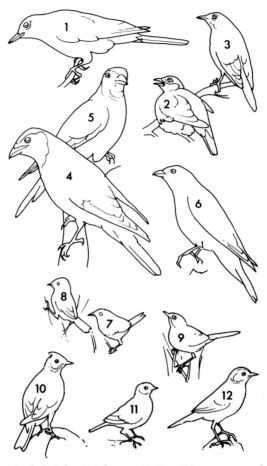

1. Olive-backed Oriole *Oriolus sagittatus*, 28 cm, a regular common breeding migrant. Page 341.
2. White-winged Triller *Lalage sueurii*, 18 cm, adult male, a common breeding migrant. Page 218.
3. White-winged Triller, adult female.
4. Black-faced Cuckoo-shrike *Coracina novaehollandiae*, 33 cm, a common resident. Page 215.
5. Black-faced Cuckoo-shrike, immature.
6. Little Cuckoo-shrike *Coracina papuensis*, 28 cm, a rare vagrant. Page 216.
7. Cisticola *Cisticola exilis*, 9-11 cm, adult male, breeding plumage, a rare breeding resident. Page 253.
8. Cisticola, adult female, breeding plumage.
9. Little Grass-bird *Megalurus gramineus*, 16 cm, an uncommon resident. Page 255.
10. Skylark *Alauda arvensis*, 19 cm, a common resident. Page 207.
11. Bushlark *Mirafra javanica*, 13 cm, a rare summer visitor. Page 205.
12. Pipit *Anthus novaeseelandiae*, 18 cm, a common resident. Page 208.

B.T.W. 1963

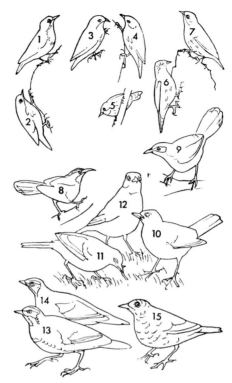

1. White-throated Treecreeper *Climacteris leucophaea,* 16 cm, adult female, a common resident. Page 287.
2. White-throated Treecreeper, adult male.
3. Red-browed Treecreeper *Climacteris erythrops,* 15 cm, adult female, an uncommon resident. Page 289.
4. Red-browed Treecreeper, adult male.
5. Orange-winged Sittella *Daphoenositta chrysoptera,* 11 cm, a common resident. Page 290.
6. Brown Treecreeper *Climacteris picumnus,* 18 cm, adult male, an uncommon resident. Page 286.
7. Brown Treecreeper, adult female.
8. White-browed Babbler *Pomatostomus superciliosus,* 20 cm, a very rare vagrant. Page 252.
9. Grey-crowned Babbler *Pomatostomus temporalis,* 28 cm, a rare resident. Page 251.
10. Blackbird *Turdus merula,* 26 cm, adult male, a common resident. Page 221.
11. Blackbird, immature.
12. Blackbird, adult female.
13. Spotted Quail-thrush *Cinclosoma punctatum,* 28 cm, adult male, an uncommon resident. Page 248.
14. Spotted Quail-thrush, adult female.
15. Australian Ground Thrush *Zoothera dauma,* 29 cm, a common resident. Page 223.

B.T.W. 1962

1.  Rose Robin *Petroica rosea,* 10 cm, adult male, a common breeding migrant. Page 230.
2.  Rose Robin, adult female.
3.  Hooded Robin *Melanodryas cucullata,* 16 cm, adult male, an uncommon resident. Page 232.
4.  Hooded Robin, adult female.
5.  Pink Robin *Petroica rodinogaster,* 10 cm, adult male, an uncommon winter visitor. Page 229.
6.  Pink Robin, adult female.
7.  Yellow Robin *Eopsaltria australis,* 16 cm, a very common resident. Page 233.
8.  Red-capped Robin *Petroica goodenovii,* 12 cm, adult male, an infrequent visitor. Page 226.
9.  Red-capped Robin, adult female.
10. Scarlet Robin *Petroica multicolor,* 13 cm, adult male, a common resident. Page 225.
11. Scarlet Robin, adult female.
12. Flame Robin *Petroica phoenicea,* 13 cm, adult male, a common resident. Page 228.
13. Flame Robin, adult female.

1. Restless Flycatcher *Myiagra inquieta,* 21 cm, an uncommon resident. Page 242.
2. Satin Flycatcher *Myiagra cyanoleuca,* 16 cm, adult male, uncommon breeding migrant. Page 240.
3. Satin Flycatcher, adult female.
4. Leaden Flycatcher *Myiagra rubecula,* 15 cm, adult male, a common breeding migrant. Page 239.
5. Leaden Flycatcher, adult female.
6. Grey Fantail *Rhipidura fuliginosa,* 16 cm, a common resident. Page 234.
7. Rufous Fantail *Rhipidura rufifrons,* 16 cm, a common breeding migrant. Page 235.
8. Jacky Winter *Microeca leucophaea,* 13 cm, an uncommon resident. Page 224.
9. Willie Wagtail *Rhipidura leucophrys,* 20 cm, an abundant resident. Page 237.

B.T.W. 1962

1.  White-fronted Chat *Epthianura albifrons,* 12 cm, adult male, an uncommon resident. Page 283.
2.  White-fronted Chat, adult female.
3.  White-throated Warbler *Gerygone olivacea,* 11 cm, a common breeding migrant. Page 262.
4.  Western Warbler *Gerygone fusca,* 10 cm, a common breeding migrant. Page 264.
5.  Little Thornbill *Acanthiza nana,* 10 cm, a rare resident. Page 267.
6.  Striated Thornbill *Acanthiza lineata,* 10 cm, a common resident. Page 266.
7.  Brown Thornbill *Acanthiza pusilla,* 11 cm, a very common resident. Page 268.
8.  Weebill *Smicrornis brevirostris,* 9 cm, a common resident. Page 279.
9.  Buff-tailed Thornbill *Acanthiza reguloides,* 11 cm, a common resident. Page 271.
10. Chestnut-tailed Thornbill *Acanthiza uropygialis,* 9 cm, a rare vagrant. Page 270.
11. Whiteface *Aphelocephala leucopsis,* 13 cm, an uncommon resident. Page 280.
12. Yellow-tailed Thornbill *Acanthiza chrysorrhoa,* 11 cm, a common resident. Page 272.

B.T.W.1962

1.  Brown Songlark *Cinclorhamphus cruralis,* 25 cm, adult male, an uncommon breeding migrant. Page 257.
2.  Brown Songlark, adult female.
3.  Rufous Songlark *Cinclorhamphus mathewsi,* 19 cm, adult male, a common breeding migrant. Page 258.
4.  Rufous Songlark, immature.
5.  Superb Blue Wren *Malurus cyaneus,* 16 cm, adult male, breeding plumage, a common breeding resident. Page 259.
6.  Superb Blue Wren, adult female.
7.  White-browed Scrub-Wren *Sericornis frontalis,* 12 cm, a common breeding resident. Page 273.
8.  Reed Warbler *Acrocephalus stentoreus,* 18 cm, a common breeding migrant. Page 256.
9.  Speckled Warbler *Sericornis sagittatus,* 12 cm, an uncommon resident. Page 277.
10. Pilot Bird *Pycnoptilus floccosus,* 16 cm, widely distributed resident in small numbers. Page 282.

B.T.W. 1962

1. Rufous Whistler *Pachycephala rufiventris,* 17 cm, adult male, a common breeding migrant. Page 244.
2. Rufous Whistler, adult female.
3. Golden Whistler *Pachycephala pectoralis,* 18 cm, adult male, a common breeding resident. Page 243.
4. Golden Whistler, adult female.
5. Shrike-tit *Falcunculus frontatus,* 19 cm, adult female, an uncommon but widely distributed resident. Page 247.
6. Shrike-tit, adult male.
7. Olive Whistler *Pachycephala olivacea,* 20 cm, an uncommon but widespread resident. Page 245.
8. Grey Shrike-thrush *Colluricincla harmonica,* 24 cm, a common breeding resident. Page 246.
9. Eastern Whipbird *Psophodes olivaceus,* 27 cm, a resident in small numbers. Page 249.

B.T.W. 1962

PARDALOTES, MISTLETOE-BIRDS
AND SILVEREYES

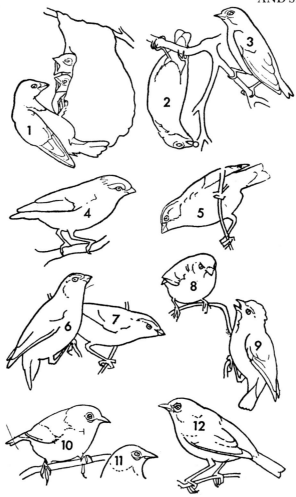

1. Mistletoe-bird *Dicaeum hirundinaceum,* 10 cm, adult male, a common resident. Page 292.
2. Mistletoe-bird, adult female.
3. Mistletoe-bird, immature.
4. Striated Pardalote *Pardalotus striatus,* 11 cm, western form, a rare resident or visitor. Page 296.
5. Striated Pardalote, Tasmanian form, a common winter visitor.
6. Striated Pardalote, eastern form, adult, a common resident.
7. Striated Pardalote, eastern form, immature.
8. Spotted Pardalote *Pardalotus punctatus,* 9 cm, adult female, a common resident. Page 293.
9. Spotted Pardalote, adult male.
10. Grey-breasted Silvereye *Zosterops lateralis,* 10 cm, a common resident. Page 297.
11. Grey-breasted Silvereye, more southern form, a common visitor.
12. Grey-breasted Silvereye, Tasmanian form, a common visitor.

1. Singing Honeyeater *Lichenostomus virescens,* 19 cm, a rare vagrant. Page 304.
2. Yellow-faced Honeyeater *Lichenostomus chrysops,* 17 cm, a common migrant. Page 306.
3. Fuscous Honeyeater *Lichenostomus fuscus,* 15 cm, an uncommon resident. Page 305.
4. Yellow-tufted Honeyeater *Lichenostomus melanops,* 19 cm, a fairly common resident. Page 308.
5. White-eared Honeyeater *Lichenostomus leucotis,* 20 cm, a common resident. Page 307.
6. White-plumed Honeyeater *Lichenostomus penicillatus,* 17 cm, a common resident. Page 309.
7. Lewin Honeyeater *Meliphaga lewinii,* 18 cm, an uncommon visitor. Page 303.

B.T.W
1962

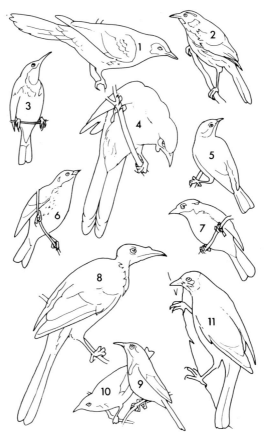

1. Regent Honeyeater *Xanthomyza phrygia*, 20 cm, a rare visitor. Page 302.
2. New Holland Honeyeater *Phylidonyris novaehollandiae*, 18 cm, a common resident. Page 317.
3. Eastern Spinebill *Acanthorhynchus tenuirostris*, 16 cm, a common resident. Page 313.
4. Red Wattle-bird *Anthochaera carunculata*, 35 cm, a common resident. Page 320.
5. Brown-headed Honeyeater *Melithreptus brevirostris*, 14 cm, an uncommon resident. Page 312.
6. Painted Honeyeater *Grantiella picta*, 16 cm, a rare breeding migrant. Page 300.
7. White-naped Honeyeater *Melithreptus lunatus*, 14 cm, a common breeding migrant. Page 310.
8. Noisy Friar-bird *Philomen corniculatus*, 33 cm, a common breeding migrant. Page 323.
9. Crescent Honeyeater *Phylidonyris pyrrhoptera*, 15 cm, adult male, a common resident. Page 315.
10. Crescent Honeyeater, adult female.
11. Noisy Miner *Manorina melanocephala*, 24 cm, a common breeding resident. Page 318.

1.  Zebra Finch *Poephila guttata,* 10 cm, adult male, a nomadic visitor.
    Page 331.
2.  Zebra Finch, adult female.
3.  Goldfinch *Carduelis carduelis,* 12 cm, a common resident. Page 335.
4.  Greenfinch *Carduelis chloris,* 15 cm, an uncommon resident. Page 336.
5.  Plum-headed Finch *Aidemosyne modesta,* 11 cm, a rare visitor.
    Page 330.
6.  Diamond Firetail *Emblema guttata,* 11 cm, a sparsely distributed
    breeding resident. Page 329.
7.  Banded Finch *Poephila bichenovii,* 10 cm, an uncommon resident.
    Page 332.
8.  Tree Sparrow *Passer montanus,* 14 cm, a rare vagrant. Page 334.
9.  Red-browed Finch *Emblema temporalis,* 11 cm, a common breeding
    resident. Page 327.
10. Beautiful Firetail *Emblema bella,* 11 cm, a very rare vagrant.
    Page 328.
11. House Sparrow *Passer domesticus,* 15 cm, adult male, a very
    common resident. Page 333.
12. House Sparrow, adult female.

B.T.W. 1959

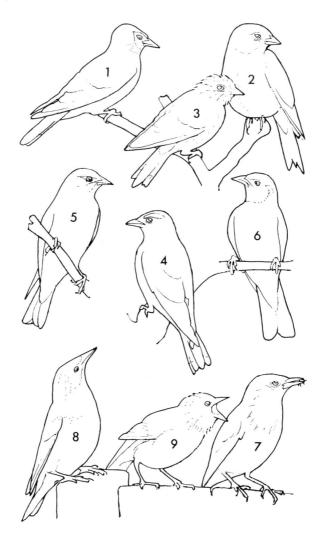

1.  Black-faced Wood-swallow *Artamus cinereus,* 18 cm, a very rare
    vagrant. Page 352.
2.  Dusky Wood-swallow *Artamus cyanopterus,* 18 cm, adult, a common
    breeding migrant. Page 349.
3.  Dusky Wood-swallow, immature.
4.  White-browed Wood-swallow *Artamus superciliosus,* 19 cm, adult
    male, a fairly rare migrant. Page 351.
5.  White-browed Wood-swallow, adult female.
6.  Masked Wood-swallow *Artamus personatus,* 19 cm, a rare migrant.
    Page 352.
7.  Starling *Sturnus vulgaris,* 20 cm, adult male, summer plumage, a very
    common resident. Page 338.
8.  Starling, early winter adult female.
9.  Starling, juvenile.

B.T.W. 1962

1. Pied Currawong *Strepera graculina,* 49 cm, a common breeding resident. Page 354.
2. Little Raven *Corvus mellori,* 50 cm, a largely nomadic breeding species. Page 363.
3,4. Australian Raven *Corvus coronoides,* 52 cm, a common breeding resident. Page 361.
5. Grey Currawong *Strepera versicolor,* 47 cm, an uncommon breeding resident. Page 355.
6. Grey Butcher-bird *Cracticus torquatus,* 30 cm, an uncommon breeding resident. Page 357.
7. Magpie-lark *Grallina cyanoleuca,* 30 cm, adult male, a common breeding resident. Page 342.
8. Magpie-lark, adult female.
9. Apostle Bird *Struthidea cinerea,* 33 cm, a rare vagrant. Page 346.
10. White-winged Chough *Corcorax melanorhamphos,* 47 cm, a common breeding resident. Page 344.
11. Black-backed Magpie *Gymnorphina t. tibicen,* 44 cm, adult male, a common breeding resident. Page 358.
12. White-backed Magpie *Gymnorhina t. hypoleuca,* 44 cm, adult female, a fairly common breeding resident.
13. Black-backed Magpie, immature.

B.T.W. 1960

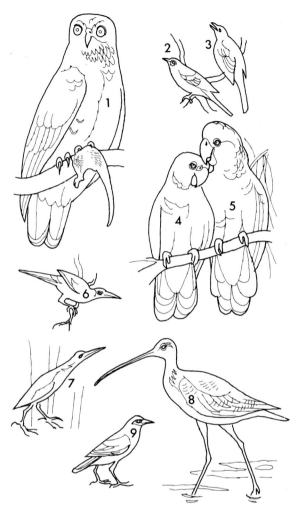

1.  Powerful Owl *Ninox strenua,* 65 cm, an uncommon breeding resident.
    Page 92.
2.  Cicada-bird *Coracina tenuirostris,* 27 cm, adult female, an uncommon
    regular visitor. Page 217.
3.  Cicada-bird, adult male.
4.  Glossy Cockatoo *Calyptorhynchus lathami,* 50 cm, adult female, an
    uncommon resident. Page 163.
5.  Glossy Cockatoo, adult male.
6.  Little Friar-bird *Philemon citreogularis,* 25-28 cm, a rare visitor.
    Page 325.
7.  Little Bittern *Ixobrychus minutus,* 30 cm, status uncertain, probably a
    rare visitor. Page 42.
8.  Eastern Curlew *Numenius madagascariensis,* 55 cm, a rare vagrant.
    Page 130.
9.  Common Mynah *Acridotheres tristis,* 26 cm, a common breeding
    resident, increasing. Page 339.

BTW
1980

1.  Black-faced Flycatcher *Monarcha melanopsis,* 25-28 cm, adult male, a common breeding migrant on coastal ranges, otherwise very rare. Page 238.
2.  Black-faced Flycatcher, immature.
3.  Large-billed Scrub-wren *Sericornis magnirostris,* 12 cm, an uncommon breeding resident on coastal ranges. Page 274.
4.  Brown Warbler *Gerygone mouki,* 10 cm, a common resident on coastal ranges, a rare vagrant inland. Page 265.
5.  Scarlet Honeyeater *Myzomela sanguinolenta,* 11 cm, an uncommon visitor on coast when eucalypts in flower; several records from Canberra. Page 299.
6.  Scarlet Honeyeater, adult female.
7.  Southern Emu-wren *Stipiturus malachurus,* 18 cm, adult female, common in coastal range heaths. Page 261.
8.  Southern Emu-wren, adult male.
9.  Heath-wren *Sericornis pyrrhopygius,* 15 cm, common in coastal range heaths. Page 276.
10. Rock Warbler *Origma solitaria,* 14 cm, uncommon in rocky areas of coastal ranges. Page 281.
11. Yellow-throated Scrub-wren *Sericornis citreogularis,* 12-15 cm, an uncommon breeding resident in coastal ranges. Page 275.

# THE HIGH COUNTRY

## THE REGION

Australia is wide and flat; the distances are unlimited and, to the traveller, the horizon is always just as far ahead as it was yesterday. The country comes in large pieces, miles of woodland, then days of saltbush or mulga; the spinifex seems to extend forever. The same kinds of birds are distributed for over 3000 kilometres.

The dweller on the inland plains forgets, or has no reason to realise, that in the south-east there is a great boomerang-shaped sweep of mountains, gullies and high plains that are a different world. Here in the one day, or less, you can climb from dripping rainforest, with tree ferns and mossy logs, to bleak, open, alpine moors — and pass a dozen different bird communities on the way. Distance ceases to be the problem and is replaced by inaccessibility, for the mountains are as trackless as any part of the continent and, to the individual, are often more remote than most. He finds the birds are more numerous than elsewhere and more varied and, for the first time, he realises that migration is a real thing, birds do move *en masse* at regular times. The accepted concepts of the origin of Australian birds begin to make more sense.

In Australia there is little high land. Apart from that in the Eastern Divide, the only country over 600 metres is small parts of the Hamersley Range in the arid north-west and the Macdonnell Range in the centre. The Eastern Divide is by far the greatest area and sweeps down the continent from north to south, separating the narrow coastal plains from the dry interior. In the far north, at the base of Cape York, the Divide is only a series of low hills but in the south-east it increases in height and culminates in Mt Kosciusko of over 2000 metres.

The highlands are the remnants of an old mountain system that has been worn and changed in past time. It has been eroded to a low level and then uplifted in parts; in places it has been intruded by granite masses and elsewhere great sheets of lava have poured; streams have cut chasms and broad valleys.

1

The geology and the climate have produced a great variety of topography and bird habitats. There are the rich tropical rainforests on the lava plateaux of the Atherton Tablelands and the Lamington Plateau, the bleak plains and *Eucalyptus* forests of the igneous hills of New England, the sandstone plateau of the Blue Mountains, the granite mountains of the south-eastern highlands and the fluted dolerite ramparts of the Tasmanian highlands. Throughout their length, the highlands form the barrier between the coastal birds and those of the inland. This book then is about the birds that live in that part of the south-east that can be called the "high country". In the broad expanse of Australia, it is difficult to define regions, unless they be unreasonably large or political, and hence equally unreal, but this one is possible. The area considered extends from near Canberra, which is on an elevated open plain up the slopes and spurs to Mt Kosciusko, and through the Snowy Mountains and the Victorian Alps. On the seaward side, the area is bounded by the sudden fall away of the mountains to the coastal plains that enjoy the spring-time warmth and growth while the ranges above are still bound in fog and sleet. In the west, the boundary is less precise for the country tails off to the slopes and the wheat belt until the inland plains roll out before us. The birds do not change much though, from the mountains, until the beginning of the plains at Wagga, New South Wales, so we can use Gundagai, 100 kilometres east of there, as a convenient and conservative boundary. In the south, the ranges, inland, drop more sharply to the Murray River or the plains and the area is better defined. The region, in ornithological literature, is the barrier that protected the "south-east refuge" where our birds survived the great arid cycles of past periods in geological time.

Although elevated, not all of the region is mountainous. Relatively flat plains occur, as around Canberra, and remnants of a flat landscape that existed in past geological time remain. It has been uplifted, dissected and eroded, leaving characteristic high plateaux. The ranges and mountains themselves are not the craggy pinnacles of other countries but are large, rounded masses of granite. Kosciusko is not a peak but the highest point of a gently rising system of ridges.

Little of the region is below 600 metres and much of it is above 900 metres; Kosciusko reaches 2250 metres and there are many differences in climate from place to place, though it is generally harsh throughout the whole region.

The temperature range during the year is great. At Canberra the mean maximum temperature in January is 27.7°C and in July 10.9°C. The extreme temperatures experienced in Canberra have been 42.7°C and −10.0°C. In the high mountains near Charlotte Pass, these extremes have been 26.7°C and −22°C.

2

Frosts are common. Canberra averages 103 each year but in the ranges there are over 140; in the alpine areas the mean monthly temperature remains below 0°C for six to eight months. Snow sometimes falls in Canberra but above 1230 metres altitude it falls every year; above 1500 metres it lies for three or four months and in the alpine areas it can lie for the whole year.

The average annual rainfall varies greatly. At Cooma, it is about 450 mm but at Canberra, 650 mm, and, in some of the high mountain areas, as much as 3000 mm in up to 150 rainy days. The northern end of the region is in a zone that is uniform in rainfall throughout the year but in the south the rain is mainly in winter and there are great annual differences. At times both winter and summer falls can be high, but other times both can fail. Occasionally drought can be sufficiently severe to cause disastrous tree mortality. In general, however, the cycle of growth is regular; it is prevented by the cold in winter, by a relatively low rainfall and high evaporation rate in summer. In spring and early summer there is abundant plant growth. (H.J.F.)

Note:    A physiographic map of the highlands of south-east Australia appears inside the front cover.

# HISTORY

EXPLORATION AND SETTLEMENT: As in much of Australia, exploration and settlement went hand in hand and much of the detailed pioneer exploration was done by stockmen seeking new pastures. The discovery of the southern highlands began in 1818 when James Meehan, Deputy Surveyor-General, discovered Lake Bathurst and the Goulburn Plains. Construction of a road to the Goulburn Plains was begun in 1820 under the supervision of Dr Charles Throsby, a retired naval surgeon, who had taken up land near Moss Vale. He sent his overseer, James Wild, on an exploring expedition which resulted in the discovery of Lake George in August 1820. Wild ascended a hill at the southern end of the lake and saw "Snowy Mountains to the S.W."; this was the first glimpse of the southern alps by a European. Governor Macquarie, anxious to see the new discoveries of fertile land, visited Lake George and named it in October 1820. Throsby and Constable James Vaughan, who were in Macquarie's party, then pushed on from Lake George and there seems to be no doubt that they discovered the Yass River and the site of the future Capital Territory. Wild, Vaughan and Throsby's nephew, Charles Throsby Smith, discovered the junction of the Molonglo and Queanbeyan Rivers, explored the future site of Canberra, and climbed Black Mountain in December 1820. In 1821, Throsby discovered the Murrumbidgee River near Tuggeranong. Captain Mark John Currie

3

and Brigade Major Ovens, with Wild as guide, traversed the Limestone Plains, the future site of Canberra in 1823. Continuing southwards, they crossed the Umeralla River, which Currie thought was the upper Murrumbidgee, and discovered the Monaro Plains.

A party led by Hamilton Hume, who had been with Meehan when Lake Bathurst was first seen, discovered the Yass Plains in 1821 or 1822 and, late in 1824, Hamilton Hume and William Hilton Hovell left Hume's outpost station near Gunning and made their epic journey to Port Phillip. Their route was along the foothills of the southern alps, and on the way they saw peaks in the Victorian Alps, one of which they named Mount Buffalo.

While settlement followed closely on these discoveries, further exploration continued. In 1834 Dr John Lhotsky, a Polish naturalist, travelled through the Monaro Plains to the Australian Alps and named, among other features, the Snowy River and the "plain of Omeo". Early in 1840, another Polish scientist, Sir Paul Edmund de Strzelecki, climbed the Alps and named Mt Kosciusko. He then continued on through Gippsland, which had been explored only a short time before by Angus McMillan, a pioneer pastoralist who had moved southwards from the Monaro. Detailed exploration of the Victorian Alps was made in the 1850s by stockmen, gold-seekers and Government servants such as the botanist, Baron Ferdinand von Mueller.

By 1823 Goulburn Plains were occupied and about that year the first settler squatted on the site of the future Canberra. James Ainslie, overseer for Robert Campbell, brought sheep in 1825 and established Duntroon on behalf of his employer. Soon after, the rest of the Limestone Plains was taken up and within twenty-five years squatting spread southwards over the Monaro and into eastern Victoria. By 1860 settlement of the region was virtually complete.

LAND USE: Many villages, connected by a network of roads and tracks came into existence early in the settlement period. A few such as Goulburn, Yass, Queanbeyan and Cooma, have grown into towns and rural cities, while others in between remain small villages to this day. Gold mining was not an important industry and the only gold discoveries of any consequence were at Kiandra and one or two places in the Victorian high country.

Although most alienated land in the region was grazed by sheep and cattle, some was cultivated for wheat from the earliest days of settlement. The original estates were of the order of 1000 to 3000 hectares, although a few were enlarged beyond this by purchase. They were unfenced and sheep were shepherded. Parts of the large estates, especially the fertile river valleys such as the Molonglo, were soon leased to tenant farmers, and many of these, together with newcomers,

4

eventually acquired their own small farms.

The pattern of land usage that evolved on the Southern Tablelands was dominated by sheep and beef cattle grazing, with communities of small farms on suitable areas. It has remained much the same throughout the history of the area. The country occupied by sheep was the drier plains at the lower altitudes, and beef cattle were grazed in the colder, wetter parts. The cold high plains near or above the snowline were grazed in summer time. Small farming was at its maximum development about a century ago and crops grown at that time were wheat, barley, oats and maize and even a little tobacco. A small amount of dairying and pig-raising and some orcharding developed on the fertile river valleys or lower warmer areas.

The major changes to the plant cover brought about by settlement were a change in the composition of the grasslands and a thinning of the tree density in the savannah woodlands. The plains were covered with an association of tall grasses, chiefly kangaroo grass *Themeda* and tussock grass *Poa*; under grazing this was transformed into a community of much shorter grasses, chiefly species of *Stipa* and *Danthonia*. The tall spreading eucalypts of the savannah woodland have gradually decreased in density through death, prevention of regeneration by grazing stock, and from clearing. Land for cropping was cleared but the area under cultivation was small. Ringbarking on grazing land was not common until well into the 1880s because many farmers believed that trees attracted rain. However, considerable amounts of timber were necessary for post-and-rail fencing, and wire-fencing was not introduced until about 1880.

In this century the most important development has been the selection of the Federal Capital Territory site and the construction of Canberra. The city was designed in 1911 but construction was slow and the Federal Parliament did not sit here until 1927. The Canberra plan, with its accent on parks, gardens, open areas and artificial lakes, has created new and different habitats for birds. Another consequence of Capital Territory development, detrimental as far as conservation of bird life is concerned, has been the destruction of considerable areas of native bush and grassland and its replacement with plantations of exotic pines.

PREVIOUS ORNITHOLOGICAL WORK: As in most parts of Australia, little systematic observation of the fauna was done during the settlement period, as the pioneers struggled to establish themselves, and only fragmentary information has been handed down.

Some of the explorers and early travellers commented on the bird life although they generally recorded only the larger or edible species. Macquarie saw "several flocks of fine large emus and some fine large turkies" on the Goulburn Plains and shot "a very fine large wild turkey" at Lake Bathurst. At Lake George he found "black swans, Native Companions and ducks"; and records that the southern end of the lake was "covered with innumerable flocks of black swans, ducks and sea gulls". Currie records the killing of a total of ten Emus and some ducks by his party during the couple of weeks they were in the country around Lake George, the future Capital Territory and the Umeralla. In 1824 the botanist Allan Cunningham visited Lakes Bathurst and George and nearby plains and remarked on the number of Emus.

Lieutenant Breton, R.N. who visited the area in the early 1830s commented on the numbers of "black swans, ducks, teal, and other wildfowl" on the surface of Lake George. He goes on to say: "It was here that I first met with the Native Companion, or Gigantic Crane: there were forty of these great birds (they are *six feet* high) in one flock, and it was an amusing sight to see them marching along in military order, like a file of soldiers: the effect was fine when they rose at once into the air. Here also there are numerous wild, or native, turkies, the Bustard of New Holland. When a person wishes to shoot this bird, he should go on horseback; it will then often permit him to approach within half a dozen yards: on foot he will seldom get more than a distant shot, which is almost useless, as it will carry off an incredible quantity of lead..."

The attitude to bird life of Samuel Shumack, a farmer who lived in the Canberra district from 1856 to 1912, was no doubt typical of the views of the rural community. In his published reminiscences, he mentions only two categories of birds — game and pests. On one occasion he shot "hundreds" of magpies which "wrought havoc" with his germinating crop, and he lists a number of species as orchard pests, including parrots, of which he once shot over five hundred in a short period. He mentions the "Eagle-hawk" as a pastoral pest. A farmer friend fired at a group of about eighty Brolgas on a Canberra farm and killed only one. Shumack records the Bustard as plentiful at Gininderra in 1859 and describes the manner in which he killed a large male. About this time a number of farmers formed a shooting party and the day's bag was five Bustards and over forty ducks. The bird life around Lake George is described in Balliere's *New South Wales Gazetteer and Road Guide*, published in 1866, in which it is stated that..."Native Companions are so numerous as to have become exceedingly destructive to the crops, and the small farmers around Bungendore have been obliged to poison them in large numbers". The vulnerable large birds, once so common on these plains, gradually disappeared under this onslaught; the Emu has not been recorded for generations, the Brolga is now a rare vagrant, and the last recorded

Bustard was seen on 21 June 1920.

Dr George Bennett, physician, naturalist, and an early associate of the Australian Museum, made two journeys to Yass and surrounding country in 1832 and recorded incidental observations on a number of birds. Until this century only occasional anecdotal reports, such as these, were published on the birds of the southern high country. The first resident ornithologist was D. P. Jones, Head Teacher at Duntroon Public School. In 1929 he published the first list of birds of the Australian Capital Territory based on his observations from 1913. The naturalist Charles Barrett visited Tuggeranong for two short periods in the early 1920s, and published a brief account of the birds he saw. These early reports are of value in that they provide evidence from which changes in status of some species can be assessed. The ornithologist G. M. Mathews, while resident in Canberra preparing a catalogue of his library which he had presented to the National Library of Australia, compiled a list of birds of the Australian Capital Territory (1943). The list owes much to Jones's previous one, but Mathews did little or no field work and the list appears to be in part little more than guesswork.

During the past twenty-five years amateur ornithologists have made an excellent contribution to knowledge of the bird life of the area. There is an active local ornithological society, the Canberra Ornithologists Group, which publishes a periodical, *Canberra Bird Notes*.

A list of the important general papers on the bird life of the area is given in the Appendix, page 369.

An important event in the history of ornithology in our area was the establishment of the CSIRO Wildlife Survey Section (now the Division of Wildlife and Rangelands Research) at Canberra in 1949, with fulltime ornithologists on the staff from 1952. CSIRO staff have made intensive studies on a number of locally-occurring species including the Black Swan and other Anatidae, Lyrebird, Blue Wren, White-winged Chough, Magpie, Raven and Little Raven, and others.

Since the pioneering days great progress has been made in wildlife conservation, and all native species of birds are now legally protected. A number of reserves have been created in the south-eastern high country, including several nature reserves in the Australian Capital Territory, the Kosciusko National Park, and other reserves in the Victorian Alps. Catchment management in the Capital Territory, Snowy Mountains and the Victorian Alps has led to the prohibition of grazing by domestic stock in much of the highlands, and more efficient fire control has lessened destruction by wild fires. Large areas in the forested high country are either water catchment or forest reserves, and in either case the mountain forest habitat is effectively preserved.

Water conservation measures, particularly by the Snowy Mountains Authority, have led to the creation of many artificial lakes, including the two immense reservoirs at Eucumbene and Jindabyne.

The great alteration to the savannah woodland is probably of little consequence as far as most birds are concerned as the species of this community seem to survive as well in farming and grazing land, providing that enough suitable nesting and shelter sites are available. Two former inhabitants of this woodland, the Emu and Bustard, have disappeared but this was largely a result of direct persecution. Another woodland species, the Stone Curlew, is now very rare and, although we do not know its former density, it is probable that interference from stock played a large part in its decline.

There can be little doubt that, providing there is no radical alteration in the patterns of land use, the future of the bird fauna in our area is assured. (J.H.C.)

## BIRD HABITATS

The vegetation of the region has been changed substantially during settlement. Grasslands have been altered in their composition, lakes have been created and swamps destroyed, woodlands have been cleared or thinned, native forests have been replaced with exotic pines in some areas and the understorey of some forests has been altered by grazing domestic and feral stock. The changes have been greatest on the plains and ridges and least in the mountains where vast areas remain in a relatively virgin condition. The changes are extensive but, by and large, habitat destruction has not been so severe as in many other parts of Australia. The native vegetation and its present condition has been summarised by Professor L. D. Pryor in *Canberra, a Nation's Capital*, edited by H. L. White, and by Dr A. Costin in *A Study of the Ecosystems of the Monaro Region of New South Wales*, published by the New South Wales Soil Conservation Service.

The region was, and still is, dominated by *Eucalyptus*, the only exceptions being the swamps, cities, pine plantations and grasslands. The main bird habitats show a very distinct altitudinal stratification in type and can be summarised in sequence from the valleys to the tops of the mountains.

LOWLAND SWAMPS: Apart from the specialised bogs in the alpine areas, there are very few swamps in the region and these are small and heavily overgrown with sedges *Eleocharis* and bulrush *Typha*. They are shallow and most are semi-permanent. They support numbers of swamphens, rails and similar birds but are not good waterfowl habitat because of the very dense vegetation. Most of the local swamps are in the grasslands between Canberra and Goulburn.

LAKES: There are some small glacial lakes in the high mountains but the most important lakes are in the lower areas: Lake George, the largest natural lake in New South Wales, and Lake Bathurst. They are large, deep, cold and windswept so that aquatic and edge vegetation is generally absent, except in Lake Bathurst, which is to some extent protected from the wind. In general, they are not good breeding places for most water birds although considerable colonies of Black Swans and grebes occur on them in favourable seasons. Numbers of birds from the inland crowd onto them in dry seasons.

The water levels in these lakes have undergone remarkable fluctuations over the years; at times they have been completely dry, and the beds were subdivided by fencing and grazed by sheep and cattle. These fluctuations have a tremendous effect on local populations of water birds. Lake George contained little water in the approximate periods 1836–51, 1856–60, 1901–15, 1917–24, 1926–49, 1982 and in some of these years even the lowest point on the lake bed was dry. It filled in 1950, a year with double the average rainfall, and except in the last couple of years since then the average depth of water in the deepest part has been about four to six metres. According to an earlier report, a depth of eight metres was attained for short periods in 1823 and 1874. Oscillations in the level of Lake Bathurst are similar to those of Lake George. The lakes lie in basins of internal drainage and their levels are governed by the normal climatic features of rainfall and evaporation.

Water conservation, hydro-electric and city beautification schemes have resulted in the construction of very large dams in the area. These include Lake Eucumbene and Lake Burley Griffin. As these filled and the water's edge spread, forming extensive shallows, they provided valuable habitat for water birds. Once filled, however, they lost much of their value to birds. They all suffer from the same difficulties as the natural lakes, being deep, cold and windswept and are not good water bird habitat. Some of them could have been very valuable waterfowl areas had appropriate planning been undertaken to provide islands and shallow parts.

STREAMS: The region is the source of some of the major rivers of the inland, the Murray, Murrumbidgee and Snowy and many tributaries. In their upper reaches these are steep and rocky rivulets but in the lower valleys the banks provide distinct bird habitats. There are swift flowing mountain streams throughout the region; the bottoms are stony or sandy, and the banks generally deeply dissected with occasional sandbeaches. In places, however, a forest of *Eucalyptus* or *Casuarina* with a dense undergrowth of shrubs, blackberries and ferns, provides useful habitat for many nectar feeding birds, finches, silvereyes and other small passerines.

**GRASSLANDS:** The grasslands generally occur below 600 metres. Originally, they were dominated by *Themeda* and *Poa* but only very small areas of these grasses now remain and over vast areas they have been replaced by *Danthonia, Stipa* and many other grasses and herbs. Parts of the former grasslands are now devoted to cereals, lucerne, and cities. The Emus and Bustards that roamed these plains have gone but numerous birds remain, perhaps even helped by the change from tall to shorter grass; these include the Pipit and Bushlark. The cultivations support abundant quail at all seasons.

**GARDENS:** The construction of Canberra, with its accent on open space within the city and the extensive plantings of trees and shrubs, both in public places and private gardens, has provided a very rich distinctive habitat for birds. The plantings include flowering *Eucalyptus, Acacia, Banksia* and *Grevillea* as well as numerous exotic berry-bearing shrubs and trees and other plants that have greatly increased and diversified the food and cover for birds. Most cities are dominated by introduced birds but in Canberra, although these also occur, the most prominent birds are the native species. It is probably the only Australian city where large colourful cockatoos feed in the city parks and suburban gardens in numbers or through which major migration routes follow the plantings of the streets and lake foreshores.

**SAVANNAH WOODLAND:** Below 700 metres altitude, the main tree formation is a savannah woodland of *Eucalyptus*. The trees rarely exceed twenty-two metres but can be up to twenty-eight metres and are widely spaced, giving a parkland appearance. Nowadays, the trees have been thinned out and the ground cover is degraded native grasslands or exotic improved pastures but, as has been mentioned already, the birds characteristic of savannah woodland are fairly resilient and have suffered the change very well indeed. Some of the edible and the "harmful" species have been destroyed but most birds have adapted to the change and are still numerous.

**DRY SCLEROPHYLL FOREST:** At altitudes of 760 to 900 metres, the most extensive formation is dry sclerophyll forest of Red Stringybark *E. macrorhyncha*, Broad-leafed Peppermint *E. dives*, Scribbly Gum *E. rossii* and Brittle Gum *E. mannifera*. The dominant trees rarely exceed twenty-two metres in height and they form a closed canopy. There are some tall shrubs and small shrubs of one metre or less that form a more or less continuous layer. The dry sclerophyll has been and is still often damaged by fire but on the whole is much closer to its original condition than the savannah woodland.

PINE PLANTATIONS: Much land, particularly that formerly carrying dry sclerophyll forest, has been cleared and replanted with exotic conifers. In 1926, the Australian Forestry School was begun in Adelaide and in 1927 transferred to Canberra. In 1915, some pine plantations were established on Mt Stromlo and planting on a commercial scale was begun in 1926. By 1954, there were 7700 hectares of pine plantations and, in 1967, 13,000 hectares of which 12,000 were *Pinus radiata*. There are smaller plantings of other species including Yellow Pine *P. ponderosa* and Corsican Pine *P. laricio*.

The extensive clearing of the native trees has meant the destruction of much bird habitat; its replacement by a forest of single exotic species, to which no Australian bird has been able to adapt, has not compensated for this loss. When the pines are small and many plants grow between them, the plantations support birds, but as the trees grow and the canopy closes this all changes. The undergrowth disappears and the ground is covered with dry pine needles. The birds leave. In a mature plantation, a few birds travel through or camp but very few live in it except along the scrubby creeks or in clearings where a few native trees and plants remain.

WET SCLEROPHYLL FORESTS: This forest grows on southern and eastern slopes between 830 and 1500 metres. Below 1100 metres, the forest is of Brown Barrel *Eucalyptus fastigata*, Narrow-leafed Peppermint *E. radiata* and Manna Gum *E. viminalis*, above 1100 metres it is of Alpine Ash *E. delegatensis* and Mountain Gum *E. dalrympleana*. The dominant trees grow to forty metres and have butt diameters of up to one and a half metres; the canopy is closed. There is a substratum of *Acacia melanoxylon* up to eighteen metres tall and lower strata of broad-leafed shrubs, providing a very rich habitat for birds. Along the streams and damper gullies, there is a rainforest of shrubs and tree ferns, and the logs and stones are moss covered and the ground litter deep and rotted. It is the haunt of the Superb Lyrebird, Ground Thrush, Rufous Fantail, Pilot Bird, Yellow Robin and Eastern Whipbird.

SUB-ALPINE WOODLAND: Above the forests, over 1600 metres altitude and up to at least 1800 metres, there is an alpine woodland mainly of Snow Gum or *Eucalyptus pauciflora*. The trees are small, seldom more than ten metres in height and often only five metres. They have a short bole but the heads are often windswept and distorted by the incessant mountain winds. There is a ground cover of small shrubs and herbs, some very colourful in spring. The sub-alpine woodlands form the tree line. Tree growth generally ceases at 1800 to 2000 metres in the Kosciusko area but between 1700 to 1770 metres in

11

the more southern Victorian Mountains.

ALPINE COMMUNITIES: Above the tree line are several typical alpine communities. These include tall alpine herbfields, feldmark, sod tussock grasslands, heaths, bogs and ferns. None of these is of much importance to birds but they are visited by Pipits and others from the lower levels during the summer.

Doubtless, as development of the Canberra district continues, there will be further changes in bird habitats. In the past, the changes have been bearable to most nature lovers and the future developments coming in an age of increased conservation awareness should not be retrogressive, provided biologists take their place in the planning stages. (H.J.F.)

# BIRD GEOGRAPHY

There is no distinctive mountain bird fauna in Australia, probably because the altitudes involved are not very great, but the region nevertheless has a very rich and diversified assemblage of birds.

A total of 281 kinds of birds have been recorded in the region. A large number of seabirds, naturally, do not come to the area but, apart from these, only thirteen of the families that occur in Australia have not been recorded in the region. These are the family Casuariidae, cassowaries; Megapodiidae, moundbuilders; Jacanidae, jacanas; Haematopodidae, oystercatchers; Phalaropidae, phalaropes; Glareolidae, pratincoles; Psittacidae, typical parrots; Opopsittidae, fig parrots; Pittidae, pittas; Atrichornithidae, scrub birds; Pycnonotidae, bulbuls; Nectariniidae, sunbirds and Dicruridae, drongos.

Of the birds in the region, many are residents but quite a large number of species also visit the area regularly as migrants or as nomadic visitors or vagrants from the coast or the inland plains.

The status of the birds can be summarised as follows:

| | |
|---|---:|
| Residents | 135 |
| Migrants from Northern Hemisphere | 17 |
| Migrant from New Zealand | 1 |
| Migrants within Australia | 37 |
| Vagrants and nomads | 88 |
| Birds formerly present | 4 |
| Total: | 281 |

The generally accepted theory of the evolution of the Australian bird fauna rests on the existence of a number of "refuge areas" during past geological cycles. These were important, particularly during the Pleistocene age, when there were several glaciations and much of the area would have been snow-covered, and during warm, dry interglacial periods. In the arid cycles, the birds that ranged the continent were forced back into the refuge areas. Those species that survived, or species that had evolved from them, later expanded back throughout the continent. The classical refuges were places where mountains with valleys provided some shelter or where, because of their proximity to the sea, the general climatic conditions were less severe.

Some writers have suggested many refuge areas of varying value and certainty but all are agreed that there were four of major importance. These are in the south-east, the south-west, and the north-west of the continent, and an area in the centre around the Macdonnell Ranges. Of these, when judged by the richness and diversity of the birds, especially those endemic to it, the south-east was by far the most important. The south-eastern highlands were the shield between the arid interior and the wetter coast, which was the major refuge; for much of the time it was probably ice covered and supported few birds. Since then, however, the coastal birds have spread inland again and occupied the ranges and parts of the western slopes and birds from the south-west have advanced across the continent to the eastern highlands.

As long ago as 1896, Professor Baldwin Spencer pointed out that, in Australia, there were three regions, or provinces, each with a very distinctive fauna. He named these the Torresian in the north and north-east, the Bassian in the east and south-east and the Eyrean in the inland. Since then, the importance of these primary divisions has remained unshaken but later work has shown that the south-west of Western Australia has a fauna that is a mixture of Bassian and Eyrean elements. It has also been shown that the boundaries between the various faunas are continually shifting and so they are best considered not in terms of static zoogeography but as faunas that were evolved within the regions and which are now on the whole still characteristic

**The faunal subregions of Australia**

of them. This is a more fluid concept; of kinds of birds rather than of geographic regions.

The boundary between the distinctive Bassian and Eyrean provinces was defined as the Great Dividing Range and this division is very real. The two faunas had an ecological basis to their differentiation for the altitude of the range itself is unlikely to be an important barrier to their spread and mingling. It is more probable that species tending to spread from the coast find the changes in habitat west of the divide too great for them to pass and that the Eyrean or inland species are on the whole unable to penetrate the habitats of the high country. So that, on the whole, the two groups of birds remain quite well separated. The Australian Capital Territory is only about sixty-four kilometres west of the Great Dividing Range and, as might be expected, the birds are of mainly Bassian origin. There is, however, a fairly strong contingent of Eyrean forms and a few Torresian invaders.

The boundaries of the regions occupied by the different faunas are not static but move about in response to long and short term changes in climate. There have probably been several considerable shifts in the boundaries in the past, and small changes are apparent even today. The fairly strong representation of Eyrean species around Canberra includes some that well illustrate the fluid nature of the boundaries. The most obvious include the Crested Pigeon, whose range just reaches the west of the highlands. Some time before 1930 there was a dry period inland and the region, as well as several places on the New South Wales coast, was invaded by Crested Pigeons. They survived for several years but did not become established and none were seen between 1945 and 1965, although a few have returned recently in response to the dry years of 1957 and 1961. The Galah was virtually unknown in the area before 1930 but in the last forty years it has gradually invaded and is now a very common breeding species. Less successful invaders include the Crimson Chat, which has bred here at least once, the Yellow-tailed Pardalote, Little Quail, Chestnut-tailed Thornbill and White-backed Swallow.

The Torresian or tropical element is very much less obvious. There are frequent movements southwards of Torresian birds but these, probably in response to their habitat needs, remain on the coast and seldom come inland as far as the ranges. The few that have successfully invaded the region and now breed here include the Dollar Bird, Banded Finch, Olive-backed Oriole, Satin Flycatcher, Leaden Flycatcher and Rufous Fantail. Some others are vagrants like the Channel-billed Cuckoo, Koel and Grass Whistle-duck.

The birds of the region are, however, overwhelmingly of south-eastern or Bassian origin and this is exemplified by the Lyrebird, the Crimson Rosella, Gang-gang Cockatoo, Crescent Honeyeater, Eastern

Spinebill, Superb Blue Wren, Pilot Bird, Olive Whistler, Flame Robin, Chestnut Teal, Brush Bronzewing and a great many other locally common species. (H.J.F.)

# MOVEMENTS

The birds in and around Canberra are constantly changing; some are present all the time, others come and go at regular times during the year and others at irregular intervals. The first frosts of autumn are followed by the sudden appearance in the city of hordes of currawongs that flop in the trees, stalk the gardens and lawns and vie with household pets for their food; at about the same time, Gang-gang Cockatoos "grate" their way over the city and wheel and swoop into windbreaks and suburban hedges. Flocks of honeyeaters hurry through, from tree to tree, until they disappear in the east. The paddocks become sprinkled with the red breasts of robins, almost as though they had sprung from the ground, and Golden Whistlers become common about the city. In the city's ornamental lakes, Black Ducks appear in numbers, large groups of cormorants pass along its length and move on, Mountain Ducks pause there and Wood Ducks take up station on the verge to graze the lawns and gardens.

In spring and summer it all changes: the currawongs and cockatoos go back to the ranges, the honeyeaters drift back and flocks of Rainbow-birds suddenly wheel overhead at the same time as kingfishers begin to pipe and bronze cuckoos to trill. The Pallid Cuckoo suddenly appears on the same fence post as he did last year at the same time. The ducks mostly move away from the lake and their place on the edge is taken by small grey waders that walk in the shallows after their long flight from Siberia.

Some birds are able to live in the one place throughout the whole year, finding all the things they need to sustain life at all seasons, but many cannot do this and during the seasons that are unfavourable they move elsewhere, to return later. These movements are covered by the term "migration". The word really refers to regular movements that include the whole or a large part of a population from one area to another at fixed times in the year. The movement can be in any direction so long as it is constant and regular. It can be from one altitude to another in one small district, or from a district in southern Australia to northern Siberia or any intermediate distance. It can include the whole population and then the migration is said to be total, or part of it, when it is said to be partial. Great regularity in the time of departure and return is normal and the return of the same experienced individual to the same piece of bush or even nest site that it had left, is common.

15

Migration in Australia has been known ever since the first observers came to the country, but its true extent has been hidden by the more prominent irregular mass movements, nomadism, of many of the birds. The full extent of the true migration within the continent and beyond it is only now becoming realised and two recent developments have helped this appreciation. In recent years there has been resurgence of systematic work by the more progressive bird watchers who have formed new organisations and banded themselves into effective working groups, recording the birds in their districts month by month; this work is the essential base to future progress. The other event was the beginning of the Australian Bird Banding Scheme in 1953 by the CSIRO Division of Wildlife and Rangelands Research; birds are permanently marked with numbered bands on their legs so that their movements can be traced. Both these developments have been important, and are complementary.

In the highlands, migration is very prominent; perhaps more so than elsewhere in the continent. This is probably due to the great annual range of temperatures which is, on the whole, reasonably regular. Every stage exists, from long range transequatorial migrants to those that only move to northern New South Wales and every degree from total migration to partial.

1   TRANSEQUATORIAL MOVEMENTS: The largest and most obvious group that annually moves from Australia to the Northern Hemisphere are the waders of the families Scolopacidae and Charadriidae. They breed in northern Asia and spend the northern winter in Australia. They include the sandpipers, curlews, snipe, godwits and some plovers. Over forty species have been recorded in Australia. Our area is probably off the main migration routes and has only a few suitable swamps anyway, so very few of them come here. Five are regular visitors, the Japanese Snipe, Greenshank, Red-necked Stint, Sharp-tailed Sandpiper and the Curlew Sandpiper; ten others occasionally turn up. The only other transequatorial migrants that visit our area are the two swifts from Asia, the Spine-tailed Swift and the Fork-tailed Swift. In all these species the movement is total.

2   TRANS-TASMAN MOVEMENTS: A few birds appear in our area that have migrated from New Zealand, across the Tasman Sea. The most regular is the Double-banded Dotterel. This bird breeds in New Zealand and each autumn moves to eastern Australia and some of the islands in the South Pacific. It reaches Australia in February or March and leaves again in September or October; a few straggle inland to our area and along the main inland rivers. They have been seen around Canberra between early April and late August. The Golden Bronze

Urban Environment Of the large centres of populations, Canberra is unique. It has an overall planning authority and, as a result, the city, with a present population of over 200,000, is noted for its gardens and large number of both exotic and native trees. Native bushland remains adjacent to the central city area. This was not planned for the birds but it has enabled them to remain in numbers right within the most densely populated areas. How long this situation will remain unaltered is not known as some introduced birds are increasing perhaps to the detriment of native species. There seems little doubt however that the city plantings will remain a great attraction to altitudinal migrants from the ranges whilst ever native forest remains there. (E.S.)

2. *Grasslands:* Large expanses of treeless flat to slightly undulating country, surrounded by mountains, characterise the landscape about Canberra and the Monaro. Low temperatures preclude tree growth and before grazing by sheep the climax community was kangaroo grass *Themeda australis* and snow grass *Poa* sp. Surrounding the grassland is a narrow zone of Snow Gum *Eucalyptus pauciflora* and Candle Bark *E. rubida* which is replaced by savannah woodland on higher ground. The grassland community has been much altered by grazing activity and no longer supports Emus and Bustards, birds known to have once occurred in the habitat. Quail. larks and pipits, birds-of-prey, ravens and parrots are now the chief residents or visitors to the grasslands. (E.S.)

3. *Lakes:* Two important lakes are contained in the region: Lake George, the largest natural lake in New South Wales, and Lake Bathurst. Numerous waterfowl and other species from the inland frequent them, particularly during dry seasons in the interior. Water conservation, hydro-electric and city beautification schemes have added several more, notably Lakes Eucumbene and Burley Griffin. The photograph above shows a rocky island in Lake Bathurst on which Chestnut Teal breed among the rocks, Black Swans on the beaches, Silver Gulls and cormorants on the rocks, occasional hawks in the air, and introduced Starlings in the crevices. (E.S.)

4. *Savannah Woodland:* The woodland about Canberra is open and dominated by the eucalypts, Yellow Box *Eucalyptus melliodora* and Red Gum *E. blakeleyi.* The understorey is essentially one of grassland which in the virgin state was kangaroo grass *Themeda.* A few low shrubs occur such as *Bursaria spinosa* and these provide nesting sites for small passerine birds. One hundred years or more of grazing has altered some areas of this woodland considerably, but despite grazing pressures the bird population is varied. Some species such as magpies, parrots, cockatoos and Wood Ducks seem to have adapted to the rural changes that have taken place, some may have even increased in numbers. A modified savannah woodland occurs in the southern sections of the Australian Capital Territory and beyond where the dominant trees are Snow

5. *Dry Sclerophyll Forest:* The dry sclerophyll forest is extensively developed at altitudes of 700-880 metres, where the rainfall is slightly higher than the requirements for savannah formations. Stringy Bark *Eucalyptus macrorrhyncha* and Scribbly Gum *E. rossii*, the species illustrated here, are the dominant trees, although other eucalypts also occur. Sometimes the Grass Tree *Xanthorrhoea* is present. The ground cover is sparse consisting mainly of clumps of the grass *Poa*. Litter, bark fragments, and leaves provide favourite feeding areas for the small insectivorous birds in this habitat. Fairy wrens, flycatchers and thornbills are the more obvious bird occupants. (E.S.)

6. *Wet Sclerophyll Forest:* Below the Alpine Ash community of the higher slopes and between the altitudes of about 800 and 1,150 metres the dominant tree species of the wet sclerophyll forest are Manna Gum *Eucalyptus viminalis* and Brown Barrel *E. fastigata.* Associated with this slightly lower rainfall area of the wet sclerophyll zone is *Acacia melanoxylon,* reaching up to about 18 metres in height. Often there is a dense shrub layer. This forest is particularly rich in bird species. Honeyeaters, thornbills, whistlers, the Whipbirds, Satin Bower-birds, Wonga Pigeons and Lyrebirds occur in abundance. Along streams and tracks the Red-browed Finch and many small species live in the undergrowth. (E.S.)

7. *Wet Sclerophyll Zone:* Fern gullies are well developed in the wet sclerophyll zone especially towards the southern limits of the highland region where the rainfall is high. In places the fern gullies have reached the density of a temperate rainforest. The tree ferns *Dicksonia antarctica* and *Cyathea australis* are the dominant features of this habitat. The ground is usually clear but covered with deep litter, mosses, and fungi. It is the main feeding area for Superb Lyrebirds, Pilot Birds, Yellow Robins, White-browed Scrub Wrens and many others. The dominant eucalypt locally is the Alpine Ash *Eucalyptus delegatensis* but further south, in Victoria, it is Mountain Ash *E. regnans,* which prefers the higher rainfall available in the southern part of the highland region. (E.S.)

8. *Wet Sclerophyll Forest:* Above the Manna Gum and Brown Barrel forests, on the steep mountain slopes between 1,150-1,500 metres, where the rainfall is 1,000-1,300 mm per annum and snow falls each year, there is a forest of Alpine Ash *Eucalyptus delegatensis.* There is an understorey of shrubs and ferns, and snow grass provides a ground cover. There are numerous birds in this forest but many are restricted to the treetops. The Lyrebird extends into the zone from the gullies and lower slopes and along the mountain spurs territories are developed and many display mounds may be found. Nests of the Lyrebird are often placed on rocks and tree stumps where the forest borders the wetter gullies. (E.S.)

9. *Pine plantations:* The considerable reafforestation now going on in the region has had a serious effect on the bird life. Replacement of native trees with a forest of single exotic species has created areas which few birds inhabit. The Monterey Pine *Pinus radiata* is the most favoured species and has been planted up to 1,220 metres around Canberra; some higher plantations nearly reach the 1,800 metre level. In places all the main woodland habitats have been replaced with pine forest, and further large areas of virgin native forest are being felled for subsequent pine planting. (F.S.)

10. *Alpine Zone:* Mountain swamp communities are broad depressions at heads of gullies in the alpine woodland zone and are very characteristic features of the region above 1,500 metres. Botanically the mountain swamps consist of a succession of plant communities ranging from aquatics and sphagnum moss to a typical heath flora. *Stylidium, Epacris, Richea, Prosthanthera, Grevillea* and *Leptospermum* occur, surrounded by Snow Gum *Eucalyptus pauciflora.*

Mostly the bird fauna is that of the alpine woodland proper and, as the swamps are usually snow covered in winter, the birds that occur here in summer move to tree cover or to lower altitudes in the colder weather. Japanese Snipe have been seen at about 1,500 metres on Ginini Flats illustrated here. (E.S.)

11. *Alpine Zone:* Alpine woodland consists of a single dominant tree, the Snow Gum *Eucalyptus pauciflora* that grows above 1,600 metres altitude in the Australian Capital Territory. In the high alpine environment the tree varies in form depending upon whether it is in a sheltered situation where it may reach nine metres in height or in exposed places where it has a short stunted growth. In summer the alpine woodland is inhabited by birds including Pied Currawongs, Ravens, Crimson Rosellas, Yellow-tailed Black Cockatoos and many smaller species, but most of them depart for lower regions in the winter months leaving the woodland almost deserted.

In the alpine country to the west of Canberra are a number of aestivation sites of the Bogong Moth *Agrotis infusa* and it is said these places are regularly visited by ravens seeking the moths as food. The truth of this is not known and this lack suggests the need for more bird observations in the high elevations. (F.S.)

12. *High Alpine Herbfields:* The treeless glaciated Kosciusko Plateau is an unfavourable habitat for birds. Covered with snow for a greater part of the year this high alpine environment cannot support a resident population. Pipits nest here in the summer months and Japanese Snipe have been reported, together with some vagrant Mountain Ducks on Blue Lake, a well-known glacial feature, but most birds prefer altitudes that are below the tree line. The summer months, after the snows melt, bring a rapid cycle of growth and reproduction in the plant and animal communities that occur here. During this time a census of bird species in this rather hostile environment would prove of considerable interest.

The illustration shows Club Lake with its lateral moraines, and Mt Kosciusko, the highest land surface on continental Australia, is in the background. (E.S.)

Cuckoo has two races that are distinctively coloured, when in the hand; one breeds in New Zealand and one in southern Australia. The New Zealand race migrates in the autumn to the Solomon Islands, that is in a stream more or less parallel to that of the Australian race which travels north to New Guinea and Indonesia. The edge of the stream from New Zealand apparently sweeps the eastern coast of Australia and odd birds straggle inland as far as Canberra. Several other birds migrate from New Zealand and nearby islands to Australia but these are mainly seabirds and never come inland.

3   CONTINENTAL MOVEMENTS: The commonest migratory movements are between southern and northern Australia and some of the islands of the north. Information on some of these birds is not complete but it seems that about thirty birds of this region undertake movements of this type and the movement is total in eighteen of these. Many birds are total migrants in this area but partial migrants in other places. The total migrants include the Dollar Bird, Sacred Kingfisher, Rainbow-bird, Pallid Cuckoo, Black-eared Cuckoo, Brush Cuckoo, Golden Bronze Cuckoo, Tree Martin, Fairy Martin, Leaden Flycatcher, Satin Flycatcher, Rose Robin, Rufous Fantail, White-winged Triller, Brown Songlark, Rufous Songlark, Cicada-bird, White-browed Wood-swallow, Dusky Wood-swallow, Painted Honeyeater, Noisy Friar-bird and the White-throated Warbler. Those in which only part of the population is involved include the Fan-tailed Cuckoo, Horsfield Bronze Cuckoo, Rufous Whistler, Black-faced Cuckoo Shrike and Welcome Swallow.

A few birds migrate to our area from more southern districts each winter. Some merely pass through on their way north but some winter here and return south in the spring. Some do both; in winter birds in the Canberra area move north. Birds from the south arrive in the area; some individuals remain and others move through to more northerly places. Of these the Silvereye is a good example. Each winter birds from Tasmania, easily recognised by their brown flanks and grey throats, arrive in our area. Some, traced by banding, pass through northwards, and others remain in the area. Whilst this is happening, local banded birds also move north although many of them remain around Canberra through the winter. The Yellow-faced Honeyeater and the White-naped Honeyeater provide spectacular examples of almost total movement. Both are common, both around Canberra and farther south. In autumn, usually March, they congregate and leave the Canberra area. The departing flocks early in the season are composed mainly of Yellow-faced Honeyeaters, but by May they are mainly of White-naped Honeyeaters. When the movement is at its height many thousands of birds pass a given point each day. The same move-

17

ment has been reported from many places in south-eastern Australia. Other honeyeaters are swept up in the movement and travel in the mixed flocks.

It is possible that some of the robins seen around Canberra in the winter are from Tasmania and southern Victoria but this has not been proved by banding. The Flame Robin is very common in Tasmania and it is thought that some move across Bass Strait and spread through Victoria, southern New South Wales and parts of South Australia each winter; these birds could form part of the local winter populations. The Pink Robin is seen in the ranges each winter but is known to breed only in Tasmania and the damp fern gullies in eastern and southern Victoria; it seems possible that some of the local winter population is from these places. The Tasmanian form of the Striated Pardalote is a clearer case of migration from Tasmania. It breeds in that State and there are no well documented records of breeding on the mainland, but each winter it spreads throughout the south-east to as far north as south-eastern Queensland. It becomes common in our area, arriving about May and leaving again in early August. There are some indications that the Spotted Pardalote and the eastern form of Striated Pardalote are also partial migrants.

4 ALTITUDINAL MOVEMENTS: This is very marked and many birds leave the ranges in autumn to spend the winter at lower altitudes around Canberra and elsewhere, many probably moving on to the coast itself. During winter, the number of birds, both species and individuals, increases very greatly in Canberra and the nearby valleys. From the life history data recorded in this book, the scale of the total or partial altitudinal movements can be seen. Its magnitude was also shown in a study by D. W. Lamm and S. J. Wilson (*Emu*, Volume 65, 1966) at 1100 metres near Canberra. Of sixty-three species of birds only nineteen were year-round residents and twenty-two were summer residents. Only one, the Pink Robin, was exclusively a winter resident.

The most obvious altitudinal migrants at the lower levels are the Pied Currawong, Gang-gang Cockatoo and the Flame Robin. None of these is very common in Canberra during the summer but all are widely distributed in the ranges. In the winter they move into the city and the lower valleys and the numbers then are quite remarkable. Less spectacular movements involve the Sulphur-crested Cockatoo, King Parrot, Crimson Rosella, Golden Whistler, Crescent Honeyeater, Red Wattle-bird and many other birds.

At the highest levels, although some magpies, Yellow-tailed Black Cockatoos and a few individuals of other species remain at the tree-line, the area above it is deserted in winter by all but a few ravens, that apparently depend on garbage and refuse from ski resorts. In summer other birds move to the very tops; these include honeyeaters, Pipits, Japanese Snipe and Goldfinches.

It is strange that, despite its prominence in the area and the ease of observation, there has been little systematic study of altitudinal migration in the highlands.

5   NOMADIC MOVEMENTS: The movements of many birds in Australia follow no strict seasonal pattern but are erratic or multi-directional and are determined by the availability of food as this changes with the season or weather. In the non-breeding season most of the local birds have this tendency on a small scale but in many the movements are on a wide scale, some individuals wandering over the whole continent.

Typical of the small scale wanderings are those of the Scarlet Robin, White-fronted Chat, Little Grass Bird and Brown Quail that occur within the district. The lorikeets provide a good example of nomadic birds whose movements can be extensive and are tied to the changing supply of food, in this case the flowering of *Eucalyptus*. The flowering tends to have a seasonal regularity and so the movements of the birds have a superficial regularity. They appear in each district in turn as different eucalypts flower. Some honeyeaters also are large scale nomads that follow their food supply; these include the Regent Honeyeater, and the Little Wattle Bird that wanders up from the coast in search of *Eucalyptus, Banksia* and *Grevillea*.

The best examples of large scale nomadic movements are given by several of the waterfowl; the Grey Teal, the Coot and the Pink-eared Duck particularly. These birds are adapted to breed in shallow temporary water and their main breeding areas are on the inland plains of the Murray-Darling river system. The extent of the habitat varies enormously in accordance with the degree of flooding of the rivers, from month to month and year to year, so the birds must wander widely. They congregate briefly and then disperse widely in all directions. In general, however, water is more abundant inland in winter than in summer so there is a general movement from the inland plains each summer and concentrations of waterfowl in our area are normal in that season. From time to time, however, the inland is unusually dry and then the exodus or irruption is really extensive and vast numbers of birds congregate here. The waterbirds include Freckled Ducks, Black Ducks, Grey Teal, Pink-eared Ducks, Shovelers, Hardheads, White Ibis, Straw-necked Ibis, Coots and many others. Numerous landbirds are also involved and these include species rarely seen on the highlands such as Cockatiels, Crested Pigeons, Zebra Finches and Wood-swallows. (H.J.F.)

# BREEDING SEASONS

These are timed to occur at the season when the chances are greatest that the young can be successfully reared. This means that breeding is nicely adjusted to the environment and to a considerable extent controlled by it, and generally varies from region to region according to the climate. In the coastal districts of the Northern Territory where there is a very dry winter and a summer wet season the main breeding season is related to the wet season. In much of the inland where rainfall is erratic and unpredictable, so is the general breeding season and many birds breed at any time of the year that rain falls. In southern coastal districts, where the seasons are on the whole regular and the rainfall adequate and predictable, the general breeding season is in the spring and early summer when plant growth is at its greatest.

The systematic collection of data on the breeding seasons of birds of the Canberra district has only recently begun so it is not possible to define the breeding seasons of many birds precisely. Nevertheless, the information provided in *A Field list of the Birds of Canberra and District*, published by the Canberra Ornithologists Group, and some unpublished records, when summarised, do show the general season. The following diagram shows the numbers of species of birds found breeding in each month of the year.

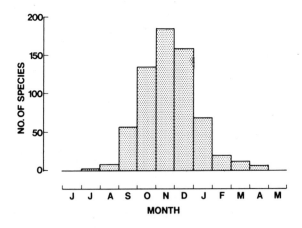

**The numbers of different species of birds breeding in each month of the year near Canberra**

In the Capital Territory breeding is a spring and early summer phenomenon. It begins in July when the winter-breeding Lyrebird lays its egg, although in some years the very early breeding Black-shouldered Kite may have nested before that. Few other species breed until the warmer months of September and October come. The month of greatest activity is November when 186 species of birds are nesting. After January, there is relatively little breeding among the local birds. The data presently available are not sufficiently precise to compare the breeding seasons of different ecological groupings of birds but they do suggest that the season of the seed-eating species begins later than that of the other groups and extends well into the autumn. That of the water birds reaches its peak relatively early, in October. (H.J.F.)

# BIRD FAMILIES

## EMUS

Originally there were three species of emu. In addition to the mainland species, which had a distinct race in Tasmania, there were two smaller, darker species on Kangaroo Island and King Island. All of these island forms are now extinct. The fate of these three insular emus demonstrates the disadvantage of being a large, flightless bird on an island during the pastoral invasion of the place.

Family Dromaiidae — Emus
EMU *Dromaius novaehollandiae*

PLATE I

IDENTIFICATION: Length, 200 cm. The largest Australian bird; the legs are very long, as is the neck, but the head is small. Plumage: very dark brown to light grey-brown, fading with age; head and neck feathers, black, short, sparse and hair-like; bare skin of the head and throat, bluish; the strong legs and feet are dark grey-brown, and in adaptation to the running habit the hind toe is absent; bill, dark brown to black; iris, pale to dark brown. Females are larger than males. In the first half of the year the nuptial plumage allows pairs to be sexed. The female acquires a dense covering of black feathers so the head and neck and the general body colour darkens. The male remains very pale with a conspicuous blue neck, in contrast to the dark female with a black neck. The blue skin on the female's neck is darker than that on the male's neck but is covered by the black feathers.

For the first two months the chicks are dark brown with a rufous tinge and bold off-white to yellow longitudinal stripes. They moult into adult plumage but do not attain full size for eighteen months or so, depending on feeding conditions.

VOICE: The voice is a deep guttural grunt in both sexes and the

22

female also makes a deep, rhythmic "booming" or "thumping" that seems to come from her heart.

DISTRIBUTION: The Emu was formerly distributed over most of the continent probably avoiding only the densest forests on the coast. It still maintains its numbers in many places but has been destroyed by close settlement over very large areas, particularly in eastern Australia. In New South Wales, for instance, it is now numerous only on the far western plains. It formerly occurred on the highlands and was reported to be common on the Limestone Plains, that part of Canberra that now supports several suburbs, a drive-in theatre, a race course, a crematorium and the CSIRO Division of Wildlife Research. Its demise in that locality was expected but it has disappeared elsewhere also. In our area it occurs, and then only in very small numbers, in alpine woodland around Cabramurra and Kiandra in the Snowy Mountains.

HABITS: In the highlands Emus are rarely seen and then only as pairs or individuals in the ranges. Where it is abundant, inland, it lives in small bands, or sometimes large flocks. It is flightless and runs very swiftly, forty to fifty kilometres per hour, with an ungainly gait. It is not easily frightened and is inquisitive and unless disturbed it can often be induced to come close — reversing the roles of watcher and watched. It has the unfortunate habit of forcing its way under or through fences and of running through flocks of lambing ewes, and wheat crops, but in the east it is now generally tolerated and spared the destruction that other large animals in the inland suffer. In the west, however, it is still considered vermin in wheat-growing districts and destroyed accordingly.

BREEDING: In its mainland range it breeds regularly in the winter, eggs being laid in May and June. In the highlands eggs have been found in August, presumably laid in July. Breeding at this time would often involve eggs being incubated in snow. The nest is usually in open country and is a bed of grass and leaves trampled down. The clutch size in the Riverina, New South Wales, varies from seven to eleven but eight or nine eggs is commonest. The eggs are dark green and granulated, and average $14 \times 9$ cm. The male incubates and cares for the young. The incubation time is eight to nine weeks.

FEEDING: Emus feed mainly on plant material; the seeds, fruits and leaves of a wide variety of plants and trees. They readily eat cultivated cereals where these are grown. Plague grasshoppers and caterpillars and doubtless other small animals are eaten when they are available. (H.J.F.)

# GREBES

Grebes are waterbirds of moderate to large size that are very highly adapted for an aquatic life. Their bodies are streamlined and the legs are set at the extreme rear of the body and flattened laterally to cut the water efficiently. The toes are equipped with prominent lobes for swimming, and propulsion is entirely by means of the feet. The plumage is very compact and dense and the birds are able to suddenly compress the feathers tightly, expelling the air, so that aided by the feet they sink very rapidly. They also eat their own feathers and feed them to their young for some unknown reason, apparently associated with digestion. The wings are small and the flight weak. They build floating nests and seldom come on to land.

Most grebes are dark above and pale below and many have conspicuous head colours or ornaments; both sexes have distinct breeding plumages. They indulge in mutual courtship displays that are often very spectacular.

The relationships of the various grebes is very much in need of revision. In the meantime, about twenty species are recognised of which three occur in Australia and have been seen in the region considered in this book.

Family Podicipedidae — Grebes
## LITTLE GREBE *Tachybaptus novaehollandiae*
PLATE II

IDENTIFICATION: Length, 28 cm. Breeding plumage: general colour above, dark brown; head and neck, black; face, black, *chestnut stripe on side of neck and a yellow spot before the eye*; chin and throat, black; remainder of under-parts, silver-grey; bill, short and sharp, black; legs and feet, grey; iris, yellow. The sexes are similar. Non-breeding and juvenile birds are alike and similar to Hoary-headed Grebes but the face markings, although pale, can still be detected.

VOICE: It has a shrill, prolonged chatter.

DISTRIBUTION: It extends throughout New Guinea, the Solomons, Celebes, and Moluccas, in addition to Australia. In Australia it is found throughout the continent and Tasmania wherever suitable water conditions exist. It is a freshwater species and is found in lakes, streams, swamps and stock dams. Around Canberra it is found on all the lakes. Despite its apparently weak powers of flight, it is very nomadic and appears on temporary waters far out on the plains soon after they are formed, but the true nature of its movements is not known. It has been suggested that in the north it is to some extent migratory.

HABITS: It is usually singly or in pairs and rarely in groups, although in areas of suitable swamp loose breeding colonies can occur. It dives frequently, with hardly a ripple, and remains underwater for up to sixteen seconds. It is rather shy and dives to escape attention. When pursued it escapes by pattering along the water and diving; it can be induced to fly only with great difficulty, unlike the very similar Hoary-headed Grebe. It apparently moves from place to place at night.

BREEDING: The breeding season in Canberra begins in early October and concludes in mid-January. The nest is a floating heap of swamp vegetation that can be more than thirty centimetres in diameter. The eggs are laid in a small depression in the centre and are so low that they are frequently wet. When the bird is not brooding, she covers the eggs with nest material and even pauses to do so when disturbed. The eggs are pale bluish-white with a thin, white, limy coating when laid but quickly stain brown from the decaying material of the nest. They average $35 \times 25$ mm in size. The incubation period is twenty-one to twenty-five days. Both sexes share in incubation and caring for the young which take to the water soon after hatching and are frequently carried on the parent's back.

FEEDING: The bird feeds mainly by diving but has been seen picking material from the surface. The composition of the food is not known but is usually assumed to be plant and animal material. (H.J.F.)

## HOARY-HEADED GREBE *Poliocephalus poliocephalus*
PLATE II

IDENTIFICATION: Length, 30 cm. General colour above, dark grey-brown; head, brown-black; wings have pale wing bar; throat, grey; upper breast, pale rufous; remainder of under-parts silky white; bill short and sharp, blackish-grey; legs and feet, olive-green; iris, black, mottled cream. The sexes are similar. In breeding plumage the *head and neck are covered with long white hair-like feathers*, giving a "hoary" appearance.

VOICE: Unlike the Little Grebe which has a loud shrill chatter, the Hoary-headed Grebe is silent, except for a thin squeak when tending young.

DISTRIBUTION: It has a much more restricted distribution than the Little Grebe. It is found in south-western Western Australia and in the south-east. In the west it seldom travels north of Point Cloates; in the east its northern limit of distribution is southern Queensland but vagrants occur along the coast to as far north as Cairns. It is most

25

numerous in south-western New South Wales. In our area it is very common on all large water areas and congregations of several hundred occur. Its movements are not understood but experience in western New South Wales, as well as the local changes in numbers, suggest that it is highly nomadic. It favours swamps and lakes and visits saltwater estuaries far more often than does the Little Grebe.

HABITS: It is found singly, in pairs or small groups but in dry times forms very large flocks. It is more gregarious than the Little Grebe. Its general habits are similar to those of the Little Grebe but it flies more readily than that species which can hardly be induced to leave the water. When on the wing it flies swiftly and low over the water.

BREEDING: Present information suggests that it breeds in the period November to January, that is later than the Little Grebe. It tends to breed in colonies and up to four hundred nests have occurred in one part of Lake Bathurst. It chooses places where there is thick submergent vegetation and builds a floating nest usually a little smaller than that of the Little Grebe. The clutch size is four or sometimes as many as six. The eggs, when fresh, are greenish-white in colour and average $40 \times 28$ mm in size.

FEEDING: Nothing is known of the food of either of the small grebes. As they are almost identical in size and general habits a comparison of the food eaten would be of great interest as a possible indication of how they manage to live together in large numbers on the same lake or swamp. (H.J.F.)

## GREAT CRESTED GREBE *Podiceps cristatus*

PLATE II

IDENTIFICATION: Length, 50 cm. General colour above, dark grey-brown; wing, dark grey with a white band; face, white; there is a double tuft of *elongated, almost black feathers on the head*; underparts, silky white; bill, long and pointed, dark brown above, carmine below; legs and feet, olive; iris, crimson. The sexes are similar. In the breeding season both sexes have a prominent chestnut ruff of elongated feathers around base of skull and upper neck. Juveniles are generally similar to non-breeding adults but the crest is much reduced in size.

VOICE: The Great Crested Grebe has a variety of harsh calls, described as rattling, barking or moaning, sometimes used as part of its complicated display actions.

DISTRIBUTION: The species has a very wide distribution, in several races, and ranges across Europe, Asia, North Africa and Australia. The Australian race occurs in south-west Western Australia where it is rare but it is quite common in parts of the east. In the east it extends down the coastal districts from north Queensland to South Australia and Tasmania. It is found throughout New South Wales, and Victoria, ranging inland to follow the swamps of the major river systems. Elsewhere in Australia rare vagrants appear from time to time. In the Canberra area it is a relatively common breeding species on the large lakes. The numbers fluctuate from time to time but nothing is known of its movements.

HABITS: It is usually solitary or in small groups but six to eight hundred have been seen in one flock in a lignum swamp on the Lachlan River in the inland. It is usually in deep water with the body low and the long neck fully extended. When startled it dives quickly and smoothly, and surfaces a long way off. When taking flight it patters along the water a long distance before take-off; on landing it hits the water breast first, unlike the ducks. Its flight is low and laboured with very rapid wing beats and the neck and head are depressed. There are spectacular displays in the breeding season, both sexes shaking the head and ruff, arching the neck, diving and "dancing" breast to breast and fairly erect on the water.

BREEDING: The breeding season near Canberra is in November to January, and up to 200 pairs have bred on Lake Bathurst. The nest is a great floating mass of aquatic vegetation and can be sixty to ninety centimetres in diameter; it is rather flat and the eggs are often wet. It is often built among rushes or submergent vegetation and so is tethered. As with the other grebes, the eggs are covered with nest material when the parents leave them. The usual clutch is three or four but it can be as great as six. The eggs are pale green with a coating of lime but quickly stain dark brown; they average 50 × 35 mm in size. The incubation period is about twenty-eight days and the young are habitually carried on the parent's back.

FEEDING: There has been no study of the food in Australia, but in England they eat mainly fish, insects and crustacea and some (15% of total) aquatic plants. (H.J.F.)

# PELICANS, CORMORANTS AND DARTERS

Pelicans, cormorants and darters form a group of closely related water-birds which have diverged mainly in their methods of catching aquatic prey. Pelicans reach down from the water surface or plunge dive for food, cormorants surface dive and pursue their prey underwater, and darters surface dive or sink and stalk prey underwater. As a result of the necessary anatomical modifications for these different feeding methods the adults differ markedly in silhouette. The naked chicks on hatching look virtually identical except for size.

Chicks obtain food by prodding a parent's throat which stimulates the regurgitation of food for them. They tend to nest in colonies containing several species of waterbirds. Males select the nest sites and bring in nest material and the females build the nest. Both males and females take turns in guarding the nest, incubating the eggs and feeding the chicks.

They are large to medium sized birds with long necks and short legs. Unlike other waterbirds in our area all four toes are united in a web. The throat is extendible down a gullet to the stomach, and is partly naked thus forming what is called a gular pouch. Fish and other prey are swallowed whole, head first, and the head of a large one may be partly digested in the stomach while the tail is still in the mouth. Chicks obtain food by reaching into the mouth and throat of a parent.

Authors differ on whether cormorants and darters should be in the same or separate families but we prefer to keep them separate.

### Family Pelecanidae — Pelicans

There are seven species of pelicans in the genus *Pelecanus* which occurs on all the continents except Antarctica. There is only one species of pelican in Australia. It differs from others by its face being feathered between the bill and the eyes which have naked circles around them. Pelicans are large waterbirds with very long bills and enormous gular pouches. Their legs are short and stout and their feet are large with all four toes united in a web. In breeding birds, especially at the time of pair formation, the feet and gular pouches are brilliantly coloured. The pouches are used as dipnets for fishing and they are also used as cooling surfaces during hot weather. During courtship the long bills and extended pouches are used as flags in several display patterns.

### PELICAN *Pelecanus conspicillatus*

PLATE II

IDENTIFICATION: Length, 163 cm. General body colour, white; primaries, secondaries, primary coverts, leading edges of wings, shoulders, sides of rump and tail, black; some other black feathers irregularly distributed on wings and rump; long bill and gular pouch, pinkish-yellow; naked skin around eye, yellow; legs and feet, slate-blue; iris, brown. Females, smaller with shorter bill. Immatures, shorter white wing coverts. Juveniles, white and brown plumage.

VOICE: It is normally silent but gruntlike sounds are made at the nesting colonies.

DISTRIBUTION: It occurs in Australia, including Tasmania, and disperses to Indonesia, Caroline Islands, New Guinea and New Zealand. The pelican frequents inland fresh and saltwater lakes and lagoons, swamps, estuaries and bays. Around Canberra it occurs regularly on larger bodies of water such as Lakes Bathurst, George and Burley Griffin.

HABITS: They usually occur in groups but sometimes singly. They tend to fly in formation and to soar on thermals and updrafts. The take off is laborious and heavy but the gliding landing, with a long taxi to a halt, is very graceful. They are often seen swimming in formation, apparently driving fish into the shallows, or roosting in very dense groups on the water's edge.

BREEDING: The breeding season is greatly affected by rainfall but in northern Australia tends to be in autumn and in southern Australia in the spring. Breeding places are mainly on the inland rivers, but occur also on some offshore islands.

They normally nest in dense colonies on sandy islands. Occasionally nests are dispersed in lignum and then large platforms are built of sticks and other vegetation. The eggs are white with a limy coating and their average size is $90 \times 59$ mm. The clutch size is normally two and rarely three. The only local breeding records were abortive attempts to breed on Lake George in 1963 and 1968. Pelicans readily desert their nests when disturbed by dogs or people. Their eggs then fall prey to crows and gulls and naked chicks may then die of exposure.

FEEDING: The food consists of fish, shrimp and other aquatic animals which are captured in shallow water. Like most pelicans it feeds by reaching down from the water surface with the long neck and bill. On very rare occasions it has been seen plunge-diving. This is the usual feeding method of the Brown Pelican of America.

(G.F.vT.)

## Family Anhingidae — Darters

There are two species of darter, one in the New World and one in the Old World, including Australia. They are both in the same genus *Anhinga*. Some authors consider them all the same whereas some divide the Old World darters into several species. Darters frequent swamps, estuaries and lakes in those parts of the world where such water bodies are rarely, if ever, covered by ice.

They are specialised for the stalking and spearing of fish and other aquatic prey underwater. Thus they are the avian counterpart of the modern spearfisherman. A special hinge mechanism at the eighth neck vertebra enables the neck muscles to dart the small head with stout and pointed bill rapidly forward to puncture and stun fish and other prey. Because of this hinge the neck is G-shaped.

In the water darters use their feet for propulsion. As in other diving birds the legs are short and situated at the rear of the body. This rear position of the legs gives them an upright posture when on land. All four toes of the feet are united in a web.

## DARTER *Anhinga melanogaster*

PLATE II

IDENTIFICATION: Length, 90 cm. Male: general body colour, glossy black, with pale streaks on the upper-wing coverts and the scapulars; head and upper neck, brownish-black with a white stripe extending down the sides of the neck from below the eye, and a short white stripe near the lower mandible; neck is very long; naked skin around the eyes and on the throat, yellow; legs and feet, flesh-yellow; iris, yellow. Females, grey above and white to pale buff below. Immatures, like females, but with less distinct side of neck stripe and shorter upper-wing coverts.

VOICE: Clicking sounds away from nest area, where cawing, whistling, purring and hissing sounds are made.

DISTRIBUTION: It occurs in Africa south of the Sahara, Madagascar, the Middle East, India through Indonesia, lowland New Guinea, and Australia. In Australia it is found wherever there are suitable bodies of water. It is rare in southern mainland Australia and absent from Tasmania. It frequents lakes, swamps, rivers and sheltered coastal inlets, preferring placid rather than turbulent water. There are regularly a few birds at Lakes George and Burley Griffin.

HABITS: The plumage is permeable to water; this permeability is for reducing buoyancy. As buoyancy is reduced the body sinks slowly beneath the water surface until the back is awash. When it thus swims with only head and neck above water it resembles a swimming snake and consequently darters are often called snakebirds. Reduced buoyancy also facilitates slow and deliberate movements during stalking underwater. Out of the water the plumage is water repellent largely due to the oily secretions of the preen gland above the tail.

After swimming they are often seen with their wings spread, presumably to dry them in the sun. Normally darters perch and nest in trees above water. At some treeless swamps they also rest and nest in reed beds. In flight they tend to soar on thermals and updrafts. With their long wings, tails and necks they resemble flying crosses.

BREEDING: In northern Australia the breeding season is in the wet season but in the south-east it occurs in the spring. Darters breed in small groups on trees which stand in water. The nests are mere platforms of sticks but they are sometimes quite bulky. In our area they nest at Lake Burley Griffin.

The eggs are pale green with a limy coating and their average size is 56 × 34 mm. The clutch size varies between three and five.

FEEDING: Darters feed mainly on fish, insects and occasionally young tortoises (G.F.vT.)

Family Phalacrocoracidae — Cormorants
There are thirty-four species of cormorants in two or more genera which occur throughout the world including both polar regions. Cormorants feed in all types of fresh and salt water but they rarely go out of sight of land. Provided there is open water available containing aquatic animals, cormorants thrive and breed as well in areas covered by ice and snow as in hot tropical deserts. There are five species of cormorants in Australia. All of them feed in the sea, but only four frequent inland waters, including those in our area.

They are adapted for the underwater pursuit and grabbing of fish and other aquatic prey. Like darters, their body plumage is water-permeable under water and water-repellent out of the water and they are often seen with their wings spread, presumably to dry and sun them. They also have long necks and at the rear of their bodies short legs with all four toes united in a web. Cormorants differ from darters in having sinuous, rather than G-shaped, necks, larger heads, and strong hooks at the ends of their upper mandibles.

Most cormorants are black dorsally and either black or white ventrally. Several species have black-bellied and white-bellied colour phases. Mostly white, but in some species also black, nuptial plumes occur on the head, neck, back or rump of adult birds at the beginning of the breeding season.

## BLACK CORMORANT *Phalacrocorax carbo*

PLATE II

IDENTIFICATION: Length, 79 cm. *General colour, black with a bronze-brown gloss*; behind bare skin of face and throat is a white border; in breeding plumage white nuptial plumes occur all over the head and upper neck and on the sides of the rump; *bare skin around eyes, and on face and throat, yellow*; bill, dark grey and lower mandible is paler than the upper mandible; legs and feet, black; iris, green. The sexes are similar. Immatures are brown dorsally and white mottled with brown ventrally. Juveniles have brown iris which changes in immatures through yellow to green.

VOICE: It is normally silent but at the nest a variety of croaking and gargling calls are made. During courtship females become hoarse and almost silent. After egg-laying female voices become louder and indistinguishable from the raucous male voices.

DISTRIBUTION: Black Cormorants occur in a broad band from the east coast of Canada, Greenland, Iceland and northern Norway, across Europe and Afro-Asia to Japan and Australasia, including Tasmania and New Zealand. In Australia they are common only in the south-east and disperse to New Guinea, and islands in the Tasman Sea and the Southern Ocean. They frequent mainly marine bays, estuaries, rivers and lakes. Occasionally they also visit ponds and dams. They are numerous on Lakes Burley Griffin, George and Bathurst.

HABITS: In flight they often alternate a series of wing strokes by gliding or coasting a short distance. Groups of them often fly in formation like geese and other waterbirds do. They perch in trees and on poles and logs.

BREEDING: On lakes near Canberra, most breeding is in the period November to April. Black Cormorants nest in colonies in trees, in swamps, or on ledges of precipitous cliffs, or on the ground on islands. Even on the ground they build stick nests composed of branches and other plant material. Material is continually added to the nest until the chicks fledge and nests may be used several years in succession. The usual clutch size is four but some birds may lay as many as six eggs. The eggs are pale blue-green with a limy coating and their average size is 63 × 40 mm. In the Netherlands, young of the Black Cormorant start to fly seven weeks after hatching and they become independent of their parents twelve to thirteen weeks after hatching. In our area they breed at Lake Bathurst and have bred on Lake George.

FEEDING: They feed mainly on fish and shrimp but they also take other arthropods. (G.F.vT.)

## PIED CORMORANT *Phalacrocorax varius*

PLATE II

IDENTIFICATION: Length, 76 cm. *General plumage, black above and white below*; outer parts of thighs, black; tail, black; forehead, crown and back of neck, black; remainder of head and neck, white. *Naked skin in front of eye, yellow or orange*, remainder of face below and throat, greenish-blue; bill, horn colour; legs and feet, black; iris, green. The sexes are similar. General plumage of immatures is brown above and mixed brown and white below.

VOICE: Silent away from roosts and nests where males are loud and raucous and females softly hiss.

DISTRIBUTION: It occurs in mainland Australia and New Zealand. It is a bird of large water bodies such as bays, estuaries, inlets, lakes and rivers. In Australia it inhabits the marine bays and inlets and the larger inland lakes and rivers. In our area a few are occasionally seen on Lakes George and Burley Griffin.

HABITS: In flight they often alternate a series of wing strokes by gliding or coasting a short distance. Groups of them often fly in formation like geese and other waterbirds do. They perch on dead trees, boats and poles.

BREEDING: They nest in trees, mangroves, cliff ledges and small offshore islands. Even on the ground they build stick nests composed of branches and other plant material. The clutch size varies from one to five. The eggs are greenish-white with a limy coating and their average size is $60 \times 38$ mm. The Pied Cormorant is not known to breed in our area.

FEEDING: They feed mainly on fish, and to a lesser extent on shrimp and insects. (G.F.vT.)

## LITTLE BLACK CORMORANT *Phalacrocorax sulcirostris*
PLATE II

IDENTIFICATION: Length, 62 cm. *General colour, entirely black*; in breeding plumage white nuptial plumes occur irregularly and sparsely on head, neck and back, concentrated in stripe over eye and tuft behind eye; *bare skin of face, blue-grey*; upper mandible black above, remainder, grey; legs and feet, black; iris, dark green. The sexes are similar. Immatures have brown feathers in their general plumage. Juveniles have a brown iris which changes in immatures through yellow to green.

VOICE: They are normally silent but at the nest males have a variety of grunts and croaks.

33

DISTRIBUTION: It occurs from Borneo and Java through New Guinea to Australia, including Tasmania, and is found also in New Caledonia and New Zealand. It occurs throughout Australia where there is suitable habitat — estuaries, inlets, rivers, lakes and occasionally dams. In our area individuals are regularly seen along the Murrumbidgee and around the lakes.

HABITS: In flight they often alternate a series of wing strokes by gliding or coasting a short distance. Groups of them often fly in formation like geese and other waterbirds do. They perch on dead trees, boats, rafts and cables.

BREEDING: They nest in colonies in trees in shallow lakes and swamps. The nest is a platform of sticks. The usual clutch size is four but clutches may include as many as five eggs. The eggs are pale blue with a limy coating and their average size is $47 \times 32$ mm. It is not known to breed locally.

FEEDING: They feed on fish, shrimp and insects. (G.F.vT.)

## LITTLE PIED CORMORANT *Phalacrocorax melanoleucos*
PLATE II

IDENTIFICATION: Length, 58 cm. *General colour, black above and white below*; outer part of thighs, white in most, black in a few; forehead, crown and back of neck, black; remainder of head and neck, white; *naked skin around eye and throat, yellow*; bill, mostly yellow, brown on upper-parts; legs and feet, black; iris, brown. In breeding plumage there is a black tuft on the forehead and white tufts on sides of black crown. The sexes are similar. Juveniles have black above eyes and on thighs.

VOICE: They are normally silent, but make cooing sounds at the nest.

DISTRIBUTION: It occurs from Sumatra through Indonesia to New Guinea and the Solomon Islands, Australia, including Tasmania, New Caledonia and New Zealand. This is the most abundant and widely distributed of the Australian cormorants and is likely to be found on any body of water, large or small, marine or fresh, even on ephemeral bodies of water in the far inland. In our region it is very common on the lakes and rivers and is often seen on dams.

HABITS: In flight they often alternate a series of wing strokes by gliding or coasting a short distance. Groups of them often fly in formation like geese and other waterbirds do. They perch on dead trees, boats, rafts, poles, wires and cables.

BREEDING: They nest in colonies on trees in shallow lakes and swamps. The nest is a platform of sticks. Clutch size is usually four or five. The eggs are pale blue with a limy coating, and their average size is 47 × 32 mm. They breed on the lakes around Canberra.

FEEDING: They feed mainly on crustacea including crayfish, and occasionally on small fish and other aquatic animals. (G.F.vT.)

# HERONS, STORKS, IBISES AND SPOONBILLS

Herons, egrets, bitterns, ibises and spoonbills form a group of closely related waterbirds that have diverged mainly in their methods of catching aquatic prey. They are large to medium sized birds with long necks and long legs. The long legs are an adaptation for wading in shallow water and walking through tall grass. Their toes are not united in a web. Fish and other large prey are swallowed head first.

The parental behaviour patterns are very similar to those of the pelicans, darters, and cormorants, described in the previous section.

They differ when foraging in that herons, egrets and bitterns stalk, storks capture prey animals while walking through marsh vegetation or grassland, ibises probe, and spoonbills sift for prey animals. Bitterns differ from herons, ibises, and spoonbills in rarely moving out of dense marshes, having relatively shorter legs, tending to be solitary in feeding and nesting, and in adopting a characteristic vertical posture when alarmed. As a result of the necessary anatomical modifications for the different feeding methods they differ markedly in silhouette when fully grown but the chicks in the nests are very similar in shape.

### Family Ardeidae — Herons, Egrets and Bitterns

There are approximately fifty species of herons and approximately twelve species of bitterns spread throughout most of the world except the polar regions. They are medium to large sized birds with relatively long necks and legs. They are adapted for stalking large invertebrate and small vertebrate prey in grassland, marshes, and shallow water. Their long necks are G-shaped due to a special hinge mechanism at the sixth vertebra. This hinge permits a rapid extension of the neck and thus a stout straight bill is shot forward to grab an unwary prey. Long naked legs permit slow deliberate stalking through tall grass and shallow water. Frangible feathers called powder down, which occur in tufts at various locations on the body, provide a powder which, during preening, helps to clean the slime from fish, amphibia and molluscs off their plumage.

During pair-formation and courtship prior to breeding, species and individual recognition is helped by distinctive patterns of nuptial plumes. The nuptial plumes of egrets (white herons) were formerly marketed as ornaments for ladies' hats. The depredations by egret hunters in the breeding colonies caused a public outcry which helped start bird protection movements and legislation. The trade in and wearing of egret plumes is now prohibited in most parts of the world.

The coloration of face, bill, legs and feet vary markedly with age, season, nutrition, locality and individual. During courtship iris, face, bill and upper legs of egrets may briefly go bright red.

In Australia there are six species of herons of which three occur in our area, five species of egret four of which occur, and there are three species of bitterns of which two occur in our area.

## WHITE-NECKED HERON *Ardea pacifica*

PLATE III

IDENTIFICATION: Length, 91 cm. *General plumage, dark slate* glossed with green above; *head, neck and upper breast mainly white* with some black-tipped feathers in front and with chestnut spots and patches on crown, hind neck and upper breast; lower breast, abdomen and under-tail, dark slate streaked with white; primaries, black; *white patch at bend of dark wing* conspicuous in flight; long thin nuptial plumes on back, maroon; bill, legs and feet, black; face, blue; iris, yellow-green. The sexes are similar. Non-breeding birds lack nuptial plumes, are spotted grey instead of chestnut on crown, hind neck and upper chest, and have more black spots on front neck than breeding birds.

VOICE: When startled they utter a loud croak. A variety of guttural calls are made at the nest.

DISTRIBUTION: It occurs throughout Australia wherever there is suitable aquatic habitat. It is a rare vagrant in Tasmania and also in New Zealand. It frequents the margins of lakes, swamps, rivers and dams. In our area usually single birds are seen.

HABITS: In flight the neck is folded, the head is close to the body and the legs trail beyond the tail feathers. They perch, rest and roost in trees.

BREEDING: In northern Australia it breeds in the summer wet season but in the south-east in spring. The nests are built in trees which are normally in or hanging over water. Usually single nests are found and they do not form nesting colonies but occasionally a number of birds will nest in groups of adjacent trees. Nest platforms are loosely constructed of sticks, and eggs and chicks are visible through the structure from below. Clutch sizes vary from one to six but are usually four. The eggs are green, and their average size is $53 \times 38$ mm. It bred near Canberra in 1968.

FEEDING: They feed by wading in shallow water and stalking through wet grass in search of prey. Their diet consists mainly of insects, crustacea, fish and amphibia. (G.F.vT.)

## WHITE-FACED HERON *Ardea novaehollandiae*
PLATE III

IDENTIFICATION: Length, 67 cm. *General plumage, light blue-grey*; primaries, black; *forehead, face and throat, white*; long thin nuptial plumes on back reaching almost to end of tail; chestnut spots and patches only on upper breast; bill, black; in front of eye, greenish-yellow; iris, yellow; legs and feet, olive-yellow. The sexes are similar. Immature birds lack nuptial plumes, white face and chestnut on breast.

VOICE: When startled they utter a loud croak. A variety of guttural calls are made at the nest.

DISTRIBUTION: It occurs throughout Australia, including Tasmania, and nearby islands including Celebes, Lesser Sunda Islands, New Guinea, New Caledonia and New Zealand. In Australia it is common or at least of regular occurrence wherever there is suitable aquatic habitat. It frequents lakes, swamps, estuaries, mangroves, dams, tidal mudflats and grasslands. In our area it is the heron most frequently seen, either alone or in small groups.

HABITS: In flight the neck is folded, the head is held close to the body and the legs trail beyond the tail feathers. They perch, rest and roost in trees. They are seen usually singly or in pairs stalking in shallow water.

BREEDING: The breeding season around Canberra is in the spring and early summer, mid-October to January. The nests are built in trees which are not necessarily near water. Normally single nests are found and they do not form nesting colonies, although occasionally several nests are found in adjacent trees. Nest contents are visible through the structure from below. The clutch size varies from one to seven, usually

37

about four. The eggs are pale blue, and their average size is 48 × 35 mm.

FEEDING: They feed by wading in shallow water and stalking through grass in search of prey. Their diet consists mainly of insects, crustacea, fish, amphibia, and occasionally small reptiles, birds and mammals. (G.F.vT.)

## WHITE EGRET *Egretta alba*

PLATE III

IDENTIFICATION: Length, 83 cm. Breeding plumage: general colour, white; *nuptial plumes only on back*, extending beyond tail; *face, blue-green, bill, black or black with yellow base*; legs and feet, black to light brown; iris, yellow. The sexes are similar. Non-breeding birds lack nuptial plumes, and have greenish-yellow face and yellow bill.

VOICE: When startled, they utter a low-pitched loud croak. A variety of guttural calls are made at the nest.

DISTRIBUTION: It occurs in the tropical and warm temperate regions of all continents including Australia, Tasmania, and New Zealand. It is likely to be found in association with water anywhere in Australia. It frequents lakes, swamps, estuaries, mangroves, and dams. Usually single birds are seen from time to time on large and small water bodies in our area but on the northern and eastern coasts immense congregations occur.

HABITS: In flight the neck is folded, the head is held close to the body and the legs trail beyond the tail feathers. They perch, rest and roost in trees.

BREEDING: The nests are normally in colonies in trees standing in water, but in some localities in reed beds. Nest platforms are made of sticks. The clutch size is usually three or four but occasionally up to six. The eggs are pale greenish-blue, and their average size is 53 × 38 mm. It is not known to breed in the Canberra area.

FEEDING: They feed mainly by standing in shallow water watching for prey. Their diet consists mainly of small aquatic animals including insects, crustacea, fish, amphibia, and occasionally mice and other small mammals. (G.F.vT.)

38

## PLUMED EGRET *Egretta intermedia*

PLATE III

IDENTIFICATION: Length, 62 cm. *Neck as long as body*. Plumage, white; *bill, yellow*; face, greenish-yellow; upper legs, flesh-colour or brown; lower legs, black; iris, yellow. The sexes are similar. Nuptial plumes on back and breast, and face blue-green in breeding birds.

VOICE: When startled, they utter a loud croaking sound. A variety of guttural calls are made at the nest.

DISTRIBUTION: It occurs from Africa through southern Asia and Indonesia to northern and eastern Australia. It is uncommon in southern Australia. It frequents lake shores, swamps, estuaries, mangroves, and dams and is occasionally seen in our region.

HABITS: In flight the neck is folded, the head is held close to the body and the legs trail beyond the tail feathers. They perch, rest and roost in trees.

BREEDING: The nests are normally in colonies in trees standing in water. Nest platforms are made of sticks. The clutch size varies from three to six but is usually four. The eggs are sea-green or blue-green, and their average size is $46 \times 33$ mm. It does not breed in our region. On the north coast of New South Wales the breeding season is in the period October to November.

FEEDING: They feed by wading and searching in shallow water. Their diet consists mainly of small aquatic animals including insects, crustacea, fish and amphibia. (G.F.vT.)

## LITTLE EGRET *Egretta garzetta*

PLATE III

IDENTIFICATION: Length, 56 cm. *Neck as long as body*. Plumage, white; *bill, black*; face yellow; legs and top of feet, black; soles, yellow; iris, yellow. The sexes are similar. Nuptial plumes on back and breast, and two long, narrow plumes on nape in breeding birds. Immatures have black soles.

VOICE: At the nest a variety of croaking and bubbling calls are made.

DISTRIBUTION: It occurs from southern Europe and Africa through southern Asia and Indonesia to northern and eastern Australia. In southern Australia it is more often seen on the inland swamps. It is a rare vagrant in Tasmania and New Zealand, and uncommon in our

39

area. It frequents lake shores, swamps, estuaries, mangroves, and dams and seems rather more nomadic than other egrets.

HABITS: In flight the neck is folded, the head is held close to the body and the legs trail beyond the tail feathers. They perch, rest and roost in trees.

BREEDING: The nests are normally in colonies in trees standing in water, but in some localities they are also in reed beds, on cliff ledges or on small rocky islands. Nest platforms are made of sticks. Clutch sizes vary from one to five, usually three or four. The eggs are bright bluish-green, and their average size is $43 \times 31$ mm. It does not breed in the Canberra area.

FEEDING: They feed by wading and searching in shallow water. Their diet consists mainly of small aquatic animals including insects, crustacea, fish, and amphibia. Occasionally they join flocks of Cattle Egrets to feed in grassland near large grazing mammals. The mammals serve to flush insects and other prey for them. (G.F.vT.)

## CATTLE EGRET *Ardeola ibis*

PLATE III

IDENTIFICATION: Length, 53 cm. *Neck shorter than squat body.* Plumage, white; *bill, yellow*; face, greenish-yellow; legs and feet, dark greenish-yellow; iris, yellow. The sexes are similar. Buff-coloured nuptial plumes on crown, nape, throat and back in breeding birds.

VOICE: A variety of guttural calls are made at the nest.

DISTRIBUTION: Formerly it only occurred in southern Europe and Afro-Asia. During the last hundred years it has spread to the Americas and Australasia. The spread is due to vagrant and introduced birds establishing themselves in man-made cattle country. It established itself in Australia within the last fifty years, spread in 1965 to Tasmania, and in 1975 one was found on Macquarie Island. In our area it is a common visitor.

HABITS: Normally small flocks feed around and perch on large grazing animals. In flight the neck is folded, the head is held close to the body and the legs trail beyond the tail feathers. They perch, rest and roost hidden in the dense foliage of trees and shrubs.

BREEDING: The nests are normally in colonies in the dense foliage of trees and shrubs near or in water. Nest platforms are made of sticks.

40

Clutch sizes vary from one to four, usually three or four. The eggs are white with a slight blue-green tinge, and their average size is 45 × 33 mm. It does not breed in our region.

FEEDING: They feed mainly on grasshoppers and other insects that are flushed by grazing animals, and to a lesser extent on a variety of small aquatic animals and on external parasites of grazing animals. (G.F.vT.)

## NANKEEN NIGHT HERON *Nycticorax caledonicus*
PLATE III

IDENTIFICATION: Length; 59 cm. *General plumage, chestnut-brown above and white below*; eyebrow streak beginning at base of bill; chin and throat, white; sometimes a buff wash on white feathers; *crown and nape, black*; long white nuptial plumes project from nape down back; bill, black; face, greenish-yellow; legs and feet, yellow; iris, yellow. The sexes are similar. Immatures are *brown streaked with white and pale buff*, including crown and nape; bill, grey; legs greenish-yellow. Non-breeding birds lack nuptial plumes.

VOICE: Harsh croaks are uttered at night.

DISTRIBUTION: It occurs in Indonesia, Philippines, Bonin Islands, New Guinea, New Caledonia, south-western Pacific Islands, Australia, Tasmania and New Zealand. In Indonesia it is extending its range north-westwards across that of the closely related Black-crowned Night Heron, *N. nycticorax*, which occurs from the Greater Sunda Islands across southern Asia, Africa and Europe to the Americas. In New Zealand the Nankeen Night Heron is a vagrant and attempts to introduce it as a breeding bird have failed. It is found in Australia wherever there is permanent aquatic habitat. It frequents the wooded margins of swamps, estuaries, rivers and lakes. It is uncommon in our area.

HABITS: In the daytime it usually perches in heavily foliaged trees in or near water, and it is usually seen when it is flushed from cover. It then flaps heavily to the nearest alternative cover.

BREEDING: The nests are normally in colonies on trees standing in or near water, and are loosely constructed of sticks. The clutch size varies from one to five but is usually two or three. The eggs are light bluish-green, and their average size is 52 × 36 mm. In the tropics it breeds in the summer wet season and in southern Australia in spring. It has bred on the Molonglo River near Lake Burley Griffin.

41

FEEDING: They feed at night in wet swampy areas on insects, crustacea, fish and amphibia. (G.F.vT.)

## BROWN BITTERN *Botaurus poiciloptilus*

PLATE III

IDENTIFICATION: Length, 71 cm. *General plumage, brown mottled with buff-yellow above and pale yellow-buff with dark brown below*; crown and hind neck, dark brown with some pale mottling; thin broken transverse brown bars on sides of neck and outer surface of thighs; upper mandible dark brown; lower mandible, greenish-yellow; face, pale green; legs and feet, pale green; iris, yellow. The sexes are similar. Immatures are paler than adults.

VOICE: At night a loud braying or booming of several notes betrays its presence. This sound is thought by some to be the origin of the bunyip legend of the Aborigines.

DISTRIBUTION: It occurs in south-western Australia, from north-eastern New South Wales to south-eastern South Australia, Tasmania, New Zealand and New Caledonia. It frequents swamps and the margins of rivers and lakes. It is rarely seen in our area.

HABITS: It seldom shows itself outside of reed beds. When flushed it flies heavily for a fairly short distance and "crashes" back into reeds. It has the well-known reaction, when surprised, of facing the intruder and pointing its neck and beak directly upwards, thus making it hard to see among the reeds.

BREEDING: Nests are mere platforms of bent-over reeds and rushes and occur singly in dense cover. The usual clutch size is six. The eggs are olive-brown, and their average size is $52 \times 38$ mm. It has not been recorded as breeding in our region but this is almost certainly due to lack of observation. In south-eastern Australia the usual breeding season is in the period October to January.

FEEDING: They forage from a feeding platform made of matted reeds and rushes on a variety of aquatic animals including insects, crustacea, yabbies, fish and frogs. Feeding platforms are normally littered with the hard parts of their prey. (G.F.vT.)

## LITTLE BITTERN *Ixobrychus minutus*

PLATE XXXV

IDENTIFICATION: Length 30 cm. Male: general plumage, *black above and brown below*; there is a buff or chestnut patch on upper wing; sides of head, neck and upper breast, chestnut or buff; tail, black above and white below; bill, greenish-yellow; legs, green; iris, yellow. Female: generally duller than male, brownish on back and plumage streaked. Immature: buff and brown streaked.

VOICE: Hoarse croaking calls are uttered.

DISTRIBUTION: It occurs in Africa south of the Sahara, Europe, western Asia, the Himalayan mountains, and the coastal regions of Australia. It is a vagrant to New Guinea and New Zealand, and has not been recorded in Indonesia and Tasmania. It is doubtful that the Australian birds are the same species as those that occur in Africa and Eurasia, and those that died out shortly after European settlement in New Zealand. The Little Bittern was first recorded in our area on 6 January 1969 at Molonglo River flats, Canberra. There have been subsequent infrequent sightings in extensive reedbeds around parts of Lake Burley Griffin and larger ponds.

HABITS: It lives in dense reed beds and is rarely seen.

BREEDING: The nests are solitary and are made by placing plant material on bent-over reeds. Often the reeds are bent over a leaning branch or stick. The usual clutch size is four. The eggs are white and their average size is 30 × 25 mm. It has not been recorded as breeding in our region but this is probably due to lack of observation. In south-eastern Australia the usual breeding season is in the period October to December.

FEEDING: The Little Bittern forages on a variety of aquatic animals including insects and crustacea. (G.F.vT.)

Family Ciconiidae — Storks
This is a small family of only seventeen species found in Europe, Asia, Africa and central and South America. One species reaches Australia. The storks are large birds with long necks and legs, long broad wings, large bills and short tails. They fly with necks outstretched and legs trailing behind. Most species live near water and feed on small animals captured while the birds are walking through swamp vegetation or grassland. A few species live on dry open plains, and three subsist largely on carrion.

BLACK-NECKED STORK *Xenorhynchus asiaticus*

IDENTIFICATION: Length, 130 cm, wing span about 200 cm; head, neck, tail, and a broad band across back extending to upper and lower surfaces of wings, glossy black; rest of bird, including the wing tips, white; bill, black; legs and feet, pink to red; iris, black in male, yellow in female; otherwise sexes similar.

Immature is duller and browner than adult, has black legs and feet and a dark brown iris.

VOICE: Generally silent with occasional dull booming; sometimes rattles the bill.

DISTRIBUTION: From India, through South-east Asia and New Guinea to Australia. In Australia it is relatively common from about Port Hedland, Western Australia, across the tropical north to about central coastal Queensland. Uncommon or a rare vagrant south of these areas. The species can be found in all aquatic habitats and at times on dry floodplains.

The sole record of this species from the local region is of a single bird seen and photographed in the swamplands at the eastern end of Lake Burley Griffin in May 1981.

HABITS: The species is better known as the Jabiru. It is usually seen singly or in pairs, although groups may be seen at the end of the dry season in the north, on drying pools where there is an abundant food supply. It will often use thermals for gliding to great heights.

BREEDING: A large stick nest is built in a live or dead tree, generally in the vicinity of water. The nest is constructed by both members of the pair. The clutch size is two to five whitish eggs, measuring about 71 × 52 mm. Both birds share incubation duties and feeding the young. The breeding season in northern Australia is from about March to June.

Some years ago a pair was reported to have nested near Nowra, New South Wales.

FEEDING: Fish and other aquatic animals such as crabs and frogs are the main food. Reptiles, small mammals such as rats, and carrion are also eaten. (M.C.)

### Family Plataleidae — Ibises and Spoonbills

There are about twenty-six species of ibises in seventeen genera, and six species of spoonbills in an Old World and a New World genus. They occur throughout the tropical and temperate land masses of the world. In Australia there are three species of ibises and two species of spoonbills, all of which occur in our area.

44

They are medium to large sized birds with relatively long bills, necks and legs. Ibises are adapted for probing with long down-curved bills in grass, mud, and shallow water for food, while spoonbills have long spoon-shaped bills with which they filter shallow water for food. Both ibises and spoonbills feed on a wide variety of small animal matter.

## STRAW-NECKED IBIS *Threskiornis spinicollis*
PLATE IV

**IDENTIFICATION:** Length, 72 cm. *General plumage, black with bronze and green metallic sheen; neck, white with dark mottling; black band across upper breast and tuft of stiff yellow straw-like plumes on it*; rest of under-parts, white; head and upper neck, naked, black; bill, black with pale brown transverse marks on basal portion; skin patches under-wings, yellow; upper legs, red; lower legs, black; iris, brown. The sexes are similar. General plumage of immatures is dull, and they lack yellow straw-like plumes.

**VOICE:** Grunt-like sounds are made when flushed and when squabbling with other members of a flock.

**DISTRIBUTION:** It occurs throughout Australia in suitable habitat and occasionally in southern lowland New Guinea and in Tasmania. It frequents swamps, shallow lake margins and both wet and dry grasslands. It is usually common in our area, and may be seen near water or in dry fields. It is much less tied to water than the White Ibis and is often seen foraging in dry fields far from any water.

**HABITS:** In flight the neck is extended and the legs trail beyond the tail feathers. Rapid wing beats alternate with long glides. Straw-necked Ibis fly in formations of lines or Vs. They perch, rest and roost in trees. They are very gregarious and form mixed flocks with White Ibises.

**BREEDING:** Normally the nests are in colonies. The nests are platforms of twigs, reeds, rushes, and other material among reeds, rushes, lignum and in tea trees and occasionally other kinds of trees. Breeding takes place any time of the year and depends on swamps being flooded. Near our area they have bred at Lake Cowal, New South Wales. They are not known to breed in our area. Clutch size is usually four to five. Eggs are dull white, and their average size is $63 \times 43$ mm.

**FEEDING:** They forage in shallow water, mud and both wet and dry grasslands for molluscs, insects, crustacea, fish, amphibia, and occasionally reptiles and mammals. As it utilises a greater variety of habitats than the White Ibis, its diet contains a greater diversity of invertebrates and it is less dependent on aquatic animals. (G.F.vT.)

## WHITE IBIS *Threskiornis aethiopica*

PLATE IV

IDENTIFICATION: Length, 71 cm. *General plumage, white; wing tips, black.* Long narrow feathers on lower neck; head and upper neck, naked and black; bill, black; iris, dark brown; transverse pink bands on back of head; red skin patches under wings; upper legs, pink; lower legs and feet, bluish-grey to purple-brown. The sexes are similar. Immatures have feathers on head and upper neck and bill is shorter and less curved than in adults.

VOICE: Grunt-like sounds are made when flushed and when squabbling with other members of a flock.

DISTRIBUTION: Found in Africa, India, the Molucca Islands, lowland New Guinea, and Australia; stragglers reach New Zealand. In Australia it is common in the northern and eastern parts, and is absent from the semi-arid interior. It does not occur in the greater part of Western Australia; it is present in the Kimberleys, but apart from there, only one small breeding colony, in the south-west, is known. It is a rare straggler in Tasmania. In our area its status varies widely — sometimes it is quite common and at other times rare. It frequents swamps, shallow lake margins and wet fields. It is much more closely associated with water than is the Straw-necked Ibis.

HABITS: In flight the neck is extended and the legs trail beyond the tail feathers. White Ibis fly in formations of lines or Vs. Rapid wing beats alternate with long glides. They perch, rest and roost in trees. They are very gregarious and form mixed flocks with Straw-necked Ibises.

BREEDING: Normally the nests are in colonies. The nests are platforms of twigs, reeds, rushes and other material among reeds, lignum and in tea trees and occasionally other kinds of trees. Breeding takes place at any time of the year and depends on swamps being flooded. Near our area they have bred at Lake Cowal, New South Wales, but there is no local record. Clutch size is usually three. Eggs are dull white, and their average size is 64 × 45 mm.

FEEDING: They forage in shallow water, mud and damp grasslands for molluscs, insects, crustacea, fish, amphibia and occasionally reptiles and mammals. While it takes essentially the same food

46

organisms as the Straw-necked Ibis, its diet contains a higher proportion of freshwater invertebrates. (G.F.vT.)

## GLOSSY IBIS *Plegadis falcinellus*

PLATE IV

IDENTIFICATION: Length, 52 cm. General plumage, reddish-brown with bronze-green gloss; bill, olive-brown; legs and feet, brown; iris, brown. At a distance the Glossy Ibis looks black. The sexes are similar. Immatures are duller in colour with green gloss on wings; head and neck, brown with white streaking; bill, shorter and less curved than in adults.

VOICE: Its calls are seldom heard and consist of nasal grunts and a series of four distinct guttural notes. At the nest bleating and cooing sounds are made.

DISTRIBUTION: It occurs in southern North America, southern Europe, Africa, southern Asia, through the Indonesian islands to southern New Guinea and Australia. Rare stragglers reach New Zealand. In Australia it is likely to appear wherever there is suitable habitat. It is fairly common in the tropics but decreases in relative abundance towards the southern parts where it is rare. It is a rare straggler in Tasmania. In our region it is an uncommon visitor to the lakes and nearby swamps. It is nomadic and individuals or small groups may be seen at any time. It frequents swamps, shallow lake margins and fields near water.

HABITS: In flight the neck is extended and the legs trail beyond the tail feathers. Rapid wing beats alternate with long glides. They perch, rest and roost in trees, shrubs and mangroves. They are less gregarious than the White and the Straw-necked Ibises.

BREEDING: The nests are built in trees and shrubs standing in water, including lignum and mangroves. Normally the nests are in colonies. The nests are made of leafy branches. In some localities it nests in reeds and during the breeding season the nests of several pairs are united into a single platform of matted reeds and rushes. The clutch size is usually three or four but sometimes as many as six. The eggs are blue with a greenish tinge, and their average size is 51 × 34 mm. It is not known to breed in our region.

FEEDING: They forage in shallow water, mud and swampy grasslands for molluscs, insects, crustacea, fish and amphibia. (G.F.vT.)

47

## ROYAL SPOONBILL *Platalea regia*
PLATE IV

IDENTIFICATION: Length, 76 cm. General plumage, white; long nuptial plumes on crown and nape; *bill, black, long, straight and spoon-shaped*; fore part of head and throat, naked, black; eyelid and above, yellow-ochre; red patch on forehead; legs and feet, black; iris, red. The sexes are similar. Non-breeding birds lack nuptial plumes, red forehead patch and yellow above eye.

VOICE: At the nest it grunts and clappers its bill.

DISTRIBUTION: It occurs throughout mainland Australia and is a straggler to Tasmania. It also occurs in New Guinea and Indonesia. It breeds in Java. Recently it has established itself as a breeding species in New Zealand. It is found around swamps and shallow lake margins.

HABITS: In flight the neck is extended and the legs trail beyond the tail feathers. Slow wing beats alternate with long glides. They perch, rest and roost in trees.

BREEDING: Normally the nests are in colonies. The nests are platforms of twigs, reeds, rushes and other material among reeds, rushes, lignum and in trees not necessarily near water. Near our area they have bred at Lake Cowal but there is no local record. The clutch size is usually three or four. The eggs are dull white spotted or blotched with brown, and their average size is 68 × 45 mm.

FEEDING: They feed on small aquatic animals, including molluscs, insects, crustacea, and small fishes by wading into shallow water and moving the bill from side to side in it. (G.F.vT.)

## YELLOW-BILLED SPOONBILL *Platalea flavipes*
PLATE IV

IDENTIFICATION: Length, 89 cm. General plumage, white; long nuptial plumes on upper breast; *bill, yellow, long, straight and spoon-shaped*; fore part of head and throat, naked, bluish with pink tinge and bounded by narrow black line; legs and feet, yellow; iris, very pale yellow. The sexes are similar. Non-breeding birds lack nuptial plumes and colour of naked parts is dull flesh colour.

VOICE: At the nest it grunts and clappers its bill.

DISTRIBUTION: It occurs throughout Australia, but is rare in Tasmania and the drier and cooler southern parts of the continent. It

48

frequents swamps, shallow lakes, river margins, and dams. One or more are seen from time to time at swampy locations throughout our area.

HABITS: In flight the neck is extended and the legs trail beyond the tail feathers. Slow wing beats alternate with long glides. They perch, rest and roost in trees.

BREEDING: Normally the nests are in colonies. The nests are platforms of twigs, reeds, rushes and other material among reeds, rushes, lignum and in tall trees, not necessarily near water. Near our area they have bred at Lake Cowal, but they have not been found breeding locally. Clutch size varies from one to four and is usually two or three. Eggs are dull white, and their average size is $68 \times 45$ mm.

FEEDING: They feed on small aquatic animals, including molluscs, insects, crustacea and small fishes by wading into shallow water and moving the partly-opened bill from side to side through the water. (G.F.vT.)

# WATERFOWL

The waterfowl are web-footed, aquatic birds, typically with flattened bills. The word is a very old one and has different meanings in different parts of the world but in Australia it usually refers to the wild ducks, swans and geese although occasionally, but not in this book, coots and waterhens are included.

The family is large and cosmopolitan, there being 148 species distributed throughout the world. The Australian continent is the poorest of all with respect to numbers of waterfowl; there are only nineteen native species, and two introductions. Two very rare vagrants also reach the country occasionally from the Northern Hemisphere. Many Australian waterfowl are closely related to species that occur elsewhere but there are six genera restricted to this continent that are not. These are Cape Barren Goose *Cereopsis*, Magpie Goose *Anseranas*, Freckled Duck *Stictonetta*, Pink-eared Duck *Malacorhynchus*, Wood Duck *Chenonetta* and Musk Duck *Biziura*.

Most waterfowl are nomadic. Their movements are extensive and erratic being controlled by the rainfall and flooding. At times great irruptions occur from the inland and, less frequently, from the north so that local populations of waterfowl can be greatly increased at any time by an influx of nomadic birds. In our area there are eight resident breeding species, three common visitors, two of which have not been recorded breeding, and there have been records of two rare vagrants.

Family Anatidae — Swans, Geese and Ducks
## GRASS WHISTLE-DUCK *Dendrocygna eytoni*

PLATE V

IDENTIFICATION: Length, 50 cm. General colour above, brownish-black; rump and tail, dark brown; wings, brown; *breast, chestnut barred with black*; abdomen, buff; long *lanceolate black-edged plumes* arise from the flanks; bill, pink; iris, yellow. The sexes are alike.

In flight the posture, with *depressed neck and trailing legs*, is very characteristic and the white rump is less obvious than in the Water Whistle-duck. It whistles incessantly in flight.

VOICE: A shrill whistle and a musical twitter.

DISTRIBUTION: The main range is in tropical Australia but isolated breeding colonies also occur inland to as far south as the Murray River and nomadic flocks can be seen at times almost anywhere in south-eastern Australia. The occurrences around Canberra were restricted to occasional birds and small groups that visited the captive flock formerly held by the Division of Wildlife Research at Canberra.

HABITS: In the north they occur in very large flocks but in the south rarely are more than twenty seen together. They are found in dense groups on the edges of lagoons, dams and lakes, flying out to feed elsewhere in the late afternoon. They walk very gracefully but swim slowly and awkwardly; the flight is slow and the wings whistle in flight. They fly with the neck extended and depressed and the long legs trail behind. On alighting the legs are lowered and neck steeply depressed as they come down. They perch in trees occasionally and can dive but rarely do so.

BREEDING: In the tropics the breeding season is in the summer wet season but in the south occurs in the spring, August to October. There is no breeding record around Canberra.

The nest is a scrape in the ground in long grass usually far from water. It is lined with a few pieces of grass. The eggs are pure white, oval and pointed, and vary from 44–51 × 33–38 mm. The average is 48 × 36 mm. The clutch size varies from eight to fourteen eggs. Incubation time is twenty-eight days.

FEEDING: The Grass Whistle-duck feeds entirely on land. The food consists mainly of grass blades and grass seeds but the green parts and seeds of a wide variety of other plants, herbs, clovers and sedges are eaten. Stubble feeding is common in inland New South Wales. (H.J.F.)

50

## BLACK SWAN *Cygnus atratus*

PLATE X

IDENTIFICATION: Length, 129 cm. *Plumage black* often with a brownish tinge; *primaries and secondaries, pure white* very prominent in flight; bill red with a broad white band near tip; legs and feet, dark grey; iris, red. Males and females are similar in size and appearance. *Juveniles are grey brown in colour* and the *primaries are black tipped.*

VOICE: A musical honk, bugling; the sound is often heard at night.

DISTRIBUTION: Throughout the continent, but particularly in the south-east and south-west; only vagrants occur in the centre and extreme north. In the Canberra area it is found on all water areas, lakes, swamps and streams, particularly Lakes George and Bathurst. Elsewhere it is found also in billabongs, floodwaters, brackish water and saltwater estuaries.

HABITS: Swans are found in pairs, family parties or large flocks; they are usually seen on water or overhead but often come ashore and graze. The flight is undulating and slow but powerful and graceful. At most times of the year, but particularly after breeding, flightless moulting birds are found on large water areas, particularly Lake George. They cannot rise from the land and do so from the water with some difficulty for they need a long take off distance.

BREEDING: The breeding season is mainly in the late spring and early summer but is subject to very great variation; in some years breeding is continuous for the whole year, in others very few nests are started. There is evidence that the timing of the breeding season is related to changes in the nutrition of the birds associated with extensive blooms of algae and the growth of submergent plants due to factors that are, at present, unpredictable.

Black Swan nests are concentrated and form colonies in areas of suitable habitat. Where reedbeds of moderate density occur the nest is a large floating heap of aquatic vegetation; in other places they are built on islands and are smaller.

The eggs are coarse shelled and pale green when laid but are soon nest stained. The size varies from $95-115 \times 50-70$ mm. The average is $105 \times 67$ mm. The clutch size varies from three to ten around Canberra but five and six are the commonest numbers of eggs laid and the average clutch size is 5.5 eggs. The incubation time is thirty-five days to forty-five days.

FEEDING: Black Swans feed mainly in water grazing on, or uprooting,

51

submergent plants. In deep water they upend to reach a depth of one metre or more. They also collect floating plants from the water surface and often leave the water to graze grass and herbage some distance away. The food is entirely vegetable. (H.J.F.)

## FRECKLED DUCK *Stictonetta naevosa*

PLATE V

IDENTIFICATION: Length, 56 cm. Colour of plumage, *dark brownish-black uniformly freckled with white or buff*; breast, darker than abdomen; wing, dark brown above but the under-side has dark primaries with white wing lining; bill, very heavy and dished above, slate grey; legs and feet, slate-grey; iris, brown; head has a high pointed crown. Sexes are similar but males are darker particularly around head; in breeding season the bill of male is red at the base.

In flight the dark breast, light abdomen and white under-wings distinguish it.

VOICE: Sounds are seldom heard in the wild but it does have a number of soft grunts and hisses.

DISTRIBUTION: Major breeding areas are probably located in the vast lignum swamps of inland southern Queensland, northern South Australia and New South Wales. Other localities are in south-west Western Australia, the south-east of South Australia and the Riverina, New South Wales. In our area they are regular visitors to Lakes George and Bathurst and other large water areas in the district; flocks as large as two hundred sometimes occur.

HABITS: They usually associate with other ducks and can easily be overlooked. During the day they rest in dense cover where it is available but otherwise very characteristically sit on rocks, the tops of stumps and posts protruding from the water, one bird to each post. At dusk they fly to the edge and cruise inshore, feeding.

BREEDING: The main breeding season is in the spring, September to December, but this is influenced by rainfall and flooding and, like several other inland ducks, they can breed at any time of the year that flooding provides suitable conditions. There is no record of breeding in the Canberra region.

The nests are well built, bowl-shaped constructions of lignum and fine sticks placed in emergent lignum or other bushes, at water level. They are also built in fallen timber and flood rubbish at the base of flooded trees.

52

The eggs are unlike other duck eggs; they are more oval shape and the shell is thick and soft. They are cream or ivory in colour. The length varies from 61–66 mm and the breadth from 45–48 mm. The average size is 63–47 mm. The clutch varies from five to fourteen eggs but six is the commonest number found. Incubation time is twenty-six to twenty-eight days.

FEEDING: Although Freckled Ducks dabble at the edge, upend or feed from the surface, the main action is filter feeding, the bill is below water and just above the bottom. The principal food is filtered from the water and muds and is mainly aquatic animals. (H.J.F.)

## MOUNTAIN DUCK *Tadorna tadornoides*

PLATE V

IDENTIFICATION: Length, 67 cm. Male: *head and neck, black* with greenish tinge and a *white ring at base of neck*; breast, deep buff; abdomen, dark brown; under-tail, glossy black; bill, black; legs and feet, dark grey; iris, dark brown. Females are similar but breast is chestnut and there is usually a white eyespot and white at base of the bill.

In flight the bird is distinguished by *prominent white shoulders and neck ring*. From below the white lower part of wings and light breast are diagnostic.

VOICE: The identity call is a loud honk. The call of the female is very much higher in pitch than that of the male.

DISTRIBUTION: The Mountain Duck is restricted to south-west and south-eastern Australia. Canberra is near the northern extremity of its range. It is most numerous in south-east South Australia and Tasmania and uncommon in the inland generally. In our area concentrations as great as two thousand occur annually on Lakes George and Bathurst. It breeds throughout the Southern Tablelands in freshwater lakes but elsewhere is very numerous in brackish and saltwater habitats.

The movements are quite regular. During the breeding season they are widely dispersed, each pair occupying a territory to which it returns each year but after breeding they concentrate on large lakes, e.g. Lake George and big flocks of flightless moulting birds develop. After moulting the birds disperse from our area many travelling as far as Tasmania and South Australia and by May only a few residents remain. The return influx begins in November and reaches its peak in January.

HABITS: During the day the large groups rest on the edges of lakes or float in the centre and in late afternoon they fly out in long honking skeins to feed. They are very wary and alert and difficult to approach. They walk well on dry land and can dive but seldom do so. They occasionally roost in trees.

BREEDING: The breeding season is regular throughout the birds' range and the eggs are laid mainly in July and August. The nest is usually in a tree hole up to thirty metres from the ground and not necessarily near water. Some birds nest on the ground in long grass, in crevices in rocks and occasionally in rabbit burrows.

The eggs are oval, creamy white and have a close-grained lustrous shell. The length varies from 62–74 mm and the breadth from 45–51 mm. The average size is 68–49 mm. The clutch, like that of all shelducks, is large and varies from ten to twenty-two, although more than fourteen is rare. Incubation time is thirty to thirty-five days.

FEEDING: Mountain Ducks graze emergent, aquatic vegetation or crops, grasslands and improved pastures, sometimes quite far from water. In our area the food is mainly the seeds and leaves of clovers, green algae, some duckweed and pondweeds and small amounts of numerous plants characteristic of the water's edge. Insects are also found in forty per cent of the birds but these contribute little to the bulk of food. (H.J.F.)

## BLACK DUCK *Anas superciliosa*

PLATE V

IDENTIFICATION: Length 57 cm. General colour above, brown, the feathers with light brown edge; under-parts, brown; throat, white; speculum, glossy green; under-wing, white; *face, light yellow* or white *with a black line through the eye* and a shorter one below it; bill, greenish-grey; legs and feet, yellow-green; iris, brown. The sexes are similar.

In flight the *white under-wings and the face pattern are diagnostic.*

VOICE: The most familiar call of female is a loud decrescendo of quacks. A soft 'raehb' is characteristic of males. Both sexes have a range of other distinct calls associated with courtship and social displays.

DISTRIBUTION: The Black Duck is found in Indonesia, New Guinea, many Pacific Islands and New Zealand as well as throughout Australia. In Australia it is most numerous in the Riverina and on the east coast. It seldom visits the inland deserts except after rain. In our region it is common in all lakes, swamps and streams but shows a strong preference for those that are heavily vegetated.

Many individuals are sedentary but each summer large numbers of nomadic birds move into the area from the inland seeking dry season refuge; in droughts the numbers are very great as the inland swamps dry. When the birds in the summer concentrations disperse they move throughout most of eastern Australia in all possible directions.

HABITS: Black Ducks are found in pairs, small groups or large flocks. They may be on the water, mudbanks, the shore or fallen timber. They are very wary and alert and when disturbed the flight is swift and straight and they usually leave the area, unlike the teal, which commonly circle overhead.

BREEDING: In the inland the Black Duck has the ability to breed at any time of the year although most have a regular spring breeding season. On the Southern Tablelands pair forming displays begin in May and continue throughout the winter. Breeding occurs in the period July to January but most clutches have been begun by the end of November.

Nests are scrapes in the ground in long grass, sometimes quite far from water, in the tops of stumps, in deserted nests of other birds or in treeholes.

The eggs are elliptical and white or cream with a greenish tinge. They vary from $51-63 \times 37-45$ mm. The average is $58 \times 41$ mm. The clutch varies from five to thirteen but most contain between eight to ten eggs. The incubation time is thirty days.

FEEDING: Its feeding methods are similar to those of the other dabbling ducks, i.e., the Grey Teal and Chestnut Teal. They feed on plant or animal material according to its availability. In Canberra, in winter, they often leave the water and feed on the ground on the foreshores of urban lakes, usually with Wood Ducks. (H.J.F.)

## GREY TEAL *Anas gibberifrons*

PLATE V

IDENTIFICATION: Length, 45 cm. *General colour above, dark grey-brown* each feather edged with buff; *throat and face, pale almost white*; under-parts, lighter grey than back; wings, dark brown; speculum, black with a white edge above and below; bill, blue-grey; legs and feet, grey; iris, red. The sexes are similar.

In flight the light face with no lines on it and the wing pattern showing white edges to the speculum distinguish it.

VOICE: Females have a loud, chattering decrescendo of quacks repeated rapidly for fifteen or more syllables — "laughing"; the male has a loud burp call 'g-dee-oo'. There are other calls characteristic of both sexes.

DISTRIBUTION: The Grey Teal ranges from Indonesia to New Zealand and many Pacific islands. It is an extreme nomad and can be found in large numbers almost anywhere in the continent at any time. The breeding population around Canberra is not large but is augmented each summer by large numbers of nomads from the inland plains; these later disperse over the whole continent. It can be found in any water habitat in the area. Its movements are quite erratic and are controlled by rainfall and flooding. In droughts they have travelled as far as New Guinea and New Zealand.

HABITS: It can be found in pairs, groups or large flocks on the edges of water, mudbanks or clustered all over fallen timber. It is moderately tame and, when disturbed, flies in compact flocks that twist and turn in the air frequently swooping to skim the water and are reluctant to leave the area.

BREEDING: The breeding season can occur at any time but in our reasonably reliable climate occurs in the late winter and spring. They most often nest above ground usually in treeholes.

The clutch size varies from four to fourteen eggs but most are between six and nine. The eggs are oval or elliptical, cream coloured when fresh but usually nest stained. They vary from 49–58 × 35–42 mm. The average is 50 × 36 mm. The incubation time is twenty-five to thirty days.

FEEDING: Grey Teal dredge the mud in shallow water, upend in deeper water to reach the bottom and filter material from the surface; they strip seeds from plants growing in, or on, the edge of the water but seldom feed on the shore.

There has been no study in the region of the food eaten but elsewhere they have very elastic feeding habits and feed on plants or animal material according to its availability. (H.J.F.)

## CHESTNUT TEAL *Anas castanea*

PLATE V

IDENTIFICATION: Length, 45 mm. Male: *head and neck, glossy green*; back, dark brown; rump and upper-tail, jet black; breast, chestnut each feather blotched with black; under-tail, black: wing, dark brown; speculum, black with a white edge above and below; bill, blue-grey; legs and feet, grey; iris, red. The females are similar to Grey Teal but lack the white face and throat and are generally very much darker.

VOICE: Very similar to that of the Grey Teal.

DISTRIBUTION: The Chestnut Teal is mainly restricted to south-western Western Australia and the coast and highlands of south-east Australia, but vagrants occur elsewhere. The most northern regular breeding occurs around Sydney. It is typically a bird of coastal lagoons, swamps and estuaries. In our area it is found in the large lakes especially where rocky islands and rocky shorelines exist.

HABITS: They are usually seen in pairs or small groups and are commonly associated with Grey Teal, resting on mudbanks or on logs and rocks. They seldom leave the water, except to nest. The flight is swift and direct and the groups do not twist and swoop so much as the Grey Teal. Although most are fairly sedentary there is some movement and one bird from Lake George has travelled as far as western Victoria.

BREEDING: The breeding season is regular. Communal pair forming displays occur in autumn and early winter, the mated pairs separate from the flock in August and nests are begun in September and October and occasionally as late as mid-December. All the nests we have seen around Canberra have been scrapes in the ground, in short grass on islands. Elsewhere they also nest in tree holes. The eggs are very similar to those of the Grey Teal but the down covering them is very much darker in colour. The clutch varies from five to fifteen eggs but seven to nine is by far the most common. They vary from 37–57 × 35–41 mm. The average is 52 × 37 mm. The incubation period is twenty-eight days.

FEEDING: The feeding methods are the same as those of the Grey Teal but there has been no study of the food eaten. (H.J.F.)

## SHOVELER *Anas rhynchotis*

PLATE V

IDENTIFICATION: Length, 50 cm. Male: head and neck, blue-grey with green gloss; *face, grey with a white crescent before the eye*; back and rump, black; tail, dark brown; fore neck and breast, dark brown; abdomen, deep chestnut with black edges to feathers; there is a *prominent white patch on the flank*; wings, dark brown with powder blue shoulders; bill, long and spatulate, forming a straight line with top of the head, olive brown; legs and feet, orange; iris, yellow; the speculum is dark green with a white band in front. In winter males enter an eclipse plumage and resemble the females. Females are duller and lack the face crescent and green wash on the head; the iris is brown.

In flight the bill, lack of forehead, face crescent in males and orange legs are all very obvious.

VOICE: Drakes have a soft repeated 'club-it' call used in display but it is seldom heard.

DISTRIBUTION: The Shoveler is found in New Zealand as well as in south-west Western Australia and south-eastern Australia. It is no-where common but in earlier days was abundant on the New South Wales north coast. In the districts discussed in this book it is occasionally seen and breeds in the large lakes. There is an increase in numbers each summer and up to several thousand have been seen on Lakes George and Bathurst.

HABITS: They are usually found as widely dispersed pairs. They are very wary and jump vertically and fly away swiftly with a very distinctive whirr of the wings.

BREEDING: Few nests have been seen here but they suggest that the breeding season is regular and in the spring and early summer. The nest is a scrape in the ground in long grass, in this district often on an island in a lake, and is usually close to the water edge. The eggs are elliptical and smooth, creamy white in colour with a greenish tinge. They vary from 51–57 × 36–40 mm. The average is 54 × 37 mm. The clutch size varies from nine to eleven and the incubation period is twenty-four days.

FEEDING: The Shoveler feeds only in water and almost entirely at the surface. It cruises with the large shovel bill immersed, filtering the water. They also dive for food, and chase insects across the water and sometimes stand in the shallows dredging mud. Three-quarters of the food eaten is of animal origin and consists mainly of aquatic insects but also includes small shells, crustacea and ostracods. The plant material is whatever is floating in the water and includes seeds of aquatic and dry land plants and algae. (H.J.F.)

## PINK-EARED DUCK *Malacorhynchus membranaceus*
PLATE V

IDENTIFICATION: Length, 42 cm. General colour above, brown;

side of head, white with a dark brown patch around the eye; there is a small pink patch behind the eyes; neck and under-parts, white with brown lines; under-tail, buff; wings have a white trailing edge and there is a subterminal white bar on the tail; *bill is grey, enormous and spoon-shaped* with membranous flaps near tip but *there is a distinct forehead*; legs and feet, lead grey; iris, brown. The sexes are similar.

In flight the white edge to the wings and tail is diagnostic even without the enormous bill. They twitter in flight.

VOICE: A musical chirrup in both sexes is most commonly heard but a variety of similar calls is given.

DISTRIBUTION: This is the extreme nomad and can be found anywhere in the continent although it is most typically a bird of the shallow floodwaters of the vast inland plains, particularly of the Riverina. A few are present at all times on Lake George and other large lakes in our area but in the summer the numbers increase to several hundred and in drought several thousand may seek refuge here.

HABITS: Pink-eared Ducks are found in pairs or flocks on large bodies of water. They are usually with Grey Teal but are less commonly seen on the edge than that species. They are often tame and allow close approach. When flushed they fly in dense flocks chirruping continuously. Pink-eared Ducks seldom leave the water except to climb onto fallen timber and never dive except when wounded or moulting.

BREEDING: There is no breeding record in our region. Inland the breeding season is erratic and can occur at any time of the year. The sexual cycle is geared to gross changes in water level so that breeding begins after extensive flooding, as the water on the plains recedes. In years when there is no flooding very few, if any, birds breed. In times of extensive flood really vast breeding concentrations develop on the inland plains.

The nest can be placed in a treehole, thick bush, on a fence post, flat branch, tree fork or in the nest of another waterbird; anywhere that will provide support. It is a rounded mound of greyish down that encloses the eggs when the bird is not sitting.

The eggs are oval but more pointed than those of other ducks. They are smooth, white or creamy-white and greasy in texture. The size varies from 46–53 × 34–38 mm. The average is 49 × 36 mm. The clutch varies from three to eleven eggs but most are between five and eight and the mean clutch size is 6.7 eggs. The incubation period is twenty-six days.

FEEDING: The enormous bill is fringed with very fine lamellae that act as a filter. The Pink-eared Duck feeds almost entirely by filtering the surface water. They cruise slowly in arrowheads, echelon or sometimes in circles, each bird with its bill immersed up to its eyes, beside another's flank filtering the water and retaining edible items. They occasionally stand in shallow water and dredge the mud or upend. The food collected is mainly microscopic animals and plants—plankton, and whatever larger insects and seeds are swept up and through the filter. (H.J.F.)

## HARDHEAD *Aythya australis*

PLATE V

IDENTIFICATION: Length, 49 cm. Male: general colour above, rich dark brown; under-parts, throat and neck, similar to back; breast, dark rufous brown, lower breast, white mottled with brown; abdomen, brown; *under-tail coverts, white*; wing, above brown with broad white band at rear, below white edged with brown all around; bill, black with slate blue tip; legs and feet, grey; iris, white. Females are similar but much paler and have a brown eye.

The flight is very distinctive. Positive identification from below is by the wings, which appear translucent, and the pale abdomen. From above the white band on the wing is distinctive.

VOICE: Although males have a soft wheezy whistle and females a harsh croak these are rarely heard.

DISTRIBUTION: The Hardhead is found in New Guinea, some Pacific islands and eastern Indonesia as well as Australia. It formerly also occurred in New Zealand. In Australia it is found throughout the continent but is most numerous in the Murray-Darling Basin where it is characteristic of deep permanent swamps and streams. A few are found in the large lakes in this district each summer and one nest has been found at Lake Bathurst.

HABITS: It is nearly always seen on deep water, seldom on the shore and never in trees. It swims swiftly and dives frequently to reappear travelling rapidly. It is very wary and alert and springs from the water almost vertically, then flies very swiftly with a characteristic rapid wing beat.

BREEDING: In the inland, breeding occurs in summer, a little later than the Black Duck. Nests are usually built in dense reeds or bushes and are well constructed, bowl-shaped structures of woven plant material but they are sometimes placed on the ground in long grass.

The eggs are creamy white and measure 49–65 × 37–45 mm. The average is 57 × 42 mm. The clutch varies from six to eighteen but nine to twelve is the commonest. The incubation period is twenty-five days.

FEEDING: Much of the food is gathered under water; the birds dive deeply and remain below for over one minute. They also dabble the surface and feed on emergent vegetation but never come ashore. Seventy-five per cent of the food is of vegetable origin and comprises the seeds of aquatic grass, smartweeds and other edge plants and many submergent plants of deep water. The animal food is mainly aquatic insects but the birds also secure many molluscs and yabbies from the bottom of the lake. (H.J.F.)

## WOOD DUCK *Chenonetta jubata*

PLATE V

IDENTIFICATION: Length, 48 cm. Male: head and neck, brown with *mane of black feathers*; lower back and tail, black; scapulars, grey with black edges to feathers; upper-wing coverts, grey; speculum brilliant green edged with black; breast, mottled grey, black and white; abdomen and under-tail, black; sides of breast and flanks, grey with very fine, wavy, black lines; bill, olive brown; legs and feet, olive brown; iris, brown. Females differ in having head brown-grey; quills, brown, not black; flanks, white. Immatures of both sexes resemble the female.

Overhead the speculum appears as a white triangle near the body and is diagnostic; flying away there are prominent white wing patches on the rear part of the wing near the body.

VOICE: The female has a long drawn out, plaintive "mew" extending to $1\frac{1}{2}$ –2 seconds. The call of the male is higher in pitch and shorter.

DISTRIBUTION: The Wood Duck is found throughout the continent but is most numerous on the tablelands and the western slopes of eastern Australia. It is not necessarily associated with water and is found throughout lightly timbered and grassy areas as well as on the margins of swamps, lakes and rivers.

HABITS: They are usually found in flocks, sometimes very large, on the ground. Individuals occasionally perch in trees. They are very shy and wary and when encountered have always seen the observer first and either freeze with head erect, or fly silently away, low down, through the timber. On land they run about swiftly and nimbly but swim awkwardly. The flight is easy and slower than other ducks. In the winter they congregate in camps, the location of which is traditional,

61

and disperse in early summer to breed throughout the eastern high-lands and slopes. Many return to the same camp site the following year. The pairs remain mated for long periods, probably for life.

BREEDING: The breeding season is regular but is influenced by rain-fall and in dry years there is little breeding. On the Southern Table-lands the breeding season is August, September and October. The nests are in tree hollows, often far from water. The ducklings jump to the ground and are then shepherded to the nearest pool or lake. The nest down is light grey. The eggs are cream or creamy-white and measure 53–62 × 40–45 mm. The average is 57 × 42 mm. The clutch size varies from nine to eleven. The incubation time is about twenty-eight days.

FEEDING: Wood Ducks feed on green herbage on land, emergent vegetation in water, and plants on the edge; they often feed in stubble also. The main plants eaten are leaves and seeds of grasses, clovers and sedges. (H.J.F.)

## MUSK DUCK *Biziura lobata*

PLATE V

IDENTIFICATION: Length, male 66 cm, female 55 cm. A large male can weigh nearly 3 kg. General colour, black-brown with numerous fine lines of brown; lower breast, whitish-brown; head, large, black and prominent; bill, black with a *large pendulous lobe* beneath; legs and feet, dark grey; iris, brown. Females and juveniles resemble the the male but are smaller and the pendulous lobe is absent.

VOICE: When in display the male makes several sounds including a shrill whistle followed by a deep "plonk" made with the feet.

DISTRIBUTION: Musk Ducks are found throughout southern Aus-tralia wherever densely vegetated swamp occurs, to as far north as Rockhampton, Queensland. They have been recorded breeding on Lake Burley Griffin and in the non-breeding season are found in small numbers on all the large lakes.

HABITS: They inhabit dense reeds in the breeding season but are found on open lakes at other times. They are usually solitary and float far from the shore, diving frequently and effortlessly without a splash. They are seldom seen to fly and do so very awkwardly, needing a long take off distance and landing with a crash. They never leave the water except to slither on to a log or clump of reeds.

BREEDING: The breeding season is very regular September to November. The nest is built in a clump of rushes or in flooded bushes in deep water and the eggs are often wet. It is a rough cup of beaten down and woven rushes, with a canopy of broken rushes overhead. The eggs are greenish-white and have a coating of lime when fresh but soon stain dark brown. They are rather large measuring 71–88 mm (average 79) × 48–58 mm (average 54). The clutch varies from one to ten but mostly is one to three. The incubation time is twenty to twenty-one days.

FEEDING: Food is collected by diving in deep water and consists mainly of animals. It includes numerous insects both adults and larvae, crayfish, and freshwater mussels. They occasionally eat the young of other waterbirds. (H.J.F.)

## BLUE-BILLED DUCK *Oxyura australis*

PLATE V

IDENTIFICATION: Length, 41 cm. Male: *head and neck, glossy black*; foreneck, upper breast, flanks and back, rich chestnut; rest of underparts, brown; under-tail, black; wings, dark brown; *bill, bright blue*; legs and feet, grey; iris, dark brown. In winter males assume eclipse plumage losing the glossy black of the head and much of the chestnut of the body; the bill is then slate grey. Females are duller, blackish-brown above with a black tail; chin and throat, brown; under-parts, mottled light brown and black; bill, grey-brown; legs and feet, grey-brown; iris, brown. Immatures resemble the females but have grey-green bills.

VOICE: There is a low quack but this is rarely heard.

DISTRIBUTION: The Blue-billed Duck is widely distributed in south-east and south-west Australia, mainly in the inland, wherever deep permanent heavily vegetated swamps occur. There are few records in our area but it is of regular occurrence on Lake Bathurst.

HABITS: In summer they live in very dense swamps, are secretive and seldom seen but in winter they congregate into large rafts on clear lakes in the more southern parts of their range. They are completely aquatic and swim and dive expertly, never coming on land. The flight is laborious until they are aloft but then is swift, though the posture appears tail heavy.

BREEDING: The breeding season is regular and occurs in July to October but is sometimes extended to November. The nest is built in dense vegetation in deep water and may be in a deserted nest of another waterbird but more usually a clump of reeds is broken down and a deep cup is built on this platform with top cover provided by breaking down other reeds. Breeding has been recorded at Lake Bathurst.

The eggs are large averaging 66 mm (64–72) × 48 mm (46–51). They are coarse shelled and light green in colour. The clutch varies from three to twelve but the commonest is five or six. The incubation period is twenty-six to twenty-eight days.

FEEDING: Most of the food is secured by diving in deep water and is of equal parts of animal and vegetable material. The plants include numerous submergent species such as watermilfoil and algae, as well as other swamp plants. The animals are all less than one and a half centimetres in diameter and are nearly all insects, particularly larvae of midges. (H.J.F.)

# BIRDS-OF-PREY

The birds-of-prey or "raptors" are the owls on the one hand and the hawks, eagles and falcons on the other. Strictly speaking these two groups of birds belong to very distinct orders which are not closely related. However, they have much in common as they live on animal food and have sharp curved talons and strong hooked bills, adaptations for catching and tearing-up prey. Popularly the owls are the "nocturnal birds-of-prey" and the hawks the "diurnal birds-of-prey". As might be expected, there are occasional exceptions to the rule and a few species of owls hunt by day and occasional hawks are crepuscular or hunt by night.

## Diurnal Birds-of-Prey

This order is large, comprising 270 species, grouped into several families, and is cosmopolitan in distribution. The Australian fauna is an impoverished one containing only twenty-four species. Only seven species are endemic to the continent although a further twelve are endemic in the sense that they are of Australian origin but have reached as far as New Guinea, the eastern Indonesian islands, the western Pacific and New Zealand. The majority of Australian species are contained in genera that are widespread in the world.

Only three genera are endemic: *Hamirostra*, the Black-breasted Buzzard, and *Lophoictinia*, the Square-tailed Kite which are aberrant kites, and *Erythrotriorchis*, the Red Goshawk, which is little different to the ordinary goshawks of the genus *Accipiter*. Five species that are found in Australia are widespread in the world and two of them, the Osprey and Peregrine Falcon, share with the Barn Owl the distinction

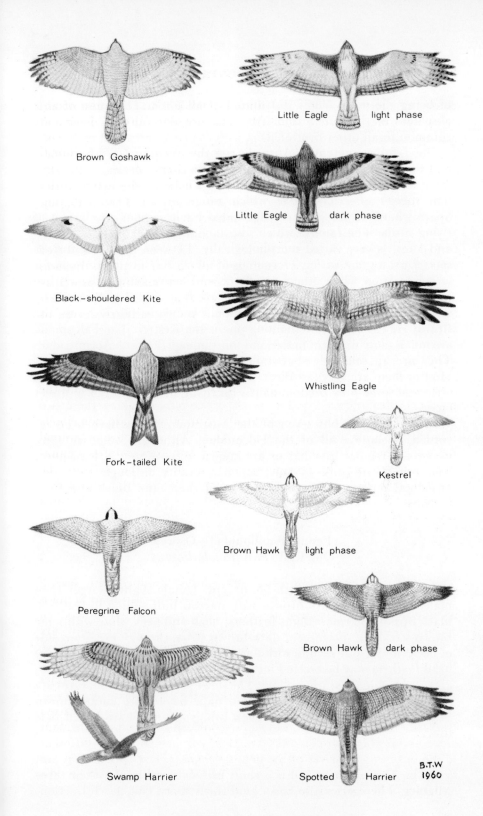

Brown Goshawk

Little Eagle      light phase

Little Eagle      dark phase

Black-shouldered Kite

Whistling Eagle

Fork-tailed Kite

Kestrel

Peregrine Falcon

Brown Hawk      light phase

Brown Hawk      dark phase

Swamp Harrier

Spotted Harrier

B.T.W
1960

**Recognition of raptors overhead**

of being the most widely distributed of all birds. The most notable absentees of this order from Australia are the vultures, which are common in all other continents.

The families present in Australia are the Accipitridae, Falconidae, and Pandionidae, the last containing but a single species, the Osprey *Pandion*, which occurs in all continents. There are seventeen Australian species of Accipitridae which range in size from the small Sparrowhawk to the great Wedge-tailed Eagle, among the largest of flying birds. The family, which also includes the harriers, goshawks and kites, is very varied morphologically. Between them the various species eat a great variety of animals of all classes. The diet of some is largely carrion while others are fierce and active hunters which live largely on flying birds. The Falconidae are represented in Australia by six species of *Falco*. Four are commonly known as falcons, one, the Brown Hawk, and the remaining one is the Kestrel. The Falconidae are much more uniform in size and morphology than the Accipitridae. They are all relatively short-tailed birds with sharp-pointed wings. Most of them are very fast fliers. They all live on small animals caught alive and some prey predominantly on flying birds captured in direct chase.

In our area all but seven of the Australian hawks have been recorded, including all of the Falconidae. Although some are rare, twelve are regular breeders or are known to have bred at least once. The others are rare or uncommon vagrants although there are anecdotal reports of breeding in two of these, the Black and Grey Falcons.

## Family Pandionidae — Osprey
## OSPREY *Pandion haliaetus*

IDENTIFICATION: Length 55–63 cm, female slightly larger than male. Upper-parts dark brown, with narrow buff edging to feathers; black tips to outermost flight feathers; head and neck white with some brown streaking; prominent dark-brown stripe through eye down side of neck; under-parts white with dark-brown band across upper breast; head feathers may be erected into small crest; bill, black; cere, bluish-grey; legs, pale grey; iris, yellow. The sexes are similar. Immatures are similar to adults but the crown and nape have more darker brown flecks, and the feathers of the back, wings and tail have broad pale tips.

VOICE: The common call is a short musical whistle of two or three syllables. The species also has a loud shrill alarm call.

DISTRIBUTION: The Osprey is found around most of the Australian, including Tasmanian, coast, and offshore islands. It follows
up the estuaries and lower reaches of the larger rivers, but is found
inland only as a vagrant. It is more common in northern Australia.
There are two local records, a bird seen over Lake George on 2
February 1969, and another at Lake Bathurst on 20 June 1982.

HABITS: Ospreys are usually seen singly or in pairs. They are mostly
observed flying back and forth over inshore waters searching for fish.
Occasionally they hover briefly while searching. They are also seen
perched quietly on trees or rocky headlands, presumably after feeding.

BREEDING: The breeding season appears to depend on latitude; in
northern Australia it is late winter and spring. The nest is a large one
made of sticks and seaweed with a shallow depression on top. It may be
added to year after year and in time becomes a very bulky structure. It
may be built in trees, including dead ones, or on a rocky headland or
stack. The clutch size is two to four, usually three. The eggs are bluntly
oval with a rough texture, and are dull white marked, often heavily,
with reddish or brown blotches. They average $60 \times 45$ mm in
dimensions. As the breeding season approaches, the pair soar above
the nest site, and they also have a plunge-diving display interspersed
with soaring flights above the water.

FEEDING: The diet consists almost wholly of fish caught alive. When
attacking fish the Osprey plunges feet first into the sea. Fish are carried
in their talons to a tree or rock for eating. (J.H.C.)

Family Accipitridae — Hawks and Eagles
## BLACK-SHOULDERED KITE *Elanus notatus*

PLATE VII

IDENTIFICATION: Length, 36 cm. General colour above, pale grey;
wing quills darker grey; black patch at "shoulder" of wing; head and
neck, white except for small black patch in front of eye; under-parts,
white, except for a small black patch just in from "bend" of wing,
which is seen in flight; bill, black; cere, greenish-yellow; legs and feet,
yellow; iris, orange-red. The sexes are similar.

Juveniles are somewhat darker on the upper-parts; wing feathers are
mottled with white and pale brown; the black area is small and broken
with white and brown marks; crown, nape, and hind neck are light
buffy-brown with some white and brown streaks; under neck and
upper breast, pale buffy-brown; iris, brown. The adult plumage is
acquired in the first year.

67

VOICE: It has two common calls. One is a series of rapidly uttered sharp whistles, and the other is a wheezing call rather like that of the Silver Gull. The latter call is used mostly when attacking other birds or defending the nest.

DISTRIBUTION: This kite is found only in mainland Australia, and is widely distributed in all States. Its preferred habitat is the woodland areas and it appears in forested country only after the forest has been partially cleared. It is fairly common in local woodland and several pairs are resident close to Canberra.

HABITS: Black-shouldered Kites are seen alone or in pairs. They are usually perched in low trees or on telegraph posts, or hovering over open fields. They are accomplished hoverers and this is their normal method of searching for prey. They fly with fairly rapid wing beats or glide for short distances. When gliding the wings are straight and held in a low V-shape. They do not seem to fly very high into the air.

BREEDING: It is a seasonal breeder in southern Australia. At least some birds in our region breed twice in the one season; the first clutch of eggs is laid in late May or June and the second in September. The nest is built from ten to fifteen metres from the ground in a thick-foliaged tree. The nest is made of sticks and lined with leaves. The clutch size is three to four. The eggs are oval in shape and dull white in colour, blotched with brown, sometimes heavily. The average dimensions are 40 × 30 mm. The nest is vigorously defended.

FEEDING: The Black-shouldered Kite feeds on small mammals, birds, reptiles and insects. It searches while hovering and drops or flutters down on the prey. House mice are an important food and other items taken include small lizards, grasshoppers, and occasional birds such as Starlings. (J.H.C.)

## LETTER-WINGED KITE *Elanus scriptus*

IDENTIFICATION: Length, males 34–37 cm, females slightly larger. General colour above, medium grey; wing quills slightly darker; some white on forehead; broad black patch at "shoulder" of wing; black ring around eye; under-parts white except for large black under-wing stripes resembling the letter "W" or "M", seen in flight; bill, black; cere, brownish; legs and feet, cream to pale yellow; iris, red. The sexes are similar.

Juveniles are grey-brown on the upper-parts; the forehead is brown; the "shoulder" patch is mottled black; under-parts, pale buffy-brown; throat, white; iris, light brown.

This species is distinguished from the Black-shouldered Kite, particularly by the distinctive black under-wing patch. The Letter-winged Kite is also darker grey on the back, has much less white on the head and a complete black eye ring.

VOICE: It has a whistling call similar to that of the Black-shouldered Kite but louder and harsher. It also has a harsh, repeated jarring call again somewhat similar to that of its congener.

DISTRIBUTION: Normally this kite is found only in western Queensland and the adjacent Barkly Tableland in the Northern Territory south to the Lake Eyre region of South Australia. The range consists of semi-arid grassland and desert shrublands intersected by watercourses lined with trees, particularly coolabahs (*Eucalyptus microtheca*). Its distribution coincides with that of the long-haired rat (*Rattus villosissimus*), its chief food item. The rat is normally quite uncommon but during runs of good seasons it increases enormously in numbers, and the kites' numbers increase at the same time. Eventually the food supply of the rats is exhausted, and they move out over the countryside in large plagues, sometimes for hundreds of kilometres, and die off. When this happens the starving surplus kites also leave the area and are observed in places where they do not normally occur.

Letter-winged Kites are known to have reached our region on two occasions following collapse of rat plagues. A couple were seen about 1970, and occasional ones were observed in Canberra and near Lake George in the summer and autumn of 1977. One was found dead at Lake George in March 1977. At this time large numbers of kites were recorded in southern Victoria and other coastal localities in southern Australia.

HABITS: In its normal range this kite is a gregarious species and lives in large groups. During daytime they are largely inactive and roost in groups in trees. They normally hunt at dusk and during the night but when food is scarce they also hunt in daylight. They fly slowly and circle around at ten to forty metres from the ground and also hover. When gliding the wings are held in a low V-shape.

BREEDING: Breeding takes place at any time of the year, the amount depending on the quantity of food available. In years when rats are abundant breeding is virtually continuous. Breeding is communal and colonies of five to twenty or more pairs build nests in a group of trees along a watercourse; sometimes there are several active nests in the one tree. The nest is made of twigs, usually from low shrubs, and lined with green leaves. New nests may be built on old ones. Old nests are covered

69

with accumulations of rat fur. Refugee kites outside their normal range seldom attempt breeding and no successful breeding has been reported. The clutch size is two to six. The eggs are oval and dull white to pale buff with red-brown blotches, usually concentrated on the larger end. The average dimensions are 45 × 33 mm.

FEEDING: In its normal range the Letter-winged Kite is highly adapted to living on the long-haired rat. When these are scarce they supplement their diet with grasshoppers and perhaps reptiles. Outside the normal range their diet consists of small mammals, particularly house mice, and insects. When captured, mammalian food is taken to a tree for eating. (J.H.C.)

## FORK-TAILED KITE *Milvus migrans*

PLATE VII

IDENTIFICATION: Length, male 52 cm, female slightly larger. General colour above, dark brown; wing quills, black; other wing feathers edged pale brown; tail, brown with black bars, shallow fork at end; crown of head and hind neck, paler brown with dark streaking; sides of face and throat, pale grey with dark markings; rest of underparts, rufous-brown with black streaking; bill, black, grey at base; cere, yellow; legs and feet, yellow; iris, brown. The sexes are similar but young birds are a lighter brown.

It is distinguished in flight by the dark colour and the shallowly-forked tail.

VOICE: The Fork-tailed Kite is quite vocal and has a variety of squealing and whistling notes.

DISTRIBUTION: It is widely distributed from Europe and northern Africa through southern Asia and Indonesia to New Guinea and Australia. In Australia it is most abundant in the tropics and the dry northern inland but occasionally irrupts in considerable numbers to southern Australia. It seems to be fairly uncommon in the woodlands and savannahs but is abundant near habitations.

In our region it is a rare vagrant and the few Canberra records were usually associated with irruptions following droughts in the inland or tropics.

HABITS: Fork-tailed Kites may be seen alone but are more usually found in groups, sometimes in large numbers. They congregate around rural human habitations, stockyards, and particularly slaughter houses and refuse tips, where they perch in trees or on fence posts, roofs or on the ground for long periods, watching and squabbling. Their flight is very slow, consisting of slow wing beats and glides. The tail, used for equilibration, is constantly moving and twisting. When gliding the wings are held horizontally but are bowed upwards in the centre. Fork-tailed Kites congregate on suitable upcurrents and soar to great heights. They gather at grass and scrub fires and soar upwards over the fire. They are tame and inoffensive birds.

BREEDING: The Fork-tailed Kite may build its own nest but usually renovates an old nest of a crow or other hawk. Soft lining such as bark or animal hair is added. The clutch size is two or three. The eggs are rounded oval in shape and are white with a few red markings. They are very variable in both size and colour. They average $51 \times 42$ mm in dimensions. The incubation period has been determined as thirty-four days. There are no breeding records in our area.

FEEDING: The Fork-tailed Kite is a scavenger and eats carrion of any kind. It also catches some small mammals, insects, and reptiles, and congregates at rodent, grasshopper and caterpillar plagues. Grasshoppers are sometimes caught in the air. The bird catches them in its feet and transfers them to its bill. (J.H.C.)

## WHISTLING EAGLE *Haliastur sphenurus*

PLATE VII

IDENTIFICATION: Length, male 53 cm, female slightly larger. Wings and back, brown; wing quills, dark brown to black; inner wing feathers, tipped with pale brown; tail feathers, paler brown than back; head and neck, brown, heavily streaked pale buff; rest of under-parts, buff streaked with brown. There is considerable variation in the colour of the head, neck and under-parts. Some specimens are so pale in these areas that they appear creamy-white while at the other extreme some are quite brown. Bill and cere, brown; legs and feet, pale grey; iris, brown. The sexes are similar.

The juvenile is somewhat darker than the adult and has some dorsal spotting. The spotting is lost and the back becomes paler at the end of the first year.

In flight the ends of the primaries are dark, long, and well spread, the tail is long and rounded, and there is a dark sub-rectangular area at the trailing edge of the wing adjacent to the body.

Although it is usually called an eagle, the Whistling Eagle is in fact a kite.

VOICE: It is quite vocal and has a whistling call, uttered on the wing or when perched. The call consists of a loud whistle usually followed by a rapid series of short notes on an ascending scale.

71

DISTRIBUTION: It occurs in New Guinea, the Solomons, New Caledonia, and mainland Australia. It is found in all parts of Australia but is most common in open woodland country near water, swamps, rivers, lakes and the seashore. Around Canberra it is quite common along the rivers and around lakes and is sometimes seen floating over open countryside.

HABITS: Whistling Eagles are seen alone, in pairs, and larger groups. In the non-breeding season these groups can be very large, up to several scores. Usually they are seen perched in open trees or on fence posts, flying with slow wing beats, or gliding slowly at low altitudes. When gliding the wings are held horizontally but they are bowed upwards in the centre. They sometimes soar to considerable heights. Their movements in the air are slow and leisurely. Whistling Eagles are confiding and inoffensive birds.

BREEDING: It apparently breeds at any time of the year in warm regions where food supply is abundant but in our region it is a spring breeder and eggs have been found in September. It builds a large stick nest thirteen metres or more high in a tree, usually by a river. The nest is lined with fresh green leaves. The clutch size is two or three; the eggs are oval in shape and have a rough texture. They are bluish-white in colour sparingly marked with reddish-brown blotches. Average dimensions are 57 × 44 mm. The Whistling Eagle does not defend its nest.

FEEDING: It is a scavenger and feeds on any sort of carrion, much of which is mammals, birds and reptiles, killed on roads by traffic. It also kills some of its food, e.g., occasional rabbit kittens and young water birds. It has been seen feeding on dead water rats and platypus which it may have killed. It also eats larger insects such as grasshoppers and caterpillars and catches some freshwater crayfish, or finds them dead on river and lake shores. Dead fish are eaten when they are cast up on shore or are picked from the water. (J.H.C.)

## BLACK-BREASTED BUZZARD *Hamirostra melanosternon*

IDENTIFICATION: Length, female 56–68 cm, male slightly smaller. A medium to large, squat, heavy-looking hawk occurring in two phases, dark and light, of which the former is the commoner. Head, back, wings, throat and breast mostly black, remainder, including nape and edge of "shoulders", chiefly reddish-brown; tail, grey-brown, short and square. Light phase mainly reddish-brown with dark centres to wing coverts and black streaks on breast feathers. Bill, pale grey with black tip; cere, off-white, sometimes with bluish tinge; legs, pale grey; iris, brown. The sexes are similar. Immatures mainly reddish-brown, somewhat darker than the light phase. This large hawk is second only to the Wedge-tailed Eagle and White-breasted Sea Eagle in size. It is readily distinguished in flight by its large size, dark colour, short, square tail and broad upswept wings with a prominent circular white patch towards the ends of the wings.

VOICE: This species has a short sharp two- or three-syllable call, sometimes repeated rapidly. It also produces a loud harsh call occasionally when attacking prey.

DISTRIBUTION: The Black-breasted Buzzard is found in small numbers over the greater part of mainland Australia but is absent from most of the eastern and southern coastal areas. It is more common in the arid inland and in the tropical northern parts of Australia. Its habitat is chiefly the woodlands and lightly timbered plains. In arid, relatively treeless country it is associated with the trees along watercourses. There is one local record, an immature in flight forty kilometres south of Yass on 20 February 1970.

HABITS: This hawk is found singly, in pairs, or occasionally in small groups. It is usually seen in flight soaring in wide circles with only very infrequent wing beats. A side-slipping action over treetops when searching for prey, has been reported. Individuals are occasionally seen standing motionless on the ground in open areas. They also sit quietly in trees for long periods after feeding.

BREEDING: The breeding season is late winter and spring. The nest is a large stick structure with a shallow egg chamber, built in a tree fork ten to twenty or more metres above the ground. The chamber is lined with fresh green leaves. The same nest may be used and added to year after year. The clutch size is two to four. The eggs are rounded oval in shape, and are dull white to pale buff marked with reddish, brown and purplish blotches. The average dimensions are 62 × 48 mm. Usually only one young is reared.

FEEDING: The food consists of a variety of animals, usually caught alive, including small mammals, some birds, reptiles and large insects such as grasshoppers. Rabbits are an important food in some areas. Carrion is also eaten at times. The Black-breasted Buzzard is also said to break the eggs of large ground-nesting birds such as the Bustard and Emu, by dropping rocks on to them. The contents are then eaten. (J.H.C.)

73

## GREY GOSHAWK *Accipiter novaehollandiae*

PLATE VI

IDENTIFICATION: Length, male 42 cm, female 52 cm. General colour of upper-parts, pale grey; head, white with grey barring; under-parts, white with grey barring on throat, neck and sides of breast; grey-brown bars on tail; bill, black; cere, orange-yellow; legs and feet, orange-yellow; claws, black; iris, red or reddish-brown. The sexes of same phase are similar in colour.

There is also a white phase in which the entire plumage is pure white, and a coloured phase with a dark grey back and a brown breast. The white phase occurs in Australia but the coloured phase does not. Usually the grey phase is observed in our region.

VOICE: According to David Fleay the Grey Goshawk utters "deliberate, mellow and rather pleasing call-notes of rising inflexion".

DISTRIBUTION: It ranges from eastern Indonesia through New Guinea to the Solomons and Australia, including Tasmania. In Australia it occurs only in the higher rainfall parts from eastern South Australia to Queensland, Northern Territory and the Kimberley Division of Western Australia. In Australia it inhabits rainforest, wet sclerophyll forest, and sometimes the drier forest and denser vegetation along rivers. It is rare in our area but has been seen occasionally in the wetter forest and along the Murrumbidgee River.

HABITS: Grey Goshawks are seen alone or in pairs. They fly swiftly and directly when chasing prey, or slowly when moving about or searching for prey. They are said to be very wary but at least some individuals seem to be fairly confiding.

BREEDING: There are no breeding records in the region but elsewhere the breeding season is in the spring and summer. It builds a large stick nest in a tall tree or occasionally uses an old nest of a raven. The nest is lined with green leaves. The clutch size is two, rarely three. The eggs are oval in shape, and pale bluish-white in colour, occasionally with a few brown markings, and measure about 41 × 38 mm.

FEEDING: The Grey Goshawk feeds on birds, small mammals, including rabbits, reptiles and large insects such as grasshoppers. It chases birds among trees and has been seen pursuing pigeons just above the treetops in rainforest. (J.H.C.)

## BROWN GOSHAWK *Accipiter fasciatus*

PLATE VI

IDENTIFICATION: Length, male 40–43 cm, female 46–56 cm. General colour above, slaty-grey; a broad reddish-brown collar around back of neck; tail with brown barring; sides of face, pale grey; throat, almost white with pale grey-brown barring; under-parts, reddish-brown crossed with numerous fine white bars; bill, black; cere, bluish; legs and feet, yellow; iris, yellow. The sexes are similar in colour. Juveniles are brown above with the feathers edged with rufous-brown. The under-parts are white with broad brown streaking on throat and chest, and broad brown bars on the breast and abdomen. In the fledgling the feet are bright yellow, they then fade to pale yellow and finally develop to bright yellow again in the adult. Full adult plumage is attained in the second year.

The Brown Goshawk is distinguished in flight by the broad rounded wings which are held horizontally when gliding. Male Brown Goshawks cannot be separated from female Sparrowhawks without handling. Female Brown Goshawks are distinguished by their large size and male Sparrowhawks by their very small size. Other distinguishable characters are found in the feet. In the Brown Goshawk the tarsus is relatively thick, and the third joint of the middle toe is level with or behind the base of the claw of the outer toe. In the Sparrowhawk the middle toe is slender and the third joint is beyond the base of the claw of the outer toe.

VOICE: It utters a shrill chattering call when alarmed, defending its nest, or approaching its mate on the nest, but is generally silent.

DISTRIBUTION: The Brown Goshawk ranges from Christmas Island in the Indian Ocean through eastern Indonesia to New Guinea, Fiji, New Caledonia and Australia, including Tasmania. It is Australia-wide in distribution where there are trees. It reaches its greatest abundance in sclerophyll forest and woodland. In our area it is common.

HABITS: Brown Goshawks are found alone or in pairs. Their flight is direct with fairly rapid wing beats and is rather slow except when chasing prey. They often soar in spirals on warm still days. They are usually found perching silently in leafy trees and appear to be rather wary.

BREEDING: The breeding season is from September to January. The nest is built of sticks and lined with green leaves and is situated on the outer limbs of trees from six up to thirty metres from the ground. Occasionally an old nest of a raven is used and lined with leaves. The clutch size varies from two to five and is usually three. The eggs are rounded oval in shape; white in colour, with a bluish tinge and are lightly marked with red blotches. The average dimensions are 47 × 37 mm. Only the female broods the eggs and the incubation period is thirty days. The nest is fiercely defended by both parent birds.

FEEDING: The food consists of small mammals, particularly rabbits, birds, reptiles, and larger insects. Its chief food is birds which it actively pursues in short fast bursts through trees and shrubs. Locally this hawk has been seen to catch rosellas, Domestic Pigeons, Pipits, Skylarks, Starlings, and rabbits. It is a raider of fowl runs and also enters pigeon lofts after Domestic Pigeons.

It is greatly feared by most birds; its appearance causes immediate alarm reactions in many species. For example, Starlings bunch together and fly around rapidly, Galahs rise in a tight group and screech, small passerines fly into dense bushes and honeyeaters utter alarm calls continuously. (J.H.C.)

## SPARROWHAWK *Accipiter cirrocephalus*

PLATE VI

IDENTIFICATION: Length, male 28–33 cm, female 36–39 cm. General colour above, dark slaty-grey; tail, with dark brown bars above; sides of face, grey; reddish-brown collar around back of neck; under-parts, reddish-brown crossed with numerous fine white bars; bill, black; cere, bluish; legs and feet, yellow; iris, yellow. The sexes are similar in colour.

The plumage of both adults and young is very similar to that of adults and young of the Brown Goshawk. They are very difficult to separate but male Sparrowhawks are readily distinguished because of their very small size. The separation of the Brown Goshawk and the Sparrowhawk is discussed under the Goshawk.

VOICE: The Sparrowhawk is generally a silent bird but it has calls similar to those of the Brown Goshawk.

DISTRIBUTION: It is found in New Guinea, Aru Islands, and Australia, including Tasmania. It is widespread in Australia and favours woodland and the drier forest country. In our region it is found in woodland and forests and in river-side vegetation, at the lower altitudes. Its status is difficult to determine because of confusion with the Brown Goshawk but judging from the number of males seen it is a less common resident species than the Goshawk.

HABITS: Sparrowhawks are seen singly or in pairs. Their general habits are similar to those of the Brown Goshawk.

BREEDING: The breeding season is from September to December. It makes a nest of small sticks, in a tree, and lines it with green leaves, or takes over and lines an old raven's or magpie's nest. The clutch size is from two to four. The eggs are rounded oval, white in colour with a few red-brown blotches, and measure about $38 \times 31$ mm. The incubation period has been recorded, probably incorrectly, as about nineteen days. The birds defend the nest.

FEEDING: The Sparrowhawk hunts and feeds on small animals, birds, and larger insects. Its chief prey is small birds and its hunting methods are similar to those of the Brown Goshawk. The reactions of other birds to the presence of the Sparrowhawk are similar to their behaviour at the sight of the Brown Goshawk. (J.H.C.)

## LITTLE EAGLE *Hieraaetus morphnoides*

PLATE VI

IDENTIFICATION: Length, male 48 cm, female 56 cm. The plumage is very variable but there are well-marked light and dark phases. General colour above, brown; wing quills, black; pale bars on wings; upper-tail feathers, greyish-brown crossed with dark brown bars, almost white at tip; head, neck and upper chest may be chestnut-brown or dark brown with black streaks; black streak below eye; short erectile crest on crown with black tips to feathers; under-parts may be white with a few chestnut streaks, buff to chestnut with darker streaks, or dark brown with black streaks; legs feathered right down to feet, white, buff or reddish-brown; bill, blue-grey or brown; cere, grey; feet, greenish-white or blue-grey; claws, black; iris, brown. Sexes of the same phase are similar in plumage.

Light phase birds have a small triangular dark patch near the front of the wing, a broad oblique white band below this, and a dark triangular area at the back of the wing. In dark phase birds the dark patch at the front of the wing is much more extensive and the oblique band, if visible at all, is greyish. In flight the Little Eagle is distinguished by broad wings and dark-tipped primaries, held horizontally when gliding, the short tail with square-cut end, and under-wing pattern.

VOICE: The Little Eagle is quite a vocal species. Its normal call uttered when perched or flying is a soft whistling two or three-syllable note with the second and third syllables lower in pitch and of shorter duration than the first. These notes may be written "choo-oo" and "choo-oo-oo". The bird also has a long call only used when perched. It consists of a monotone of five or six notes uttered relatively slowly, and generally followed by six or seven notes of shorter duration emitted at a faster rate on a descending scale. This call may be written "chew-chew-

chew-chew-chew-choo-oo-oo-oo-oo-oo-oo-oo". Normally the calls are soft and rather plaintive but in certain circumstances, e.g., during display flights, or in threat situations, they may be loud or harsh, or different in the duration of the component notes.

DISTRIBUTION: It is found in New Guinea and mainland Australia. In Australia it is usually in woodland and lightly timbered plain country but is also found in forested country where there are open areas in which it can hunt. In the highlands it is thinly scattered over the woodland, open grazing country and along forest edges at the lower altitudes.

HABITS: Little Eagles are seen alone or in pairs. They are generally gliding or flying around rabbit-infested areas or perched in thinly-foliaged trees, but they are occasionally seen standing on the ground. On suitable days they soar in fairly tight spirals to great heights. The normal progression consists of flying with relatively slow wing beats alternating with periods of gliding. They are often heckled by other birds such as magpies, ravens, and Magpie-larks. Prior to breeding and during the breeding season the male performs an undulating display flight from a hundred to several hundred metres above its territory. It flies rapidly upwards at a steep angle, then plummets down with folded wings and repeats the manoeuvre over and over. During the display a loud variant of the normal call is uttered often.

BREEDING: In southern Australia the breeding season extends from August to November. Eggs have been found in the region in September and October. The nest is built in a tree from thirteen up to fifty metres from the ground. It builds a large stick nest lined with green leaves or uses an old nest of a raven or another species of hawk. The clutch is one or two. The eggs are pale bluish-white in colour marked with reddish-brown streaks or blotches, oval to rounded oval in shape and averaging $55 \times 45$ mm in dimensions. Some birds defend their nests.

FEEDING: It feeds on small mammals, reptiles, birds, occasionally carrion, and large insects, such as grasshoppers. Its chief diet in rabbit-infested country is young rabbits up to about one-third grown. It searches for prey while flying slowly over suitable areas such as rabbit warrens, or from a commanding perch on a tree. The prey is eaten on ground where it is killed, or it may be carried to a more sheltered position on the ground, or a stout branch of a tree. (J.H.C.)

## WEDGE-TAILED EAGLE *Aquila audax*
PLATE VI

IDENTIFICATION: Length, 90 cm, male slightly smaller than female. General colour, dark brown to black; nape, and hind neck, chestnut-brown, streaked black; pale edges to feathers of wing coverts; tail, long and wedge-shaped; legs feathered down to feet; bluish-white bare skin in front of and above eye; bill, mostly pale grey; cere, almost white; feet, almost white; iris, yellow. The sexes are similar in plumage. Immature birds are mainly golden-brown or reddish-brown with black tails and wing quills. Full adult plumage is not acquired until the sixth year.

In flight the Wedge-tailed Eagle is distinguished by its great size, wedge-shaped tail, and wings held in a low V-shape.

VOICE: The Wedge-tailed Eagle is not heard very often but it has a variety of calls. The normal call is a shrill rather weak double-syllabled note. Other shrill calls are associated with greeting and territoriality. There is a very loud "bleating" scream which appears to be an alarm call. The female has a loud double-note mating call.

DISTRIBUTION: It occurs in southern New Guinea and Australia, including Tasmania. It is Australia-wide in distribution and occurs in all habitats. It is quite common in our region, particularly in the open woodland and is found up to the highest altitude.

HABITS: Wedge-tailed Eagles are sometimes seen alone but are usually in pairs. They are generally seen gliding or soaring over the countryside, or perched silently on dead or sparsely-foliaged trees. When gliding the wings are straight and are held in a characteristic low V-shaped carriage. Wedge-tailed Eagles are often pursued by other birds, particularly magpies and ravens. They are wary birds.

Display flights have been observed in early winter. One bird, presumably the male, performs an undulating display flight fairly high in the air, flying steeply upwards and plummeting downwards with closed wings, and then repeating the manoeuvre. In another display both birds fly close together one above the other. Every now and again the lower bird turns over in the air and both birds touch, or almost touch, claws. Sometimes the upper bird, presumed to be the male because of its smaller size, has a stick in its claw.

BREEDING: In southern Australia, including our area, mating behaviour of the Wedge-tailed Eagle begins in June and the eggs are laid in August. If the eggs are taken or are infertile, further clutches may be laid as late as October. The nest is a huge stick structure lined with green leaves; fresh leaves are constantly added to the nest until the young leave. The nest is usually built fairly high in a tree but in semi-arid and treeless country small trees, the ground or rocks are used. Nest building begins in late June or July; both sexes participate but the male is the chief builder. The clutch size is one or two. The eggs are dull white in colour with reddish-brown spots, blotches and streaks, and are oval or rounded oval in shape. They measure about 73 × 58 mm. Apparently only the female broods the eggs. The nest is not defended.

FEEDING: The Wedge-tailed Eagle has a diverse diet of mammals, birds and reptiles. A considerable proportion of its food is carrion and it will feed on dead vertebrates of any size. Its most important foods in southern Australia are rabbit and sheep, the latter largely carrion. Some lambs are killed but the killers seem to be mostly foot-loose unestablished immatures which tend to move in nomadic groups. Rabbits, young kangaroos, wallabies, young foxes, some birds, and reptiles are also captured. Searching is done while flying or gliding slowly. When attacking, the eagle either folds its wings and plummets down steeply, or flies rapidly after the prey. Pairs often hunt co-operatively. Among birds killed and eaten are Kookaburras, Galahs, and magpies; reptiles eaten include stumptailed lizards, blue-tongue lizards, bearded dragons, goannas, and carpet snakes. The Wedge-tailed Eagle also takes advantage of road casualties and is also known to steal food from other predatory birds. (J.H.C.)

## WHITE-BREASTED SEA-EAGLE *Haliaeetus leucogaster*
PLATE VI

IDENTIFICATION: Length, male 76 cm, female 84 cm. Wings, back, and most of the tail, dark ashy-grey; apical third of tail, white; head, neck, and under-parts, including under-tail, white; not feathered to toes; bill, blue-grey, black at tip; cere, greyish; legs and feet, off-white; claws, black; iris, brown. The sexes are similar in plumage.

First-year birds are light brown above, with buffy-white tips to feathers; head and neck, light buff; tail feathers, very pale buff becoming deep brown towards the tips; chest, brown with buff margins to feathers; abdomen, mottled brown and buff. In the second-year the bird is much lighter brown all over, the head is pale buff, and the tail is virtually white all over. Full adult plumage is attained at about three and a half years of age.

In flight the bird is distinguished by its large size, very broad wings held in a fairly high V-shape, short rounded tail, and pale colour in the adult.

80

VOICE: It has a loud clanging call, and usually sustained duets are performed. They are much more vocal during the breeding season.

DISTRIBUTION: The White-breasted Sea-eagle ranges from India and southern China through Indonesia to the New Guinea area and Australia, including Tasmania. It is associated with sea-shores and large lowland rivers and lakes. It is seen sometimes around Lakes George and Bathurst and occasionally over Lake Burley Griffin and the Murrumbidgee River.

HABITS: They are seen singly or in pairs, usually gliding or flying with fairly slow wing beats, over water or along the shore. They perch in open positions on trees, rocks or headlands, or sometimes on the shore, although in the latter case they are probably investigating cast-up possible food items. They appear to maintain permanent territories. They are chased by gulls, terns, and oystercatchers if they come near these birds' nesting sites, and also by ravens and magpies and other land birds.

BREEDING: In southern Australia eggs are laid from June to September generally. Breeding behaviour begins in autumn when nest-building commences. The nest is a huge stick structure usually built high up, thirty metres or more, in a tall tree and is used annually for long periods. The White-breasted Sea-eagle also nests in smaller trees in inland swamps, or on the ground or rocks on treeless islands. The nest is lined with stems of green leaves which are added to while the young are present. The clutch size is two. The eggs are oval, white in colour and unmarked, and measure approximately $71 \times 53$ mm. The female does most of the brooding but the male relieves her for periods during the daytime. Both birds defend the nest vigorously and the male is particularly aggressive. It has bred at Lake Bathurst and has nested on at least one occasion in a tall manna gum on the shore of Lake George. The latter was unsuccessful, as one of the birds was shot by a vandal.

FEEDING: It feeds on a variety of food including fish, other sea animals, birds, mammals and reptiles and will eat all of these as carrion. It is an accomplished fisher and catches surface swimming freshwater and marine fishes. It can also capture sea-snakes. Birds killed include Coots, ducks, and Black Swans. Mammals eaten include rabbits, and domestic stock, including lambs, as carrion. One of its habits is to harry Ospreys, terns, and other birds until they drop their prey which it then snatches up. (J.H.C.)

81

## SPOTTED HARRIER *Circus assimilis*

PLATE VI

IDENTIFICATION: Length, male 53 cm, female 60 cm. General colour above including tail, bluish-grey; wing quills, black, brown bars on outer wing coverts; inner wing coverts, reddish-brown, spotted white; head, grey with red-brown striations; facial ruff, reddish-brown; under-parts, reddish-brown spotted white; tail, with several blackish-brown bars and narrow white tips to feathers; under-tail, grey with several white bars; bill, black; cere, green-grey; legs and feet, yellow; claws, black; iris, yellow. The sexes are similar in plumage.

In flight distinguished by the reddish body and under-wing coverts heavily spotted with white, the dark edges to the primaries, and the barred tail.

VOICE: It is generally silent but does have short shrill "squealing" notes which are sometimes uttered when attacking prey.

DISTRIBUTION: The Spotted Harrier is found in Celebes, Lesser Sundas, Timor, and mainland Australia, and is vagrant in northern Tasmania. It is absent from New Guinea. In Australia it is found in the more open country and is absent from forested areas. It occurs in greatest numbers in the warmer lower-rainfall country, and is sometimes found around swamps. It is occasionally seen around Canberra, Lake George, and the open countryside.

HABITS: Spotted Harriers are found singly or in pairs. They generally fly low, mostly alternating gliding with slow wing beats. When gliding the wings are straight and held in a low V-shape. They perch in trees but are often seen standing on the ground. In display flight they soar to great heights, and return to earth in slow spirals, or side-slips, or sometimes plummet with half-closed wings.

BREEDING: It is not known to breed in our region but elsewhere the breeding season is from July to October. It builds a bulky flat stick nest in a low tree and lines it with green leaves. The clutch size is two to four. The eggs are white to bluish-white and unmarked but they become very nest-stained. They are oval to rounded oval in shape. The egg dimensions are approximately 53 × 41 mm.

FEEDING: The Spotted Harrier glides low over the ground and cane grass swamps, and beats around bushes, searching for prey. Prey is killed on the ground but is usually taken to a tree for eating. It feeds on young rabbits and other small mammals, birds, reptiles, larger insects such as grasshoppers, and occasionally carrion. (J.H.C.)

## SWAMP HARRIER *Circus aeruginosus*

PLATE VI

IDENTIFICATION: Length, male 50 cm, female 58 cm. General colour above, dark brown with brownish-yellow streaking to head, nape, and rump; ends of primaries, blackish-brown; conspicuous broad white bar at base of tail; under-parts, buff with dark-brown streaking; bill, black; cere, greenish-yellow; legs and feet, greenish-yellow; claws, black; iris, brown. The sexes are similar in colour. There is some variation in colour; some birds, presumably young ones, are very dark and the pale rump is sometimes difficult to see.

In flight it appears uniformly dark-brown with the white rump bar conspicuous.

VOICE: It is generally silent but utters a loud single-note whistle, and shrill screaming notes, particularly when attacking prey. When the birds are displaying high in the air the high-pitched call has a plaintive quality.

DISTRIBUTION: This is a wide-ranging hawk and occurs in southern New Guinea, Fiji, New Caledonia, Lord Howe and Norfolk Islands, New Zealand and Australia, including Tasmania. In Australia it is widely distributed but is more abundant in the areas where there are extensive swamps. It is usually found around swamps, estuaries, and other open bodies of water. Around Canberra it is uncommon but is a breeding species. It can generally be found around Lakes George and Bathurst, and other large areas of water. In at least the southern part of its range, the Swamp Harrier is migratory.

HABITS: Swamp Harriers occur singly or in pairs or in larger groups. It is probable that larger groups are not social units but are drawn together because of suitable habitat or food abundance. They are generally seen flying low over swamp vegetation or hay and wheat fields. They mostly glide or fly with slow wing beats and when gliding, the wings are straight and held in a low V-shape. They often perch on the ground or drop into swamp vegetation or standing crops. They also perch on stumps or fence posts close to swamps or crops.

BREEDING: The Swamp Harrier breeds from September to December. It nests on the ground in standing crops, rushes, or long tussocky grass, or in swamp vegetation standing in water. It sometimes builds on an old swan's nest. The nest is made of rushes, dead thistles and small diameter sticks, and is lined with finer plant material. The clutch is from three to six, usually four or five. The eggs are bluish-white in colour and oval in shape, and average 53 × 40 mm in dimensions.

Nests have been found in the region in wheatfields and reedy swamp vegetation, including cumbungi on the shore of Lake Burley Griffin within the Canberra city area. Eggs have been found in September and October, and young have been observed on the wing in late December.

FEEDING: The Swamp Harrier searches for prey while gliding or flying low over swamps and open fields. It feeds on waterbirds, small mammals, such as young rabbits, and Water-rats *Hydromys chrysogaster*, reptiles, large insects, and occasionally on carrion such as dead rabbits. It is often seen making determined attacks on broods of ducklings and smaller waterbirds such as Coots and grebes, and will hurl itself uttering screaming calls, at swamp vegetation in which birds are hiding. (J.H.C.)

## Family Falconidae — Falcons and Kestrels
## PEREGRINE FALCON *Falco peregrinus*

PLATE VII

IDENTIFICATION: Length, male 38 cm, female 48 cm. General colour above, blue-grey with dark cross-bars to the feathers; pale margins to smaller wing feathers; tail with dark cross-bars and a pale tip; crown, nape, and sides of head and cheeks, black; throat to breast, pale chestnut-buff with a few black spots on the lower breast; rest of under-parts, chestnut-buff crossed with numerous black bars; bill, grey-blue with black tip; cere and naked skin around eye, blue; legs and feet, yellow; iris, brown. The under-parts of females have a richer chestnut colour.

Juveniles are generally dark brown above with rufous margins to most of the feathers; head and cheeks, dark brown; under-parts, rufous-buff; throat and breast, paler with longitudinal dark brown streaks which go farther up the breast than the dark breast markings of the adult.

VOICE: The Peregrine is quite a vocal falcon. It utters loud, shrill, harsh and repetitive screams on the wing. It is particularly noisy when defending its nest.

DISTRIBUTION: Except possibly for the Osprey the Peregrine Falcon is the most widely distributed of all hawks and occurs in North America, Europe, Africa, Asia and Australia, including Tasmania. It is found in all parts of Australia but is not common anywhere. It is most often seen in hilly country or around cliffs and escarpments. It is observed occasionally around Canberra, along the fault scarp at Lake George or in the open woodland country.

HABITS: Peregrines are seen alone or in pairs, usually flying past with rapid wing beats at low to medium altitudes, or harassing other birds. They commonly soar to fairly high altitudes with outstretched wings. They are also seen standing quietly and alert on commanding positions on trees or cliffs. They are very wary birds.

BREEDING: It is a seasonal breeding species; eggs have been found in the region in September and October. It does not build a nest but lays its eggs in hollows of tall trees, cliff recesses, and large abandoned nests of other species. Two clutches near Canberra were found in old nests of a Wedge-tailed Eagle and an Australian Raven. The clutch size is two or three, usually three. The eggs are oval to rounded oval in shape and are a pale buff colour, marked with blotches of red and reddish-brown. Average dimensions of the eggs are 51 × 41 mm. Both sexes defend the nest vigorously and noisily. The young stay with the parents for some time after fledging.

FEEDING: The chief foods are birds and mammals, particularly the former. It is an active, fierce and very fast hunter and overhauls its victims in direct pursuit and usually attacks from above in a power dive. It kills birds larger than itself by striking them out of the air with a talon. Sometimes it will bind to the victim and drop down with it. Peregrines often hunt in co-operation. It also catches ground mammals, and patrols likely hunting grounds, such as concentrations of rabbit burrows, by flying rapidly over them close to the ground. Usually it carries its prey to safe places for plucking and butchering.

No species of small or medium-sized birds are immune from attack and among local records of species killed are the Eastern and Crimson Rosella, Domestic Pigeon, White-winged Chough and Grey Thrush.

Reactions of other birds to the presence of this falcon are similar to their behaviour at the sight of the Brown Goshawk. (J.H.C.)

## LITTLE FALCON *Falco longipennis*

PLATE VII

IDENTIFICATION: Length, male 30 cm, female 33–35 cm. General colour above, dark slaty-grey with black streaks to centres of feathers, pale margins to smaller wing feathers; tail feathers with dark bars and pale tip; crown and nape, black with bluish gloss; sides of face, almost black; forehead, throat and collar at sides of neck, slightly rufous, almost white; rest of under-parts, rufous-brown with dark streaking; bill, grey-blue with black tip; cere, bluish; legs and feet, yellow; iris, brown. The sexes are similar.

Juveniles are generally dark brown above including the crown, the feathers margined with buff; under-parts, rufous-brown with indistinct streaking. The adult plumage is acquired within the first year.

VOICE: The Little Falcon has a shrill, repetitive twittering call. When attacking or defending its nest it utters a shrill, harsh chatter.

DISTRIBUTION: It is found in the Lesser Sunda Islands and in Australia, including Tasmania. Some Australian birds migrate to New Guinea during winter. It is widely distributed in all Australian States. Around Canberra it is fairly common in woodland, open forest and built-up areas where there are trees.

HABITS: They are seen singly or in pairs, sometimes perched but more generally flying swiftly with very rapid wing beats at low to medium altitudes. They hover occasionally in a rather clumsy manner, soar at times and glide downwards very rapidly. They are very wary birds.

BREEDING: The Little Falcon is a seasonal breeder and eggs have been found near Canberra in November. It uses old nests of other birds such as ravens, magpies and Little Crows and lines them with leaves or other plant material. It also has the un-falcon-like habit of building its own stick nest. The clutch size is two or three, the eggs are a pale buff colour with reddish markings. The average dimensions of the egg are $46 \times 34$ mm. This species defends its nest very fiercely.

FEEDING: The chief prey is birds and large insects which are caught in flight. Its hunting methods are direct pursuit and fast power dives. It will attack and strike and often kill birds such as ducks and Galahs, which are larger than itself, but generally the birds it hunts are the smaller passerines such as Starlings and finches. It catches grasshoppers, dragonflies, winged ants, and other insects on the wing. Just before dusk it hunts and sometimes catches early-flying bats.

Reaction of other birds, at least the smaller kinds, at the appearance of this falcon are rather like their reactions to the presence of the Brown Goshawk. (J.H.C.)

## GREY FALCON *Falco hypoleucus*

IDENTIFICATION: Length, male 34 cm, female 43 cm. General colour above, pale blue-grey; tail feathers barred darker grey; black tips to primaries; narrow ring of black feathers surrounding eyes; under-parts, pale ashy-brown; bill, blue-grey; cere and naked skin around eye, yellowish; legs and feet, orange; iris, brown. Tail relatively short when compared with other falcons. The sexes are similar. Imma-

86

tures have brownish backs and heavy brown streaking on the foreneck and abdomen.

VOICE: The Grey Falcon is quite vocal and has a harsh repetitive chattering call. It also produces a clucking call, presumably for contact purposes.

DISTRIBUTION: It is restricted to mainland Australia and occurs in the drier parts of all States, particularly the lightly timbered plains. There are occasional occurrences in lower altitude open woodland in the northern part of the area.

HABITS: They are seen singly or in pairs. The flight is rather slow and flapping and the short tail is frequently flicked from side to side, presumably for equilibration. They can fly fairly rapidly when attacking prey. They often perch on trees for long periods, and at other times soar to great heights. Grey Falcons are rather tame and confiding birds.

BREEDING: Little is known about the breeding of this species; but it seems to breed in the late spring. The Grey Falcon uses the old nest of a crow or other species of hawk. The nest is lined with soft material such as animal hair or bark. The clutch size is two to four, usually three. The eggs are pinkish-buff in colour, heavily spotted with reddish-brown markings. They are blunt oval in shape and the average dimensions are 51 × 37 mm. The nest is defended vigorously and noisily. There is an anecdotal record of breeding near Canberra some years ago.

FEEDING: It feeds on small mammals, birds, reptiles, and insects, mostly collected from the ground. It flies slowly, close to the ground and above small shrubs, and pounces on its prey. It also spends a considerable amount of time perching on trees watching for prey. Among the mammals caught are juvenile rabbits and mice. The Grey Falcon catches considerable numbers of flying grasshoppers and other insects in its talons and transfers them to its bill whilst still in the air. Small mammals and birds are usually taken to a tree for butchering and eating. (J.H.C.)

## BLACK FALCON *Falco subniger*

PLATE VII

IDENTIFICATION: Length, female 54 cm, male slightly smaller. General colour appears black but is dark sooty brown, except for whitish forehead, cheeks and throat; bill, blue-grey; cere, pale bluish-white; legs and feet, blue-grey; iris, brown. The sexes are similar.

VOICE: The Black Falcon has a chattering call, and utters loud, harsh screaming notes when swooping on prey.

DISTRIBUTION: It is restricted to mainland Australia and is found chiefly in the more open lower rainfall country inland. It is apparently nomadic and occasionally appears in southern coastal higher rainfall areas. It is fairly commonly seen in the region, in the lower altitude open woodland.

HABITS: Black Falcons are seen either alone or in pairs. They have a slow flapping flight and glide in an undulating fashion at low altitudes, but fly very rapidly when attacking. Their appearance and flight characteristics when not hunting remind observers of crows. At times they soar to great heights.

BREEDING: Little is known about breeding of the Black Falcon. It uses an old nest of a crow or other species of hawk. Eggs have been found from June to December. The clutch size is two to four, usually three. The eggs are rounded oval, and in colour are pinkish-buff, heavily spotted with red-brown markings. The average dimensions are 54 × 40 mm. The nest is defended, the parent birds attacking silently in nearly vertical swoops. A pair of Black Falcons are reported to have nested for a number of years in the Cooma district.

FEEDING: The food is mainly birds, with some mammals. It swoops from a height in a fast gravity dive and then pursues the prey with rapid wing beats. When swooping and attacking it utters loud chattering screams which apparently intimidate the prey. Birds which have taken refuge in bushes are often frightened out by the Black Falcon which flies rapidly at the bush, screaming. Species of quail and Starlings are common prey and it also attacks larger birds such as Galahs, pigeons and ducks. These are struck repeatedly with the talons until they drop to the ground. It also takes small mammals, such as juvenile rabbits, and is said to prefer catching them on the run rather than in a squat. The Black Falcon usually carries its prey to a tree for butchering and eating. (J.H.C.)

## BROWN HAWK *Falco berigora*

PLATE VII

IDENTIFICATION: Length, male 45 cm, female 50 cm. The plumage is very variable; there are light and dark phases and intermediates. *Light phase.* General colour above, reddish-brown narrowly streaked black; quills, dark brown; wings, spotted rufous; tail feathers, grey-brown barred rufous; thighs, reddish-brown with paler streaks; crown, pale reddish-brown narrowly streaked black; lower forehead, off-white; sides of face, white; throat, pale buff; black streak across face from base of beak to below eye; breast, pale buff, abdomen almost white, both streaked black. *Dark phase*. General colour above, dark brown with pale margins to most feathers; head and nape, brown narrowly streaked black; throat almost white narrowly streaked black; black streak across face as in light phase; almost white narrow stripe outside black streak; dark bar beneath pale throat patch; rest of under-parts, dark brown with pale margins to feathers; bill, blue-grey; cere, pale blue; legs and feet, pale blue. Both sexes of the same phase are similar in colour.

Juveniles of both phases are dark, have a feebly barred tail, and golden-buff colour on the nape, throat, and cheeks. Most dark birds seen are juveniles.

VOICE: It is quite a vocal bird and utters loud repetitive cackling calls.

DISTRIBUTION: It is found in central and eastern New Guinea as well as all parts of Australia, including Tasmania. It occurs in most habitats and is probably the commonest bird-of-prey. In the southern part of the range at least some Brown Hawks are migratory.

HABITS: Brown Hawks are seen alone, in pairs, or several may be seen in close proximity in the non-breeding season. They are fairly slow fliers with relatively slow wing beats, and the flight is erratic at times. They glide a lot with the wings held in a fairly low V-shape, and sometimes soar to great heights. They frequently hover but not very efficiently. Usually they are seen perched on telegraph poles and trees watching for prey. Brown Hawks are generally rather wary but, if unmolested, they become fairly tame around human habitations.

During the breeding season the Brown Hawk performs a display flight. Two or perhaps three birds fly very rapidly around in circles and spirals, and perform side-slips and other manoeuvres including gliding around with the wings held in a fairly high V-shape. Loud cackling calls are uttered during these performances.

BREEDING: It is a seasonal breeder; eggs have been found around Canberra in September and October. It generally lays its eggs in the deserted nest of another species of hawk or a corvid, but sometimes in an open tree hollow. Both the Brown Hawk and the Little Falcon build their own nests at times, an unusual habit for a falcon. They are large

89

stick nests lined with finer material. The clutch size is two to five, usually three. The eggs are rounded-oval or oval, and in colour are pale buff blotched with red-brown markings. The average dimensions are $50 \times 38$ mm. The female broods and, as with some other falcons and other hawks, is fed by the male. She usually leaves the nest as he approaches, giving a cackling call, and takes the food from his talons in the air. When brooding small young she feeds them with the food taken from the male in the same way. The nest is not defended and both birds leave the area if the nest is molested.

FEEDING: It does not actively pursue its prey as do other falcons. Its chief searching method is to perch quietly on a post or high stump or tree and watch; when prey is seen it is pounced on. Some searching is done while it is flying or gliding slowly at low altitudes. Its chief prey is small mammals, some small birds, reptiles, insects and other invertebrates. It catches a fair number of house mice, and occasional rabbit kittens newly emerged from breeding burrows. It also commonly preys on small lizards and snakes. Probably its most important food is invertebrates such as grasshoppers, crickets, beetles, and caterpillars. It sometimes chases grasshoppers on the ground and catches them in its bill as well as in its talons. (J.H.C.)

## KESTREL *Falco cenchroides*

PLATE VII

IDENTIFICATION: Length, male 31 cm, female slightly larger. Male: general colour above, pale rufous; head with black streaking; wing quills, almost black with pale streaks; black tips to few wing feathers near primaries; tail feathers, pale grey, unbarred, tip white, black subterminal band; face and under-parts, white; thin black streak above eyes; black stripe arising near front of eye down side of throat; breast and flanks with pale rufous wash; few black streaks on breast. Female: generally similar to male but has considerable amount of brownish-black marking in wing feathers; upper-tail rufous, somewhat paler than back with black bars and broader subterminal black band. Bill, blue-grey; cere and eye ring, yellow; legs and feet, orange-yellow; iris, brown.

VOICE: The Kestrel's call is a shrill repetitive "ki-ki-ki..." uttered when perched or flying.

DISTRIBUTION: It occurs in Australia, including Tasmania, New Guinea, and a few nearby islands. There are several records of stragglers to New Zealand. It is Australia-wide in distribution and occurs in all habitats except the denser forests. It reaches its greatest abundance in the more open forests. There is some evidence that at least part of the population is migratory in the southern part of the range.

HABITS: They are usually seen alone or in pairs but several may be seen in proximity in the non-breeding season. They are most commonly seen hovering, sometimes for long periods, over open areas; after a while they move to another spot and begin hovering again. They have rapid wing beats but are not fast fliers. They sometimes glide and soar to fair heights. Quite often they are seen perched on telegraph posts, dead trees, haystacks, ledges of city buildings, etc. Kestrels are rather tame birds.

BREEDING: In southern Australia at least it is a seasonal breeder and eggs have been found around Canberra in October and November. The eggs are laid in deserted nests of other birds such as ravens, in tree hollows, recesses on cliff faces, or city buildings. The clutch size is three to seven, usually five. The eggs are rounded oval and in colour are very pale buff or pink, liberally blotched with brownish-red. Average dimensions are 38 × 31 mm. When the female is incubating she will leave the nest in response to the calling male and take food from his talons in the air.

FEEDING: The Kestrel does not pursue prey but searches from a hovering position, or a perch, and drops down on the prey. Its food is small mammals, particularly the house mouse, reptiles, birds and insects. Birds are not an important item and are small ones, such as swallows and chats, occasionally picked up in the air. Small skinks and dragon lizards are often caught. Perhaps its most important food consists of insects such as grasshoppers, crickets and beetles collected on the ground. It is seen attacking dragon-flies, butterflies, and grasshoppers on the wing. (J.H.C.)

## Nocturnal Birds-of-Prey

Owls are nocturnal birds-of-prey feeding exclusively on animal food. They are adapted for locating live prey by their sounds. Among their peculiarities are large round heads, capable of an extraordinary degree of rotation, prominent facial discs, large forward-projecting eyes, short tails, legs feathered to feet, soft plumage and noiseless flight.

The order containing the owls consists of two families and about 134 species and is worldwide in distribution. With only eight species, Australia is the poorest in owls of all continents. The family Tytonidae, the Barn Owls, consists of only two genera and eleven species. Australia is inhabited by four species of *Tyto*, one of which is virtually world-wide in distribution, another occurs from southern Asia to Australia, and the other two are found in Australia, New Guinea, and nearby islands. Three have been found in our area. None is seen very often but one is of fairly frequent occurrence. The family Strigidae, the Typical Owls, contains about 123 species. It is poorly represented in Australia, by only one genus and four species. One species is restricted to Australia, two others reach New Guinea and nearby islands, and the final one ranges from Timor, through New Guinea and Australia, to New Zealand. Three species occur in our area, all of which occur regularly but only one is commonly seen or heard.

## Family Strigidae — Typical Owls
## POWERFUL OWL *Ninox strenua*

PLATE XXXV

IDENTIFICATION: Length 65 cm, male larger than female. General colour above, dark brown barred with white and pale brown; tail feathers, dark brown barred with dull white; throat and under parts, whitish, barred with brown chevron-shaped markings; bill, black; feet, yellow; iris, orange-yellow. Plumage of female somewhat duller than that of male.

VOICE: The normal call is a slowly uttered, rather mournful, loud, double-syllabled note, written as "woo-hoo". About ten seconds elapse between each "woo-hoo". The call of the male is lower pitched and slower than that of the female. It calls at any time of the year but is much more vocal in the breeding season. It occasionally begins calling before sunset during the breeding season.

DISTRIBUTION: The Powerful Owl is confined to a 160 kilometre wide stretch of the coast of south-eastern Australia; from Portland in south-western Victoria to the Dawson River in south-eastern Queensland. It is a bird of the wetter, heavily-timbered ranges. It has been heard and observed in wet sclerophyll forest at Mount Tidbinbilla and the Brindabella Range. It is a resident breeding species in these forested ranges.

HABITS: Powerful Owls live permanently in pairs. They rest by day in trees which are not necessarily densely foliaged; the roosting sites are apparently chosen as much for quick escape as for shelter. Each pair has a number of daytime roosting-sites and alternates between them. The individual birds do not always roost together but are always within calling distance of each other. The Powerful Owl is a much shyer bird than other Australian owls.

BREEDING: The nesting site is a large hollow in the limb or trunk of a tree situated in dense forest, up to twenty-five metres or more from the ground. Eggs are laid in late May or June. They are laid on the rotten wood in the nesting hollow. The usual clutch size is two, the eggs being rounded oval in shape, dull white in colour, and measuring approximately 55 × 46 mm. The incubation period is thought to be about thirty-eight days. Only the female broods, and the male makes no effort to defend the nest. There are no nesting records in our region but this is surely a matter of lack of observation.

FEEDING: The chief prey of the Powerful Owl are mammals but a proportion of its diet consists of birds. The most commonly eaten animals are members of the possum family, the Greater Glider *Petauroides volans*, and the Ringtail Possum *Pseudocheirus peregrinus*. The Greater Glider has been seen in a Powerful Owl's clutches; it is the most common arboreal mammal in our area and is probably the most important item of food. Other mammals taken are the Sugar Glider *Petaurus breviceps*, and less commonly, rats, rabbits, flying foxes *Pteropus*, and juvenile Brush Possums *Trichosurus*. Birds killed and eaten include Kookaburras, magpies and ravens. The victims are torn apart and eaten piece-meal. The Powerful Owl has the habit of going to roost holding the rear part of his prey. This is carefully placed on the roosting limb, held in the talons all day, and eaten in the late afternoon. (J.H.C.)

## BARKING OWL *Ninox connivens*

PLATE VIII

IDENTIFICATION: Length, 38–43 cm, male larger than female. General colour above, dark grey, some white blotches on wings and lower back; tail feathers, grey brown, barred with and tipped pale brown; under-parts appear mottled brown and white, the feathers being white with a broad central brown streak; bill, grey; feet, dull yellow; claws, black; iris, yellow. The sexes are similar in colour.

VOICE: The normal call is a rapid two-syllable repetitive barking that sounds like "wook-wook". The male's call is considerably lower-pitched than that of the female. A chorus of barking may begin or be interspersed with "growling" sounds. The Barking Owl is a noisy bird that calls frequently and is vocal all year round. Rarely it produces a loud high-pitched tremulous scream. This terrifying call is heard usually in autumn and has led to the bird being called the "screaming-woman" bird.

DISTRIBUTION: It is found in Australia and New Guinea to the northern Moluccas but not in Tasmania, and there are no records for central Australia and mid-Western Australia. It occurs in quite heavily forested country but its optimum habitat is savannah woodland. The few records from the Canberra area were in savannah woodland.

HABITS: Barking Owls are almost always found in pairs. They rest by day in leafy trees although they are not necessarily well hidden. They have more than one roosting site but usually patronise a favourite one. They are the least nocturnal of Australian owls and occasionally call in the daytime. On dull winter days they may begin hunting some time before sunset.

BREEDING: The nesting site is a hollow in a tree from a metre up to ten metres from the ground. Eggs are laid in July and August, on the dust or rotten wood in the hollow tree. The clutch size is two or three, usually three. The eggs are dull white, rounded oval in shape and measure approximately $46 \times 41$ mm. The incubation period has been determined as thirty-seven days. Only the female broods the eggs. The male becomes very aggressive at this time. There are no breeding records in our area.

FEEDING: The Barking Owl is not a great deal longer than the Boobook Owl but it is a much larger and heavier bird and is capable of killing much larger prey. It takes some insects and other invertebrates but the bulk of its prey is mammals and birds, particularly the former. An important food item is the rabbit and it is capable of killing quite large young. Other mammals eaten are rats, mice, young hares, Ringtail Possums, and bats. This owl also kills and eats birds up to the size of the magpie. The larger prey, at least, are torn apart and eaten piece-meal, and the rear halves of victims are sometimes found beneath the roosting trees. (J.H.C.)

## BOOBOOK OWL *Ninox novaeseelandiae*

PLATE VIII

IDENTIFICATION: Length, 35 cm. The sexes are about the same size or the female may be a little larger than the male. General colour above, medium to dark brown with white spots on wings and back; wing quills, barred with shades of brown; tail, brown, feathers barred with shades of brown, tips of feathers, pale; forehead with pale brown streaks; facial disc, paler than general colour, with dark patch behind eye; under-parts, cream to buff with broad dark-brown streaks; bill, blue-grey; feet, pale blue-grey; iris, yellow in adults and brown in juveniles. The sexes are similar in colour.

VOICE: The well-known two-syllabled call is generally written as "mo-poke" or "more-pork". The call may be heard at any time of the year but it is more common in winter than in summer in this area.

DISTRIBUTION: It is found over the whole of Australia, including Tasmania, from Timor to southern New Guinea, Norfolk Island, and New Zealand. The ecological distribution is very broad and ranges from dense forest to desert. Although not often seen it is quite common locally and occurs in all habitats including built-up areas.

HABITS: Boobook Owls are found singly or in pairs; single birds appear to be more usual in daytime retreats. They roost quietly by day in trees with dense foliage and attention is often drawn to them by the noisy mobbing of small birds, particularly honeyeaters. In relatively treeless country they may roost in daytime in caves. Each bird or pair appears to have a number of daytime roosting sites and can usually be found at one or other of these.

BREEDING: Like other members of the genus *Ninox*, the Boobook Owl is a seasonal breeder and eggs are laid about September. The nest-site is a hole in a tree and may be anything from one to twenty metres from the ground. The eggs are laid on wood-dust or rotten wood. The clutch size is from two to four, usually three. The eggs are rounded oval in shape, dull white in colour and measure 40–43 × 34–36 mm. Brooding is done by the female.

FEEDING: The Boobook Owl is probably more insectivorous than other Australian owls. It feeds on a variety of insects active at night, particularly moths and beetles, and takes other invertebrates such as spiders. In June these owls may be seen at night hunting hepialid moths at Canberra street lights. Other than invertebrates the Boobook Owl feeds on small mammals, particularly the House Mouse, and small birds up to the size of sparrows. (J.H.C.)

Family Tytonidae — Barn Owls
## BARN OWL *Tyto alba*
PLATE VIII

IDENTIFICATION: Length, 32 cm. General colour above, light grey, with numerous fine darker lines on the feathers; pale spots with dark edgings near tips of back- and wing-feathers; buff markings on wings and back; tail feathers, pale buff with brownish-grey cross bars and fine flecks; facial disc, white, dark mark at front of eye, buff and black tips to feathers of facial disc; under-parts, white with dark flecks at tips of some of the feathers; bill, off-white; feet, yellowish-white to brownish; iris, black. The sexes are similar in size and colour.

VOICE: It appears to call infrequently, and the main call is a drawn out rasping screech. The courtship call of the male at the nest is a shrill repetitive twittering.

DISTRIBUTION: The Barn Owl is one of the most widespread of birds and occurs on all continents and large islands. It is found over the whole of Australia, including Tasmania. It is much more abundant in open woodland than in forested country. It is subject to large fluctuations in numbers; during mouse plagues, for example, it sometimes becomes very common. After the plague has collapsed considerable numbers of dead emaciated birds may be found. Around Canberra its status appears to be variable, it is more common at certain times than others. In general it is rarely seen and most records are of dead birds found on roads.

HABITS: Barn Owls are found singly or in pairs. They usually roost by day in tree hollows but in country lacking hollow trees may be found in out-buildings, caves, thick foliage, or down wells. When disturbed they fly off, usually pursued by other birds, and perch in trees. When surprised in the roosting hollow or on the nest, and escape is not possible, they react by swaying from side to side, moving the head in a circular fashion, crouching, spreading the wings, snapping the bill, hissing or sometimes making a rasping call.

BREEDING: The Barn Owl breeds at any time of the year depending on food supply. There are no observations of its breeding in our area. It nests in tree hollows and the eggs are laid on rotten wood or on accumulations of regurgitated pellets or food residues. The nest is a noisome affair as it becomes covered with pellets and unconsumed fragments of prey. The clutch size is from three to six, usually three or four. The eggs are smooth and white, oval to rounded oval in shape, and average $43 \times 32$ mm. Brooding is done by the female. The incubation period is about thirty-four days.

FEEDING: It locates food by flying close to the ground, or by listening from a perch, and pouncing. Food is usually swallowed whole. As with all owls, indigestible parts, bones, hair, feathers, chitinous fragments, etc. are regurgitated some time after the meal. No studies of food habits have been done in the region but elsewhere in Australia the food consists of small mammals, small birds, nightflying insects, particularly beetles and moths, and other small animals active by night. Probably the most important food item in southern Australia is the introduced House Mouse, *Mus musculus*. Other small mammals taken include marsupial mice, *Sminthopsis*. The House Sparrow is a fairly common food item. Large numbers of scarabaeid beetles are eaten. (J.H.C.)

## MASKED OWL *Tyto novaehollandiae*

PLATE VIII

IDENTIFICATION: Length, male 38 cm, female 45 cm. General colour above, including upper-tail, blackish-brown, each feather closely and finely freckled with white on the apical portion and having a single white spot near the tip; buff barring in wing and back feathers; under-parts, white, sometimes with tinge of very pale buff, some black spots on breast and flank; facial disc, white, somewhat rufous around eyes, feathers on edge of facial disc, tipped buff and black; bill, white; feet, off-white to brownish; iris, brown. Except for size discrepancy, the sexes are similar.

VOICE: The calls are similar to those of the Barn Owl but the normal call is probably a little louder.

DISTRIBUTION: It occurs in southern New Guinea and some nearby islands, and over most of Australia, including Tasmania, except central Australia and the arid parts of Western Australia. This owl is usually found in forest and savannah woodland but it also occurs it treeless areas such as the Nullarbor Plain where it can find daytime shelter in caves. Around Canberra it is apparently a rare species and there are very few records.

HABITS: Masked Owls are very similar in their habits to Barn Owls, except that they do not seem to use buildings for daytime shelters. They are often found in caves. Their reactions to disturbance are similar to those of the Barn Owl.

BREEDING: Very little is known on breeding in this species. It nests in tree hollows in a similar manner to the Barn Owl. The usual clutch size is two or three. The eggs are rounded oval and dull white, and are approximately 45 × 36 mm. Brooding is done by the female. The incubation period has been determined for the large Tasmanian race as thirty-five days.

FEEDING: The Masked Owl's food habits are generally similar to those of the Barn Owl except that it can catch larger prey and consequently young rabbits, which are rarely taken by the Barn Owl, are commonly caught by the Masked Owl. The large Tasmanian form can kill adult rabbits. (J.H.C.)

## GRASS OWL *Tyto longimembris*

IDENTIFICATION: Length, 33-36 cm, female larger than male. General colour above, dark grey to black or dark chocolate brown, white tips to feathers, buff bars on wings; underparts cream to pale buff, with some brown spots; feathers on lower half of legs reduced to a few bristles; facial disc, white to pale buff, edges of disc dark brown on top, buff on sides and lower edge; distinctive brown mark in front of eye; bill, white with a pink or grey tinge; legs, pale greyish or yellowish brown; iris, deep brown. The sexes and juveniles are similar.

It is distinguished from the Barn Owl by its darker upperparts, buff underparts, longer legs and smaller eyes.

VOICE: Grass Owls are rather silent owls. They have a variety of calls similar to those of the Barn Owl but the screeching call is not so loud.

DISTRIBUTION: This owl occurs from India and southern China through Indonesia to Australia and some south-west Pacific islands. In Australia it is permanently resident in swampy grassland areas along the coast from north-eastern New South Wales to Cape York, and apparently also in moister areas of tussock grassland in the eastern part of the Northern Territory, central western Queensland, and north-eastern South Australia. The Grass Owl resembles the Letter-winged Kite, in that it increases greatly in numbers during periodical rat plagues and when these collapse the starving owls disperse widely. Vagrants have been found rarely in many parts of Australia far from its normal range.

The only local record was an emaciated injured bird found on the ground in a windrow, near Murrumbateman, about 30 km north of Canberra, on 23 October 1982.

HABITS: Grass Owls are found singly or in pairs in areas of tall tussock grasslands or sedges, including swamps. During daylight hours they roost on the ground, hidden among tussocks. When flushed during daytime they fly for twenty metres or so with the legs dangling, and drop back into the grass. When disturbed Grass Owls behave like other *Tyto* species, and crouch, spread their wings, sway from side to side, hiss and snap their bills.

BREEDING: The Grass Owl breeds at any time of year depending on food supply. The nest consists of a platform of trampled grass hidden among dense tussocks. It is entered from runways or tunnels in the grass. Clutch size is three to eight; larger clutches are usual when food is plentiful. The eggs are rounded oval, smooth and dull white in colour, and measure $40-44 \times 30-33$ mm. Brooding is done by the female.

FEEDING: The chief food is ground-living rodents. In the grassland areas the owl inhabits permanently, native rats are the commonest small mammals and often occur in high densities. Small marsupials, birds and some kinds of insects are also eaten. (J.H.C.)

# QUAILS

The birds known as "quail" in Australia are a diverse group and some of them are not very closely related. Members of two major divisions of birds are included under the general loose term; the Galliformes and the Gruiformes. The former includes quails, pheasants, grouse, guinea fowls, turkeys, megapodes, hoatzins and curassows; the latter includes bustard-quails, cranes, rails, bustards and several other dissimilar groups.

Despite their distant relationship the quails and bustard-quails have evolved in a convergent manner to produce birds that are very similar in size, shape and general behaviour. In Australia they are all thought of as "quail" by most people so it is convenient to discuss them together here.

### Family Phasianidae — Quails and Pheasants

The family contains many of the most valuable birds in the world from the points of view of economics and beauty, and as game birds. As well as quail, it includes the pheasants, partridges and peacocks, and domestic poultry and turkeys have been developed from wild fore-fathers. There are over 170 members of the family.

Among the quail there are two groups, one confined to the Americas and the other confined to Europe, Asia, Africa and Australia. The latter group is numerous and widespread but only three species have reached Australia, all of which occur, one abundantly, in our area.

The Australian quail are all small and, except for the King Quail, dull coloured. They are terrestrial and have short, strong bills, small rounded wings and inconspicuous tails. They are all more or less nomadic and two, the Stubble Quail and Brown Quail, are important game birds in some places. Despite this, however, little is available on their life histories.

### STUBBLE QUAIL *Coturnix novaezelandiae*
PLATE IX

IDENTIFICATION: Length, 18 cm. Male: upper-parts, *generally blackish-brown* with transverse pale buff markings and *with creamy-*

*white lanceolate stripes* in the centre of each feather; flight feathers, brown; head and nape, black with small brown tips to the feathers, a white line down the centre of the head and a white stripe above each eye extending to back of neck; throat and sides of face, light chestnut; black patch on chest, remainder of chest and abdomen, white, streaked black down centre. The adult female differs from the male in that the throat is off-white and sides of face and neck are pale buff with dark spots, breast pale buffy-white with longitudinal dark markings; bill, dark, almost black; legs and feet, flesh-white; iris, red-brown.

VOICE: A loud, clear whistle is often heard in the late afternoon. It has been described quite well as "two-to-weep" or "churchy-whit", with the last note rising in inflection.

DISTRIBUTION: The Stubble Quail is distributed throughout Australia mainly south of the Tropic of Capricorn but moves about within this area, and at times far beyond it. It avoids the deserts, except after rain; is rarely found in forests and never in dense forests, but otherwise, is found in all habitats. It does, however, show a decided preference for flat, well drained grasslands, where the cover is not excessively dense, stubble fields and lucerne stands. In our region it is common at all seasons but the numbers fluctuate greatly. Throughout its range its numbers are subject to gross fluctuations but the reasons for this have not been studied. There is undoubtedly a strong nomadic habit that could explain the appearance of vast numbers on the inland plains immediately after rain but it is probable that many of the fluctuations in numbers on the Southern Tablelands and elsewhere are due to local breeding conditions at the time.

HABITS: It is usually in small parties or coveys. Like all quail it is terrestrial and secretive, and is seldom seen unless one has a game dog to assist in flushing it. The usual signs of its presence are its calls and the occurrence of small, round and characteristic dung in suitable places. It is more difficult to flush than the Brown Quail and runs ahead of the dog, especially in open situations, such as stubble. When flushed it flies swiftly, with a loud whirr of the wings, low over the grass before dropping and running. It usually flies farther than the Brown Quail. It is commonly found in coveys of up to twenty birds, except in the breeding season.

BREEDING: The breeding season is usually given as the summer but is subject to variation according to the rainfall. It is difficult to be precise though, as nests are not often found except by game dogs in the restricted hunting seasons. The nest is a scrape in the ground under a tussock or in a crop, and is lined with a little grass. The clutch is large, usually seven to eleven eggs. The eggs measure about 30 × 23 mm but vary greatly. They are pale buff, spotted and blotched all over with brown, chestnut and umber.

FEEDING: A thorough study of the food in the Australian Capital Territory showed that the Stubble Quail feeds mainly on the seeds of cultivated cereals, grasses and weeds and the leaves of these plants. Introduced plants (weeds and crops) are of great importance. Insects are also eaten but not in great numbers. The food in Victoria is similar. The species has benefited from the replacement of woodlands with crops and grassland. (H.J.F.)

## BROWN QUAIL *Coturnix australis*

PLATE IX

IDENTIFICATION: Length, 18 cm. Male: *upper-parts, generally brown*, the feathers marked with black and having a thin white line in the centre; forehead and crown, brown with fine black spots, a white line down the centre of head; throat and cheeks, buff; under-parts, buff with conspicuous transverse black bars some of them V-shaped; bill, bluish-black; legs and feet, yellowish-green; iris, red. The sexes are similar but the female is a little larger.

VOICE: The call is a double whistle "tu-whee" with the second syllable long, drawn out and on a rising inflection.

DISTRIBUTION: The Brown Quail is distributed throughout parts of Indonesia and New Guinea as well as coastal and near coastal districts of northern, eastern and south-western Australia. The birds are very variable in colour, even in the one locality, and although several races have been described these are not universally accepted. It is still thought by some that the Tasmanian and the mainland birds are different species. Most of our area is beyond its range but there have been several records and the recent beginning of regular surveys, using a quail dog, suggests that it is very much more numerous than was previously thought.

HABITS: Usually found in denser cover than the Stubble Quail, it "holds" for the dog better and frequently is closer to the observer when flushed. Its typical habitat is low lying or swampy places with fairly dense coarse grass, but the two species are often found together in lucerne and elsewhere. It flies quite as swiftly as the Stubble Quail but usually for a shorter distance. It often utters an alarm cackle as it rises.

BREEDING: As with other quail the breeding season is difficult to determine. Most nests in New South Wales are found in the period October to December, but in the tropical north many breed after the wet season, February to May. There is no breeding record in our area yet. The nest is merely a depression in the ground lined with grass or leaves. The eggs measure about 30 × 24 mm and are dull white in colour finely spotted all over with light brown and olive-brown. The usual clutch is seven to eleven but up to twenty have occasionally been found in a nest.

FEEDING: They feed on seeds of cultivated cereals and weeds as well as some insects but there has been no systematic study. (H.J.F.)

## KING QUAIL *Coturnix chinensis*

PLATE IX

IDENTIFICATION: Length, 14 cm. Male: general colour above, brown with black markings; wings, brown; there is a buff streak in centre of forehead; sides of head, chest and sides of body, slate-blue; *throat, black; cheeks and a crescentic band on foreneck, white; abdomen, chestnut*; bill, black; legs and feet, yellow; iris, red. The female differs from the male in lacking most of the colour; general colour above is dark brown streaked with white, the under-parts are barred with black and the throat is white; the iris is brown.

VOICE: The call is a sharp whistle of three syllables—"whit-too-whit". All the syllables are short but the third is shortest and falls in pitch.

DISTRIBUTION: It extends from India and China, through Indonesia and New Guinea to northern and eastern coastal districts of Australia and a few localities in southern Victoria. Our area is beyond its range although it is common on the coast a few kilometres east. Inclusion in this work depends on a sole recent record near Canberra. The King Quail favours very dense cover; the edges of swamps, lucerne fields that have been neglected and overgrown and the matted *Paspalum* of headlands of cultivation paddocks.

HABITS: It is very rarely seen, even though it might be quite common in the area, as it seldom flies and is very difficult to flush, exploding finally from under one's feet. It is impossible to flush the second time. In flight it is relatively weak and seems tail-heavy compared to other quails and typically cackles as it goes. It drops into the grass tail first.

BREEDING: The main breeding season seems to be in the summer. The nest is a grass-lined depression in dense cover. The clutch is usually four or five eggs which measure about 25 × 20 mm. In colour they are pale brown or olive green and are very closely covered with fine spots of blackish-brown.

FEEDING: They feed on seeds and insects but there has been no thorough study. (H.J.F.)

### Family Turnicidae — Bustard Quails

Bustard Quails, also called Button Quails, are distinguished from true quail in many ways but the most obvious external feature is that there is no hind toe. They are ground living birds of grasslands and scrub and are very secretive in habits. The female is always larger and more brightly coloured than the male and is very pugnacious towards other females. She takes the leading part in courtship and, although both birds build the nest, the male does the incubation and cares for the young. There is some evidence that the female lays several sets of eggs to be cared for by different males. The incubation period is very short, twelve to thirteen days. The young are agile on hatching and very quickly follow the male parent, who at first also feeds them. The whole family includes only fifteen species and of these the genus *Turnix* accounts for thirteen of which six occur in Australia. Three have been recorded in our area but only one regularly occurs.

## PAINTED QUAIL *Turnix varia*

PLATE IX

IDENTIFICATION: Length, 20 cm. Male: upper-parts generally, grey, upper-part of the *back feathers black tipped and barred with chestnut and with white edges*; flight feathers, greyish-blue; centre of forehead and crown, grey-black, tipped with rufous; sides of face, white with black edges to some feathers; nape, blackish with white spots on feathers; under-parts generally, grey with light buff spots, throat whitish, some feathers on side of neck and breast mottled with buff; abdomen, buff; bill, dark brown; legs and feet, yellow; iris, red. The female is larger and has a reddish collar.

VOICE: The call is a low-pitched resonant "oom" quite soft but easily heard from some distance. It calls freely both by day and night.

DISTRIBUTION: Its range extends from at least as far north as Cooktown, Queensland, along the coast to the Adelaide hills, South Australia. It extends from the coast inland to the tablelands but barely penetrates the western slopes. Canberra is about its inland limit in this district. It favours wooded areas, dry heathlands near the coast and, further inland, forests and timbered ridges. It occurs in the same

103

districts as the Stubble and Brown Quail but is usually found in a different habitat. It seems to be fairly sedentary.

HABITS: As it lives in forests and on dry ridges where the ground cover is often sparse it is more frequently seen than many quail. When disturbed it often "freezes" but at other times runs very swiftly and is very hard to flush even with dogs. When it does rise there is a very loud wing beat and the flight is swift and sure as it twists between the trees. It often flies up to six metres from the ground and travels a considerable distance. Unlike Stubble and Brown Quail that are commonly in coveys or small flocks, the Painted Quail is usually found singly or in pairs.

BREEDING: In coastal New South Wales the breeding season is in the period September to February but nests have been found at other times and breeding is probably affected by rainfall. There are no data from our area. The nest is more substantial than that of the Brown and Stubble Quail and is a scrape under a bush, tussock or fallen timber, thickly lined with fine grasses and is often partly covered. The clutch size is three to five but four is commonest. The eggs are off-white, closely covered with spots and small blotches of brown, mauve and grey. Average measurements are 28 × 23 mm. The incubation time is fourteen days.

FEEDING: It feeds on seeds and a considerable number of insects. (H.J.F.)

## LITTLE QUAIL *Turnix velox*

PLATE IX

IDENTIFICATION: Length, 14 cm. Male: *upper-parts, generally chestnut-red* with pale margins to the feathers and black barring across the feathers; hind neck and nape, somewhat paler, white line down centre of head; sides of head, reddish-buff; throat and abdomen, dull white, upper breast with rufous tinge; bill, grey brown; legs and feet, flesh colour; iris, cream. Female is larger, less streaked above and lacks the median white line on head.

VOICE: The call is a low-pitched, soft "oop".

DISTRIBUTION: Mainly a bird of the drier parts of the continent it is only common on the coast in Western Australia, or elsewhere in times of drought. In the north-west of Western Australia it is the commonest quail and is very numerous in the spinifex covered hills but, elsewhere, is usually only seen singly or small groups. It is very uncommon in our

104

area. It seems to have declined greatly in eastern Australia since the inland plains were occupied by sheep and the native grasslands degenerated. Writers in the 1890s speak as though it was a very common bird, regularly encountered in large numbers, in parts of inland New South Wales but in twelve years residence in the same district I never saw more than two or three at a time and it was rarely encountered at all until an irruption occurred in 1969.

HABITS: It sits very closely and does not flush until the observer is upon it when it flies a short distance, runs very rapidly and is hard to flush again.

BREEDING: The breeding season has not been well documented but most authors agree that, like many other inland birds, its timing is very largely determined by rainfall. There is no breeding record in our area. The nest is a scrape in the ground sheltered by a clump of grass. The clutch is four or five eggs and these are dull white or light buff thickly covered with brown, chestnut and grey spots and small blotches; they measure about 25 × 19 mm.

FEEDING: Mainly seed is eaten; those examined in north-west Queensland had been feeding entirely on spinifex and in inland New South Wales on wallaby grass. (H.J.F.)

## RED-CHESTED QUAIL *Turnix pyrrhothorax*

IDENTIFICATION: Length, 14 cm. General colour above, brown to black, the feathers with broad buffy margins and pale reddish-brown bars; forehead, black with thin white bars; nape, brown with white spots; hind neck, reddish-brown with black barrings and pale margins to feathers; *throat and under-parts, bright reddish-orange*; centre of breast and abdomen, white; bill, brown, legs and feet, yellow; iris, yellow. The sexes are alike.

VOICE: Not described.

DISTRIBUTION: It is found mainly in the inland parts of northern and eastern Australia and frequently irrupts into more coastal and southern districts. Its range is, however, not well established perhaps because of the difficulties in identifying small quail in flight. Inclusion in this work rests on a nest found near Braidwood in 1863 and a specimen captured in the grounds of the CSIRO Division of Wildlife Research in October 1968. There were several more sightings during an irruption in 1969.

105

Even in the early days of the pastoral invasion of the grasslands the Red-chested Quail seems to have been an uncommon bird. Perhaps it has further declined since then as it is now very rarely seen. It seems to have favoured denser and moister places than the Little Quail.

HABITS, BREEDING AND FEEDING: It seems to be very similar to the Little Quail but not much has been recorded. (H.J.F.)

Family Pedionomidae — Plain Wanderer

There is only one member of this family, the Plain Wanderer. It is very similar to the bustard quail and many ornithologists hold that the retention of a separate family is not necessary and that they could be grouped together. It differs from the bustard quail in having a hind toe and in some other anatomical details.

## PLAIN WANDERER *Pedionomus torquatus*

PLATE IX

IDENTIFICATION: Length, 15 cm. Male: upper-parts, generally brown with pale margins to the feathers and narrow black marks across the feathers; feathers around eye and cheeks, off-white with fine, almost-black, spotting; throat, white with black spots at the sides; *collar around neck spotted and streaked with dark brown*; upper breast and lower neck, pale buff with dark brown crescent-shaped markings, these markings extend down to the sides of the flanks; abdomen, off-white with a buff tinge; bill, yellowish; legs and feet, yellow; iris, yellow.

The female resembles the male but is a little larger. The collar, which is much more pronounced surrounding the entire neck, is black with bold white spotting; sides of head, more rufous, chestnut patch on fore neck; richer buff colouring on upper neck and sides of body, and crescent-shaped markings black.

VOICE: The call is similar to that of other bustard quails, low-pitched but resonant "ooms", heard day and night.

DISTRIBUTION: It is confined to the south-east, from Duaringa, Queensland to south-eastern South Australia but it is nowhere numerous or even common. Apparently before settlement had greatly altered the habitats of the inland it was moderately common in many places but since then has declined very greatly. Most records nowadays are in a small part of Victoria, west of Melbourne, and in the Deniliquin district, New South Wales. Inclusion in this work rests on a sight record near Canberra in 1954.

106

HABITS: It seems to prefer flat, open, grass plains and avoids scrubs and stubble fields. It runs very swiftly and is hard to flush. When hunted with dogs it often "freezes" and there are many accounts of it then being picked up by hand. It does not crouch like other button-quails but runs and stands erect.

BREEDING: The breeding season is mainly in summer but there are many accounts of nests at other periods. The nest is a scrape in the ground, lined with some grass. The clutch size is said to be usually four. The eggs are off-white or pale buff, covered, particularly at the larger end, with spots and small blotches of brown, chestnut and grey. They measure about 33 × 23 mm.

FEEDING: They apparently eat seeds and insects. (H.J.F.)

# BROLGA AND BUSTARD

Australia has two cranes, the Brolga and the Sarus Crane. The Brolga and the Bustard have suffered badly during European settlement of the continent. The Bustard has been greatly affected by stock grazing destroying its habitat and has also been over shot throughout its range. The Brolga has been poisoned and shot in large numbers as it some-times damages standing crops. It has also been affected by the exten-sive drainage of swamps and destruction of its habitat. Both remain in reasonable numbers in some northern districts but there is no doubt that both should now be considered threatened species.

## Family Otididae — Bustards

The bustards include some of the heaviest flying birds in the world, and some of the birds worst affected by close settlement. There are about twenty-three species; most of these are African but there are a few in Eurasia as well as the one in Australia. They are all large birds adapted to ground-living in deserts, grasslands or open scrubs. The habits, behaviour and life history of all the bustards are rather similar to those of the Australian species.

## AUSTRALIAN BUSTARD *Ardeotis australis*
PLATE X

IDENTIFICATION: Length, male 114 cm, female 87 cm; a male can weigh up to 14.5 kilograms; females 4.5–6.5 kilograms. Upper-parts generally, dark brown finely marked with light brown; primaries, brown; a black area occurs on the wing coverts with white tips to some feathers; forehead, crown and elongated nape feathers, black; cheeks

107

and neck, greyish-white with transverse black bars; almost black band across chest at base of fore neck; breast and abdomen, white; bill, off-white to brown; legs and feet, yellow; iris, white. The sexes are similar.

VOICE: It is normally silent but there is a deep "hoo" uttered in display.

DISTRIBUTION: It was formerly distributed throughout the continent avoiding only the denser forests of the east coast. The bustard occurred mainly in the inland plains, in south-east Australia, and only came onto the New South Wales coast in times of inland drought. There was one record near Canberra in 1920, but it was very common here before settlement, and flocks of several hundred were not unusual on the plains to the west of the area at the end of the last century.

In earlier days it was very abundant in parts of the inland, particularly in New South Wales, where at least one flock of one thousand was reported, and in western Queensland. Uncontrolled shooting, as well as the destruction of its habitat by domestic stock, has virtually wiped it out in south-east Australia generally; any that are seen there today are very rare vagrants. It still remains in some numbers in the far north of the continent, particularly Cape York, the Barkly Tableland and the Kimberley region, but even there it is not often seen in groups of more than fifteen to twenty. The Australian Bustard must be considered seriously threatened as it is still shot throughout most of its range although it is legally protected.

HABITS: Bustards are entirely terrestrial and are never in trees. They are usually seen singly or in small groups on the open plains and in the lighter scrublands and forests. They are remarkably tame in many places, stand to watch the observer and are particularly vulnerable to people in motor cars. They sometimes squat where there is some cover and so escape detection but more often remain erect. They seldom fly but prefer to walk from place to place. When they do fly the flight is strong, though heavy, and the bird needs quite a long run before it is airborne.

The male has a spectacular display in the breeding season. The neck is inflated and the long feathers spread to form an impressive front that almost touches the ground. The wings are drooped to the ground, the head is bent backwards and the tail spread elevated. In this posture he struts about booming.

BREEDING: The breeding season is said to be in the period July to November, but is much affected by the rainfall. The single egg, or occasionally two, is placed on the ground in the open or near a bush with sometimes a few sticks placed around it. It is light brown-green or olive-green with spots and blotches of brown over the whole surface. The eggs measure 75–81 × 52–55 mm. The chick moves off with the female very soon after hatching.

FEEDING: The food has not been studied in detail but is mainly seeds, leaves and fruits of various plants. It also eats large numbers of insects, small reptiles and other animals, including small rodents and young birds. (H.J.F.)

## Family Gruidae — Cranes

There are fourteen species of cranes in four or five genera which occur in North America, Europe, Africa, Asia and Australia, but not in South America. They are large water and grassland birds with long legs and necks. Their bills are stout, straight and pointed. Inner secondaries form elongated plumes which are called the "tail" of a crane. They feed in swamps and flood plains on both animal and plant matter, including large invertebrates, small vertebrates, green shoots, tubers, cereals and fruit.

Until recently, the Brolga was the only crane known in Australia but within the last twenty years the Sarus Crane *Grus antigone*, a common species in south Asia has become well established in north Queensland. The source and significance of these birds is not known.

## BROLGA *Grus rubicundus*

PLATE X

IDENTIFICATION: Length, 116 cm. General plumage, silvery-grey; back, grey with slight brownish wash; primaries and primary coverts, black; ear coverts, grey; head, except for ear coverts but including throat and top of hind neck, naked; crown, olive-green, and remainder of naked area, red; bill, olive-green; legs and feet, grey-brown; iris, yellow. The sexes are similar.

Sarus Cranes differ by being slightly bigger (length 125 cm); grey on back paler; "tail" bends under more; naked red area of head extends much further down neck; legs and feet are pink.

VOICE: Harsh grating or trumpeting sounds are made in flight and on the ground.

DISTRIBUTION: It occurs in northern and eastern Australia. The range was formerly from the Kimberley region, across the north, down the east and west, throughout Victoria to south-east South Australia. It preferred coastal districts but it did extend inland along the major river systems of the south-east. Recently it has extended its

109

range south to Carnarvon in Western Australia. In the east it has been virtually eradicated by settlement in the southern parts of its range; a Brolga in New South Wales, Victoria or South Australia is a rare event. In southern Queensland it is now uncommon. In our area it was formerly common but is now virtually extinct. A recent sight record in Canberra was the first in many years. It frequents marshes, lagoons, wet meadows and the shores of lakes and rivers.

HABITS: In the breeding season they are seen in pairs, but in the non-breeding season they congregate into flocks, which can be very large. They tend to fly in V-shaped flocks. Flight is slow and ponderous with head and neck stretched forwards and the legs trailing beyond the tail. Occasionally they soar up to, and glide down from, great heights. At the beginning of the breeding season pairs perform a characteristic dance in which two birds of opposite sex face each other and hop up and down as mirror images of each other. The dance is elicited by other Brolgas approaching a mated pair. The dancing serves to inform others that the pair bond has been formed and presumably helps to strengthen it. This dance is a common feature of the mating behaviour of cranes generally.

BREEDING: In the north breeding occurs in the wet season but in south-eastern Australia it occurs in the spring. Single pairs nest at small water holes and ponds in grasslands. The nest tends to be a small island which is built up of sedges and grass tufts and looks like a small swan's nest. The Brolga is incorrectly reported in many books as the only crane that does not build a nest. Possibly in some places where nest material is scarce and the substrate is soft, the Brolga may lay on bare ground. The clutch size is usually two. The eggs are creamy-white, spotted with brown and purple, and their average size is 92 × 61 mm. The incubation period is about thirty-two days. Both sexes incubate the eggs and guard the chicks.

FEEDING: They feed on a large variety of large invertebrates, small vertebrates, green shoots including wheat, tubers including potatoes, and seeds including cereals such as wheat. Farmers complain and have persecuted them because of damage to crops. (G.F.vT.)

# RAILS AND WATERHENS

This family consists of a rather homogeneous group of 132 species which usually run well and are semi-aquatic. They have long toes and relatively powerful legs. The tail is short and the body rather narrow.

Distribution is cosmopolitan and fifteen species occur in Australia. One genus and four species are restricted to Australia, and six others occur otherwise only in New Guinea and/or New Zealand. The family can be divided into the crakes and rails, the waterhens, and the coots. The crakes and rails are usually drab coloured birds but some, in other countries, are quite brightly coloured. In Australia they are dwellers in swamps and wet places but elsewhere some live in quite dry forests.

Crakes and rails are very secretive and are seldom seen, hence there is very little recorded about them and it is difficult to plot their exact range as they often escape notice in a district. Waterhens are larger, plumper and often more highly coloured; greens and purples are common. Generally they are more obvious than crakes and rails are. Although usually living in dense swamp vegetation, they often walk in the open and flush from the reeds relatively easily. The coots are highly adapted to a life in open water and are as aquatic as many ducks. They dive more abruptly than most ducks and swim quite as fast; much of their food is secured under water.

The five crakes and rails which occur in our area are of very uncertain status. The construction of reservoirs and artificial lakes has increased the population of our two waterhens, the Dusky Moorhen and the Eastern Swamphen, and these are common, as is the Coot.

Family Rallidae — Rails, Crakes, Waterhens and Coots
## LEWIN WATER RAIL *Rallus pectoralis*
PLATE XI

IDENTIFICATION: Length, 20 cm. *Upper-parts, dark brown with black streaks*; throat and breast, greyish; abdomen, black barred with white; bill, reddish-brown; legs, dirty-pink; iris, brown. Female is slightly smaller and the grey band on the breast is duller. The juveniles have all the upper-parts a dull brown, duller under-parts and a whitish throat.

VOICE: A loud "crik crik" alarm call and a low-pitched grunting are known.

DISTRIBUTION: It occurs in New Guinea, New Zealand, eastern, southern and south-western Australia, and Tasmania. In Western Australia it is seldom seen and its status is unknown; in eastern Australia it extends from south-eastern Queensland through inland New South Wales and Victoria to South Australia but nowhere has it been proved to be common. It has been recorded rarely from Lake Burley Griffin, the Murrumbidgee River and one or two other places in our region. It inhabits swamps, lagoons, watercourses and other wet places with dense semi-aquatic vegetation.

HABITS: It is shy, keeps closely to dense cover and is difficult to see. It sometimes feeds near water or wet places, singly or in pairs and runs well but rarely flies. It flicks its tail when alarmed as do many of the family.

BREEDING: The breeding season is from August to December in south-eastern Australia. The nest is built low, or actually on the ground, in rushes in wet situations. It consists of a well-woven cup of grass a few centimetres in diameter which may be roofed, after incubation has begun, by the interlacing of stems above. It often has a distinct entrance track leading up to it. It is very well concealed. The clutch is usually between four and six. The eggs are dull white with reddish, brownish, purplish and greyish blotches. They measure about 35 × 26 mm.

FEEDING: It eats insects, small molluscs and probably other invertebrates, but there has been no systematic study of this or the other four rails in Australia. (M.G.R.)

## BANDED LANDRAIL *Rallus philippensis*

PLATE XI

IDENTIFICATION: Length, 31 cm. *Upper-parts, greenish-brown with white spots*, and nape rich chestnut; throat, grey; buff across breast; rest of under-parts, black with white bars; bill, brown; legs, brown; iris, brown or red. The sexes are similar.

VOICE: A harsh call and a high-pitched call are known.

DISTRIBUTION: It occurs in Australia, northwards through the islands to the Philippines, including New Guinea; also Lord Howe Island, Norfolk Island and New Zealand, and Tasmania. On the mainland it extends from Northwest Cape throughout south-west Western Australia, and in eastern Australia from South Australia to north Queensland. It is mainly coastal and is seldom seen in the inland. It is rare and seldom seen in our region although it has bred here.

It inhabits swamps, lagoons, watercourses and other wet places with dense semi-aquatic vegetation and also thick grass and scrub in low-lying places.

HABITS: It keeps closely to dense cover and is very shy. It flicks its tail when alarmed. It runs well but rarely flies and feeds near water or wet places, singly or in pairs. It is most often seen towards the end of the day.

112

BREEDING: The breeding season is from September to January in south-eastern Australia. The nest is a thick pad of grass beneath a tussock of grass or reeds and is usually near water. The clutch size is usually five to eight eggs, but up to eleven have been recorded. They are cream, blotched with reddish-brown and purplish-grey, and measure about 36 × 28 mm.

FEEDING: It eats insects, small molluscs and some fine vegetable matter. (M.G.R.)

## SPOTTED CRAKE *Porzana fluminea*

PLATE XI

IDENTIFICATION: Length, 17 cm. *Upper-parts, greenish-brown with white streaks*; breast, dark grey; abdomen and flanks, black with white bars; bill, green with red patch at base of upper mandible; legs, green; iris, rufous. The sexes are similar.

VOICE: A sharp metallic call is known.

DISTRIBUTION: It is confined to Australia and is found in the east and south-west as well as Tasmania. In the east it extends from southern Queensland to south-east South Australia and in south-western Australia its range extends as far north as Moora. Its distribution is very uncertain due to difficulties of observation and it seems to be mainly coastal, although there are a few inland records. It is rare around Canberra and very seldom seen. Like other crakes it is found in rank herbage in low-lying places and around swamps and watercourses.

HABITS: It keeps to dense cover but feeds in the open if undisturbed. It runs fast and flight is infrequent and laboured. It also swims. When alarmed it flicks its tail. It feeds near water, singly or in pairs.

BREEDING: The breeding season is from August to December. The nest is an open cup of coarse grass and rushes lined with finer grass. It is usually built close to water on the ground, among rushes or grass with a little track leading to it. It normally lays four or five eggs, which vary in colour from pale grey to brownish-olive and have reddish and purplish spots or blotches. They measure about 31 × 23 mm.

FEEDING: It eats insects and probably other invertebrates. (M.G.R.)

## MARSH CRAKE *Porzana pusilla*

PLATE XI

IDENTIFICATION: Length, 17 cm. *Upper-parts, dark olive brown with black and white streaks*; chest, grey; abdomen, black barred with white; bill, brown with green base, legs, greenish-brown; iris, red. The sexes are similar. The young have face and under-parts buff-coloured.

VOICE: It calls mainly at night, when it makes a purring, trilling noise. A "creek creek" call and a high-pitched note in flight are also known.

DISTRIBUTION: This species is widespread, occurring in Africa, Europe, Asia and New Zealand, as well as Australia and Tasmania. Its detailed distribution is not well recorded but it occurs in coastal districts throughout the whole continent. It is more commonly reported in southern districts than in northern but this could be due to the greater concentration of observers in the south. It inhabits swamps, lagoons, watercourses and other wet places with dense semi-aquatic vegetation. There are very few records from our region.

HABITS: It keeps to dense cover, but will feed in the open if undisturbed, especially in the evening. It runs fast, rarely flies, often swims, and only dives when in danger. When alarmed, it flicks its tail. It feeds near water, singly or in pairs.

BREEDING: The breeding season is from October to January. The nest is a flat cup of rushes, with grass, among rushes and close to water. It is about ten centimetres in diameter. The clutch is generally four to five. The eggs are olive-brown either uniform or with dark flecks. They measure about 28 × 20 mm.

FEEDING: It eats insects, molluscs, green vegetation and seeds. (M.G.R.)

## SPOTLESS CRAKE *Porzana tabuensis*

PLATE XI

IDENTIFICATION: Length, 20 cm. Upper-parts, dark olive-brown with head and under-parts grey, giving an *overall uniform appearance*; beak, black; legs, dull brown; iris, red. The sexes are similar. Young have white marks on shoulder, side of head pale, a dull white patch on throat.

VOICE: A harsh "creek creek" is the sound most usually heard.

114

DISTRIBUTION: It extends from the Philippines and Tonga through Malaysia and islands south to New Zealand, Australia and Tasmania. On the mainland it is widely distributed in eastern Australia, from north Queensland to south-eastern South Australia, and also the south-western corner and some offshore islands. It is seldom seen around Canberra. It inhabits swamps, lagoons, watercourses and other wet places with dense semi-aquatic vegetation. Occasionally it is found away from water.

HABITS: It keeps close to dense cover and is shy and skulking. It runs well, but rarely flies, trailing its legs when it does so. When alarmed, it flicks its tail. It can swim, and feeds near water, singly or in pairs.

BREEDING: The breeding season is from October to January. The nest is cup-shaped and made of grasses, loosely woven. It is placed on a small platform on the ground, or low in a tussock of reed or grass, close to, or sometimes over water. It generally lays a clutch of five but this varies from four to seven. The eggs are dirty greenish-white, lightly mottled with brown. They measure about 31 × 22 mm.

FEEDING: It feeds on insects, and probably on other invertebrates. (M.G.R.)

## DUSKY MOORHEN *Gallinula tenebrosa*

PLATE XI

IDENTIFICATION: Length, 38 cm. General colour above, dark olive-brown; *head and under-parts, dark grey with slight bluish tinge; conspicuous white patches beneath tail*; forehead (plate), red; bill, *bright red with brilliant yellow tip*; legs, green with central patch of dull red; iris, brown. The sexes are similar. Young birds are paler and have dull green bills.

VOICE: It is rather silent, but utters a sharp "kurk".

DISTRIBUTION: It occurs in New Guinea, eastern, southern and south-western Australia. In Western Australia it is restricted to the south-west corner. It is more widely distributed in the east where it extends from Cape York through south-east Queensland, most of inland New South Wales, Victoria, and the southern parts of South Australia, but not in Tasmania. It is fairly sedentary but, in the inland, does undertake nomadic movements to appear in freshly flooded swamps on the plains. It is resident around Canberra in significant numbers. It lives in swamps, reedy pools and the thickly timbered fringes of water-

115

courses. It prefers cover to open water. It sometimes walks some distance from water to feed near cover.

HABITS: It normally occurs in pairs, or families, feeding on grass near water, or swimming and dabbling in the water. It runs quite well but flies only when abruptly disturbed. The flight is laboured and the legs trailed. It flicks its tail when alarmed. It is territorial and fights vigorously against intruding moorhens. It is fairly secretive, except where constantly exposed to human presence, when it becomes quite confident and will swim in the open well away from cover.

BREEDING: The breeding season is from November to February. The nest is a moderately bulky platform of aquatic vegetation with a slight cup, placed among rushes in or beside water. It is about forty centimetres in diameter. Supernumerary nests are also built in exposed positions. The clutch is usually seven to nine, but occasionally up to eleven. The eggs are dull cream wtih brownish and greyish spots and blotches. They measure about 53 × 36 mm.

FEEDING: It eats aquatic vegetation and seeds, and also aquatic insects and other invertebrates, frogs and tadpoles. It tilts to dabble for prey and vegetation beneath the surface of the water. (M.G.R.)

## EASTERN SWAMPHEN *Porphyrio porphyrio*
PLATE XI

IDENTIFICATION: Length, 44 cm. Upper-parts, black; under-parts, *rich dark blue*; forehead (plate) and *massive bill, blood-red*; legs, blood-red; iris, red. The sexes are similar.

VOICE: A harsh grating call, and squealing, is given during aggressive behaviour, but otherwise it is rather silent.

DISTRIBUTION: It occurs from Southern Europe and Africa through Southern Asia to Australia, New Zealand and the South-west Pacific. Although it can be said to extend throughout the continent it is very rare in the dry interior. It is most common on the coast and in the denser swamps of the inland rivers of New South Wales. It is very common in all suitable swamps around Canberra. It inhabits permanent water with a fringe of semi-aquatic vegetation, such as lakes, rivers and deep swamps.

HABITS: It normally occurs as pairs, in trios, or in families, feeding on herbage near water, sometimes walking some hundreds of metres from the edge. Swamphens run and fly quite readily over short dis-

116

tances, though the flight is heavy and the legs are trailed. It scrambles over swamp vegetation and is often seen in low timber above the water. It also swims. It can be confiding if not harassed. It flicks its tail when alarmed, exhibiting a conspicuous white patch beneath it. It is territorial in the breeding season and fights vigorously against intruding swamphens.

BREEDING: The breeding season is from August to December. The nest is a shallow cup on a platform of rushes and grass, usually near the base of a clump of rushes in water. Supernumerary nests are built. The clutch is five to seven. The eggs are pale brownish or greenish with dots and blotches of reddish-brown. They measure about 50 × 36 mm.

FEEDING: The food is chiefly vegetable, though some insects, molluscs and other invertebrates are taken. It favours the succulent bases of water plants and seeds. The Swamphen has the most unusual eating habit of grasping vegetation in one foot and then holding it up while pecking it, but it also feeds normally. (M.G.R.)

## COOT *Fulica atra*

PLATE XI
IDENTIFICATION: Length, 38 cm. Sooty black above and dark grey below; *white forehead* (plate) is conspicuous; bill, bluish-grey; legs, grey with lobed toes. The sexes are similar. The young are dark grey tinged with brown and have white on throat and breast.

VOICE: A sharp clinking note is given when alarmed. The commonest note is a loud "kowk". A high-pitched repeated note may be associated with aggression.

DISTRIBUTION: It extends through Europe, Asia, New Zealand and Australia. In Australia it is found throughout the continent but is much less common in the far north than in the south. It is highly nomadic and appears on newly formed inland swamps following rain, almost as quickly as do some of the ducks. It prefers waters of appreciable area and depth such as lakes and big swamps, or extensive floodwaters. Near Canberra it is chiefly found on the lakes on the plains and is very numerous.

HABITS: The Coot is a thoroughly aquatic bird, normally seen swimming and diving in the open on large bodies of water. Occasionally it leaves the water to graze a short distance on the surrounding herbage. It is not shy. The Coot flies only rarely. During the breeding season pairs are territorial and repel trespassing Coots by fighting and chasing them with a characteristic splattering run along the surface of the water. At other times they may be seen in flocks of up to a few hundred.

BREEDING: The breeding season is usually August to February but is greatly affected by rainfall. The occurrence of non-breeding flocks during the breeding season is not uncommon, but their significance is not yet understood. The nest is a bulky mass of rushes and reeds in the water among aquatic vegetation. It measures about forty centimetres across and the cup about twenty-one centimetres; the top is generally ten centimetres above the water. The clutch is usually seven to nine. The eggs are pale white with small brown spots. They measure about 50 × 34 mm.

FEEDING: It eats mainly vegetable matter with some aquatic insects, molluscs and other animals. Water weeds of various kinds are predominant in the diet and are obtained by diving, sometimes in deep water. It seldom leaves the shallows to feed but commonly walks on the water's edge collecting wave-washed food items. (M.G.R.)

# WADERS

A very large group of birds that are mainly found on the seashore and edges of swamps and lakes are included under this general term. Although some are resident in Australia, many are summer visitors only and migrate here from their breeding places in northern Asia. Mostly they arrive in the southern parts of the continent in early September and move away again in April. The main lines or streams of migration follow the coastlines of the east and west, and although many birds do move inland the numbers that pass through the Southern Tablelands or breed here are small and most of the species are rare in this locality. This is also, of course, associated with the fact that the muddy shores and swampy flats favoured by waders are not well developed in the region.

Most of the migratory waders have two distinct plumages, a relatively bright breeding plumage which often includes black and rufous, and a drab grey non-breeding plumage. The breeding plumage is worn in the Northern Hemisphere but many birds of some species begin to assume it before leaving Australia and some retain traces of it on their arrival here. The accurate identification of the smaller waders is beset with special difficulties because of the general similarity of appearance, variability in respect to different possible plumages and, from the practical point of view, the general lack of cover in the birds' haunts and their wariness.

Family Rostratulidae — Painted Snipe

There are only two species, one in southern South America, the other ranging from Africa through southern Asia to Japan, Malaysia, Philippines and Australia, including Tasmania. Both species are cryptically patterned above and have broad wings and a short, weak tail. The male is duller and smaller than the female, who apparently mates with several males (polyandrous). In Australia the species is nomadic rather than migratory, and may suddenly appear in numbers and nest after heavy rains.

## AUSTRALIAN PAINTED SNIPE *Rostratula benghalensis*
PLATE XIII

IDENTIFICATION: Length, 25 cm. Female: top of head, greenish-brown with a median stripe of golden buff; *prominent white eye-ring prolonged into a white stripe behind the eye*; upper-parts, bronzy green, finely barred black; flight feathers, barred black, with spots and bars of golden buff on the outer webs; tail, greyish with broad pale buff bars narrowly edged with black; *throat and neck, dark chestnut, darkening into a broad black pectoral collar separated by a broad white band from a dark patch on each side of breast*; rest of under-parts, white; bill 5 cm, slightly downcurved at tip, greenish-yellow, brown at tip; legs and toes, pale olive green; iris, deep brown. Male: slightly smaller, and *without any chestnut in the plumage*; general tone of upper-parts, light brown with an olive sheen; foreneck and breast, greyish-brown mottled with white; dark breast patches reduced; *wing coverts with large squarish twin-spots of golden buff.*

VOICE: The Painted Snipe's calls are virtually unknown; the only ones on record are an alarm note, "kek" or "kak" repeated three or four times at intervals of less than a second, and a soft musical "booo" given by a captive female at the conclusion of a threat display.

DISTRIBUTION: In Australia the Painted Snipe has been recorded from all States, including Tasmania, and the Northern Territory. It is nowhere common and is sporadic in occurrence, e.g. in the Melbourne district it was not recorded between 1897 and 1951, nor again until 1963. The first local record was of four birds caught and banded at Lake Burley Griffin in January 1964, when the lake was filling. Since then there have been several records from Lake Burley Griffin and Lake George.

HABITS: Painted Snipe are found singly, in small family groups, and in post-breeding flocks. In Australia they favour flooded and marshy areas, both coastal and inland, with perhaps a preference for samphire *Salicornia* swamps. They have been observed "creeping about under

119

bushes in shallow water". When flushed they do not fly far and can generally be approached closely and flushed again. The flight is moderately swift and straight, not twisting as in the true Snipe. In response to danger they will often "freeze" rather than fly, maintaining the attitude they happen to be holding at the moment. There is an elaborate threat display in which the head and breast are lowered, the tail fanned, and the wings spread, showing the markings on the quills — the whole effect suggesting a huge butterfly.

BREEDING: In southern Australia eggs have been found from October to December and in north Queensland towards the end of the wet season, March to April. One female mates with several males, but it is not known how many clutches she lays in a season. The male does the nest-building and incubation, and cares for the young.

The nest is a simple platform of grasses under the shelter of a samphire bush or tuft of grass, placed on hummocks a little above water level. Occasionally the nest is woven from grasses or rushes growing in water. The eggs are a blunt pear-shape; the ground colour varies from creamy-white to yellow-stone, boldly marked with blotches of dark brown and black, with some spots and lines of the same colours. They vary in length from 30–35 mm and in breadth from 23–27 mm. The normal clutch is four. Incubation time is about twenty days.

FEEDING: The Painted Snipe feeds mainly on aquatic insects, which it gets by probing in shallow water and mud. Like other waders, it probably also takes some seeds of aquatic plants. (W.B.H.)

## Family Charadriidae — Plovers and Dotterels

The family is world-wide, with about sixty species, of which eight breed in Australia, one is a winter visitor from New Zealand, and five are summer visitors from the Northern Hemisphere. They range in size from 15–39 cm. The plumage is grey, brown or black and white, many with a conspicuous collar-mark, and often with the head and neck boldly marked. They are usually white underneath (some black in breeding plumage), sometimes with one or two bands of colour. The wings often have a conspicuous pattern in flight. Some have crests, facial wattles and wing-spurs. The bill is straight and short, with a swollen tip (compare Scolopacidae). The legs are rather short to long; tibia, partly bare and the toes are not webbed, the hind toe is lacking or vestigial. The eyes are large and prominent. The sexes are alike or nearly so.

They are mostly gregarious and terrestrial; the flight is strong and they can run swiftly. The young are cryptically patterned and run soon

120

after hatching. Most species are migratory. In our area there are four breeding species.

## MASKED PLOVER *Vanellus miles*

PLATE XIV

IDENTIFICATION: Length, 34 cm. General plumage, pale olive-brown above and white below; head, white with black crown; black line down hind neck, rest of neck, white; shoulders and sides of breast, black; wing coverts, olive-brown on top and white below; primaries and outer secondaries, black; tail, white with a broad black band near the tip; iris, yellow; *from yellow eye ring a yellow wattle* extends forward in broad rounded lobe which extends below the base of the bill; bill, yellow with brown tip; *spurs at wing angles*, yellow with black tip and shaped like rose thorns; legs, long, naked and purple-red, four toes present. The sexes are similar. Front lobes of the wattles overlap above the bill in adult birds when perturbed. Just before breeding, the old, blunt wing spurs are shed to expose needle-sharp new ones. Juveniles have partially developed spurs and wattles and are brown with irregular dark and light spots above, including top of head.

The above description applies to the southern and local race *V. m. novaehollandiae* known as the Spur-winged Plover. The northern race *V. m. miles* known as the Masked Plover differs by having white, not black, on hind neck, shoulders and sides of breast and a thin olive-brown stripe occurs on the hind neck in some birds. The Masked Plover has a third lobe to the yellow wattles, which is pointed and extends backward from above the eye. Intermediates have a poorly developed third lobe and some black on shoulders and sides of breast.

VOICE: Both sexes utter a loud penetrating stutter "keer kick ki ki ki" on land and in flight, whenever they are disturbed. Sometimes a single "keer" sound is made. There is no racial difference in these calls. Male Spur-winged Plovers make a soft purring sound just before copulating.

DISTRIBUTION: Formerly the two well marked races were considered separate species, the Masked Plover with a nesting distribution confined to northern Australia and the Spur-winged Plover with a nesting distribution confined to south-eastern Australia. Both races and intermediates breed together at Townsville, Queensland. They frequent wet grasslands and readily settle on man-made habitats such as improved pasture, sports grounds, airfields and even grass strips beside urban and suburban roads. Consequently since white settlement there has been a substantial increase in nesting distribution, including a spread to Tasmania and New Zealand by the Spur-winged Plover and recently to New Guinea by the Masked Plover. In western Queensland pasture irrigation by town sewer effluents is causing a breeding range extension north-westward by the Spur-winged Plover. Presumably before white settlement the two races were kept apart by a zone of unfavourable habitat.

Non-breeding birds of both races roam widely all over Australia, New Guinea and some islands of Indonesia. Spur-winged Plovers and intermediates have recently been seen in New Guinea. Mixed and pure flocks of both races are regularly seen in south-western Australia from where there are no breeding records yet.

HABITS: In flight the wings are flapped slowly. When not breeding they tend to form flocks of up to a hundred which roam the country-side. At night the flocks roost standing in large expanses of shallow water or on small islands. In Victoria and Tasmania they recently have started to roost and even breed on roofs in cities and towns.

BREEDING: Plovers require wet weather for breeding, consequently they breed in summer and autumn in northern Australia and winter and spring in south-eastern Australia. In and around the Australian Capital Territory nests with eggs have been found from August to November. Both sexes together defend a large nesting territory, build the nest, take turns in incubating the eggs and defend their brood. Nests are often on pieces of higher ground in large, wet meadows. On airfields they tend to nest beside the runways. In Canberra nests have been found in parking lots and school yards, one pair hatched its eggs between a road and a footpath just outside a public hall, and another pair nested on an office roof.

The nest consists of a scrape lined with straws and small stones. The incubation period is about thirty days. When the young hatch the parents lead them from exposed nest sites to the shelter of rough pasture and dry ditches. Parents and brood wander freely and the vacated nest territory may be taken up by a second pair later in the same season. Pairs are loud and aggressive before eggs are laid and they chase crows, gulls and other egg-predators from the nesting area. During incubation they are silent and unobtrusive. At hatching, and subsequently, they become loud and aggressive again and then dive and scream at people and animals that come too close to their off-spring.

The clutch size is normally four. The eggs vary in colour from brownish-olive through yellow-olive to olive-green, with many irregular dark spots. They average about 49 × 36 mm.

FEEDING: When available they feed on worms, insects and other small invertebrates. At low tide they feed on intertidal invertebrates. During dry and cold weather they also feed on seeds. On wet ground they shuffle one foot and stand on the other, and they thus flush prey animals. Like gulls they go to recently ploughed and cleared land to feed on exposed soil invertebrates. (G.F.vT.)

## BANDED PLOVER *Vanellus tricolor*

PLATE XIV

IDENTIFICATION: Length, 26 cm. General colour above, brown with purple sheen; under-parts, white below; *head, black with a white stripe from eye to eye across back of head*; crown, black; *broad black band* from eyes down sides of neck and covering entire breast; wing coverts, brown with purple sheen above and white below; primaries, black; outer secondaries, black and white; inner secondaries, brown; thick cover of white feathers down most of upper legs; tail, white with broad black band near tip; iris, yellow; from a yellow eye ring a *bulbous red wattle* lobe extends forward; legs, relatively short compared to the Masked Plover and coloured purple-red. They lack spurs on wings and rear toes on feet. The sexes are similar. Wattles of juveniles are only partly developed and the head and breast are mottled black and brown.

VOICE: When disturbed their call is a melodious and chime-like "a chee chee chee".

DISTRIBUTION: The breeding distribution is confined to Australia south of the Tropic of Capricorn and includes Tasmania. Non-breeding birds range north of the Tropic of Capricorn and have been seen at Mount Isa, Queensland during dry weather. It frequents dry marginal and unimproved pasture near a source of water and occasionally forages on mudflats and shores of lakes and dams which are drying and lack vegetation. Its legs are too short to negotiate dense grass that is more than lawn height and in wet grass the plumage becomes wet, bedraggled and matted, unlike that of the Masked Plover. Consequently, where pastures are improved the Banded Plover is replaced by the Masked Plover with its longer legs. Whereas the Masked Plover is a bird of wet coastal areas, the Banded Plover is a bird of the dry interior. In better watered areas it is reasonably sedentary but in the dry inland it is very nomadic.

HABITS: In flight the wings are flapped slowly. They tend to congregate in localised colonies, where they feed, roost and breed. Like the other plovers, they are quite active at night.

123

BREEDING: Although they are a dry country plover, they require rain for breeding. Throughout much of their range rain falls in winter and they breed in winter and spring. After good but unusual summer and autumn rains breeding in autumn has been noted. In and around the Australian Capital Territory nests with eggs have been found from August to November. Banded Plovers nest much closer together than do Masked Plovers. The nests are scrapes on patches of bare ground and are often located in a concentration of dung of grazing stock. The nest is lined with pieces of dry vegetation, dung and dirt.

Both parents build the nest, incubate the eggs and guard the chicks. The chicks leave the nest with their parents shortly after hatching. In addition to diving and calling at people and animals that come too close to their brood the parents also, like many wader species and other birds with precocial chicks, perform distraction displays consisting of walking with a trailing wing. The clutch size is normally four. The eggs are pale brown sometimes with an olive-green tinge and they are covered by irregular dark brown spots. They average about 44 × 32 mm.

FEEDING: When available they feed on insects and other small invertebrates. During dry and cold weather they feed on small seeds of grasses and herbs. Like Masked Plovers they also shuffle one foot to flush prey on damp ground. (G.F.vT.)

## PACIFIC GOLDEN PLOVER *Pluvialis dominica*
PLATE XIII

IDENTIFICATION: Length, 25 cm. *Upper-parts, blackish-brown, mottled with golden-buff*; tail and rump, like back, without any white; pale buff eyebrow stripe; throat and breast, grey-brown suffused with yellow; abdomen, white; *under-wing coverts and axillaries, pale grey-brown*; bill, black; legs, blackish-brown; iris, brown. The sexes are similar. Some birds show traces of the breeding-plumage, which may be partly attained before they leave for their nesting grounds in the Northern Hemisphere; in this plumage, the under-parts are black and the golden mottling on the back is more intense.

VOICE: Call notes have been rendered as "too-wheet" with an upward inflection and an alarm call "tlui" or "tlu-ee". In display flight, a "rippling trill" is given.

DISTRIBUTION: This form of the Golden Plover nests in north-eastern Siberia and western Alaska. It leaves its breeding grounds in the northern winter, migrating through eastern Asia to New Guinea,

124

the south-west Pacific, New Zealand, Australia and Tasmania. It is found in southern Australia between November and May and in the north in June and July. It is occasionally recorded from the larger lakes in the region.

HABITS: The Golden Plover occurs in scattered flocks. It has an alert, upright stance, and a fast, straight flight. In Australia it is usually coastal — on beaches, estuaries, mudflats and salt marshes. It may occur inland on passage, as in New Guinea, where it is not uncommon on open areas, such as airfields, at quite high altitudes.

BREEDING: The nest is a scrape in the tundra, lined with some plants and moss. Four eggs are laid.

FEEDING: The food consists of a variety of small aquatic animals including molluscs, worms, crustacea and insects. These are picked from the surface of beaches and mud-flats, or along the water's edge at the tide-mark. (W.B.H.)

## RED-CAPPED DOTTEREL *Charadrius ruficapillus*
PLATE XII

IDENTIFICATION: Length, 15 cm. Upper-parts, light grey-brown; *top of head and nape, cinnamon-rufous*; a white band on forehead, separated from crown by another band of black; lores, black; *sides of rump, upper-tail coverts and outer tail feathers, white*; under-parts, white. In the female the crown and nape are much paler, less rufous; the lores are rufous and the white and black bands on the forehead are narrower; bill and legs, black; iris, dark brown.

VOICE: It has a rather shrill alarm note and other softer notes. It also has a trilling song, with a rising cadence.

DISTRIBUTION: In Australia and Tasmania it is mainly coastal and less common inland, where it may be nomadic. It is generally a resident species. There are a few records from Lake Burley Griffin, but the species is regularly seen on Lakes George and Bathurst where it breeds.

HABITS: It occurs in pairs or small flocks on ocean beaches and around the margins of salt and freshwater swamps and lagoons. It is a rather "tame" species. It runs swiftly and flies strongly with a motion that alternately shows the white under side, then the dark back. Like most dotterels it "bobs" its head frequently.

125

BREEDING: No nest is made, the eggs being laid in a slight depression in the sand, above high-water mark, sometimes "decorated" with a few chips of shell or wisps of dry seaweed. Inland, the eggs are laid on the ground around the margins of swamps or on islets in a swamp. The breeding season extends from August to March in eastern and southern Australia, but eggs may be found in any month of the year in the tropics and inland. The clutch is nearly always two. The eggs vary from short oval to pyriform in shape, the shell is close-grained and slightly lustrous. The ground colour varies from yellowish-stone to yellowish-brown, with irregular-shaped freckles, spots and streaks of black and blackish-brown, and some underlying ash-grey markings. The average dimensions are 30 × 24 mm. The incubation time is about eighteen days.

FEEDING: It has been recorded as taking chironomid (mosquito-like flies) larvae and adults, weevils and larvae of water-beetles. It almost certainly eats small molluscs and crustacea too in marine habitats. (W.B.H.)

## DOUBLE-BANDED DOTTEREL *Charadrius bicinctus*
PLATE XIII

IDENTIFICATION: Length, 18 cm. Eclipse plumage: upper-parts, greyish-brown; *sides of rump, white, the tail-rump pattern in flight showing a dark centre with white either side*; under-wing, white; faint sandy-buff line from base of bill, through eye; under-parts, whitish. Birds arriving in autumn are in this eclipse plumage (they may be juveniles or adults); breeding plumage is usually acquired during the winter, and by July birds may be seen with the "double-band": *a black one across the upper breast, and a broad chestnut band lower down*; the lores and cheeks become quite black; bill, black; legs, greyish-green; iris, dark brown. The sexes are similar.

VOICE: A feeble "twit-twit" or a staccato "pit-pit" alarm note.

DISTRIBUTION: It is a winter visitor from New Zealand, where it breeds; its distribution in Australia is mainly southern, including Tasmania, and eastern as far north as southern Queensland. It is normally seen between March and August, but there are earlier and later records, and possibly a few non-breeding birds stay during the summer. It has been seen around the larger lakes between April and August.

HABITS: This dotterel is gregarious and may be found on beaches, tidal flats and, more rarely, around the margins of inland swamps and lagoons. It is a rather more "chunky" bird than the Red-capped Dotterel, with which it commonly associates, and slightly larger and more active in its habits. The flight is swift, but rarely sustained for long distances, and usually close to the ground.

BREEDING: It breeds in New Zealand. The nest is a scrape in a gravel beach or river flat. Three eggs are laid.

FEEDING: The Double-banded Dotterel seeks its food from the surface of beaches and mud-flats and eats small molluscs, crustacea, spiders, beetles, ants and aquatic fly larvae. (W.B.H.)

## BLACK-FRONTED DOTTEREL *Charadrius melanops*
PLATE XII

IDENTIFICATION: Length, 16 cm. Upper-parts, brown, with darker centres to the feathers; outer wing quills, black, inner ones, white, tipped black, showing a *white panel near body in flight; a bright chestnut shoulder patch*; upper-tail coverts, rust-red; centre tail feathers, brown to blackish-brown with narrow white tip; *outermost tail feather, white*; top of head and nape, brown, bordered with a narrow white band, then a broader black band; under-parts, white, *with a crescent of black on the collar, widening to centre of breast and ending in a point*; bill, deep orange at base with black tip; legs, orange-flesh; iris, dark brown; eyelid, bright red. The sexes are similar.

VOICE: It has a high-pitched whistle, and plaintive alarm notes.

DISTRIBUTION: It is found throughout the continent, nomadic in Tasmania and is generally more common inland; small numbers are regularly found in coastal localities, but never on ocean beaches. It is resident in small numbers around all the lakes and not uncommon around stock dams or along gravelly river beds.

HABITS: It occurs singly or in pairs and favours the margins of shallow waters, dry watercourses with shingle, and similar habitats. It runs rapidly, stops and "bobs" its head like other dotterels; the flight is swift but it rarely goes far. It performs a "broken-wing" trick, like the Red-capped Dotterel, to lead intruders away from eggs or young.

BREEDING: The eggs are laid on the ground, often among stones or pebbles of the same general colour. The breeding season extends from August to January in eastern and southern Australia, but inland in any month after rains. The shape varies from oval to pyriform. The ground

127

colour is creamy-white, nearly obscured by angular freckles, spots and fine wavy lines of black; rarely, the markings form a zone at the larger end. The average dimensions are 28 × 22 mm. The incubation time is about eighteen days.

FEEDING: The Black-fronted Dotterel feeds on small freshwater crustacea, chironomid flies and their larvae, earwigs, ants, weevils, water-beetles and their larvae, and occasionally takes seeds. (W.B.H.)

## RED-KNEED DOTTEREL *Erythrogonys cinctus*

PLATE XII

IDENTIFICATION: Length, 18 cm. Head, hind neck, *and a broad band across chest, black*; throat and sides of neck, white; rest of under-parts, white, *a broad patch of chestnut on flanks*; back, wings and tail, bronzy-brown; flight feathers, darker; *broad white wing-stripe in flight*; bill, pinkish-red at base with black tip; thigh, "knee", and upper-part of tarsus, pinkish-red; lower tarsus and toes, leaden-blue; iris, brown. The sexes are similar.

VOICE: It has an alarm call, "chet-chet" and also a series of rather musical trilling notes.

DISTRIBUTION: Widely but thinly distributed over the continent but not Tasmania, it is probably most numerous in the inland portions of south-eastern Australia, occasionally reaching the coast in drought years. It is probably nomadic, but recorded as a regular spring and summer visitor to parts of inland New South Wales. In our area it is a regular visitor in small numbers.

HABITS: It occurs in pairs or small flocks. It favours the margins of shallow swamps and lagoons, especially those with cane grass and samphire cover. It runs swiftly over the mud and will hide under bushes. The flight is swift but not sustained. Its movements on the ground are generally graceful, it "bobs" its head rather frequently.

BREEDING: The nest is a slight depression in the ground, generally under a saltbush or clump of samphire, always near water. In southern Australia the breeding season extends from September to December; in northern Australia eggs have been recorded in May. The clutch is four. The eggs vary from short-oval to pear-shaped, the shell is close-grained, smooth and lustreless. They vary in ground colour from cream to pale stone, with a network of fine, black, wavy lines, interspersed with spots and freckles of black, making an excellent camouflage. The measurements are 30 × 22 mm and the incubation time is about twenty days.

FEEDING: This dotterel takes its food from the surface of mud and pools of water, or picks it from vegetation growing in shallow swamps. It eats almost all small aquatic insects, such as water-beetles, weevils, flies and their larvae, and also takes some seeds — species of *Marsilea, Medicago, Trifolium* and *Lotus* have been recorded. (W.B.H.)

Family Scolopacidae — Curlews, Godwits, Sandpipers and Snipe
The members of this family are highly migratory — often transequatorial. The family is world-wide, with eighty-two species, of which over thirty occur in Australia as summer migrants from the Northern Hemisphere; *none breeds here*. They range in size from 12–60 cm. The plumage colour is buff, grey or brown and white, with the back cryptically coloured in many species. The winter plumage (as usually seen here) is much less colourful than the breeding plumage. The bill is slender, straight (sandpipers, stints and snipe), upcurved (godwits, Greenshank and Terek Sandpiper), or downcurved (curlews and whimbrels); neck, medium to long; wings, long; tail, short; legs, short to long, tibia exposed in many species; toes, long, with hind toe, except in one species (Sanderling), and not webbed. The sexes are alike.
   They are gregarious and terrestrial. The flight is strong and swift. They mostly nest on the ground but occasionally eggs are laid in vacant tree nests, or ground burrows of other birds. The young are cryptically patterned and run soon after hatching (nidifugous).

### RUDDY TURNSTONE *Arenaria interpres*

IDENTIFICATION: Length, 23 cm. Upper-parts, dark brown mottled with black and reddish-brown; dusky grey on head; rump, tail bar and tip, shoulder bar and wing stripe, white; under-parts, white except for dark brown breast band; in breeding plumage distinctive rusty-red back, and black and white harlequin pattern on head, neck and breast. *Bill, short, stout and pointed, with upturned lower edge giving it a chisel-like profile; legs, reddish-orange to yellow brown*; iris, brown. The sexes are similar in non-breeding plumage.

VOICE: Noisy, with a twittering "kitititit" and a clear "kee-oo".

DISTRIBUTION: It breeds along the Arctic shores of America and Eurasia, and migrates south along seashores throughout the world, including oceanic islands and the Subantarctic. It is rare inland. It was recorded once from Lake Bathurst, on 11 November 1982. On that occasion large flocks of migratory waders from the Northern Hemisphere, including five other species, were also present.

HABITS: It occurs singly and in flocks, often with other species of waders on bare ground near seashores, where it prefers rock, reefs, shingles and shell beds. Flight is slow and powerful, with some gliding and side-slipping, and not as graceful as in other waders.

BREEDING: Along the Arctic shores of America and Eurasia the nest is a depression lined with small leaves on a small dry mound in open ground. Sometimes the nest is concealed by plants or other objects, or out of sight down a hole. Four eggs are laid.

FEEDING: It turns over pebbles, shells and other small objects to obtain small insects, spiders, Crustacea and molluscs. (G.F.vT.)

## EASTERN CURLEW *Numenius madagascariensis*
PLATE XXXV

IDENTIFICATION: Length, 55 cm. A very large wader with a long down-curved bill; *no pale stripe on the crown, nor a white rump*; body streaked brown and buff, darker above than below; ash-white eyebrow stripe; tail, barred dark and light brown; bill, black with pink base; legs, pale grey; iris, brown. The sexes are similar.

VOICE: It has a mournful "carr-er carr-er" and a high-pitched "kerr-lee kerr-lee" call, and short bursts of bubbling trills.

DISTRIBUTION: It breeds in north-eastern Asia and migrates south to the Philippines, Indonesia and Australasia. It is a rare vagrant inland, including our area, where it was first recorded on 9 January 1977 at Molonglo River flats, Canberra.

HABITS: It occurs singly or in small numbers on bare open ground, including sandbars, mudflats, and ploughed, grazed, mown and stubble fields.

BREEDING: Two or three pairs usually nest together. The nest is a completely exposed scrape lined with old dry grass. The clutch size is normally four.

FEEDING: The Eastern Curlew feeds by probing with its long bill, mainly for insects and crustacea; occasionally it takes worms and frogs. (G.F.vT.)

## LITTLE WHIMBREL *Numenius minutus*

IDENTIFICATION: Length, 29 cm. Upper parts, including rump, sandy brown with dark brown bars; *head pattern as in Whimbrel*, with a median buff stripe on a dark brown crown, and with a yellow buff line above a dark brown eye stripe; underparts, buff with brown marks, except for white throat and abdomen; *bill, 4.5 cm, slightly downcurved, brown with flesh-coloured base*; legs, relatively long, greenish grey; iris, dark brown. The sexes are similar.

VOICE: The contact call in a flock is a soft musical "te-te-te-te" and the alarm call is a harsh "tchew-tchew-tchew".

DISTRIBUTION: It breeds in Siberia and migrates to the Moluccas and northern Australia. Eleven were seen near Lake Bathurst in February, 1982, and a few have been seen there several times subsequently.

HABITS: It frequents grasslands in the vicinity of wetlands, often in association with other waders.

BREEDING: In Siberia the nest is on moss and lichen-covered peat.

FEEDING: While walking in a flock through short grass, it feeds on small insects, spiders, and seeds of grasses and legumes. (G.F.vT.)

## BAR-TAILED GODWIT *Limosa lapponica*
PLATE XIII

IDENTIFICATION: Length, 38 cm. Upper-parts, dark brown with paler margins; pale buffy-brown on foreneck and chest with darker shaft streaks; flight feathers, dark brown *with narrow white wing-stripe; lower back, upper-tail coverts, and tail barred white and brown*; under-parts, dull white; *bill, 8.5 cm, upcurved, basal half, flesh-coloured, rest blackish-brown*; legs, leaden-grey, not extending far beyond tail in flight; iris, brown. The sexes are similar.

VOICE: It is not very vocal but has a harsh "ku-wit", or "trrik-trrik" and an alarm call, "krick-krick".

DISTRIBUTION: It breeds in northern Europe and Asia and migrates to Africa, India, Malaysia, New Guinea, Australia and New Zealand. It is rather more coastal than inland, and more common in eastern Australia and Tasmania than elsewhere. It was recorded once from Lake Bathurst in October, 1962 and several times around Lake Burley Griffin in November 1979.

HABITS: It occurs in pairs or flocks of rarely more than twenty. It is a reasonably "tame" species. It favours tidal flats, but also occurs on seashores and, more rarely, inland lakes and marshes. The flight is strong and swift, *the neck bent up in flight*.

BREEDING: In northern Europe and Asia the nest is a depression in the ground in short grass or herbage. Four eggs are laid.

FEEDING: It probes in mud and water for food, which consists of any small marine and freshwater molluscs, crustacea, worms and insects and probably takes occasional seeds of aquatic plants. (W.B.H.)

## MARSH SANDPIPER *Tringa stagnatilis*

PLATE XIII

IDENTIFICATION: Length, 22 cm. A miniature edition of the Greenshank, but also distinguished by the slimmer, *straight bill*, and proportionately longer and finer legs which trail well beyond tail in flight; bill, black; legs, olive-yellow; iris, brown. The sexes are similar.

VOICE: The voice is quite different to that of the Greenshank—a rather soft, melodious "tee-oo" or "tew". It also has a trilling song.

DISTRIBUTION: It breeds in south-eastern Europe and central Asia, migrating in winter to South Africa, Malaysia, New Guinea and Australia, where it has been recorded from all States. In our area it is rarely recorded but has been seen on all of the larger lakes.

HABITS: It is found singly or in small flocks and inhabits mainly freshwater swamps, coastal and inland. Its movements are noticeably more graceful and dainty than those of the Greenshank.

BREEDING: The nest is a depression in the ground among grass and herbage. Four eggs are laid.

FEEDING: It probes in mud and water for aquatic insects and their larvae and also takes small molluscs. (W.B.H.)

## GREENSHANK *Tringa nebularia*

PLATE XIII

IDENTIFICATION: Length, 32 cm. Upper-parts, grey, slightly freckled white; forehead, white; *lower back and tail, white*, conspicuous in flight; under-parts, white; bill, long, slightly upcurved, black; legs, greenish-grey; iris, brown. The sexes are similar.

VOICE: It has a shrill, piping alarm call, "chewy-chewy" or "tew-tew-tew", and a more mellow song "tewi-tewi".

DISTRIBUTION: It breeds in northern Europe and northern Asia and migrates in winter to South Africa, and through eastern Asia to New Guinea, Australia, Tasmania and New Zealand. It is widely but thinly distributed in Australia, more coastal than inland. In our area it is recorded regularly in very small numbers.

HABITS: It occurs either singly or in small groups; it favours fresh-water rather than marine habitats, but is quite common on salt marshes. It is a wary species and the flight is strong and rapid; the legs extend beyond tail in flight. It "bobs" its head and tail.

BREEDING: The nest is a depression in short grass. Four eggs are laid.

FEEDING: It probes in mud and water, showing a preference for molluscs, but also takes larvae and adults of aquatic insects. (W.B.H.)

## WOOD SANDPIPER *Tringa glareola*

PLATE XII

IDENTIFICATION: Length, 23 cm. Back and wings, spotted, grey-brown; *rump, completely white*; breast, grey; abdomen, white; eyebrow, white; crown, striped; bill, black, paler at base, straight; legs, olive-green; iris, brown. The sexes are similar.

VOICE: The voice has been recorded as a three-note whistle, "chee-chee-chee"; an alarm note, "chiff-iff-iff", and a rising, liquid "flui". In song-flight, it has a musical "tleea-tleea-tleea".

DISTRIBUTION: It breeds in northern Europe and northern Asia and migrates in winter to South Africa, India, Malaysia, New Guinea and Australia, where it has been recorded from all States, but it is no-where common. It our area there are a few summer records from Lake Burley Griffin and Lake George.

HABITS: It is usually solitary, or in small groups, and frequents freshwater swamps, sewage farms, and rivers, both coastal and inland; it is not a marine species. It "bobs" its head and flicks its tail repeatedly, runs actively and can swim. It has a habit of perching on trees, fences and posts.

BREEDING: The nest is a depression in the ground near a sheltering tussock. Four eggs are laid.

FEEDING: It probes in mud and water for food which consists of aquatic insects and their larvae, small freshwater molluscs, crustacea and worms. (W.B.H.)

## COMMON SANDPIPER *Tringa hypoleucos*

PLATE XIII

IDENTIFICATION: Length, 20 cm. Upper-parts, dark olive-brown— *in sunlight showing a greenish wash*; rump, dark brown; *outer tail feathers, brown and white*; wing coverts with white tips, showing as two narrow wing-bars in flight; under-parts, white; bill, dark brown; legs, leaden-grey; iris, brown. The sexes are similar.

VOICE: Its alarm note is a shrill, piping "twee-wee-wee". It also has a rapid, trilling song.

DISTRIBUTION: It breeds in Europe and northern Asia and migrates in winter to Africa, and through eastern Asia to New Guinea, the south-west Pacific, Australia and Tasmania. It has been recorded from all States and is possibly more common in the west. In our area there is one record from Lake Burley Griffin in 1966.

HABITS: It is a solitary species and inhabits both marine and fresh-water areas, especially favouring rocky beaches and is also found inland around dams and rivers. It perches on rocks, jetties, moored boats and fence posts and has a distinctive undulating flight with wings held out stiffly. It "bobs" its head and tail like the Wood Sandpiper and Greenshank.

BREEDING: The nest is a depression in the ground with some lining of grass and moss. Four eggs are laid.

FEEDING: It probes in mud and water for aquatic insects and their larvae, small molluscs and crustacea. (W.B.H.)


## JAPANESE SNIPE *Gallinago hardwickii*

PLATE XII

IDENTIFICATION: Length, 24 cm. Upper-parts, including rump, marked brown and black; throat, neck, upper breast and under-tail, light buff; *axillaries barred black and white*; eighteen tail feathers; *bill, long* (70 mm), *straight*, black; legs, olive-yellow; iris, dark brown. The sexes are similar.

VOICE: It calls "arrk" or "krek" on flushing.

DISTRIBUTION: Breeding only in Japan (Hokkaido and Honshu) it migrates south in winter through New Guinea to Australia, Tasmania and New Zealand and is commonest in eastern Australia. It is reported in our area as a regular summer visitor, September to April, in small numbers at Lake George and Lake Burley Griffin.

HABITS: It is usually solitary or in small flocks and favours swampy localities and wet grasslands. It is secretive in habits and blends well with surroundings. It rises suddenly, flies ahead in a zig-zag manner, pitches suddenly and may fly around at a fair height before landing.

BREEDING: The nest is a depression in the ground in grass. Four eggs are laid.

FEEDING: It probes in mud and water for seeds, aquatic insects and their larvae, and worms. (W.B.H.)

## RED-NECKED STINT *Calidris ruficollis*

PLATE XII

IDENTIFICATION: Length, 15 cm. Upper-parts, medium-grey with some streaking on crown and upper back, flight feathers darker brown, with a white wing-stripe in flight; *upper-tail coverts with dark centre and white sides*; under-parts, white. Birds about to migrate in autumn often show traces of *rusty-red on the head and throat*; bill and legs, black; iris, dark brown. The sexes are similar.

VOICE: It utters sharp twittering notes, and an undulating trilling song.

DISTRIBUTION: It breeds in north-eastern Siberia and western Alaska and migrates through Asia to New Guinea, Australia, Tasmania and New Zealand. It is one of our most numerous northern waders. It is often in huge flocks and is mainly coastal but also occurs inland. It is reported in our area in small numbers around the larger lakes every summer.

HABITS: It is gregarious and is found on seashores, tidal flats, swamps and lakes. It is restless and a very active feeder. The flight is swift, usually low over water, showing white under-parts and dark back in side-long movements.

BREEDING: The nest is a depression in the ground with some lining of leaves. Four eggs are laid.

FEEDING: It probes in mud and water for small aquatic insects and their larvae — also takes some seeds (*Trifolium* and *Heliotropium* have been found in stomachs). (W.B.H.)

## PECTORAL SANDPIPER *Calidris melanotos*

PLATE XII

IDENTIFICATION: Length, 23 cm. Upper-parts, brown with dark and light stripes; rump and tail with dark-brown centre and white sides; under-parts, *breast and throat dense dark-brown streaks, sharp border with white abdomen*; bill, black with yellow base; legs, greenish-yellow; iris, brown. The sexes are similar. Breeding birds lack small boomerang-shaped marks on flanks.

VOICE: It has a reedy, creaky and variable "prit", "trip", "krick" or "kreek" call uttered as a single or double note or in series.

DISTRIBUTION: It breeds in north-eastern Siberia and north-western North America, and migrates mainly to the southern third of South America, and to a lesser extent Australia and New Zealand. Stragglers from time to time reach Greenland, Europe, Africa and islands in the Pacific Ocean. In our area there are only a couple of records from Jerrabomberra Creek, Canberra.

HABITS: It is solitary when foraging on areas of silt in estuaries and lagoons. It defends its feeding area against other Pectoral Sandpipers, but joins small flocks of them for roosting and migration.

BREEDING: The nest is a depression in the ground at a dry site with a substantial lining of lichens, birch leaves and dry grass. Four eggs are laid.

FEEDING: It probes in mud and water mainly for Diptera and their larvae, and for Amphipoda. It also takes a wide variety of other kinds of small invertebrates including spiders, grasshoppers and molluscs, as well as some grit and seeds. (G.F.vT.)

## SHARP-TAILED SANDPIPER *Calidris acuminata*

PLATE XII

IDENTIFICATION: Length, 21 cm. Upper-parts, grey-brown; *crown streaked rufous and black; rump and tail with dark-brown centre and white sides*; breast, buffish-white, streaked brown; throat and abdomen, white. Some birds show traces of breeding plumage both in summer and autumn, in which the colours are intensified above and below; bill, black; legs, olive-green; iris, brown. The sexes are similar.

VOICE: It has a sharp alarm note on flushing, "krip-krip" or "chit-chit".

136

DISTRIBUTION: It breeds in north-eastern Siberia and migrates through eastern Asia to New Guinea, Australia, Tasmania and New Zealand. It is a common wader in coastal and inland Australia. In our area it occurs regularly in summer in all suitable habitats.

HABITS: It occurs in flocks which are sometimes large and is found on the seashore, estuaries and inlets, and freshwater swamps inland. It is not so active in its movements as the Red-necked Stint, but its other habits are similar.

BREEDING: The nest is a depression in "grassy, damp, lowlying tracts of tundra". Four eggs are laid.

FEEDING: It probes in mud and water for aquatic insects and their larvae and also takes ants and some seeds (*Ruppia* and *Polygonum* recorded from stomachs). (W.B.H.)

## CURLEW SANDPIPER *Calidris ferruginea*
PLATE XII

IDENTIFICATION: Length, 20 cm. Upper-parts, greyish-brown; white eyebrow stripe; flight feathers, darker brown, *showing a white band in flight; upper-tail coverts with distinct white band*; under-parts, white. In early autumn, some birds may be seen in breeding plumage in which the head, neck and under-parts are bright russet. It is not uncommon for a few individuals to winter over in Australia; bill, black and *slightly downcurved*; legs, rather long for its size, black; iris, brown. The sexes are similar.

VOICE: It has a distinctive, rather loud "chirrup".

DISTRIBUTION: It breeds in eastern Arctic Asia and migrates in winter through Europe to Africa, and through eastern Asia to New Guinea, Australia, Tasmania and New Zealand. It is not uncommon throughout coastal Australia but is less frequent inland. In our area it has been reported regularly in small numbers at Lakes George and Bathurst in summer.

HABITS: It is usually found in flocks but is occasionally solitary. It frequents the seashore, tidal flats, freshwater swamps, and salt marshes. It is very active when feeding, with quick bill movements.

BREEDING: The nest is a scrape in the ground. Four eggs are laid.

137

FEEDING: It wades in water to feed on small aquatic animals—insects and their larvae, molluscs, crustacea and worms. (W.B.H.)

## BROAD-BILLED SANDPIPER *Limicola falcinellus*

PLATE XII

IDENTIFICATION: Length, 18 cm. Upper-parts, streaked greyish-brown; *two light eyebrow stripes; black patch at angle of wing* (not always visible); upper-tail coverts with dark centre and white sides; under-parts, white with grey streaks on breast. In breeding plumage the upper-parts are very dark with creamy streaks on back; bill, dark red-brown with yellow-brown base; legs, greenish-brown; iris, dark brown. The sexes are similar.

VOICE: It has as a contact call a subdued "chip-chip-chip", as a mild alarm call a rolling "cheridit", and on flushing a deep trilling "cherritreetreat".

DISTRIBUTION: It breeds in northern Eurasia and migrates mainly to northern Africa and southern Asia with a few going farther south to Africa and Australasia. In our area there are only some doubtful records of one or two being seen at Jerrabomberra Creek, Canberra.

HABITS: It is solitary when foraging on areas of silt in estuaries and lagoons. It defends its feeding area against other Broad-billed Sandpipers and against other small waders, but joins small flocks of them for roosting and migration.

BREEDING: The nest is a hollow in a tussock of cotton grass in an acid marsh with a lining of dry birch and willow leaves. Four eggs are laid.

FEEDING: It is relatively tame and slow when it probes in mud and water, mainly for beetles and for the larvae of Diptera. It also takes a wide variety of other kinds of small invertebrates including snails, Amphipoda, grasshoppers and ants, as well as some seeds and grit. (G.F.vT.)

Family Recurvirostridae—Avocets and Stilts
The family is found in Africa, central and southern Europe and Asia, most of the Americas, New Guinea, Australia, New Zealand and, in the Pacific, east to the Hawaiian Islands. There are seven species, of which three breed in Australia. In size they range from twenty-nine to forty-eight centimetres. Plumage, black and white or brown and white; uniform grey in one Asian species, *Ibidorhyncha*; bill, long, slender, straight (stilts) or upcurved (avocets)—down-curved in

*Ibidorhyncha.* The head is small, neck long; tail, short; legs, long; toes, partially or wholly webbed; hind toe vestigial or absent. The sexes are alike. They are gregarious and terrestrial, but swim strongly and regularly. The flight is strong. The northern species are migratory and the Australian species nomadic. They breed colonially and the young run or swim soon after hatching (nidifugous).

## WHITE-HEADED STILT *Himantopus himantopus*
PLATE XIV

IDENTIFICATION: Length, 38 cm. General colour, white, *except for black wings* (above and below), *upper back, and a patch on the nape.* Young birds have grey on the crown, nape and behind the eye. *Legs very long and pink, trailing well beyond tail in flight*; bill, black; iris, red. The sexes are similar.

VOICE: The voice is a puppy-like "bark" — unmistakable and specific and rather high-pitched.

DISTRIBUTION: It ranges from the Philippines through Java to New Guinea, the Bismarck Archipelago and Australia; accidental in Tasmania. It is common in some localities but is rare in others, especially coastal areas, and has been recorded in our area between August and April. It breeds at Lake George.

HABITS: It occurs in pairs or flocks and frequents salt marshes, swamps, rivers, lagoons and estuaries — coastal and inland. It wades in knee-deep water to feed and can swim. The flight is leisurely. It is rather wary.

BREEDING: The nest is made of twigs or aquatic grasses, with a slight hollow in the top, sometimes mortared with mud, and usually placed on an island in a shallow swamp. In southern Australia the breeding season extends from August to December, but inland it breeds in any month after rains. The clutch is normally four; the egg shape is oval to pyriform; the shell is close-grained, dull and lustreless. The eggs vary in ground colour from olive-yellow to stone-brown, tinged olive-green, covered with irregular blotches of black and brown-blackish. Their average dimensions are 42 × 30 mm and the incubation time is about twenty-one days.

FEEDING: The White-headed Stilt wades in water to feed and takes various kinds of beetles, water-bugs, water-scorpions and seeds — *Ruppia, Vitis* and *Portulaca* have been recorded. Charcoal has also been found in their gut. (W.B.H.)

139

## BANDED STILT *Cladorhynchus leucocephalus*

IDENTIFICATION: Length, 38-42 cm. Adults, white with conspicuous chestnut band across breast and belly, darkening to almost black on the lower belly; wings, black with white band, seen when in flight along the trailing edge; bill, long and slightly upcurved, black; legs and toes, pink; iris, brown. The feet are webbed. Sexes similar.

Immatures lack breast band and have grey-brown wings.

VOICE: Not unlike the White-headed Stilt; a quiet puppy-like yelp and softer wheezing notes.

DISTRIBUTION: It occurs in the southern half of the continent wherever there are brackish and saline lakes and estuaries. It is more common in Western and South Australia but uncommon in western Victoria and New South Wales. Vagrants have been recorded in coastal areas of Queensland, New South Wales and Tasmania.

The only record for the local region was an immature bird seen in the company of White-headed Stilts at Lake Bathurst in January and February 1983.

HABITS: The Banded Stilt usually occurs in large flocks, sometimes numbering thousands. Its movements are highly erratic and the species may turn up anywhere suitable habitat exists. It may be found in an area for years, then suddenly disappear, not to return until many years later.

It is generally seen wading in shallow water, often in the company of the Red-necked Avocet, and can swim well.

BREEDING: The breeding season is erratic, but if conditions are suitable it is generally from May to December. The bird breeds in huge colonies on the saline lakes of inland Western and South Australia. No nest is built, the eggs being laid in a depression in the ground. The clutch consists of three or four eggs, measuring about 53 × 38 mm. The eggs are white to fawn, with blotches and streaking of brown, black and grey.

FEEDING: The chief food of the Banded Stilt is the brine shrimp, which is found in large quantities in the saline lakes of the inland. Other small aquatic invertebrates are undoubtedly also eaten. (M.C.)

# RED-NECKED AVOCET *Recurvirostra novaehollandiae*

PLATE XIV

IDENTIFICATION: Length, 43 cm. *Head and neck, bright chestnut*; wing-tips and shoulders, black; two small black lines show on back in flight; *thin, upcurved beak is diagnostic*; remainder of plumage, white; bill, black; legs, grey-blue (no hind toe); iris, reddish-brown. The sexes are similar.

VOICE: It has a "barking" note, similar to that of the White-headed Stilt, and softer "wheezy" notes.

DISTRIBUTION: It is found throughout Australia but is rare in Tasmania and coastal areas in the eastern States. It is nomadic and has been recorded once in recent years from each of the major lakes. There are specimens from Lake George and Cooma in the Australian Museum, Sydney.

HABITS: It is usually found in flocks which are sometimes large. It swims well and feeds with head under water, but also wades in salt-marshes like the White-headed Stilt. It occurs in swamps, lakes and estuaries. The flight is leisurely with the long legs trailing behind.

BREEDING: The nest is a hollow in a clump of an aquatic plant, always near water, and usually on the margins of salt lakes. The breeding season extends from August to December in southern Australia, but eggs may be laid in any month after rains in the inland. The clutch is four; the eggs oval to pyriform, the shell close-grained and lustreless. The ground colour varies from yellowish-stone to creamy-brown, covered with spots and blotches of black, and some underlying grey markings — generally indistinguishable from those of the White-headed Stilt, except perhaps for the yellowish ground colour and slightly larger size. The average dimensions are $48 \times 32$ mm and the incubation time is about twenty days.

FEEDING: It wades or swims to feed and *moves the bill horizontally when feeding*. The food consists of any small aquatic animals — insects, molluscs, crustacea and almost certainly the seeds of aquatic plants. (W.B.H.)

## Family Burhinidae — Stone-curlews

The stone-curlews, also known in different countries as stone-plovers, thick-knees and other names, are a very small but widely distributed family. There are nine species all of which belong to the one genus *Burhinus*. Two stone-curlews occur in Australia, the Beach Stone-curlew *Burhinus neglectus*, which has an extensive range from the Andaman Islands to the beaches and rocky shores of northern and eastern Australia, and Southern Stone-curlew *Burhinus magnirostris* that is distributed throughout Australia and occurs in our area.

Stone-curlews vary from twenty-six to fifty centimetres in length and are very long legged. The "knees" are conspicuously thickened; there is no hind toe. The head is large and broad and the eyes are large and prominent, no doubt related to their largely nocturnal life. The colours are always cryptic and the sexes are alike. They fly well but generally prefer to remain on the ground and escape danger by walking or "freezing".

## SOUTHERN STONE-CURLEW *Burhinus magnirostris*
PLATE XIV

IDENTIFICATION: Length, 55 cm. Crown, back of neck and back, dark grey with fine black streaks; rump, grey; wings and tail, brown, each feather fringed with rufous and streaked with black; face, white with chestnut patch behind eye; *throat, white; under-parts, white, prominently streaked with black*; under-tail coverts, white; underside of tail, grey; iris, yellow; legs and feet, off-white, tinged with olive; bill, black. The sexes are similar.

VOICE: The usual sound is an eerie, mournful whistle "ker-loo", the second note rises in inflection and is very long drawn out, up to three seconds; it is usually uttered at night. The call is heard at widely spaced intervals but as the breeding season approaches it is repeated several times in succession with increasing speed and, apparently, excitement. Several birds sometimes join in and the performance ends in a jumble of sound.

DISTRIBUTION: The Southern Stone-curlew was formerly distributed throughout the whole of the continent and vagrants occurred to Tasmania. It has greatly declined with advancing settlement and is now only numerous in the relatively undisturbed habitats of the far north. It is generally assumed that depredations by the introduced fox have been responsible for its decline and this is doubtless partly true although destruction of its habitat by clearing and grazing are perhaps of greater importance. It is found in all habitats, sometimes even in the densest forests, but it prefers open forests and savannah woodlands with coarse grass. It is rare in our region though there are occasional records, widely spaced in time. Formerly it was abundant.

HABITS: Where common it is found in pairs and small groups and, in the tropics, these number up to thirty or forty. It is entirely terrestrial, largely nocturnal, and is particularly active on clear moon-light nights. It is very secretive and often escapes detection by freezing or stretching out along the ground with neck extended. When pursued it walks swiftly away with deliberate steps and head erect. If too closely pursued it takes wing, running quickly to gain take-off speed with wings partly spread. When aloft the flight is strong and buoyant. On alighting it "taxis" to a halt and the wings are fully opened and closed before it stalks off. When feeding it stalks very slowly and carefully, peering at the ground and sometimes scarcely seems to be moving.

BREEDING: In the tropics the breeding season is in the early wet season but in southern Australia it is generally in the spring, August to November. There are no recent records from our area. The eggs are laid on the bare ground, often in the shelter of a bush or fallen log where the ground is partly covered with broken twigs, branches and bark with which they blend perfectly in colour. When disturbed, the birds usually creep carefully away, watching the observer, but sometimes stretch out flat and remain motionless. The clutch size is two, or very occasionally three. The colour of the eggs varies greatly but is usually pale stone or buff and they are spotted and blotched with slate-grey and umber, occasionally also lavender. They measure about $56 \times 38$ mm. The incubation time is about twenty-four days and the young are able to leave the nest on the day of hatching.

FEEDING: There has been no study of the food eaten but it obviously includes much animal material. Stomachs examined have contained large insects, small lizards, spiders, centipedes and a small toad as well as a few grass seeds. Mice and scorpions have also been reported. (H.J.F.)

# GULLS AND TERNS

The family is world-wide in distribution, with eighty-two species of which three gulls and twenty-one terns occur in Australia. They range in size from the "least" terns (20 cm) to the larger gulls (76 cm). The plumage is typically grey and white but at least one species, the White Tern *Gygis alba*, an occasional visitor to Australia, is all white. Most terns have a black cap in breeding plumage, and some of the gulls are "hooded". The bill is slender and pointed in terns but rather deep and hooked in gulls. The wings are long and pointed. The tail is short and square in most gulls but rather short and slightly forked in the marsh terns and the Caspian Tern and rather long and deeply forked in other sea terns. The legs are short (terns) to medium (gulls); the toes are webbed. The sexes are alike.

143

Nearly all gulls and terns are gregarious and aquatic, both in salt and freshwater. They are migratory except in low latitudes. The Silver Gull and Marsh Tern breed in our area and the White-winged Black Tern, Gull-billed Tern and the Caspian Tern have been recorded as visitors.

## Family Laridae—Gulls and Terns
## SILVER GULL *Larus novaehollandiae*

PLATE XIV

IDENTIFICATION: Length, 41 cm. General plumage, *white; wings, grey with black and white tips*; bill, eye ring, legs and feet, red; iris, ivory. The sexes are similar. Juveniles have buff spots on back and wing, their legs are greenish-yellow to brown, and beak and iris are brown. Non-breeding birds have bill, eye ring, legs and feet, dull red-brown rather than bright red.

VOICE: It has several rapid, rasping and penetrating calls.

DISTRIBUTION: It occurs in South Africa and throughout Australia, including Tasmania, and New Zealand. Its main distribution is coastal but it regularly occurs far inland, particularly in south-east Australia. It frequents seashores, inlets, estuaries, rivers, lakes, wet meadows, refuse tips, ploughed fields and city parks. It is regularly present on all large water bodies in our area.

HABITS: Silver Gulls are gregarious and tend to fly in irregular flocks. Often they soar on thermals and updrafts. They roost at night communally on isolated islands and peninsulas, and on extensive mudflats and areas of very shallow water. In the latter they stand in water only a few centimetres deep, presumably as an additional precaution against cats, dogs and foxes. They travel daily between roosting and feeding, as much as eighty kilometres apart.

BREEDING: Gulls have very small nesting territories in colonies on small islands and peninsulas. The nests are placed in amongst tussocks, shrubs, grass and other short vegetation. Some nests are mere scrapes on flattened grass, whereas others are built of hay or seaweed brought in from elsewhere. At Devonport, Tasmania, they carry grass clippings from an airfield to their nests on an offshore island one and a half kilometres away. After the chicks hatch they normally remain within the parental territory until they fledge. When they stray out of it they are liable to be injured and even killed by other gulls. Both parents take part in building the nest, incubating the eggs and feeding the chicks. When they can fly, chicks follow their parents on foraging trips and fledglings are often fed many kilometres from the natal colony. In our area there is a large breeding colony at Lake Bathurst, where the main breeding season is from August to November. It is likely that a breeding colony may start in the near future on islands in Lake Burley Griffin. The clutch size is normally three. Egg colour varies from olive-green to blue and some are even white or pink. The eggs are covered by blotches, spots and irregular lines of black and dark brown. They average about $54 \times 38$ mm.

FEEDING: Like most other gulls, the Silver Gull is an opportunistic scavenger. At low tide it feeds on intertidal invertebrates. After heavy rain it forages on partly flooded airfields, sports grounds and city parks for earthworms, grubs and even mice. It follows ploughs and earth-moving equipment to feed on exposed soil invertebrates. It eats household refuse including bread at rubbish tips. On calm water it feeds on surfacing small fish and water surface insects. At night it has been seen feeding on insects that were attracted to harbour navigation lights, and even at drive-in theatres close to midnight on food scraps and possibly also injured moths from the screen and the flood-lights. It also follows coastal shipping and fishing boats for scraps. (G.F.vT.)

## GULL-BILLED TERN *Gelochelidon nilotica*

IDENTIFICATION: Length, 41 cm. *Similar to a gull, but with shorter legs and a forked tail, though the legs are relatively not as short and the tail not as forked as in other terns.* In breeding plumage crown of head and hind neck, jet black; general colour above, silver-grey; colour below, pure white; tips of primaries, dark grey; bill, black; legs, black; iris, dark brown. In non-breeding plumage black cap is reduced to a dusky eye-stripe and nape. Immatures are similar to birds in non-breeding plumage but are mottled above and have brownish legs.

VOICE: It calls with a repetitive double note "kuh-wuk" or "che-ah".

DISTRIBUTION: It breeds in eastern North America, Europe, Africa, southern Asia, New Guinea and Australia. It is a vagrant in New Zealand and has not been recorded in Tasmania. In our area it is a rare vagrant. It was first recorded on 17 September 1972 at Molonglo River flats, Canberra and there have been other records in 1981 and 1982.

HABITS: The Gull-billed Tern is solitary or occurs in twos and threes, except in the breeding season. It is a rare nomad over most of Australia, and is found along sea shores, on lagoons, mudflats, inland lakes, estuaries, temporary pools of water, and ploughed fields. It has a gull-like flight with more gliding and less flapping than in other terns.

It roosts on the ground and is often found far from water.

BREEDING: The eggs are laid in a scrape which is sometimes lined with twigs and soil. The species breeds in colonies. The clutch size varies from two to four. The eggs are oval, dull to slightly lustrous, and coarse-grained. The ground colour varies from grey through brown to green with splotches of brown or black. The average dimensions are 52 × 37 mm. The incubation time is about twenty-three days.

FEEDING: The Gull-billed Tern feeds on the wing by picking prey from the water, mud or bare ground surface. It takes a wide variety of small terrestrial and aquatic arthropods and vertebrates. It does not dive for food. (G.F.vT.)

## WHITE-WINGED BLACK TERN *Chlidonias leucoptera*
PLATE XIV

IDENTIFICATION: Length, 24 cm. Breeding plumage: whole *body, velvet-black*; tail and leading edge of wings, white, showing as white "shoulder" patch when wings folded; wing-linings, black. Birds in full breeding plumage are uncommon in Australia; most birds seen are "in change" from breeding to non-breeding plumage in which a varying amount of black is replaced by white on the body and underwing, *giving a distinctive mottled or speckled appearance*. In the full nonbreeding plumage the body, wing-linings and foreparts of crown are white; top of head and nape, black; upper-wings and back, grey; tail, white; bill, bright red in summer, blackish in winter; legs, orange-red; iris, dark brown. The sexes are similar.

VOICE: It is seldom vocal but the following calls have been recorded by F. T. H. Smith at Altona, Victoria; a high-pitched alarm note, "kreek-kreek" or "kreea-kik-kik", and threat calls variously rendered as "keeek-keeek-keeek", "kek-kek-kek" and "chik-a-tik-tik".

DISTRIBUTION: The species is known to breed only in southern Europe, parts of tropical Africa, and central Asia, whence it disperses both north and south outside the breeding season. It has been recorded from all Australian States, the Northern Territory and New Zealand, but only once in our area—from Lake Bathurst in 1962. The White-winged Black Tern sometimes visits southern and eastern Australia in thousands but this is at irregular intervals, usually between October and May. It is thought that seasonal conditions, especially winds, influence these sporadic appearances.

HABITS: This tern favours freshwater swamps, both coastal and inland. In Australia it has been recorded mainly from subcoastal swamps, especially in Western Australia and Victoria; in Queensland feeding flocks, probably in passage, have been seen thirty-two kilometres offshore between Cairns and Bowen. It is gregarious and commonly associates with the Marsh Tern, and occasionally with other terns. It perches freely on driftwood, small rocks, posts, etc. in the water, and roosts on the ground, often in company with other terns and gulls. It tends to be aggressive towards other species of terns and to gulls and engages in spirited and swift pursuit of them. It hovers above the water when feeding.

BREEDING: In Europe it breeds either in association with the Marsh Tern or alone, in large colonies. The nest is a scanty structure of plant material on a tussock in the water or on floating debris. Three eggs are laid.

FEEDING: Food is skimmed off the surface of the water and consists of almost any flying insect that occurs in or near water, including dragonflies (especially), butterflies, moths and flying ants. (W.B.H.)

## MARSH TERN *Chlidonias hybrida*

PLATE XIV

IDENTIFICATION: Length, 26 cm. Breeding plumage: *crown, black contrasting with white cheeks and sides of neck*; under-parts, dark grey to slaty-grey. In flight the *under-wings and under-tail coverts are noticeably white*. The upper-wings, back and tail are medium grey. The tail is rather more forked than that of the White-winged Black Tern, and the bill is longer and thicker.

The non-breeding plumage is barely distinguishable from that of the White-winged Black Tern, but the Marsh Tern has more black speckling on the forehead and the black ear coverts are joined to the black of the hind crown, the top of the head being mottled with white; bill and legs, dark red in summer, blackish in winter plumage; iris, brown. The sexes are similar in plumage but the bill of the female is shorter and stubbier.

VOICE: The voice is similar to that of the White-winged Black Tern.

DISTRIBUTION: It is distributed from Europe, Africa, central and southern Asia to New Guinea, Australia and Tasmania. A non-marine species, it is likely to be seen wherever there are freshwater swamps, lagoons and lakes. It has been recorded in our area from September to February at Lake Burley Griffin, Lakes George and Bathurst.

HABITS: Its habits are similar to those of the White-winged Black Tern, but the Marsh Tern has a less slender appearance in the field, and its flight is slightly less buoyant, with rather deeper wing beats—more like the flight action of the sea-terns of the genus *Sterna*. The Marsh Tern is nomadic, rather than migratory—its breeding is certainly influenced by availability of suitable water.

BREEDING: The Marsh Tern nests in colonies and the fragile nests are built on the water out of almost any available aquatic vegetation, e.g. grasses, rushes, samphire. In southern Australia the breeding season extends from September to December. It bred at Lake Bathurst in early November, 1963. The usual clutch is three and the eggs are pointed ovals, glossy, ranging in ground colour from greyish-olive to dark stone, spotted and blotched with dark brown, with some underlying spots of grey. They vary in size from 34–38 × 26–28 mm. The incubation time is about twenty days.

FEEDING: The feeding methods and food are similar to those of the White-winged Black Tern, but it does occasionally dive. In winter it has been observed to take locusts in Africa, and probably does likewise in Australia. (W.B.H.)

## CASPIAN TERN *Hydroprogne caspia*

PLATE XIV

IDENTIFICATION: Length, 56 cm. Wing-span 140 cm. The largest tern, unlikely to be confused with any other species. *Top of head, forehead and nape, black*, the black extending to just below the eye. All upper-parts medium grey; under-parts, white; tail not deeply forked; in flight, the quills are dark underneath. In winter, and juveniles, the black cap becomes streaked grey-black, the feathers extending below eye to the line of the gape; bill, massive, scarlet at all seasons; legs, black; iris, dark brown. The sexes are similar.

VOICE: Loud, deep notes, rendered as "kraah" or "kaah" are uttered; they have been likened to some of the calls made by crows.

DISTRIBUTION: It breeds in Europe, Asia, Africa, North America, Australia and New Zealand. In our area it has been recorded rarely on Lakes George and Burley Griffin. It is probably nomadic, rather than migratory, although coastal and island breeding colonies are vacated in winter, and there have been movements of banded birds from northern Tasmania to the mainland in winter.

HABITS: The Caspian Tern is solitary or in pairs, except in the breeding season. It is most common on sea-coasts, coastal lagoons and estuaries, but also occurs inland on the larger rivers, lakes and lagoons. It looks gull-like in flight, but is much less buoyant in the air than other terns; its wing beats are deep and deliberate. It roosts on the ground, usually with other terns and gulls.

BREEDING: The eggs are laid on the ground, on sand or pebbly banks, or on small sandy islands in estuaries and inlets. Sometimes eggs are laid in hollows scooped in the centre of a plant, such as pigface. The species usually breeds in colonies. The eggs are oval, coarse-grained and dull. The ground colour is stone-grey or light brown, sparsely blotched with greyish-black and brown. The average dimensions are $63 \times 45$ mm. The clutch is one or two, very occasionally three. The incubation time is about twenty-five days.

FEEDING: The Caspian Tern stoop-dives for its food — small to medium-sized fish in coastal seas and shallow freshwaters. It also takes the eggs and young of some shore and land birds. (W.B.H.)

## PIGEONS AND DOVES

Although its members have great diversity in form and colour, the pigeon family is a fairly compact one and all are easily recognised by the soft, dense plumage, tight bodies, small heads and the shape of the bill. Many live on the ground and some nest on it but the majority build flimsy nests of twigs. All lay one or two pure white eggs. Both parents incubate and care for the young. The young are fed by regurgitation. Most pigeons have a conspicuous bowing display and most utter booming or cooing calls.

The family is large and cosmopolitan and comprises 255 species. Of these twenty-three are native to Australia and there are also three introductions. Despite this relatively rich representation of pigeons, they are not so obvious a feature as in many Northern Hemisphere countries where pigeons in the sky are very prominent. In Australia the only places where pigeons are conspicuous overhead are near towns and these are the introduced homing pigeons. Many Australian pigeons are ground dwellers and can be very numerous and still not obvious; those that are not ground dwellers generally live below the canopy of dense forests.

In Australia the pigeons can be divided into two groups; a group of arboreal, fruit eating birds, many of them brilliantly coloured, that live in the rainforests of the east coast, and a group of ground living, seed eating pigeons that occupy all the available habitats of the continent and provide a remarkable example of adaptation. Some that live in desert grasslands have become to look so much like sandgrouse that some years ago it was seriously debated as to whether they were really sandgrouse or pigeons.

The highlands, however, are very much lacking in pigeons, both in species and numbers. There are two common breeding species, four uncommon visitors and two of the introductions. This is as poor a pigeon list as for any part of the continent.

## Family Columbidae — Pigeons and Doves
## PEACEFUL DOVE *Geopelia placida*

PLATE XV

IDENTIFICATION: Length, 20 cm. General colour above, dark grey each feather *cross barred with black*; throat, light grey; breast, light grey streaked with black; remainder of under-parts, creamy white; tail, dark grey above, black below; outer feathers white tipped; bill, pale blue; legs and feet, pink; iris, white. The sexes are similar. The juveniles are mottled rather than striped or barred.

VOICE: The usual sound heard is the contact call, a loud melodious "coo", often described as "doodle-do". There is also a soft single "coo" and a plaintive "coo coo-coo". During the bowing display there is a rapidly rolling "coo".

DISTRIBUTION: It has an extensive range from the Murchison River, Western Australia, around the northern and eastern coastal and near inland districts to South Australia. It is most numerous in the wet tropics but is quite rare in the high country, although small colonies do exist throughout. It is rarely seen in the Australian Capital Territory but is abundant on the coast a few kilometres to the east.

It is essentially a bird of the open forests but also comes into gardens and towns, where it is common.

HABITS: Peaceful Doves are well named; they are nearly always found in pairs or small groups on bare soil or roadsides walking around oblivious of the observer. They rise with a distinct whirr but seldom travel far before landing again, usually in a tree. They are very social and in the non-breeding season gather and travel in small flocks.

BREEDING: Like many other members of the family it breeds at any time of the year and, when it is abundant, nests can be found throughout the year except in the coldest months. However, in northern Australia most nests are found after the beginning of the wet season in November and December, and in southern Australia in the spring, August to October. Several successive broods may be reared by the same pair. The nest is very frail and small; it is built of twigs and is a flat saucer seldom more than about eight centimetres in diameter. It is placed in a horizontal fork or in a clump of twigs up to ten metres from the ground. Unless the bird is brooding the nest is very difficult to see. Two pure white eggs are laid; they are oval in shape and measure 21–25 mm × 15–19 mm.

FEEDING: It feeds entirely on the ground on small seeds and herbs. (H.J.F.)

## DIAMOND DOVE *Geopelia cuneata*

PLATE XV

IDENTIFICATION: Length, 20 cm. Male: general colour above, grey-brown; wings *marked with small circular white spots*; chin, throat and breast, light grey; abdomen, creamy white; tail, dark grey above; underside of tail, dark grey, outer feathers, white; bill, black; legs and feet, flesh-pink; iris, red; skin around eyes very prominent and red. Females similar but very much browner on the wings. In juveniles the wings are not spotted but are mottled grey and black.

DISTRIBUTION: It is distributed throughout the continent but is mainly a bird of the interior and seldom visits the better watered coastal districts. Its inclusion in the list for our area is based on rare vagrants but there has been no recent record. Inland it is most numerous in the thin mulga woodlands of the desert fringe; throughout its range it prefers open woodlands.

VOICE: The usual sounds heard are two rather different "coos". The first, usually heard at dawn is a low, sad, double note "coo-coo" repeated several times. The other is a double note with the emphasis on the first "cor-coo" usually repeated once or twice; it is nasal in quality. In display there is a loud, emphatic "coorh" with a rolling quality uttered during the bow.

HABITS: It is a very quiet and inconspicuous bird even when very numerous. It is usually found near sources of permanent water, which it visits frequently throughout the day. It is one of the earliest birds to call in the desert mornings and its mournful note is heard before dawn and, with those of the Crested Bellbird, are the epitome of the bird sounds of the desert fringe. It spends the early morning feeding and most of the remainder of the day quietly sitting in the bushes.

BREEDING: In the inland it breeds at any time of the year and, although there is response to rainfall, nests are found also in the driest periods. There are no breeding records from our area. The nest is a very frail platform of fine sticks, through which the eggs can be seen, placed in a bush seldom more than two metres from the ground. The two eggs of the clutch are pure white and glossy, measuring 18 to 21 mm × 14 to 17 mm; they are almost round in many cases. The incubation period is about thirteen days.

FEEDING: It feeds entirely on the ground on small seeds. (H.J.F.)

## FOREST BRONZEWING *Phaps chalcoptera*
PLATE XV

DENTIFICATION: Length, 33 cm. Male: general colour above, brown; *forehead, white or buff*; a distinct light line below eye; throat, pale brown; remainder of under-parts, brown with distinct pinkish tinge; underside of tail, dark grey; wings, dark grey with a brilliant bronze green area; bill, black; legs and feet, pink; iris, reddish. The female is similar but the forehead colour is less prominent; in juveniles it is grey.

VOICE: A soft and very deep series of "ooms", with considerable resonance, it is heard throughout the day but is very difficult to locate.

DISTRIBUTION: The Forest Bronzewing is found throughout the continent avoiding only the rainforests. It is, however, most numerous in the arid and semi-arid zones and is distributed throughout the whole of our area in small numbers. It is very nomadic and moves about a lot in response to changing food availability. The most marked and obvious movement is in winter when numbers of the birds leave the ranges to live and feed in the lower, more open country. At this time they become not uncommon in the city of Canberra itself and can be found in streets and public parks feeding under the ornamental plantings of *Acacia*. These birds remain in the city throughout the winter but are rarely seen in summer.

HABITS: It is nearly always seen singly or in pairs walking along bush tracks or roadsides or flying swiftly and low through the forest. It is very wary, flushes with a loud wing clap and usually travels a considerable distance before landing in a tree though it does sometimes pitch to the ground. Unless disturbed it spends most of the day in the one small area feeding and roosting but at last light or just after it flies to water, sometimes travelling a long distance. It lands some distance from the water, studies the area then walks in, drinks and flies silently away.

BREEDING: In the inland it breeds throughout the year and nests are found in every month. In our area no doubt the same situation exists as nests have been found in both winter and summer. The nest is a flat

152

saucer of fine sticks twelve to fifteen or sometimes up to twenty-five centimetres in diameter. It is placed on a horizontal fork or at the base of a branch and is seldom more than three metres from the ground. The two pure white eggs are elliptical and glossy and measure about $33 \times 24$ mm. Each pair raises two or three broods in the year if conditions are suitable.

FEEDING: It feeds entirely on the ground and eats a wide variety of seeds and berries. It is particularly partial to the seeds of *Acacia* and of saffron thistle, and visits stubble fields if these are near forested ridges. It also eats considerable quantitities of the leaves and seeds of clovers and medics. (H.J.F.)

## BRUSH BRONZEWING *Phaps elegans*
PLATE XV

IDENTIFICATION: Length, 30 cm. General colour above, brown; *nape and sides of neck, rufous*; crown, blue-grey; chin, chestnut; remainder of under-parts, blue-grey; there is a rufous line below the eye; wings, rich chestnut with metallic bronze green speculum; bill, black; legs and feet, pink; iris, brown. The female only differs in that the forehead is grey.

VOICE: A low, mournful "coo" with a higher pitch and lower resonance than that of the Forest Bronzewing. It is commonly heard in the late afternoon.

DISTRIBUTION: It extends from about Fraser Island off the Queensland coast, down the coastal plains to South Australia and is widely distributed in Tasmania. In Western Australia it has a restricted range in the south-west corner. Its true status in our area is not known but small numbers are regularly encountered in the region. Perhaps they are nomadic from the coast or perhaps small local breeding populations exist. It has a predominantly coastal range and is overlapped throughout most of it by the Forest Bronzewing. Although they do occur in the same place there is a tendency towards separation by habitat. The Brush Bronzewing perfers heath and the denser coastal scrubs but the Forest Bronzewing, where it is in contact with the Brush Bronzewing in coastal areas, prefers the drier, more open, tall forests.

HABITS: The general behaviour is similar to that of the Forest Bronzewing but it is probably more confiding and that would not be really difficult.

BREEDING: The breeding season is not well recorded. The nest is similar to that of the Forest Bronzewing in structure and location but is sometimes placed on the ground in thick scrub. The eggs are also very similar in size, 31 × 24 mm, and appearance to those of that species; the incubation period is fifteen to eighteen days. The clutch is two. A possible wild hybrid between the two species has been reported in Tasmania.

FEEDING: It feeds on the ground and secures seeds and berries but, as with the other pigeons, there are no detailed data. I was surprised recently to receive a complaint that Brush Bronzewings were hindering re-afforestation work in Tasmania by eating the planted seed. (H.J.F.)

## CRESTED PIGEON *Ocyphaps lophotes*

PLATE XV

IDENTIFICATION: Length, 33 cm. Back and rump, grey brown; head, grey with *a long erect crest*; wings, pale brown with prominent black bars and a metallic green and purple speculum; under-parts, pale blue-grey; bill, black; legs and feet, red; iris, orange. The sexes are similar.

VOICE: A loud, startled "wok" is the usual call heard.

DISTRIBUTION: The Crested Pigeon is a widely distributed inland species and is found throughout the continent except in the extreme south-west and north. It occurs on the east coast in several places but some of these populations are known to have developed since settlement cleared the coastal forests. It prefers lightly timbered country and is seldom found far from water. The western edge of our area touches its range but it only penetrates the Australian Capital Territory as rare vagrants. One of these "rare vagrants" lived outside an aviary containing other Crested Pigeons, in Canberra. Some years ago, however, it was quite common near Canberra, perhaps as the result of an earlier irruption.

HABITS: It is usually found in small parties hurrying across the ground with crests bobbing and, when disturbed, flies with a clatter of wings to cluster on dead timber before making off with swift direct flight. In flight the wings make a loud, characteristic and musical whistle. The flight is characteristic, a few beats of the wing and then a glide, then a few more wingbeats and so on. On landing the tail is momentarily swung up and over the back as the body swings forward and downwards.

BREEDING: West of our area some Crested Pigeons breed in every month of the year but the greatest numbers are in spring when most of the population is involved. The usual type of pigeon's nest is built in a low shrubby bush or tree; usually it is low down but can be six metres from the ground. The two eggs are oval and measure 30 × 22 mm. The incubation period is nineteen days.

FEEDING: It feeds entirely on the ground on grass seeds and those of other plants. It consumes large numbers of leaves, and burrs of clovers and medics and sometimes caterpillars. (H.J.F.)

## WONGA PIGEON *Leucosarcia melanoleuca*
PLATE XV

IDENTIFICATION: Length, 39 cm. General colour above, *dark slate-grey*; forehead, white; chin, white; throat, slate-grey; remainder of under-parts, white mottled except on breast with black; *a broad white band extends from side of the neck* to join white of upper breast; bill, red; legs and feet, pink; iris, red. The sexes are similar. Juveniles resemble adults but lack the white forehead and are generally duller.

VOICE: A very loud, high pitched and resonant "coo" that is uttered for long periods throughout the day all year round. The syllables are deliberately spaced and there can be 250 or more in the one sequence. It can be heard at over two kilometres. It calls from tall trees, on the ground and often from the nest whilst brooding. There is a soft trill used during the bowing display.

DISTRIBUTION: It ranges down the east coast from North Queensland to the vicinity of Melbourne, Victoria. It is mainly found on the coast but extends up the slopes and onto the tablelands in a few places. Canberra is about the inland extremity of its range. It uses a wide variety of habitat including tropical and temperate rainforests, wet sclerophyll, dry eucalyptus ridges and sheltered gullies in heathlands and open forest. In our area it is usually in sheltered gullies in the ranges but can be seen and heard also on sheltered mountain-sides and sometimes in dry forest and even pine plantations.

HABITS: It is very wary and is more often heard than seen. It flushes with a very loud wing clap but seldom flies far before alighting on a limb where it sits quite motionless and can be very hard to detect. When it is seen on the ground it is walking rapidly with the head continually bobbing. Wonga Pigeons live on the ground and seldom fly unless disturbed but the flight is powerful. They are usually in pairs and seldom more than three or four are together but con-centrations do occur near water in dry weather.

BREEDING: The breeding season is generally in the summer but too few nests have been found to accurately delimit it. There are, however, two very distinct periods of territorial calling in the ranges, one late in spring and one early in autumn, which raises the possibility that it rears more than one brood. The nest is the usual flimsy saucer placed in a tree, usually low down but sometimes ten metres from the ground. The two eggs measure about 34 × 28 mm.

FEEDING: It feeds entirely on the ground on fallen seed, berries and a few insects; captive birds have shown a very much greater preference for fruit than is usual among ground pigeons. In early happier days on the New South Wales north coast it hindered pioneer corn plantings by congregating on them in numbers and destroying the seed and young plants. (H.J.F.)

## SPOTTED TURTLEDOVE *Streptopelia chinensis*
PLATE XV

IDENTIFICATION: Length, 23 cm. General colour above, grey brown but for back and sides of *lower neck and nape which are black spotted with white*; under-parts, light brown with chestnut tinge; tail, dark brown above, below, black each feather tipped with white; bill, grey-black; legs and feet, red; iris, yellow. The sexes are similar, but juveniles are duller and lack the spotted black collar.

VOICE: The courting note of the male is "kookeroo kookeroo..." with the accent slightly on the last syllable; there is one syllable at each bow. At other times the contact call is a slow, drowsy coo, "kookoo kroo kroo..." of six or seven syllables.

DISTRIBUTION: This bird was introduced from Asia to Australia in about 1870 and since then there have been several introductions to various parts of the continent; the last known being in Queensland in 1912. It has now spread throughout the coastal districts of the eastern states, including Tasmania, and in south-west Western Australia. In Western Australia it is restricted to the parks and gardens of Perth and a few large country towns but in the east it is very widespread in towns and has invaded a few of the more highly developed agricultural districts, where it comes in contact with, and perhaps competes with, the native Bar-shouldered Dove *Geopelia humeralis*. In the large cities it is one of the commonest birds. It is apparently still spreading, has reached Goulburn in our area and occasional vagrants appear in Canberra. In India it is a bird of "dry jungles of low country", a very different habitat to that occupied here.

HABITS: It is usually found in city parks and streets roosting in ornamental trees and to a visitor from the country its call is one of the characteristic sounds of capital cities, being heard at all times in all places. When it flies the tail is spread showing the prominent white outer feathers until it is well aloft. It has a quite spectacular courtship flight, soaring high over the buildings and then suddenly swooping down.

BREEDING: Nests are found in every month but are most common in spring and summer. The nest itself is a flat platform, fifteen centimetres in diameter, of a few sticks placed in a low bush or tree up to six metres from the ground. The two eggs are pure white and oval, measuring 29 to 30 × 21 to 24 mm. The incubation period is sixteen days.

FEEDING: It feeds entirely on the ground on small seeds, insects and city refuse. (H.J.F.)

## DOMESTIC PIGEON *Columba livia*
PLATE XV

IDENTIFICATION: Length, 34 cm. General plumage very variable in colour. Forty to fifty per cent of the feral pigeons in Canberra are similar to the ancestral Rock Dove of Europe. Head, dark bluish-grey; neck and breast, dark blue-grey with green and purple sheen; back, most upper-wing coverts, abdomen and upper legs, light bluish-grey; under-wing coverts and rump, white; two black bars on upper-wing; primaries, dark slate-grey; tail, dark slate-grey with black terminal bar; bill, black; cere, white; legs and feet, red; claws, black; iris, orange. Plumage colour varies irregularly from black through grey, blue and brown to white in individual birds almost anywhere on the body. Some individuals have feathers extending down onto the lower legs and even feet. The sexes are similar. Juveniles differ by having cere, buff; legs and feet, reddish-brown; iris, dark brown.

VOICE: The male has a characteristic cooing call, "oo-roo-coo".

DISTRIBUTION: It occurs throughout the world mainly near human habitations. The ancestral Rock Dove frequented rocky offshore islands, alpine mountain tops and dry stony areas in western and southern Europe, northern Africa and southern Asia. In Australia feral pigeons occur in most towns and cities and especially near docks and railway yards. Undoubtedly they are descendants of strays from domestic flocks and, of lost homing pigeons. Interbreeding with domestic birds probably maintains the high percentage of odd

157

coloured birds against the selective forces in the environment which tend to cause feral flocks to revert to the ancestral colour pattern.

HABITS: Flight is rapid and frequently it glides on horizontal wings. In display flights near the nest "clacking sounds" are made with the wings and they often glide with the wings forming a "V". They tend to roost on wide ledges of old-fashioned buildings, which are sheltered from prevailing winds.

BREEDING: The nest is made of sticks in sheltered locations on and in buildings, on seaside cliffs, on rocky offshore islands, and in tree cavities. They breed in our area throughout the year but during the hot summer months most chicks fail to survive due to heat exposure, mainly from hot metal roofs behind ornamental stone parapets. Rain showers wash nests, droppings and leaves down the gutters to the drain pipes which tend to become blocked by this debris. When the pipes block up, the parapets retain almost two metres of water behind them on the roof and the first sign of this happening is water leaking into the building. Elimination of this type of roof design would remove most of the available nest sites for pigeons in Canberra. The clutch size varies from one to three and is usually two. Eggs are shiny white, and their average size is 36 × 28 mm. The incubation period is about fifteen days and the chicks remain in the nest for about thirty-one days.

FEEDING: They forage for seeds, cereals and bread scraps at railway yards, parks, sports fields, beaches, city streets and household refuse tips. After harvest they pick up fallen seeds in wheat fields. (G.F.vT.)

# LORIKEETS, COCKATOOS AND PARROTS

Probably no group of birds is more familiar to even the most casual observer than the parrots. Their rich, colourful plumage, amusing mannerisms and ability to imitate the human voice have made them popular in captivity for many centuries.

They are sharply set apart from all other groups. One conspicuous characteristic is the short, blunt, rounded bill with the curved upper mandible fitting neatly over the lower. It is attached to the large, heavy skull by means of a "hinge-like" arrangement thus allowing extra movement of both mandibles. The resulting increase in leverage enables parrots to crush the seeds and nuts that constitute the diet of so many species. The tongue is thick and prehensile, and in some species is furnished with elongated papillae for extracting nectar from blossoms. On the foot two toes point forward and two are turned backwards.

Parrots vary in size from the tiny pigmy parrots of only ten centimetres or less in length to the large black cockatoos, which average almost seventy centimetres, and the giant macaws with a length of about 100 centimetres. There are approximately 350 species distributed throughout the tropics and the Southern Hemisphere, principally in Africa, Australasia and South America. The greatest number of species is found in Brazil, but in Australia there is more diversity of types. The cockatoos and lorikeets are restricted to this region and only five of the genera found in Australia are not endemic to the continent. In our area there are eight resident species and nine uncommon visitors. One other, the Purple-crowned Lorikeet, also probably visits the area sometimes but has not been reliably reported. Mathews recorded the Red-tailed Black Cockatoo around Canberra but this was probably a misidentification.

Family Loriidae — Lorikeets
## RAINBOW LORIKEET *Trichoglossus haematodus*
PLATE XVI

IDENTIFICATION: Length, 29 cm, the largest lorikeet. General colour above, green; *head, mauve-blue*; narrow yellow-green nuchal collar; breast and flanks, orange-red; abdomen, dark violet-blue; lower under-parts, yellowish-green; under-wing coverts, yellow and orange; tail, green above and dusky yellow below; bill, coral; legs, greenish-grey; iris, orange-red. The sexes are alike. Juveniles have pale brown irides and brownish-black bills.

VOICE: A sharp, rolling screech. Feeding is accompanied by a high-pitched chattering.

DISTRIBUTION: Northern and eastern Australia from the Kimberleys, Western Australia, to Cape York Peninsula, Queensland, eastern South Australia and Kangaroo Island. A rare vagrant in Tasmania. Also widely distributed in the New Guinea region. In New South Wales it is restricted to the coast and adjacent tablelands and is an uncommon visitor to the eastern parts of our area.

HABITS: In most areas it is nomadic, its arrival coinciding with the flowering of eucalypts. Its presence is generally betrayed by the continual screeching. In our area the Rainbow Lorikeet is seen in pairs or small parties, but elsewhere congregates in flocks and frequents the flowering eucalypts, climbing amongst the branches extracting nectar from the blossoms. It is often observed in the company of other lorikeets. When feeding they remain oblivious to the approach of an intruder. The direct flight is very swift.

159

BREEDING: To some extent climatic conditions and the availability of food govern the breeding season, but most nesting takes place between August and November. The nest is in a hollow limb or hole in a tree, usually a living eucalypt, generally at a considerable height. The two white, rounded eggs are laid on decayed wood dust lining the bottom of the hollow. They average 28 × 23 mm. Although the male may spend a great deal of time in the nesting hollow it seems that he does not assist with incubation. Incubation lasts about twenty-six days and it is a further eight weeks before the young leave the nest.

FEEDING: The Rainbow Lorikeet feeds on nectar from the blossoms of eucalypts, various native trees and shrubs, particularly banksias and some introduced trees, and also eats fruits, berries and seeds, being frequently seen clinging to the seeding heads of grass-trees. In our area the species is not common enough to be troublesome in orchards, but elsewhere is considered a pest by fruit-growers. (J.M.F.)

## MUSK LORIKEET *Glossopsitta concinna*

IDENTIFICATION: Length, 22 cm. General colour, both above and below, green; forehead, lores and band behind the eyes, red; crown, blue; nape and mantle, bronze-brown; yellow patches on flanks; *under-wing coverts, yellowish-green*; tail, green above, below dusky yellow washed with orange-red at the base; *bill, black tipped coral*; legs, greenish-brown; iris, orange. The sexes are alike. Juveniles have black bills.
   May be distinguished from the Swift Parrot by the all-green under-parts and the yellowish-green under-wings; the latter is diagnostic in flight.

VOICE: A discordant screech. Distinguished from the call of the Rainbow Lorikeet by its noticeably higher pitch.

DISTRIBUTION: From southern Queensland to Tasmania, the Mt Lofty Ranges, in South Australia and Kangaroo Island. In New South Wales it is widely distributed from the coast to the western slopes. In our area it has been recorded at rare intervals, but the difficulty in distinguishing it from the Swift Parrot in the field could explain at least some of these reports. Care should be taken with identification, as the Swift Parrot is more likely to be seen in Canberra in winter.

HABITS: Similar to those of the Rainbow Lorikeet, with which it frequently associates. The direct flight is so swift that the whirring noise made by the wing beats can be heard as the bird passes overhead.

BREEDING: The breeding season is from August to December. The nest is in a hollow in a tall tree, usually a living eucalypt growing near water. The two white, rounded eggs are laid on decayed wood dust. They average 26 × 20 mm. The incubation time is approximately twenty-one days and only the female broods. The young leave the nest six weeks after hatching.

FEEDING: The feeding habits resemble those of the Rainbow Lorikeet. As well as nectar, fruits, berries and seeds are eaten. Flocks have been seen feeding on ripening wheat and sorghum crops. Where plentiful they are often troublesome in orchards. (J.M.F.)

## LITTLE LORIKEET *Glossopsitta pusilla*

PLATE XVI

IDENTIFICATION: Length, 16 cm, the smallest lorikeet. General colour, both above and below, green; forehead, lores and cheek-patches, red; nape and mantle, bronze-brown; under-wing coverts, green; tail, green above and dusky yellow below; bill, black; legs, greenish-grey; iris, yellow. The sexes are alike.

VOICE: A very high-pitched screech. Feeding is accompanied by a shrill chattering.

DISTRIBUTION: From northern Queensland to Tasmania and south-eastern South Australia. In New South Wales it is dispersed throughout the coastal districts, the adjacent tablelands and along the edge of the inland plains and is the lorikeet most frequently seen in our area. During autumn flocks have been reported from near Lake George. It prefers open forest and timber bordering water courses, but may also be found in mountain forests.

HABITS: This lorikeet is nomadic and often travels great distances searching for flowering eucalypts. In Canberra pairs or small parties are occasionally seen flying overhead but it is rarely found feeding within the city limits, except on Black Mountain and Mt Ainslie. When climbing amongst the branches of a eucalypt their small size and predominantly green plumage makes detection difficult even though the constant chattering leaves no doubts about their presence. It becomes fearless when feeding and is easy to approach. The direct flight is very swift, the wing beats producing a "whirring" noise.

BREEDING: The breeding season is from August to December. The nest is in a hollow or hole in a living eucalypt and three or four white, rounded eggs are laid on a layer of decayed wood dust. These average

$20 \times 17$ mm in size. Incubation lasts about eighteen days and only the female sits. Some thirty days after hatching the young leave the nest and remain with their parents to form the family parties frequently observed.

FEEDING: It feeds almost exclusively on nectar from the blossoms of native or introduced trees and shrubs but also eats native or cultivated fruits and berries. (J.M.F.)

## Family Cacatuidae — Cockatoos
# YELLOW-TAILED BLACK COCKATOO
*Calyptorhynchus funereus*

PLATE XVI

IDENTIFICATION: Length, 65 cm. General colour, brownish-black; ear coverts, bright yellow; feathers of the under-parts, margined with yellow giving a "barred" effect; across the outer tail feathers there is a broad yellow band marked with numerous brownish-black "flecks"; bill, dark grey; legs, brown; iris, dark brown. The female has a horn-coloured bill.

VOICE: A strange, drawn-out "kee-aah"; cannot be mistaken for that of any other species. When alarmed a harsh screech, not unlike that of the more familiar Sulphur-crested Cockatoo. A grating noise often accompanies feeding.

DISTRIBUTION: From northern Queensland to King Island and Tasmania, south-eastern South Australia west to Eyre Peninsula, and Kangaroo Island. In New South Wales it inhabits the forests of the coast and adjacent tablelands. In our region it is a bird of the mountain forests, but occasionally is seen in open country, especially near Lake George and to the west of Captain's Flat.

HABITS: Pairs or small flocks are usually seen flying across the mountain valleys or slowly moving from one tree to another along the highest ridges, their wailing cries always attracting attention. They are wary and difficult to approach. Most of the day is spent tearing into the branches of eucalypts or *Acacia* in search of the wood-boring larvae of cossid moths or feeding on the seeds of trees and shrubs. They are birds of the treetops and only rarely come to the ground. The flight is heavy and laboured with slow wing beats. Long distance flights are undertaken at a considerable height, the birds travelling far apart and calling continuously to each other. After alighting the short crest is raised and the tail fanned.

162

BREEDING: The breeding season is variable; eggs have been found as early as March and as late as January. The nest is in a large hollow in a tall tree, generally a living or dead eucalypt standing in a clearing in a mountain forest. Although two eggs are laid only one nestling is reared to maturity, the other failing to hatch or being neglected by the parents. The eggs are white, oval shaped and average 45 × 37 mm. Little is known about incubation or the rearing of the young. After leaving the nest the young is fed by the parents for many months.

The only breeding record for our area appears to be a report that in 1963 a nestling was taken from a hollow in a tree felled by forestry workers in the Brindabella Ranges.

FEEDING: It feeds largely on the larvae of cossid moths, which are dug out of the branches and exposed roots of eucalypts or *Acacia* with the massive bill. Smaller branches are sometimes chewed right through or subsequently break off during a windstorm. It also eats the seeds of eucalypts, *Banksia, Acacia* and introduced pines. Some minor damage in pine plantations has been reported by the Australian Capital Territory forestry authorities. (J.M.F.)

## GLOSSY COCKATOO *Calyptorhynchus lathami*

PLATE XXXV

IDENTIFICATION: Length 50 cm, smaller than other dark cockatoos except Gang-Gang. Male: general colour above, dull black; head and under-parts, dusky; outer tail feathers with broad red band; inner pair of feathers, black; short rounded crest; bill, grey; legs and feet, grey; iris, dark brown. Female: same as male, except that the red parts of the tail feathers have yellow outer edges, and narrow black barring; and there are some yellow feathers on the sides of head and neck. Juveniles are similar to the female but have some yellow spots on wings, and there is much less yellow on the head and neck.

VOICE: It has a prolonged, rather soft wheezing call.

DISTRIBUTION: The Glossy Cockatoo is found from south-eastern Queensland to far eastern Victoria, and there is an isolated population on Kangaroo Island, South Australia. It occurs in wet and dry eucalypt forests, woodland, and rainforest fringes, its distribution being strongly influenced by the presence of *Casuarina* trees.

In our region it is observed occasionally in the Tinderrys–Tharwa area. From March 1983 groups of up to fourteen birds have been seen on Mt Ainslie in Canberra, and the species may be a regular visitor to this area.

163

HABITS: The species is usually seen in pairs or small groups feeding quietly in *Casuarina* trees in the understorey of eucalypt forests. Occasionally groups of ten or more may be seen. They are seldom seen on the ground. They fly relatively slowly with slow wing beats. Glossy Cockatoos are confiding birds and usually allow a close approach.

BREEDING: The breeding season is in autumn and winter. The nest site is in a hollow limb or trunk of a tall, dead, forest tree. The entrance may be twenty metres above the ground. A single egg is laid in a slight depression in powdered decayed wood. The egg is oval and white and measures about $45 \times 34$ mm.

FEEDING: The staple food is the seeds of *Casuarina* trees but seeds of other kinds of forest trees may be eaten. The *Casuarina* seed-capsules are pulled from the branches and torn apart for the seeds. Plentiful shredded seed-capsules below *Casuarina* trees indicate their presence in an area. The clicking noise made by their mandibles when feeding also betrays their presence. (J.H.C.)

## GANG-GANG COCKATOO *Callocephalon fimbriatum*
PLATE XVI

IDENTIFICATION: Length, 35 cm. General colour, both above and below, grey; all feathers margined with greyish-white giving a "scaled" appearance; *head and filamented crest, flame red*; wing coverts, washed with green; bill, horn-coloured; legs, grey; iris, dark brown. Female has the head and crest grey and the feathers of the under-parts broadly margined with orange and yellow. Juveniles resemble the female, but males have the crest tipped with red.

VOICE: A prolonged, rasping screech ending with an upward inflection; it cannot be mistaken for any other species: When feeding a soft "growling".

DISTRIBUTION: South-eastern Australia from the Blue Mountains in New South Wales to the extreme south-eastern corner of South Australia. It inhabits the heavily timbered mountain ranges and nearby coastal valleys. In our area it breeds in the mountain forests, but during the non-breeding season may be found in almost all habitats.

HABITS: Because of its remarkable tameness and peculiar call-notes, it is one of the most conspicuous birds in Canberra during winter, when flocks come down from the mountains to feed in the trees or shrubs growing in the parks and gardens. Each year they may be seen feeding in the ornamental pine trees and *Pyracantha* hedges in the heart of the city. While feeding they become completely oblivious to the approach of an intruder and can almost be touched. By September they have returned to the mountains leaving behind only small parties of non-breeding birds, generally young of the previous year.

They come to the ground only to drink or to examine fallen pine cones. For no apparent reason feeding flocks suddenly leave a tree or bush, fly in wide circles overhead, screeching all the while, then return to the same tree and continue feeding as if there had been no interruption. During the hottest part of the day they either sit amongst the branches of a eucalypt for hours without moving or sidle up to each other and indulge in intensive mutual preening. The flight is heavy and laboured with slow, sweeping wing beats.

BREEDING: The breeding season lasts from October to January. The nest is in a hollow limb or hole in a tree, usually in a decayed limb of a living eucalypt, at a great height. The birds generally enlarge and extend the hollow by chewing at the sides and scraping out the chips. On a layer of decayed wood dust and chips two white, rounded eggs are laid. They average 34 × 28 mm. Incubation lasts four weeks and both parents brood. The young leave the nest about seven weeks after hatching and are fed by the parents for a further four to six weeks.

FEEDING: It feeds largely on the seeds of eucalypts, wattles and native pine *Callitris* trees but has become very fond of the berries of hawthorn and *Pyracantha* bushes and the seeds of introduced pines. They are methodical feeders and will return to the same tree or bush each day until the food supply is exhausted. (J.M.F.)

## GALAH *Cacatua roseicapilla*

PLATE XVI

IDENTIFICATION: Length, 36 cm. Forehead and crown, white with pink bases; cheeks, nape, neck and *under-parts, deep pink*; back, wings and under-tail coverts, grey; rump and scapulars, very pale grey; tail, grey, light above, very dark below; naked skin around the eye, red; bill, horn-coloured; legs, grey; iris, dark brown. The female has a reddish iris. Juveniles are duller and have the breast washed with grey.

VOICE: A disyllabic, metallic screech; characteristic of the species. When squabbling a series of sharp, grating shrieks.

DISTRIBUTION: Throughout most of the Australian mainland, but chiefly in the interior. In New South Wales it is absent from the densely forested mountainous regions, but has extended its range through the open or cleared tablelands on to the coast. In our area it is widespread in all lightly-timbered areas below 1300 metres.

HABITS: Within the last fifty years the Galah has built up its numbers so rapidly in the Canberra district, where it was formerly a rare visitor, that it has now become one of our most common birds and even breeds in trees in suburban gardens. Pairs or flocks are usually seen on the ground searching for grass seeds or roosting in eucalypts, idly stripping leaves and nibbling twigs. On the ground they walk with an amusing waddling gait.

They are strong fliers and seem to delight in aerobatics. Soon after sunrise or during a rainstorm they are often seen twisting and turning between the trees and circling overhead, the pink and then the grey being exposed to the observer below. The flight is moderately fast with full, rhythmic wing beats.

BREEDING: The breeding season varies from June to November in the north of the continent to August to January in the south. The nest is in a hollow limb or hole in a living or dead tree, generally a eucalypt growing close to water. The bark is stripped from around the entrance and the bottom is lined with a layer of *Eucalyptus* leaves on which are laid two to five, normally three, white rounded eggs. They average $35 \times 25$ mm. Incubation lasts approximately four weeks and both parents brood. The young leave the nest five to six weeks after hatching. Throughout our area the begging cries of young Galahs sitting in the treetops is an integral part of the summer scene.

FEEDING: They feed on the seeds of grasses and shrubs, grain, nuts, berries, bulbous roots and corms and leaf buds and are particularly fond of clover seeds. In Canberra flocks often congregate on sports fields and lawns. Unfortunately, they also raid wheat crops causing considerable damage. (J.M.F.)

## SULPHUR-CRESTED COCKATOO *Cacatua galerita*

PLATE XVI

IDENTIFICATION: Length, 51 cm. General colour white; undersides of wings and tail, washed with yellow; bases of ear coverts, yellow; narrow, forward-curving crest, yellow; bill, grey-black; legs, grey; iris, dark brown. The sexes are alike.

VOICE: A loud, harsh screech. While roosting or preening a shrill, piping whistle.

DISTRIBUTION: Northern, eastern and south-eastern Australia from the Kimberleys in Western Australia to Tasmania and south-eastern South Australia. It also inhabits New Guinea and the adjacent islands and has been introduced to New Zealand. In New South Wales it is widely distributed from the coast to the western plains. In our area it is found in all habitats but prefers lightly-timbered areas below 1300 metres. In the Southern Alps many birds seem to leave the higher areas at the beginning of winter and return in September.

HABITS: A noisy, conspicuous bird seen in pairs during the breeding season or in flocks at other times. Is very wary and difficult to approach. While the flock is feeding a few birds perch in surrounding trees and screech loudly at the appearance of any intruder and immediately, the entire flock rises into the air.

Each flock has its own roosting site, which is rarely deserted even if long flights to feeding grounds become necessary. The noise in these roosting trees is great as birds jostle for positions and squabble with each other. It is long after sunset before the screeching subsides. Soon after sunrise the noise recommences when the birds fly off to feed.

Until mid-morning they are usually seen on the ground feeding on seeds. During the hottest part of the day they sit in trees near the feeding area idly stripping the leaves or bark. In the afternoon they feed again and then return to the permanent roosting trees for the night. Until the food supply is exhausted they come back every day to feed in the same area.

The flight comprises shallow wing beats interspersed with brief periods of motionless glide. Going to or coming from the roosting site they fly at a considerable height.

BREEDING: Throughout the southern parts of the continent the breeding season lasts from August to January, while in the north it may begin as early as May. In our area eggs are rarely laid before October. The nest is in a hollow limb or hole in a large tree, generally a eucalypt near water. It is not easy to locate a nest because at the approach of any intruder the sitting bird will leave the hollow quietly and remain unnoticed until she is flying overhead, screeching loudly. On a layer of decayed wood dust lining the bottom of the hollow two white, elliptical eggs are laid. They average 48 × 33 mm. Incubation lasts four weeks and both sexes brood. The young leave the nest approximately six weeks after hatching.

FEEDING: They feed on the seeds of grasses and herbaceous plants, grain, bulbous roots and corms, berries, nuts, leaf buds and insects and their larvae and unfortunately, cause considerable damage to

167

crops, particularly oats and maize. On the outskirts of Canberra they may be seen feeding on hawthorn berries. (J.M.F.)

## Family Polytelitidae — Long-tailed Parrots
## COCKATIEL *Nymphicus hollandicus*

PLATE XVI

IDENTIFICATION: Length, 30 cm. Male: general colour both above and below, grey; forehead, sides of the head and *the narrow tapering crest,* yellow; a bright orange spot below the eye; a white patch extending across the wing coverts; tail, dark grey becoming almost black on the undersides; bill, dark grey; legs, grey; iris, dark brown. Females are duller with the facial markings much reduced and the undersides of the tail feathers irregularly barred with yellow. Juveniles resemble the female.

In flight the white patches on the wings are diagnostic.

VOICE: A pleasant warbling call terminating with an upward inflection. Will usually be heard before the bird is sighted.

DISTRIBUTION: Widely distributed throughout the interior of Australia, but generally more numerous in the north. In New South Wales it is found west of the Dividing Range. In our area it occasionally visits the partly cleared lands in the western areas. Most of the pairs or odd birds seen in Canberra are almost certainly aviary escapees. Cockatiels are nomadic, their movements being largely governed by the availability of food and water. During periods of severe drought they approach the coast and may be seen as far east as our area.

HABITS: Pairs or small flocks are usually seen on the ground or amongst the outermost branches of a tree or shrub feeding on seeds. In the north they congregate in large flocks of up to several hundred birds. Their soft colouring makes them difficult to detect while foraging on the ground under the shade of a tree. Throughout the day they often undertake long flights from the feeding grounds to water. The flight is swift and direct. They have the strange habit of perching lengthwise along the stout limb of a dead tree.

BREEDING: The breeding season normally lasts from August to December, but nests can be found at any time of the year following rains. The nest is in a hollow limb or hole in a tree, preferably a large hollow in a dead eucalypt standing near water. On decayed wood dust lining the bottom of the hollow four to seven, usually five, white, rounded eggs are laid. They average 26 × 20 mm. Incubation lasts twenty-three days and both parents brood. The young leave the nest approximately four weeks after hatching. Young males acquire the bright yellow facial markings when six months old, but the barred tail is retained until the first complete moult.

FEEDING: Feeds on the seeds of grasses, herbaceous plants, trees and shrubs. Occasionally attacks ripening wheat. (J.M.F.)

## KING PARROT *Alisterus scapularis*

PLATE XVII

IDENTIFICATION: Length, 41 cm. Male: mantle, back and wings, dark green; scapulars, pale green; lower back, rump and narrow band on the hind neck, deep blue; head, neck and under-parts, scarlet; tail, bluish-black; bill, red tipped with black; legs, grey; iris, yellow. The female has the head and breast dull green; tail, dark green and black; scapulars, dark green; bill, greyish-black; iris, white. Juveniles resemble the female but have pale brown eyes.

VOICE: A harsh metallic note repeated four or five times. Males also utter a soft, disyllabic, bell-like call.

DISTRIBUTION: Eastern Australia from Cooktown and the Atherton Tablelands, northern Queensland, to southern Victoria. In New South Wales restricted to the coast and adjacent tablelands. In our area it is confined to the forests of the ranges during most of the year, but in winter descends to the lowlands. King Parrots, including fully-coloured males, may be seen all year round in the suburbs of Canberra where parks and gardens are well established. Their numbers are considerably augmented with birds from the ranges during winter.

HABITS: Pairs or small flocks are usually seen feeding amongst the outermost branches of eucalypts, the shrill call-notes always betraying their presence. They are rather wary and decidedly more difficult to approach than are the rosellas. When disturbed they take to the wing calling loudly. The flight is heavy and laboured with slow, rhythmic wing beats.

BREEDING: The breeding season extends from October to January. The nest is in a hollow limb or hole in a living or dead eucalypt. A marked preference is shown for a large hollow in the trunk of a tall tree. The bottom of the hollow may be near ground level and the entrance at a height of ten metres or more. On a layer of decayed wood dust three to five, usually three, white, rounded eggs are laid. These average 33 × 28 mm. Incubation lasts approximately twenty days and

169

only the female broods. The young leave the nest about five weeks after hatching. Towards late autumn young birds tend to band together in flocks. Adult male plumage is acquired through a slow moult beginning when the bird is a little over sixteen months old and continuing for a further fourteen or fifteen months, but males have been found breeding while in immature plumage.

FEEDING: Feeds on the seeds of shrubs and trees, particularly *Acacia* and eucalypts, berries, nuts, fruits, nectar and vegetable matter. A favoured food is the acorns of the introduced pin oak *Quercus palustris* grown extensively in Canberra streets and parks. They are fond of cultivated fruits. Unfortunately, they also raid maize crops to feed on the ripening grain. (J.M.F.)

## SUPERB PARROT *Polytelis swainsonii*

PLATE XVII

IDENTIFICATION: Length, 40 cm. Male: upper-parts, including upper-side of the *long, narrow tail*, rich green; forehead, throat and cheeks, yellow; a wide scarlet band on the fore neck; under-parts, yellowish-green; underside of the tail, black; bill, coral; legs, mealy-grey; iris, yellow. The female has sides of the head pale bluish-green; chin and throat, greyish-green; thighs, orange-red; underside of tail, rose-pink. Juveniles resemble the female.

VOICE: A prolonged warbling call ending abruptly; characteristic of the genus. May be distinguished from the call of the Cockatiel by its deeper tone and the absence of an upward inflection at the end.

DISTRIBUTION: Restricted to riparian areas in northern and southern New South Wales and northern Victoria. The Castlereagh-Namoi Rivers population in the north seems to be isolated from that of the Murray-Murrumbidgee-Lachlan Rivers region in the south. Our area is on the eastern fringe of the range of the southern population, hence the species is more frequently seen in the western parts. Near Canberra it has been found breeding at Ginninderra and Gundaroo. Despite the restricted range, this species appears to be partly nomadic, its arrival in some areas coinciding with the flowering of eucalypts.

HABITS: The Superb Parrot is generally seen singly, in pairs, or in small parties on the ground foraging for grass seeds or amongst the branches of a flowering eucalypt searching for nectar. When a lone bird is seen it will almost inevitably be a fully-coloured male. Normally, they are rather timid and will not allow a close approach. The swift, direct flight seems effortless, the narrow, pointed wings being moved with deliberate precision. On long flights the birds travel at a considerable height.

BREEDING: The breeding season lasts from September to December. The nest is in a hollow limb or hole in a tree, generally a living eucalypt growing near water, and is almost invariably at a great height. On decayed wood dust lining the bottom of the hollow four to six white, rounded eggs are laid. These average 28 × 24 mm. Incubation lasts twenty-three days and only the female broods. During this time, and for the first ten days after the young hatch, the male feeds his sitting mate at frequent intervals throughout the day, but thereafter usually assists by feeding the young. The young leave the nest about four weeks after hatching. When about six months old young males show some yellow on the face and red on the fore neck; the full adult plumage is gradually acquired over the next six to nine months.

FEEDING: Feeds on the seeds of grasses, shrubs and trees, especially *Acacia* and eucalypts, nectar, fruits, berries and leaf buds. They occasionally visit farmlands to feed on grain, particularly wheat and oats. (J.M.F.)

Family Platycercidae — Broad-tailed Parrots
## CRIMSON ROSELLA *Platycercus elegans*
PLATE XVII

IDENTIFICATION: Length, 36 cm. General colour both above and below, rich crimson; violet-blue cheek-patches; feathers of back, black edged with crimson; wings and under-wing coverts, blue; tail, green strongly washed with blue; bill, greyish-horn; legs, grey; iris, brown. The sexes are alike. Juveniles are dull green with red on crown, breast and under-tail coverts.

VOICE: A piping whistle of three notes on an ascending scale. When alarmed a series of shrill screeches and while feeding in the treetops a soft chattering. All calls are of a deeper tone than those of the Eastern Rosella.

DISTRIBUTION: From Atherton Tablelands, Queensland, to south-eastern South Australia and Kangaroo Island. Introduced to Norfolk Island. In New South Wales it is confined to the coast and adjacent tablelands and in our area is distributed in the more heavily timbered habitats. During the winter flocks of immatures come into the open forest to feed. It is not uncommon in the parks and gardens of Canberra.

HABITS: A brilliantly-coloured, conspicuous bird usually seen on the ground searching for grass seeds or amongst the branches of eucalypts feeding on blossoms and seeds. Immatures tend to band together in flocks, but adults remain in pairs or small parties. They are quite confiding and will allow a close approach. In summer during the hottest part of the day they sit amongst the foliage of a eucalypt, chattering softly or idly stripping twigs and leaves from their perch. Frequently seen in the company of the Eastern Rosella, but when a mixed flock is disturbed the species separate in flight and take cover independently, often in opposite directions. It travels close to the ground with undulating flight, gliding upwards into the trees. When alighting the tail is fanned.

BREEDING: The breeding season extends from September to January, but on the Southern Tablelands eggs are not laid until November.

Nests are in a hollow limb or hole in a living or dead eucalypt and may be either a metre or so from the ground or at a great height. On decayed wood dust lining the bottom of the hollow five to eight, usually five, white, rounded eggs are laid. These average 29 × 24 mm. Only the female sits and during the three weeks incubation period she leaves the nest for brief periods in the morning to feed with, and be fed by, her mate. The young leave the nest about five weeks after hatching. During the winter red feathers appear on the head, rump and under-parts; the adult plumage is acquired when approximately sixteen months old.

FEEDING: Feeds on the seeds of grasses, shrubs and trees, especially eucalypts, fruits, berries, nuts, nectar and insects and their larvae. They are fond of the seeds of clover and scotch thistle. Throughout the fruit-growing areas near Batlow and Tumut they raid orchards to feed on ripening apples and pears. In Canberra they are frequently seen feeding on the berries of hawthorn and *Pyracantha* bushes; the latter is widely used for ornamental hedges. (J.M.F.)

## EASTERN ROSELLA *Platycercus eximius*
PLATE XVII

IDENTIFICATION: Length, 32 cm. Head and upper breast, red; lower breast, yellow merging into pale green on the abdomen; vent and under-tail coverts, red; cheek-patches, white; feathers of the back, black broadly margined with bright pale green; rump and upper-tail coverts, green; wings and under-wing coverts, blue; tail, green washed with blue; bill, greyish-horn; legs, grey; iris, brown. Female and juveniles are much duller with less red on the head and breast.

VOICE: A tuneful whistling call on an ascending scale and a disyllabic piping note. A shrill metallic screech when alarmed. All calls are very similar to those of the Crimson Rosella, but may be distinguished by their noticeably higher pitch.

DISTRIBUTION: Widely distributed in south-eastern Australia from southern Queensland to Tasmania and south-eastern South Australia. Has been introduced into New Zealand. In New South Wales it is distributed from the coast west to the fringe of the inland plains. In our area it is abundant in lightly-timbered and open habitats, being replaced in the forests by the Crimson Rosella. It is rarely found above 1200 metres, whereas the Crimson Rosella ranges up to more than 1800 metres.

HABITS: Pairs or small parties can be flushed from the ground along roads in most parts of our area and they are not infrequently killed by cars. In Canberra they are commonly seen in the parks and gardens feeding on *Pyracantha* berries. Most of the day is spent on the ground foraging for seeds of grasses or amongst the branches of a eucalypt searching for seeds and nectar. They are not timid and will allow a close approach. They are often observed in the company of other parrots, particularly the Crimson Rosella and the Red-rumped Parrot. The flight resembles that of the Crimson Rosella.

BREEDING: The breeding season is from August through to January, but in our area eggs are not laid until late October. The nest is similar to that of the Crimson Rosella. The clutch comprises four to seven, usually five, white, rounded eggs. These average 27 × 22 mm. Incubation lasts about twenty-two days and only the female broods. The young leave the nest approximately thirty days after hatching and generally remain with their parents for many months. In the autumn and winter more red feathers are acquired, but full adult plumage is not assumed until the first complete moult when a little over twelve months old.

FEEDING: They feed on the seeds of grasses, shrubs and trees, especially eucalypts and *Acacia*, berries, nuts, fruits, nectar and insects and their larvae and are troublesome in the fruit-growing areas near Batlow and Tumut. On the other hand they are responsible for the destruction of great quantities of seeds of thistles and weeds. (J.M.F.)

### RED-RUMPED PARROT *Psephotus haematonotus*
PLATE XVII

IDENTIFICATION: Length, 25 cm. Male: crown and upper breast, rich green; forehead, cheek-patches, back, wings and upper-tail coverts, bluish-green; under-wing coverts and edges of primaries, blue; shoulder-patches and lower breast, yellow; *rump, red*; abdomen, the vent and under-tail coverts, white; tail, green and blue above, white below; bill, black; legs, grey; iris, brown. The females have head, back and wings pale olive-green; rump, upper-tail coverts and upperside of the tail, green; shoulder-patches and edges of primaries, pale blue; under-parts, white; bill, grey. Juveniles resemble the adults, but young males are much duller.

VOICE: A shrill, disyllabic whistle; also a pleasant warbling call, almost a song. When squabbling a soft chattering is emitted.

DISTRIBUTION: South-eastern Australia, chiefly the interior of southern Queensland, New South Wales and south-eastern South Australia. Also found in the Lake Eyre region in northern South Australia. In New South Wales it is widely distributed from the table-lands west to the Darling River and its tributaries and seems to be extending its range towards the coast, particularly in the north and in the Hunter River districts. Around Canberra it is widespread in lightly-timbered areas below 1000 metres. Often seen in the parks and gardens of Canberra, especially along the shores of Lake Burley Griffin and in the National University grounds.

HABITS: A brightly-coloured, familiar bird generally found in pairs or small flocks but in western New South Wales, where the species is more abundant, large flocks are often encountered. Much of the time is spent on the ground searching for grass seeds. They frequently congregate around haystacks or in stubble paddocks to feed on fallen grain. On the ground they are very active, individuals scurrying here and there and fluttering from the shade of one tree to that of another. Within the flock the pair bond is strong and when roosting in trees during the heat of the day, males will be seen sidling up to their mates and initiating mutual preening. During the breeding season males move about in small parties while the females brood. The flight is relatively swift and direct with some undulation, but this is not so marked as in the flight of the rosellas.

BREEDING: The breeding season is from August through to December or January, but in our area eggs are rarely laid before October. The nest is in a hollow limb or hole in a living or dead eucalypt, preference being shown for a tree near water. The bottom of the hollow is lined with a layer of decayed wood dust on which are laid four to seven, usually five, white, rounded eggs. These average 23 × 19 mm. Incubation lasts about twenty days and only the female broods. She sits very tightly and can sometimes be lifted from the hollow. The male feeds her at frequent intervals throughout the day. The young leave the nest thirty days after hatching and remain with the parents for some time. Adult plumage is acquired through a complete moult when three to four months old.

FEEDING: Feeds on the seeds of grasses and herbaceous plants. Grit and small pieces of charcoal are taken to aid digestion. They are fond of green food, particularly crowsfoot and thistles of various kinds. (J.M.F.)

## BLUE-WINGED PARROT *Neophema chrysostoma*

IDENTIFICATION: Length, 21 cm. Male: nape, mantle, back, rump and upper-tail coverts, dull olive-green; *crown, dull golden-yellow*; frontal band, deep blue; under-wing coverts and wings, rich blue; throat and breast, pale green; remainder of underside, yellow; central tail feathers, blue; lateral feathers, blue tipped with yellow; bill, greyish-horn; legs, grey; iris, brown. Female has the crown dull olive-green; smaller frontal band; abdomen washed with dull green. Juveniles are duller than females and have no blue frontal band.

VOICE: A plaintive, but penetrative, "tinkling" call; somewhat similar to that of the common Yellow-tailed Thornbill.

DISTRIBUTION: South-eastern Australia and Tasmania; apparently breeding has not been recorded from New South Wales where the species is a migratory visitor during autumn and winter, being more common in the south and far west. It was first recorded in the Capital Territory on 4 May 1965, when a single bird was seen near Weetangera. However, prior to this, small parties had been seen near Adaminaby and Chakola, in the Monaro region, and near Collector. Favours sparsely-timbered country and open grassland.

HABITS: Because of its sombre coloration the Blue-winged Parrot may pass unnoticed unless flushed from the roadside or seen perched on a fence wire. In pairs or small flocks they spend most of the time feeding on the ground. They are tame and easy to approach. When disturbed they fly to a nearby tree or fence post, but if in open grassland away from cover they usually rise high into the air, calling all the while, and soon disappear from sight. The surprisingly swift, direct flight is somewhat erratic, but with little undulation.

175

BREEDING: The breeding season lasts from October to January. The nest is in a hollow in a tree, a stump or a log lying on the ground. On a layer of decayed wood dust lining the bottom of the hollow four to six white, rounded eggs are laid. These average 22 × 19 mm. Incubation lasts about twenty days and only the female broods. The young leave the nest approximately thirty days after hatching. Adult plumage is acquired during the following September or October.

FEEDING: Feeds almost entirely on grass seeds procured on the ground. (J.M.F.)

## SWIFT PARROT *Lathamus discolor*

PLATE XVI

IDENTIFICATION: Length, 25 cm. Upper-parts, rich green; crown, dark blue; forehead, lower cheeks and throat, red; lores, yellow; shoulder-patches, innermost coverts and *under-wing coverts, bright red;* wings, blue; under-parts, yellowish-green; *under-tail coverts, dull red; tail, very narrow, pointed,* pale blue strongly washed with dull brick-red, especially on the central feathers; bill, brownish-horn; legs, brown; iris, pale yellow. The sexes are alike. Juveniles are duller, have less red on the face and under-tail coverts and have pale brown eyes.

In flight the red under-wings and under-tail coverts are diagnostic.

VOICE: A strong, metallic "clinking" note repeated several times in succession. A soft chattering when feeding. Very distinct from the screeching calls of lorikeets.

DISTRIBUTION: It apparently breeds only in Tasmania; moves to south-eastern Australia in March and returns in September. Widespread in Victoria, in New South Wales it is confined chiefly to the coast and adjacent tablelands. It is nomadic and its presence in any area is governed by the flowering of eucalypts or the abundance of psyllid lerps. Around Canberra it could be found in almost any timbered area; it has been seen near Mt Ainslie, on Black Mountain and in suburban gardens.

HABITS: They are generally seen in pairs or small parties, often in the company of lorikeets, frequenting the outermost branches of eucalypts, and rarely come near the ground. Their coloration blends well with the foliage but the noise and movement as they climb amongst the branches reveal their presence. When feeding they are oblivious to the approach of an intruder. The direct flight is extremely swift, the wing beats producing a "whirring" noise.

BREEDING: The breeding season lasts from late September to early January. The nest is in a hollow limb or hole in a tree, usually at a great height from the ground. Four, or rarely five, white, rounded eggs are laid on a lining of decayed wood dust. These average 25 × 21 mm. The nesting period remains undetermined but is said to be nearly as long as that of the larger lorikeets.

FEEDING: Feeds on nectar, insects and their larvae, particularly lerps and caterpillars of various kinds, fruits, berries and seeds. In Hobart's parklands they occasionally come to the ground to feed on the fallen seeds of introduced elm trees. (J.M.F.)

## BUDGERIGAR *Melopsittacus undulatus*

PLATE XVII

IDENTIFICATION: Length, 10 cm. General colour, green; entire upper-parts barred with black and yellow; wings fringed with white; forehead, lores, throat and foreparts of cheeks, yellow; some feathers of the cheeks tipped with blue; a series of black spots across the throat; central tail feathers, greenish-blue, outer feathers green with a yellow band across the centres; bill, olive-grey; cere, blue; legs, greyish-blue; iris, white. The female is similar but the cere is pale blue in the non-breeding season and brownish when in breeding state.

VOICE: The contact call given in flight is a pleasant, prolonged warbling and will generally be heard before the bird is sighted. When alarmed it has a subdued, disyllabic screeching and while feeding occasionally emits a sharp chattering.

DISTRIBUTION: Australia generally, chiefly the interior, but normally absent from the extreme south-western corner and most of the east coast. In New South Wales it is widely distributed west of the Dividing Range. In our area it occasionally visits the sparsely-timbered grasslands in the western areas but most of the odd birds seen in Canberra are almost certainly aviary escapees. Budgerigars are highly nomadic, their movements being governed by the availability of water and food. In times of severe drought they move towards the coast and may be seen as far east as our area.

HABITS: The very large flocks of Budgerigars seen in the interior of the continent have become almost legendary; but elsewhere only small parties are generally encountered. Normally these birds are not timid and will allow a close approach. They feed and drink early in the morning and towards late afternoon, passing the remainder of the day sitting in trees or tall bushes. The swift, erratic flight is characterised by remarkable precision, the entire flock twisting and turning as one.

BREEDING: Although breeding is usually between August and January in the south and from June to September in the north, the birds will breed at any time of the year following good rains. They react very quickly to rainfall and soon commence nesting activities. Each pair may rear several broods in succession. The nest is in a hollow or hole in a tree, stump, fence post or even in a log lying on the ground. Several nests have been found not only in the same tree, but in the same branch of a tree. On a layer of decayed wood dust lining the bottom of the hollow four to six, occasionally up to eight, white rounded eggs are laid. They average 19 × 14 mm. Incubation lasts about eighteen days and only the female broods. The young leave the nest approximately thirty days after hatching and are fully independent within a few days. It has been shown that males may produce spermatozoa within sixty days of leaving the nest.

FEEDING: It feeds almost entirely on the seeds of grasses and herbaceous plants procured on or near the ground. Important items in the diet are the seeds of spinifex *Triodia* and Mitchell grass *Astrebla*. It occasionally attacks ripening wheat crops. (J.M.F.)

# CUCKOOS

The cuckoo family is a large and diversified one of 127 species distributed throughout the world. In Australia there are twelve species and eight have visited our area, although of these, two are vagrants. The parasitic habits of cuckoos, laying their eggs in other birds' nests, are very well known but it is less widely appreciated that many birds, other than cuckoos, also have this habit and that of the cuckoo family little more than one third of the species are parasitic. Cuckoos come in very many shapes and forms and range in size from the tiny Bronze Cuckoo, 17 cm long, to the giant Channel-billed Cuckoo, 64 cm long. They are mainly arboreal but some are ground dwellers such as the Australian Pheasant Coucal, a non-parasitic form. Most Australian cuckoos are more or less migratory.

### Family Cuculidae — Cuckoos
### PALLID CUCKOO *Cuculus pallidus*

PLATE XVIII

IDENTIFICATION: Length, 33 cm. Male: *general colour above, ashy-brown with the wing coverts edged with dull white*; main flight feathers of the wings and tail are notched and barred with white; *under-parts are dull grey*; iris, brown; bill, dark olive-brown; legs, olive. The female is similar to the male but is spotted and marked with chestnut and buff on the upper-parts. The juvenile has broader whitish margins to the feathers of the upper-parts and darker markings about the face and neck.

VOICE: The call of the male Pallid Cuckoo is a conspicuous sound of spring. The bird calls loudly and monotonously from the time of its return in the last days of August or September until the end of the breeding season. The chief call is an ascending series of notes frequently repeated and given throughout the day and sometimes at night. Juveniles are conspicuous in summer and early autumn with harsh repeated begging calls. The female call is a single harsh note.

DISTRIBUTION: This species is found throughout Australia, including Tasmania, wherever suitable habitat exists but is more numerous in the coastal and tableland areas than in the dry inland. Around Canberra it is not found in the forest country of the ranges but is quite common in the more open country. The migrations are well marked; the bird is not found on the tablelands in winter but is sometimes seen in southern coastal areas. After breeding, the adults move away in the early weeks of the New Year but juveniles remain until the end of April.

HABITS: The Pallid Cuckoo is usually seen singly, sitting in a large eucalypt or occasionally on wires. Its flight is undulating and it elevates the tail when alighting. It is very inconspicuous. Each pair occupies a territory during the breeding season and presumably seeks out nests to parasitise within it.

BREEDING: The season usually extends from September to December or January, but depends on those of the host species, which are many; at least eighty. The chief hosts are the honeyeaters but eggs are laid in virtually any form of open nest. The sight of a large juvenile Pallid Cuckoo being fed by a foster parent such as a White-plumed Honeyeater, less than half its weight, is a fairly common one. While adults are driven off by other species wherever possible, individual squawking juveniles have often been seen to be fed by several birds, one after another. The eggs are of a uniform flesh colour with a few dots of darker shades scattered over the shell. They measure about 25 × 18 mm.

FEEDING: The hairy types of caterpillars form the basic items of diet and grasshoppers are also taken. (S.J.W.)

## FAN-TAILED CUCKOO *Cuculus pyrrhophanus*

PLATE XVIII

IDENTIFICATION: Length, 27 cm. Upper-parts, slaty-grey with the wings brownish-grey; under-parts, rust-red except for the throat which is grey; tail, black with well marked *white notches on both edges of the feathers*; bill, black; legs, yellowish-olive; iris, dark brown; orbital ring, yellow. The sexes are similar. See also the Brush Cuckoo with which this species can be confused.

VOICE: The chief call is a downward scale of rapid trilled notes heard chiefly during the breeding season. At other times the bird is rather quiet.

DISTRIBUTION: Australia generally, except the north-west and the interior, and Tasmania. Extends to the Aru Islands and some islands of the south-west Pacific. The Fan-tailed Cuckoo is fairly common throughout the area but is probably more numerous in the forests of the ranges than in the open timbered country. It is nomadic in the cooler months and while it is present in all seasons, it is less numerous from May to August than at other times.

HABITS: The repeated call often draws attention to the bird perched high in a tree. Its general behaviour is similar to that of the other small cuckoos, and it is quite secretive. The flight is markedly undulating.

BREEDING: The breeding season extends from September to December. Like all other cuckoos in our area, it is parasitic and usually favours dome-shaped nests built near the ground but cup-shaped nests are occasionally selected. The nests of birds much smaller than itself are often used, e.g., those of the Brown Thornbill. The egg is white with small markings of dark brownish shades often tending to form a band at the thicker end. It measures 20 × 15 mm.

FEEDING: The species is insectivorous but seems to prefer caterpillars. (S.J.W.)

## BRUSH CUCKOO *Cuculus variolosus*

PLATE XVIII

IDENTIFICATION: Length, 24 cm. Upper-parts, brown washed with olive; head and mantle, dull leaden-grey; under-parts, leaden-grey strongly washed with rufous on the tips on the breast area; tail, brown and occasionally with *faint notches of white on the outer edges of the feathers*, inner web is notched with white; bill, black; legs, fleshy-

180

brown; iris, dark brown. The sexes are similar. See also the Fan-tailed Cuckoo with which this species may be confused. The diagnostic differences are the length, tail markings and calls.

VOICE: The call consists of six to eight single notes, rather slow, deliberate and mournful, and on a descending scale. It sometimes calls at night.

DISTRIBUTION: From coastal northern Australia down the east coast to Victoria, where it is rather rare. It extends as far as the higher western slopes of the Dividing Range. It also occurs in the Molucca Islands, Timor and New Guinea, and the Solomons and as far north as Malaysia and the Philippines. There is a regular migration in the southern areas and the birds usually appear in New South Wales and Victoria in October leaving during November to the end of January but juveniles are probably present until March. The Brush Cuckoo has been recorded from our area between early November and late January. The species is found in open timbered country and does not penetrate the heavily timbered slopes of the higher ranges. Near Canberra most sightings have been on Black Mountain and Mt Ainslie, within a few kilometres of the city.

HABITS: This is not a conspicuous bird and it appears to spend the hotter hours of the day perched in a tree in open forest country indulging in just an occasional short flight. Attention is usually drawn to it by the six to eight call notes.

BREEDING: The breeding season is from October to January, depending on the hosts. It is parasitic on a variety of birds which build open, cup-shaped nests, such as the wood swallows, fantails, Leaden Flycatcher and Restless Flycatcher. The eggs are white with faint purplish-brown and lavender markings usually in a band around the larger end. They measure 19 × 15 mm.

FEEDING: Like other small local cuckoos, the Brush Cuckoo is insectivorous and takes a variety of this form of food (S.J.W.)

## BLACK-EARED CUCKOO *Chrysococcyx osculans*
PLATE XVIII

IDENTIFICATION: Length, 19 cm. General colour above, *greyish-brown washed with bronzy-olive*; tail, bronzy olive-brown tipped with white with white bars on the outer feathers; top of the head, dark grey; *lores, black, as are the ear coverts*, and there is a white line above these areas; under-parts, pale buff-brown; bill, black; legs, black; iris, brown. The sexes are similar.

In the juveniles, the upper-parts are slightly darker than in the adult, the ear coverts are dark brown and the under-parts are pale grey.

VOICE: There are several melancholy calls. The main one is a single note with a downward inflection, repeated several times. The call is a quiet one.

DISTRIBUTION: The bird does not seem to be really common anywhere. It is sparsely distributed throughout the interior of Australia, extending to the coast in only a few places. It extends to the Molucca and Aru Islands also. In our area it is very rare. It is a bird of open scrub lands and does not penetrate forest areas. Its movements are not understood; it is either nomadic or migratory and appears in the southern parts of its range about August or September and disappears again in mid-summer.

HABITS: The Black-eared Cuckoo is a bird of low levels of the inland scrubs and is quite secretive, it flies low and silently and is not often seen. It spends much time sitting quietly in a low bush.

BREEDING: The breeding season is from September to January in New South Wales. Most parasitic cuckoos use a fairly wide range of host species but this is not so with this species which appears to concentrate on the Speckled Warbler, in eastern Australia, and the Redthroat in the west, although eggs have been reported in the nests of a few other species. The eggs are very similar to those of the two principal host species, a deep, uniform, dark chocolate colour. The colour can be readily rubbed off with a damp finger. The eggs measure about 23 × 18 mm.

FEEDING: The species takes a variety of insects from the foliage. (S.J.W.)

## HORSFIELD BRONZE CUCKOO *Chrysococcyx basalis*
PLATE XVIII

IDENTIFICATION: Length, 17 cm. Upper-parts, light bronze-green, not quite so vivid as with the Golden Bronze Cuckoo or the Shining Bronze Cuckoo; *crown of the head and the nape have a dull metallic bronze-brown tinge*; upper-*wing coverts and quills narrowly edged with dull white*; there are red-brown markings at the base of the tail; over the eye and extending to the sides of the nape there is a more or less well defined whitish streak; chin and throat, irregularly barred with brown; remainder of the under-parts, white and generally incompletely barred with brown; bill, black; legs, grey; iris, red-brown. The sexes are similar.

Young birds, in their first few months, have the red-brown markings on the tail and the under-parts are not barred. This barring develops from the throat downwards during their first autumn.

VOICE: There are several calls all identifiable as being those of a cuckoo by the plaintive tone. The chief call is a fairly loud, piercing whistle with a downward inflection. It sometimes calls at night.

DISTRIBUTION: Australia generally, including Tasmania. It migrates to the Aru and Molucca Islands and as far as southern Malaysia. In our area it is a bird of sometimes open forest country and penetrates the denser forests of the ranges. In most of its range in south-east Australia it is a partial migrant, individuals remaining over winter, but around Canberra the migration is complete and it is not present in the winter but is one of the earliest birds to return in spring.

HABITS: During August and September the birds often indulge in excited, noisy, mating flights through the tops of the trees in open forest country and it is then quite conspicuous. At other times, although it does sometimes call from a tall tree, it tends to keep to fairly thick cover and is quite secretive.

BREEDING: The breeding season is from September to January. It is parasitic and uses a large number of host species. The eggs are usually, but not always, placed in domed nests, built near the ground. Wrens and thornbills are often chosen as hosts. The egg is pinkish with minute spots of pinkish-red and measures about 15 × 12 mm.

FEEDING: A variety of insect food is taken, usually from the twigs and leaves of trees. Caterpillars are a favoured item. (S.J.W.)

## GOLDEN BRONZE CUCKOO *Chrysococcyx lucidus*

PLATE XVIII

IDENTIFICATION: Length, 16.5 cm. Upper-parts, vivid bronzy metallic green; crown of the *head and the nape have a dull metallic purple sheen; feathers of the wings are uniform in colour,* unlike those of the Horsfield Bronze Cuckoo; occasionally there are rufous spots in the tail; throat, barred with well defined markings as are the under-parts generally; bill, black; legs, grey; iris, red-brown. The sexes are similar. Juveniles are brown above with a slight bronze-green gloss and

183

the under-parts are dull ashy-white with slight indications of dull brown crossbars on the flanks.

The New Zealand race, the Shining Bronze Cuckoo, is distinguished by having a green (not purple) sheen on the head and nape and white flecks on the forehead.

VOICE: The calls have a plaintive quality. The chief call is long, drawn and repeated several times; a note with a strong upwards inflection at the end. At a slight distance it sounds like someone whistling a dog.

DISTRIBUTION: There are two races; one is distributed throughout Australia, including Tasmania but excluding the dry inland. It migrates to New Guinea and as far as Java and the Moluccas. The other is a New Zealand bird that migrates to the general area of the Solomon Islands. In the south-east the Australian race is widely distributed and is found in the dry open forests as well as in the wetter forests of the ranges, where it is fairly common in the spring and early summer months. In our area its migration is total. It returns about the beginning of October but becomes uncommon by the end of February. Juveniles have been recorded in early autumn. A few birds overwinter in Victoria but it is fairly common about Sydney during the colder months.

On its northern migration the New Zealand race sometimes strays and stragglers find their way to the east coast of Australia each year but little is known of its Australian distribution. The two birds are very similar in appearance so most Australian records and museum specimens refer to birds found dead. All Australian records are from the east coast strip as far inland as the Divide. There are two records from Lake George but it has not been recorded from the Australian Capital Territory. There is one Victorian record (Melbourne).

HABITS: Like most cuckoos it is unobtrusive but during the early spring becomes conspicuous as it indulges in noisy mating flights. Generally its call is given from a dead branch high in a tree.

BREEDING: The breeding season is from September to January. The species is parasitic and uses a large number of host species, chiefly, but by no means always, those which build domed nests, like wrens and thornbills. The eggs are a uniform colour and vary from pale olive-green to bronze-brown; they measure about $15 \times 12$ mm.

FEEDING: Caterpillars of several species are the favoured food but a variety of other insect foods are also taken. (S.J.W.)

184

KOEL *Eudynamys scolopacea*

PLATE XVIII

IDENTIFICATION: Length, 42 cm. Male: *whole plumage, glossy, greenish blue-black*. Female: a dull bronze-brown and black bird thickly *spotted and barred with white*. The head and back of the neck are glossy greenish-black; this species has a conspicuously long tail; bill, black; legs, slate-grey; iris, red.

VOICE: The Koel has a variety of rather loud calls and is often heard calling at night. The main call of the male birds, before the arrival of the females, is a long, repeated, monotonous "coo-ee" the note rising in inflection on the second syllable. In the mating period it is uttered in groups of eight or nine syllables in increasing pitch and speed; when the highest pitch is reached it ceases abruptly to shortly begin again. During the breeding season there is a variety of other loud, excited notes mainly from the female, but the birds become very quiet in the autumn months.

DISTRIBUTION: There are four geographic races extending from China and India to Australia. The Australian race is a bird of the tropical forests extending from Timor, Molucca and New Guinea, across northern Australia and down the New South Wales coast to about Sydney. Records in our area are vagrants. It is completely migratory, reaching New South Wales in early September and leaving in March and April; in this period it is absent from northern Australia.

HABITS: Although very noisy, it is remarkably hard to observe as it has a strong preference for densely foliaged trees and darts from one to another well ahead of the observer. It is sometimes seen in tall, more open trees but darts vertically downwards to cover when it sees the observer. It usually flies low down when moving through the forest.

BREEDING: It parasitises the nests of the larger honeyeaters, chiefly friar-birds, orioles and, occasionally also the Magpie Lark; there are about a dozen recorded foster parents. The breeding season corresponds to that of these birds, that is from October to January or February. The egg is similar to that of the friar birds; it is pale reddish-salmon covered with streaks, dots and blotches of purplish-red. The egg measures about 37 × 25 mm.

FEEDING: It feeds almost entirely on fruits, both native berries of the rainforest fringe and scrubby creeks and sometimes attacks mulberries and other cultivated berries. Contrary to the usual statements, it does not seem to favour native figs. (H.J.F.)

## CHANNEL-BILLED CUCKOO *Scythrops novaehollandiae*

IDENTIFICATION: Length, 64 cm. Head and neck, light, pearly grey; back and wings, darker grey mottled with brownish-black; under-parts, greyish-white, paler at the throat; tail, grey with a broad white subterminal bar; *bill is very large* and is yellow-brown; legs and feet, olive-brown; iris, brown. The sexes are similar.

VOICE: A very loud, raucous scream or screech, very difficult to describe but once heard never forgotten. They sometimes call at night.

DISTRIBUTION: It is distributed throughout New Guinea, New Britain and some Indonesian islands as well as in coastal and inland tropical Australia. It extends across the north of the continent from the Kimberleys to North Queensland and straggles down the coast to as far as Sydney in very small numbers. There are several records of vagrants in our area. It is a strict migrant reaching the south in September and October and leaving again in March.

HABITS: Commonly known as the Rain-bird or Flood-bird, the Channel-billed Cuckoo is supposed to forecast rain; a not unreasonable idea as its movements bring it into northern Australia at the same time as the beginning of the wet season. They are usually seen in tall timber in open country but occasionally penetrate rainforest also. They are usually solitary and are very much harried by their potential victims whenever they appear.

BREEDING: In the north it breeds throughout the early wet season laying its eggs in nests of crows and currawongs. Sometimes more than one egg is laid in the foster parents' nest, unlike most cuckoos. The eggs are dull white or buff, blotched with chestnut and purplish-brown. They measure about 42 × 30 mm.

FEEDING: They feed principally on native fruits and, because of a preference for figs, in some districts are known as Fig-hawks. (H.J.F.)

# FROGMOUTHS AND NIGHTJARS

The frogmouths and nightjars are nocturnal birds primarily adapted for catching insects on the wing although some Australian, and doubtless other, species secure much food on the ground. Consistent with their nocturnal life their plumage is soft so that the flight is silent. They are generally secretive and not often seen during the day. To escape detection they are beautifully camouflaged both in colour and posture. They vary in length from about twenty to sixty centimetres but all are solid birds with very large heads, broad wings and short, broad bills, often surrounded by bristles that doubtless assist in catching the insect food.

## Family Podargidae — Frogmouths

There are only twelve species in this small family that ranges from India through Burma, Thailand, the Philippines, Malaysia to New Guinea, Australia and Tasmania. Frogmouths are all similar in form, but vary in size from just over twenty centimetres to the large Papuan Frogmouth which is nearly sixty centimetres in length. Both grey and rufous phases occur in several species and the possession of powder down feathers on the rump, instead of a preen gland, is common to all. They are all nocturnal and some are migratory, but the species which occurs in our area, the Tawny Frogmouth *Podargus strigoides*, is sedentary. This species is widespread in Australia but the two other species that are found in Australia, *P. ocellatus* and *P. papuensis* are more restricted and range from Queensland through to New Guinea.

## TAWNY FROGMOUTH *Podargus strigoides*

PLATE VIII

IDENTIFICATION: Length, 46 cm. Upper-parts, mottled pale grey and fawn often with a rufous wash on the shoulders and wing coverts; flight feathers, dark brown with white spots on the outer webs; tail, grey, barred with dark brown; under-parts, pale grey with darker streaking; long bristles are conspicuous above the broad hooked bill, which is dark horn in colour; inside of mouth, pale green; legs and feet, dull brown; eye yellow.

The sexes are similar but the female is slightly smaller. An alternative plumage phase exists in which most of the grey of the plumage is replaced by rufous.

VOICE: The call is a monotonous "ooo-ooo-ooo-ooo" repeated about ten times and uttered at short intervals over long periods during the breeding season. Although fairly low in intensity it can cause sleepless nights for those unfortunate enough to camp within earshot. The name "Mo-poke" is sometimes applied in error to it but this name rightly belongs to one or other of the owls in the genus *Ninox*, most commonly the Boobook Owl, which gives the "mo-poke" call.

DISTRIBUTION: It is found throughout Australia including Tasmania. It is very variable in size and birds from the Northern Territory are only about 34 cm in length. It is found in a great variety of habitats, from the rain forests of the east coast to the arid scrublands of

187

the interior. Around Canberra, it is found wherever there are trees, even among the exotic vegetation of suburban areas, but it is most abundant among the mature eucalypts of the woodlands and forests.

HABITS: Frogmouths are nocturnal. They fly silently and slowly and are most often seen at night in the headlights of oncoming cars as they fly up from the roadside, when they appear very whitish. During the daytime they roost quietly on a thick sloping branch or in a fork of a tree and when alarmed, adopt a stiffened, erect attitude, with their eyes closed to slits, through which they watch an intruder intently. In this attitude, the combination of their evenly mottled plumage, together with the broken light filtering through the foliage makes them very hard to see. The resemblance to a broken-off branch is remarkable. In the Northern Territory the smaller sub-species often roosts on the ground in true nightjar fashion.

BREEDING: Breeding extends from August to December in south-eastern Australia. The nest is a platform of twigs twenty to twenty-five centimetres in diameter with a slight depression and is usually lined with leaves. It is placed on a thick, horizontal, forked branch of a rough-barked tree, usually a eucalypt. Two or three pure white, lustrous eggs form the clutch. They measure approximately 43 × 31 mm. Both sexes incubate the eggs and feed the young.

FEEDING: This species, despite its cavernous mouth, does not seem to feed on the wing. Stomach analyses have shown that it feeds mainly on ground-frequenting insects and spiders. They are often found dead on the road, presumably hit after they have flown down to seize prey illuminated by the lights of an approaching car. (G.S.C.)

### Family Aegothelidae—Owlet-Nightjars

The eight species of Owlet-Nightjars belong to the one genus, *Aegotheles*, and are restricted to the Australo-Papuan region and New Caledonia. They vary in size, ranging from about twenty centimetres to nearly thirty-three centimetres. All are nocturnal and are "soft feathered" so that they fly quite noiselessly. The most outstanding feature is their wide opening mouth surrounded by well developed bristles and in this respect they resemble the true nightjars. However, the erect stance of some species, their habit of nesting in hollow trees and their ability to turn the head around 180 degrees are all superficially owl-like characters, hence the mixed vernacular name given to the family.

Only one species is found throughout Australia and Tasmania, *Aegotheles cristatus*.

## OWLET-NIGHTJAR *Aegotheles cristatus*

PLATE VIII

IDENTIFICATION: Length, 22 cm. General colour above, mid-grey; head, buff or grey, mottled black, a collar on the hind neck black above a thinner ring of buff; wings and tail, barred pale grey and dark brown; under-parts, paler greyish-white, very finely barred; bill, blackish-brown, hooked, very short and broad with long black loral bristles; legs and feet, flesh pink; eye, large, dark brown; mouth, pink. The sexes are similar. Considerable variation exists in the plumage of individuals from the same area. Those having varying amounts of rufous on the ear coverts, nuchal collar, and around head and neck, may be immatures.

VOICE: The most common call is a short, shrill, churring note repeated three or four times. It is given all the year round, usually just after dusk, but sometimes in the daytime. This call is probably the most common of the nocturnal bird calls heard in wooded areas inland.

DISTRIBUTION: It occurs throughout Australia including Tasmania, and in southern New Guinea. It is more plentiful in drier inland areas but occurs in widely varying habitats, from coastal wet sclerophyll forest to arid scrub. It is uncommon but widespread in our region.

HABITS: Being primarily a nocturnal bird, the Owlet-Nightjar is more often heard than seen. By day, it roosts in the hollow spout of a tree but can sometimes be seen at the entrance. It will often flush from its hollow during the day if the tree is hit with a stick, and fly with a weak, fluttering flight into another nearby hollow.

BREEDING: In this region nesting occurs from October to December. Three or four white eggs are laid on a lining of small dried leaves inside a tree spout or hollow, the nest often being visible from the entrance. The eggs measure about 29 × 22 mm.

FEEDING: The Owlet-Nightjar can sometimes be seen feeding on insects around lights at night but stomach analyses have shown that ground-frequenting insects figure largely in its diet. (G.S.C.)

### Family Caprimulgidae — Nightjars

This is a large family of almost world-wide distribution. Of the seventy-odd species, Australia has only three, the Spotted Nightjar *Eurostopodus guttatus*, the White-throated Nightjar *Caprimulgus mysta-*

*calis*, and the Large-tailed Nightjar *C. macrurus*. The Spotted Nightjar is the only endemic species, and is found over most of the drier parts of Australia. It has not been recorded locally but comes close in the west. The white-throated species, one of the largest of all the nightjars, is seen around Canberra, though rarely, and ranges right along Australia's east coast. The Large-tailed Nightjar is found from northern Queensland and New Guinea to India.

Nightjars are nocturnal. Most of the tropical species are sedentary but some of those from temperate zones are highly migratory. They are all cryptically coloured birds with very wide opening mouths which they use for feeding in flight. Another feature common to all is the comb-like structure on the third toe, probably used in preening.

## WHITE-THROATED NIGHTJAR *Caprimulgus mystacalis*
PLATE VIII

IDENTIFICATION: Length, 33 cm. Upper-parts, generally mottled black, grey and rufous; forehead, grey; crown, grey with central black streaks; nuchal collar, buff and black: quills, brown-black spotted rufous, the third and fourth quills spotted white; tail, dark brown with lighter barring of buff; *conspicuous white crescent patches on sides of throat*; under-parts barred dark brown and rufous; bill, brown-black; legs and feet, red-brown; iris, dark brown.

VOICE: The call is several hoarse notes that could be described as a throaty cackle.

DISTRIBUTION: In Australia it is restricted to the strip of coastal country generally east of the Great Dividing Range from Cape York to as far as the Otway Range in Victoria. A. J. North mentioned a specimen from the Northern Territory but gave no precise locality. Outside Australia it extends to New Guinea. Forest country is the preferred habitat, generally on the drier ridges in areas strewn with fallen leaves and supporting little undergrowth. It is rarely recorded in our area.

HABITS: It is mostly observed hawking at dusk or by lights at night for flying insects. By day, nightjars roost on the ground or, rarely, low down in a tree, relying on their cryptic plumage pattern to escape detection and they will usually only flush right at one's feet. The late breeding and seasonal occurrence of this species is consistent with a bird of migratory habits, but there is no direct evidence of this yet. Some Northern Hemisphere members of the family are strongly migratory while one North American form hibernates during the winter.

BREEDING: The breeding season in south-eastern Australia is October to January. No nest is made, the single egg being laid straight on the ground. It is elliptical in shape, slightly pointed at one end and measures about 41 × 29 mm. The ground colour is cream and the few markings of black and grey are evenly distributed. The nest site chosen is among leaf and bark strewn areas in forest or woodland, often on the crest of a ridge. The brooding bird sits very closely during the day and the mate can usually be found perched close by in a tree or on the ground.

FEEDING: It feeds mostly on the wing, capturing flying insects such as moths and beetles in its mouth and swallowing them whole. (G.S.C.)

## SWIFTS

The swifts are the extreme adaptation to aerial life and rarely come to the ground. There is strong evidence in Europe that at least one species, under certain conditions, even sleeps and copulates in the air. Adults and nestlings are able to survive short periods of severe weather and food shortage by entering a state of torpidity by reducing body temperature and consequently the metabolic rate. Some cave-dwelling species manoeuvre in total darkness by echo-location, in the same manner as some bats. Most swifts use saliva to glue nest material together and attach the usually bracket-shaped structure to the chosen site. Nest materials are usually gathered on the wing, some species actually snapping twigs from trees with their feet as they fly past. A few species do not build nests, using a scrape in sand on a cave-ledge.

There are some sixty-five species, widely distributed from tropical to temperate zones of the world but only five species have been recorded from Australia. The Grey Swiftlet *Collocallia spodiopygia* breeds on the north-east coast of Queensland and two other swiftlets are rare stragglers to the Cape York Peninsula. The Fork-tailed Swift *Apus pacificus* and Spine-tailed Swift *Hirundapus caudacutus* are regular migratory species which breed in central and northern Asia and winter in Australia. Both species may be seen in the area about Canberra, but the Fork-tailed Swift is rare and may not be recorded every summer. The Spine-tailed Swift is relatively common and can be expected at any time during the summer period.

Family Apodidae — Swifts
SPINE-TAILED SWIFT *Hirundapus caudacutus*
PLATE XIX
IDENTIFICATION: Length, 20 cm. General colour, uniform sooty-brown, paler nape and centre of back; chin, throat, sides of tail,

191

undertail coverts and three or four secondaries on wing, white; pronounced greenish-purple gloss on wing, scapulars and upper-tail but less on crown and nape. *The shaft of each tail feather projects as a spine some 4 mm long.* Bill, black; legs and feet, brown-slate. The sexes and juveniles are alike.

In flight the long, sickle-shaped wings, *white throat, under and sides of tail* are diagnostic.

VOICE: The voice is a shrill twittering or chattering, continuous or intermittent and is usually heard from birds in flocks as a contact call when travelling. The attention of an observer may initially be attracted by the calls of high-flying swifts.

DISTRIBUTION: It is an Asian Palaearctic migrant wintering in the coastal plain, forested Eastern Highlands and immediate hinterland of eastern Australia. It is rarely recorded more than about 600 to 800 kilometres inland. Small numbers are recorded annually in the southeast of South Australia, and Tasmania. Rare stragglers reach the Northern Territory, Western Australia, New Zealand and Macquarie Island. Within this range the bird is highly nomadic, continually seeking optimum weather conditions for feeding purposes. They arrive in Australia from early October and finally depart by mid-April.

HABITS: Eight to ten rapid wing beats alternate with long glides and raking dives when swifts are travelling or feeding. In sharp turns or slow circling flight the tail and wings are widely fanned. It normally feeds and cruises between about fifty and one hundred and thirty km/h. High speed chases by pairs and trios may relate to courtship and a display flight in which groups of swifts repeatedly fly up and dive down in the one place has recently been described. The spines on the tail are reputed to assist as a prop when the bird clings to a vertical surface.

Swifts often associate with swallows, martins and wood-swallows when feeding, or travelling in response to a change in weather conditions. At times they will mob hawks or chase other large birds, apparently for entertainment.

BREEDING: Spine-tailed Swifts breed in Japan and north-east Asia, principally Siberia. Records include nests on a rockface behind a waterfall in Japan, and deep in tall, broken-off hollow trees in forested country in Siberia. Breeding is between May and August.

FEEDING: All feeding and drinking is accomplished on the wing. Swifts feed chiefly ahead of weather changes, preferring warm, humid and rising air where maximum movement of aerial insects occurs. Their association with summer thunderstorms is well known in Australia. They normally feed from centimetres above ground to some hundreds of metres in the mornings and evenings; during the middle of the day they tend to rest or feed at higher altitudes. Beetles, winged ants and termites comprise a high percentage of the catch. Swifts skim a water-surface at high speed when drinking. (K.G.S.)

## FORK-TAILED SWIFT *Apus pacificus*
PLATE XIX

IDENTIFICATION: Length, 17.5 cm. General colour, *blackish-brown; whitish* chin, throat and rump; white feather tips on breast, belly and under-wing coverts give a marked mottled effect in hand specimens; *tail has a deep fork which becomes conspicuous as the swift turns or banks sharply*; bill, legs and feet, black. The sexes and juveniles are indistinguishable in the field.

In flight *white throat and rump, forked tail and distinctly smaller size than the Spine-tailed Swift* are diagnostic.

VOICE: The voice is a shrill, excited twittering, somewhat comparable to the chatter of lorikeets and may be heard during any activity.

DISTRIBUTION: It is an Asian Palaearctic migrant that winters in Australia. Information is inadequate but indications are that it prefers the northern, western and generally more arid regions of the continent and is highly nomadic. Birds begin arriving in Australia from late September and early October, and have finally left again by mid-April. The exact migration route is not known. There are usually one or two major influxes annually into eastern South Australia, western Victoria and central New South Wales. The huge straggling flocks may number many thousands of individuals, often moving on a front many kilometres wide against strong, hot north winds during mid-summer. They generally swing northward well inside the mountain chain and are not often seen over the Eastern Highlands. Small numbers are occasionally reported from the Canberra area, often accompanying Spine-tailed Swifts. Rare stragglers reach New Guinea, New Zealand, Tasmania and Macquarie Island.

HABITS: Information on the behaviour and habits of this species is almost completely lacking in Australia. Existing data indicate its general aerial behaviour to be similar to that of the Spine-tailed Swift. Its flight is more buoyant and less direct than that of the larger swift.

BREEDING: It is believed to breed mainly in eastern Asia, including

Japan (but probably not Korea) from May to August. It occupies cliff ledges and crevices, buildings and similar sites for nesting.

FEEDING: All feeding and drinking activity is performed on the wing. The species of aerial insects consumed probably varies from those eaten by the Spine-tailed Swift, due to the different geographical range of the two species, but beetles and flying ants predominate. Both species are highly selective feeders and will reject insects that are distasteful or of the wrong size, despite the speed at which captures are achieved. Both species will also dash themselves against foliage of trees to snatch insects or stir them into flight. (K.G.S.)

# KINGFISHERS AND ROLLERS

The kingfishers, Bee-eater and Dollar Bird (the name Roller is not in general use in Australia) are familiar birds in much of the country. They include some highly coloured and beautiful creatures that do not spurn settled districts and towns, so are well known to all. The Order Coraciiformes also includes a number of groups that do not occur in Australia, the hoopoes, mot-mots and hornbills. Altogether the whole assemblage is large and very diverse in form and habits.

### Family Alcedinidae — Kingfishers

Kingfishers vary greatly in size, from 10 cm in the brilliant Little Kingfisher of northern Australia to 45 cm in the Kookaburra, but nevertheless all are similar in appearance. They have compact bodies with short necks and large heads, the tail is usually short but in a few the central feathers are elongated. The legs are always short. The bill is always long, pointed and very massive. It is tempting to assume that the bill is adapted for catching fish but this is not generally so as most kingfishers have no special affinity with water and do not fish. Many live in dry forests and feed on insects, small lizards, mammals and young birds.

The family is cosmopolitan and comprises some eighty species of which ten occur in Australia. In our region there are two breeding species, one occasional visitor and one other has been recorded as a vagrant.

### AZURE KINGFISHER *Ceyx azurea*

PLATE XX

IDENTIFICATION: Length, 18 cm. *Upper-parts, bright ultramarine*; sides of upper breast and tail, ultramarine; throat, whitish; a spot on the lores and on each side of the neck, buff; rest of underparts, rufous; bill, long and black; legs and feet, orange-red; iris, dark brown. The sexes are similar.

VOICE: A shrill, piping cry is uttered mainly while on the wing.

DISTRIBUTION: The Azure Kingfisher occurs from the Moluccas to New Guinea, across northern tropical Australia from the Kimberley Division to Cape York, throughout eastern Australia to south-eastern South Australia and Tasmania, extending inland along the major river systems. It is a rare vagrant in our area. It is common on the coast and also has been reported at Bungonia, New South Wales, where it is probably a breeding species.

HABITS: It is usually seen singly or in pairs frequenting tree-lined freshwater creeks, swamps and lakes. On the coast it also occurs along tidal streams and estuaries. Unlike most of the other Australian kingfishers, its preference for a diet of aquatic animals confines it to the vicinity of water. The flight of the Azure Kingfisher is swift, direct and usually close to the water.

BREEDING: In eastern New South Wales the breeding season extends from September to December. The nest is a chamber at the end of a hole burrowed into a bank of a creek. The burrow varies in length from half to one metre and usually slopes slightly upwards. The eggs are laid on the soil in the bottom of the nest chamber which usually contains a quantity of food remains. The clutch size varies from five to seven but is usually six. The eggs are rounded, glossy white and measure about 21 × 19 mm.

FEEDING: The Azure Kingfisher captures its prey by plunging headlong into the water from a vantage perch on a tree, rock or bank or while in flight. The height of the dive varies from a few metres to at least nine. Food eaten is mainly fish, some crustacea such as fairy-shrimps, small crabs and yabbies and aquatic insects, particularly water-beetles and water bugs. (J.L.McK.)

## KOOKABURRA *Dacelo novaeguineae*
PLATE XX

IDENTIFICATION: Length, 46 cm. *Upper-parts and wings, dark brown*; tail, more chestnut than upper-parts, barred black and tipped white; head, off-white with dark crown stripes and another stripe through the level of the eye; pale blue patch on wing; white patch at base of wing flight feathers, very conspicuous in flight; broad white neck collar; under-parts, white; bill, blackish above, dull cream below; legs and feet, brown; iris, grey-brown. The sexes are similar. Juveniles have the base of the upper half of the tail tinged blue.

195

VOICE: It has an unusual call very much like a jovial human chuckle. The Kookaburra is particularly vociferous in the early morning and evening. The laughing chorus is a communal affair, the entire family party or nesting group joining in the racket.

DISTRIBUTION: From inland Cape York Peninsula, Queensland, south throughout eastern and southern Australia to Eyre Peninsula and Kangaroo Island, South Australia. It was introduced into south-western Western Australia and northern Tasmania and is now well established there.

Although classed as common in our region it is not nearly so numerous as it is in nearby coastal and inland districts. In our area it is mostly found in the timbered foothills but is very rare in the more open grazing country and is only occasionally seen in the alpine areas. Kookaburras are apparently sedentary.

HABITS: Except when displaying they are rather sluggish birds and spend most of their time sitting around. The flight is quite slow and heavy. Territories are maintained throughout the year. Each territory contains several trees which are used by the family group for display and vocalising. Just prior to the breeding season the rapid display flights and bursts of laughing intensify and usually initiate similar responses from birds in all the surrounding territories. The Kookaburra social group usually comprises the adult breeding pair and their offspring. Some of the young birds remain with the adults during the next breeding season and assist in territorial defence, incubation and feeding the next brood.

BREEDING: The breeding season in our area extends from October to January. The nest is usually in the hollow of a tree or in a hole excavated by the birds in an arboreal termite nest; the eggs are laid on the loose material in the bottom of the hole. There are a few records of the Kookaburra burrowing a hole into the side of a creek bank or cliff or using a cavity in the side of a building. The adult pair bond is maintained throughout the year and the same nest may be used for several years.

The clutch size varies from two to five, usually three, and the eggs are white and rounded and measure 46×36 mm. Incubation takes from twenty-five to twenty-six days. The young birds remain in the nest for four to five weeks.

FEEDING: A true forest kingfisher, the Kookaburra is usually seen sitting on stumps or trees intently watching the ground. On sighting its prey it flies down, often travelling obliquely some distance to secure it

196

and then returns to its perch. Often the prey animal is dug, from two centimetres or more under the soil, with rapid jabs of the bill. Large prey animals are smashed against the limb several times or dropped from a height to subdue them.

The Kookaburra is well known, and widely celebrated, as a destroyer of snakes but it does not live on them alone. Studies to date, although far from quantitative, show that they eat a large variety of animals as well as whatever they can "steal" or scavenge from bush picnics. Known food items include small mammals, particularly rats and mice, eggs and nestlings of other bird species, snakes, lizards, frogs, fish, yabbies, grasshoppers, many different species of beetles and their larvae and pupae, locusts, caterpillars, bugs, spiders, snails and earthworms. (J.L.McK.)

## RED-BACKED KINGFISHER *Halcyon pyrrhopygia*
PLATE XX

IDENTIFICATION: Length, 22 cm. Back, wings and tail, greenish-blue; *crown, streaked dull green and white; rump, chestnut*; neck collar and under-parts, white; bill, brownish-black; legs and feet, greyish-brown; iris, dark brown. The sexes are similar.

VOICE: A mournful whistle is uttered at frequent intervals during the breeding season.

DISTRIBUTION: It is found throughout the more arid portions of all Australian States except Tasmania. There are several records in our region ranging from Tarago to Tharwa. In Victoria and New South Wales the Red-backed Kingfisher is a regular migrant arriving in September and departing in March. The wintering quarters of these migrants are presumed to be the more northern parts of its range. Of all the Australian kingfishers, this species is the most successful in managing to live in an arid environment. It is capable of establishing a territory and breeding successfully many miles from water.

HABITS: It is usually solitary and is encountered sitting quietly on a stump or low limb in dry forest, usually peering intently at the ground. When its prey is seen it darts rapidly down, seizes it and returns to its perch. Like most other kingfishers, its flight is very swift and direct.

BREEDING: The breeding season in south-western New South Wales is from November to January. The nest is usually an unlined chamber at the end of a hole burrowed into the side of a bank of a creek or sand ridge. On odd occasions it has been reported to drill a nest burrow into an arboreal or terrestrial termite mound. The clutch size varies from

197

four to five and the eggs are white and practically identical in size and shape to those of the Sacred Kingfisher.

FEEDING: Very little information is available on the food habits of this kingfisher but the following food items have been reported: small lizards, scorpions, centipedes, beetles and grasshoppers. (J.L.McK.)

## SACRED KINGFISHER *Halcyon sancta*

PLATE XX

IDENTIFICATION: Length, 22 cm. Upper-parts, greenish-blue; *under-parts and neck collar, buffy-white*; throat, white; bill, black; legs and feet, brown; iris, brown. The sexes are similar. Juveniles have darker under-parts.

VOICE: It has a loud "kee-kee-kee" note which appears to be territorial in function, and a sharper aggressive call.

DISTRIBUTION: The Sacred Kingfisher occurs from Sumatra and Borneo, to New Guinea, New Hebrides, some of the Pacific Islands, New Caledonia and New Zealand and throughout most of Australia. In Australia it is reasonably common everywhere except the far inland portion. It is found mainly in open forest in our region, more frequently in the vicinity of a river or lake edge. The species is a complete migrant arriving in the district in late September and early October when it immediately reveals its presence by the persistent territorial call. After breeding it departs from the area during February or March.

HABITS: Sacred Kingfishers can feed in water or on land so can be seen plunging into streams or diving to the ground and hopping rapidly in pursuit of prey. They are usually seen as solitary birds or in pairs. Their flight is direct and rapid. Although sometimes seen on the ground during the course of feeding, they are more often observed perching in an upright position on a branch or stump watching the ground for food.

BREEDING: The breeding season is from late October to early January. The nest is usually in the hollow limb of a tree, or in a hollowed out cavity in a termite nest. In some areas the species is known to excavate a nesting burrow in the bank of a creek or cliff but this habit is rare in this region. The nest is not lined. The clutch size varies from four to six and the eggs are spherical and shining white when first laid, becoming duller as incubation progresses. They measure about $25 \times 22$ mm. The young are born naked, the subsequent feathers remaining encased in their sheaths until the young are nearly ready to fly.

FEEDING: Known food items include small lizards, frogs, fish and invertebrates such as crustacea, worms and both aquatic and land insects, particularly beetles and grasshoppers. (J.L.McK.)

## Family Meropidae — Bee-eaters

In Australia there is only one kind of bee-eater, known as the Rainbow-bird, presumably to disguise any effect it might have on apiarists. The family is a very compact one of twenty-four species, mainly tropical in origin. They are all insectivorous taking their prey in flight and bees and wasps are preferred. The plumage is always bright; green and yellow are common colours. The bill is long and slender and very sharp, the legs are short and the feet small, for clinging rather than walking. They are usually gregarious, tend to breed in colonies and are usually migratory. All nest in burrows.

## RAINBOW-BIRD *Merops ornatus*

PLATE XX

IDENTIFICATION: Length, 23 cm. Crown, rufous-green; back, green; rump, turquoise blue; upperside of tail black, shot with blue; *throat, rufous with black bib; breast, green; abdomen, blue*; underside of tail, black; the two central tail feathers are elongated; wings are rufous brown underneath; there is a broad black band through eye; bill, black, long, pointed and decurved; legs and feet, grey-brown; iris, scarlet. The sexes are similar.

VOICE: A musical trill or whirr is uttered which has been rendered as "pirr pirr pirr". It sometimes calls from perches but usually on the wing, whole flocks calling together.

DISTRIBUTION: It is found throughout the continent but not Tasmania. It also occurs in New Guinea and the Solomons and Celebes Islands. It generally avoids dense forests but otherwise is found in all habitats, even treeless plains but it shows a decided preference for lightly timbered country. It is a strict migrant in southern Australia but large numbers remain in the north throughout the year. The migrants reach Perth, Western Australia, usually in the first week of October, but near Sydney, New South Wales, apparently sometimes in August. They reach Canberra in late September and leave again in mid-April. Many of the migrants arrive in Canberra quite unobtrusively but the Rainbow-bird travels in tight, noisy flocks that make their return immediately obvious. During its stay with us it is most common in open country along watercourses and in open woodland but does not penetrate the denser forests.

HABITS: They are usually seen in flocks or groups, sitting on telegraph wires or the bare limbs of trees or sometimes on fences, but very rarely on the ground. They dart into the air after insects and return to the perch. The flight is graceful with a good deal of rather erratic soaring and gliding.

BREEDING: In the coastal districts of the Northern Territory it breeds immediately before and after the summer wet season, when insects are very abundant. It breeds throughout its whole range and in the south the breeding season is in the summer; around Canberra between early November and late January. The nest is a tunnel drilled into a sandy bank or cutting or, on the plains, into flat ground at a slight angle. The tunnel is up to one metre long and ends in a chamber thirty centimetres long and about fifteen centimetres wide and ten high. The eggs are laid on loose soil on the bottom of the chamber. The clutch size is usually five but the full range is three to seven. The eggs are pearly white and almost circular. They average $22 \times 19$ mm in size. The egg chamber usually contains great numbers of insect wings, heads and other chitinous waste. The individual birds return to the same nest site each year.

FEEDING: They are entirely insectivorous and, although they do occasionally stand on the ground and catch terrestrial insects passing by, most hunting is done in the air. They dart from a perch or soar and glide for long periods. In the tropics very large numbers ascend just before dusk and remain aloft until dark. They frequently swoop close to the ground or water to secure a large insect, with an audible click of the bill. The food consists of a wide variety of insects including large dragon flies, but wasps and bees are especially favoured; the birds are not popular with apiarists and for this reason they are often harried. (H.J.F.)

### Family Coraciidae — Rollers

The Rollers are a small family of about a dozen birds mainly tropical in distribution; they are most common in Africa. All are medium-sized birds of rather stout build usually with short tails. The head is very large and the neck very short. The bill is broad, usually short and slightly hooked and the feet are small but powerful. The wings are broad. There is only one Australian representative, the Dollar Bird, that gets its name from round, light spots on the wings that supposedly resemble silver coins.

200

## DOLLAR BIRD *Eurystomus orientalis*

PLATE XX

IDENTIFICATION: Length, 27 cm. General colour above, brown-grey with turquoise tinge; under-parts as above with brilliant blue on throat; *wings*, black at tips, greenish-blue at shoulders *with a prominent light bluish-green spot in middle*; bill, pink; legs and feet, pink; iris, sepia. The sexes are similar.

VOICE: The voice is harsh and discordant and has been described as a screech and as "kak kak kak". It is sometimes uttered on the wing but more commonly while perched.

DISTRIBUTION: It extends from northern India to Manchuria, east to the Solomon Islands and south to southern Australia. In Australia it extends from the Kimberley Division across the north and down the east to eastern Victoria. It very occasionally reaches Tasmania. It is mainly coastal in distribution but extends inland to the western slopes and follows some of the rivers onto the plains. It is a strict migrant in eastern Australia and reaches our area in mid-October and, after breeding, it departs in late February. A few remain in the far north throughout the year but the majority apparently leave the country. When on the Southern Tablelands it is moderately common and is restricted to the open woodlands where there are tall trees; it occasionally penetrates the foothills of the ranges.

HABITS: The Dollar Bird does not make itself very obvious. It is usually seen singly or in pairs perched, hunched up, in a high tree or flying with a rather slow but very buoyant flight far overhead. The wing beats are slow and deliberate but it is very agile in the air. It apparently does not undertake the spectacular rolling and tumbling displays to the same extent as some of the African rollers, but does somersault in the air and makes quite impressive swoops.

BREEDING: The breeding season in our region is between early November and mid-January. The nest is in a hole in a dead tree a considerable height from the ground, usually between fifteen and thirty metres. The eggs are laid on the decaying wood or earth originally carried there by termites. There are occasional records of nests in the deserted holes of kookaburras in arboreal termite mounds. The clutch varies from three to five but four is most common. The eggs are less rounded than those of kingfishers and are pure white and lustrous; they measure about 38 × 28 mm.

FEEDING: They are insectivorous. The food is caught by darting from a perch or by hawking low over the timber, usually at dusk. They catch large insects, often cicadas, moths and beetles, and return to a perch to stun and swallow them. (H.J.F.)

## LYREBIRDS

This family is restricted to south-eastern Australia. The single genus contains two species, the Albert Lyrebird *Menura alberti*, and the Superb Lyrebird *M. novaehollandiae*. They have no close relatives but do have certain anatomical features in common with the scrub birds Atrichornithidae. These include a rather simple form of syrinx which is remarkable in a group of birds that are capable of producing a variety of complex sounds and are all competent mimics.

The two lyrebirds have similar habits and share the same alarm call. Both are shy, insectivorous, ground-living birds which rarely fly and are renowned for their loud and continuous song, which includes mimicry of the calls of other birds, and for their spectacular tail-spreading display. The Albert Lyrebird which is found only in the dense rainforests of northern New South Wales and southern Queensland, is smaller and duller in colour than the Superb Lyrebird and lacks the lyre-shaped outer tail feathers. Its display, though similar in form, is less spectacular and it does not build display mounds.

Family Menuridae — Lyrebirds
SUPERB LYREBIRD *Menura novaehollandiae*
PLATE XXI

IDENTIFICATION: Male: total length 97 cm, tail 61 cm. General colour above, dark brown; throat, rufous; under-parts, lighter brown; tail, upper-parts, dark brown and the under-parts, silvery-grey, it consists of two narrow single webbed feathers, twelve filamentary feathers and two outer lyre-shaped feathers which are silvery-grey with rufous bands. Bill, black; eyes, large with brown iris; feet and legs, black. Female: total length 82 cm, tail 47 cm. Colouring similar to the male; lacks the lyre-shaped tail, the tail feathers being all broadly webbed with the outer feathers slightly curved with rufous markings on the inner webs.

Flight is rather rudimentary, consisting either of a series of powerful leaps with flapping wings, when ascending trees, or a long glide with occasional wing flaps, when descending. On the ground they run very rapidly with the head low and the tail streaming out behind.

DISTRIBUTION: The principal habitat of the Superb Lyrebird is the wet eucalypt forests of the eastern slopes of the Great Dividing Range from Stanthorpe in Queensland to the Dandenong Ranges in Victoria. It is not native to Tasmania but was introduced there in 1934 and has become established. It is quite common in the wetter parts of the ranges in the area dealt with in this book, and is particularly numerous in the Tidbinbilla and Brindabella Ranges near Canberra.

VOICE: The song of the male is very loud and mingled with a continuous stream of mimicry which may be maintained for periods of up to forty minutes. Contrary to popular belief, the mimicked sounds are not random but are carefully selected for their acoustic properties and perform an important function as a highly directional sound beacon enabling females and rival males to locate a singing male at a considerable distance in dense vegetation. Loud and sustained song is an important factor in breeding success and, here again, mimicry performs an important function in adding individual variety to a basic song which is simple and could become monotonous with repetition. This extensive use of mimicry is possible only because the Superb Lyrebird is a winter breeder and the species mimicked are virtually silent during the peak period of song. It follows that the calls of birds which are vocal during this period of the year do not form a significant part of its repertoire.

Apart from mimicry the Superb Lyrebird has a number of loud distinctive notes of its own. The territorial call is a loud clear "choo" that can be heard at least one kilometre away on a mountainside; the full call is a series of notes deliberately spaced at first but increasing in speed and brevity, "choo — choo — choo — chuk — chuk — chuk — — —". The alarm note is a clear shrill whistle, usually heard without the bird being seen. These two calls are woven into the song, the structure of which varies greatly from place to place and region to region, and birds in districts only a few miles apart have quite different "dialects".

Other calls include a loud "pilik" which may be repeated several times and is often accompanied by display. A short high-pitched shriek signifies extreme alarm and a clucking sound, reminiscent of a frightened domestic fowl, is also given when alarmed or when fleeing. During courtship the male gives a series of "clicks" which may continue for as long as four minutes. This call which has a rather metallic quality is probably the source of many bushman's stories of the lyrebird's mimicry of axe blows, saw and other mechanical noises. Such stories have now become an accepted part of lyrebird lore but recent studies have shown that mimicry of such sounds, if indeed it occurs at all, is extremely rare.

Females occasionally produce a form of song, which consists mainly of mimicry, with an occasional clucking alarm call when disturbed in the vicinity of the nest site.

HABITS: Lyrebirds are mainly ground-living birds but roost in tall trees, sometimes as much as thirty metres above the ground. The hopping, flapping ascent at dusk is a remarkable sight, and at dawn they descend slowly in a series of glides from tree to tree pausing at intervals for song. The bird is well known for its display and this is usually performed on one of up to six mounds about one metre in diameter and fifteen centimetres high which the male prepares after clearing the undergrowth.

The male walks onto the mound and, after a few bursts of song, raises the tail which, until then, has been carried folded. It rises up and over the back until it falls forward and covers the bird; the lyre-shaped feathers are almost at right angles to the body and the filamentary feathers spread like a shimmering silver shawl between them. In this posture, prancing and turning from time to time, the male sings and the bush echoes and re-echoes to the stream of sound. At the end of the performance the bird falls silent, the tail is swept back, folded, and he stalks from the stage.

Sometimes a display mound is used year after year but new mounds are made each season. Where mounds have been tagged and inspected over a number of years, it has been found that one bird may make more than fifty over a period of seven years. During the display the male will turn to face a rival male or a female and when uttering the loud "pilik" call will make a series of short leaps. These movements, together with the trembling of the tail feathers, are sometimes referred to as a dance. Song and display sometimes take place on rocks or logs and males also sing in trees.

Except in Sherbrooke Forest in Victoria, where the birds have become accustomed to tourists, both sexes are very shy and difficult to observe. Females with young in the nest, however, often become quite tame and have been known to take food from an observer. Males are strongly territorial during the breeding season from April to October but non-breeding males sing and display on mounds at the beginning and end of the season, and during the summer groups of birds may be seen together wandering through the forests.

BREEDING: Although eggs have been found from May to October, the main egg-laying period is in June and July. It is not known for certain whether the birds are polygamous or promiscuous, but the male takes no part in nest building, incubation or the feeding of the young. The single egg which is purple-brown in colour streaked and blotched with black, 64 × 45 mm, is laid in a large domed nest which may be built high in a tree, in an old tree stump, on a rocky ledge or on the ground. The nest takes several weeks to build and is usually finished three weeks or more before the egg is laid. It is built of coarse sticks, up to thirteen-millimetres in diameter at the bottom, but of finer sticks, fern leaves and green mosses above. It is lined with fine wiry rootlets and a few feathers from the female's breast are added immediately before or immediately after the egg is laid. Despite the size of the nest, they can be very inconspicuous and hard to find. During the six weeks of incubation the tail of the female becomes bent owing to the restricted area of the nest and nesting females can readily be identified by this feature. The young bird remains in the nest for a period of six weeks after which it continues for some time in the company of the female.

FEEDING: The food is worms, millipedes, land crustacea, grubs and small snails from the deep litter of the forest floor. It is obtained by scratching with powerful feet. Rotting logs and termite nests are also probed for food. No thorough study of the food of the adults has yet been made but food brought to young birds includes earthworms, insect larvae, centipedes, collembola and other arthropods. (F.N.R.)

# LARKS AND PIPITS

Larks and pipits are not very closely related but live in the same places, have very similar habits and resemble one another in appearance. Without exercising care, it is easy to confuse the Australian members of the two families so they are best considered together.

## Family Alaudidae — Larks

Larks are small, brownish birds with long legs that live in grasslands and open scrubs but never in forests. There are representatives in all the continents except South America, and Africa is particularly rich. There is only one native species in Australia but for some obscure reason another was imported from Europe last century and established here. Many larks are renowned for their song, and singing on the wing is a feature of the whole group. They sometimes sing on the ground or from a low bush but more commonly soar far overhead pouring out continuous flute-like notes.

## BUSHLARK *Mirafra javanica*

PLATE XXII

IDENTIFICATION: Length, 13 cm. General colour above, dark brown, streaked black; wings, edged rich rufous; under-parts, cinnamon; upper breast and throat, streaked black; bill, brown; legs and feet, grey-brown; iris, cinnamon. The sexes are similar.

It is smaller than the Pipit and considerably smaller than the Skylark. It has a stubby tail and a noticeably stouter bill; the body patterns are more boldly marked than either Skylark or Pipit and the calls and song also differ.

DISTRIBUTION: It extends from the Minilya River, Western Australia, around the north of the continent, down the east coast to the edge of the Nullarbor Plain in South Australia. It does not occur in Tasmania. It extends inland a considerable distance and is absent only from the central deserts and mulga scrubs; it probably invades these also in good seasons. Unlike many African members of the genus that live in open scrubs the Bushlark tends to avoid these and is most common on open grass plains, particularly the Mitchell grass of the treeless Barkly Tableland and the wallaby grass of inland New South Wales. It is also found in open glades in forest country and in some of the more open coastal scrublands. In general, the name Bushlark is something of a misnomer and Fieldlark, a name sometimes used, is more appropriate.

Around Canberra it is found in small numbers in open areas; lucerne fields, grasslands, playing fields and parklands. In the north it is always present but in parts of southern Australia it is a migrant. It arrives in this district in early November and disappears again in late February. Near Sydney it remains throughout the year but its numbers vary seasonally.

VOICE: On the ground it has a sharp "chirrup" or "chip" but its best known song is that uttered during aerial display. This song is a long, continuous, outpouring of clear, slightly shrill notes formed into a rich, melodious song. The song is often given during a quivering descent to a lower perch or the ground and during undulating song flights. It sings from low perches and the ground, and is commonly heard during clear, still nights.

HABITS: It is usually in small groups in this area but elsewhere large congregations are common. It is terrestrial and runs swiftly when disturbed, more or less crouching on the run and pausing frequently to take stock. When it does fly it does so with a sharply jerky flight and seldom goes far before dropping to the ground and running.

BREEDING: There is little information on its breeding season but what there is suggests that in south-east Australia it breeds relatively late, in the period November to January. The nest is well concealed in long grass or under a tussock. It is a hollow scratched into the ground and lined with a thick layer of grass; frequently the grass extends above so that the nest is almost dome-shaped with a wide entrance. The clutch is usually three but occasionally four. The eggs measure about

206

18 × 14 mm, are greyish-white in colour, and are freckled all over with olive, dark grey and brown. They are very similar to those of the Pipit, though somewhat smaller.

FEEDING: They feed entirely on the ground, apparently on small insects. (H.J.F.)

## SKYLARK *Alauda arvensis*

PLATE XXII

IDENTIFICATION: Length, 19 cm. General colour above, brown, streaked with darker brown or black; wings, brown; under-parts, very light brown; upper breast, streaked black; bill, mid brown; legs and feet, brown; iris, brown. The sexes are similar.

The Bushlark and the Skylark are rather similar but the Skylark is very much larger and is pale underneath whereas the Bushlark is quite a rich light brown. The Skylark is distinguished from the Pipit by a stockier build and less pronounced white eye stripe. Slight crest and pale trailing edge to wings are also useful field marks.

VOICE: It is renowned for its song which is similar to that of the Bush-lark but is probably more robust. The call is a liquid "chirrup", and the song is a high-pitched, melodious trilling delivered during a characteristic sustained song flight. The bird ascends, soars and descends on quivering wings, but the song ceases with the short plummet to the ground. Song is rarely given from a low perch on the ground.

DISTRIBUTION: It is naturally distributed throughout Eurasia and was introduced by misguided enthusiasts to Victoria in the 1850s. It is now well established in that State, particularly in pastures and agricultural areas in the southern half. It has also reached Tasmania, south-east South Australia, the southern New South Wales coast and the Southern Tablelands but has not invaded the drier inland plains. Near Canberra it is common throughout the year in open grasslands and city parks. It has clearly established itself but whether this is at the expense of the native Bushlark is not known.

HABITS: In its general habits it is very similar to the Bushlark.

BREEDING: The local breeding season is in the period September to December. The nest is built on the ground in the shelter of a tussock, and is similar to that of the Bushlark. There are no local data on the clutch size but in England this is three or four or occasionally up to seven. The eggs are greyish-white spotted and speckled with olive and brown and average, in size, 24 × 17 mm. Incubation is eleven days and the young leave the nest after ten days.

FEEDING: It England it feeds on both seeds and insects in about equal quantities; there are no local data. (H.J.F.)

### Family Motacillidae — Pipits and Wagtails

The wagtails included in this family have nothing to do with the familiar Willie Wagtail, which is quite different and a flycatcher. True wagtails are Northern Hemisphere birds and at least three species occasionally reach Australia on their southern migration but do not breed here. The pipits mostly belong to the one genus, *Anthus* and there are about forty species. They are a very homogeneous group of similar birds. All are small and brown with long legs and live on the ground. They are superficially similar in appearance and behaviour to the larks that occur in Australia. The sole Australian pipit is very widespread and is common in our area at all times.

## PIPIT *Anthus novaeseelandiae*

PLATE XXII

IDENTIFICATION: Length, 18 cm. General colour above, brown, mottled with darker brown; under-parts, light brown; breast, spotted or streaked with darker brown; wings, brown; tail, brown with outer feathers white; bill, brown; legs and feet, yellow-brown; iris, brown. The sexes are similar.

The Pipit can be confused with the Bushlark but with care can be easily separated. The Pipit is much less rufous in colour, and does not soar nearly so much. The song is much weaker and more intermittent than that of the Bushlark. Its flight is more undulating and it does not pitch to the ground so suddenly. When running the Pipit jerks its tail up and down but the Bushlark and Skylark do not.

VOICE: The Pipit does not soar so expertly as the larks but does fly high and utters a much less elaborate trilling song. The contact call is a thin "zwee".

DISTRIBUTION: It is found throughout Australia including Tasmania but generally avoids the driest parts of the inland and does not enter the forests and dense scrubs. It is most numerous on the coast, tablelands and the inland slopes. Its preferred habitat is open grassland, pastures, cultivation paddocks and, on the coastline, thinly grassed sand dunes. It is very common in the open parts of our area but does not penetrate the forested slopes of the ranges although it is found on the high moors and in the cleared valleys. It seems to be sedentary and its numbers do not fluctuate much.

SWALLOWS

HABITS: It is seldom seen perched but is nearly always running rapidly and nimbly across the ground. It is quite hard to flush as it runs swiftly ahead of the observer; when it does fly the white outer tail feathers are very obvious. It is usually in pairs but in the winter small flocks develop.

BREEDING: The breeding season is throughout the summer months. The nest is a depression scratched in the ground in the shelter of a bush or tussock and lined with fine grasses to give a deep cup about five centimetres in diameter and up to eight centimetres deep. The clutch is usually four, and occasionally three or five. The eggs, which average 23 × 17 mm, are greyish-white spotted and freckled all over with dark grey, brown and umber.

FEEDING: It catches insects on the ground and on the grass and pursues them vigorously across open ground. It also eats some small seeds. (H.J.F.)

# SWALLOWS

The swallows and martins form a very uniform group. They all have short necks, slender bodies and long, pointed wings; the tail is usually moderate in length but is sometimes elongated and is usually forked. The legs are short and the feet small. The bill is always short, flattened and has a wide gape. The plumage is usually dark but the rump is very often light in colour. Swallows and martins are insectivorous and take all their food on the wing; the flight is erratic, strong and swift. Water is often taken by scooping with the bill as the bird flies low across its surface. They seldom land on the ground except to gather nest materials. Many are gregarious and breed in colonies, the nests are often closely packed together. Many are migratory. There are about eighty-five species and these are distributed throughout the world except in the highest latitudes and on a few islands. Until recently there was no swallow in New Zealand but the Welcome Swallow now breeds regularly. The Australian Tree Martin is occasionally recorded. In Australia there are six recorded species and, of these, four occur in the area discussed in this book.

Family Hirundinidae — Swallows and Martins
**WHITE-BACKED SWALLOW** *Cheramoeca leucosternum*
PLATE XIX
IDENTIFICATION: Length, 14 cm. Forehead and crown, white; nape and back of the neck, brown-white; *mantle and upper back, white*; remainder of the upper-parts, black; lores, black with a brown

209

line below the eye to the nape; *throat and upper breast are white*; remainder of the under-parts, black; legs and feet, pinkish; iris, reddish-brown. The white markings are quite diagnostic. The sexes are similar.

VOICE: This is a rather quiet bird with a subdued single note, "chip", uttered on the wing.

DISTRIBUTION: The White-backed Swallow is mainly a bird of the inland and is common on the coast only where the dry country touches it, as in Western and South Australia. In Western Australia it extends to the Kimberley region but in the east usually does not go so far north and is generally rare north of about the latitude of Alice Springs. In south-east Australia it is rare beyond the inland plains and seldom goes south of the Divide in Victoria or on to the Southern Tablelands. It is common west of Wagga, New South Wales, and small numbers regularly reach the slopes and the edge of the Australian Capital Territory. It rarely reaches the New South Wales coast.

In the inland it is usually found near water in the lightly timbered country, the box and belah woodlands. It especially favours the timbered watercourses. The details of its movements are not known but there is obviously a strong nomadic element.

HABITS: It is usually found in small groups of ten or a dozen hawking over or alongside timber; apparently large flocks do not occur. It is very graceful; though the flight is swift it is not so swift as the Welcome Swallow. It quite often rises from the ground beside pools of water. It is said to roost in groups in old nesting burrows.

BREEDING: The breeding season in inland New South Wales is in the period August to December. The nest is a tunnel drilled into a sandy bank. Sand-dunes, creek banks and road cuttings are used. The tunnel varies from about thirty to eighty centimetres in length and is up to five centimetres in diameter. A chamber is built at the end and a rudimentary saucer-shaped nest of grass and dead leaves built in it. The clutch is four or five or very occasionally up to seven eggs. The eggs are pure white and measure about 17 × 12 mm.

FEEDING: Like the other swallows, it feeds on the wing on small insects. (H.J.F.)

## WELCOME SWALLOW *Hirundo neoxena*
PLATE XIX

IDENTIFICATION: Length 15 cm. Upper-parts, steel-blue; wings and tail dark brown; abdomen, whitish; forehead, chin, cheeks and *throat, chestnut; tail, deeply forked,* and has a subterminal row of white spots, except for the central pair of feathers; bill, black; iris, dark brown; legs, brownish-black. The sexes are similar.

VOICE: A constant twittering chatter is maintained by a pair as they hawk for insects and this reaches a crescendo when young are fed. This call serves largely to maintain contact between fast flying individuals, but is also an aggressive call, becoming more strident in that role.

DISTRIBUTION: It is widely distributed throughout southern Australia, including Tasmania, but has a restricted distribution in the north. In the east it extends along the coast to Cape York and in the west to Port Hedland, but in the inland generally it is rare as far north as 25° latitude. It avoids the inland deserts and only rarely visits the Alice Springs district, for instance. It is migratory but the extent of the movement varies greatly from place to place. In Tasmania apparently most leave in the winter but in inland New South Wales, although there is no obvious exodus, passage migrants pass through and some remain. Near Canberra the numbers decline greatly at the end of May and increase again in late August but some birds are always present. One colour-banded bird first caught near Canberra as an adult in 1961, raised young in the same nest for at least six years.

HABITS: These very strong, fast fliers gather their food while flying, an activity so familiar that it needs no further description. They find that houses provide excellent nest sites and are therefore common in both suburbs and bush.

BREEDING: Nest building and egg laying usually start in September near Canberra and may continue well into December in suitable (wet) years. This species is one of the few that has thrived since settlement, finding houses, bridges, culverts, and mine shafts suitable for nest sites. The mud-cup is plastered to a (usually) vertical surface, one to four metres from the ground; both members of the pair build and it takes four to five days to complete. The eggs are white, speckled with brown and are laid on successive days; the clutch size is four or five. The eggs measure 18–20 × 13–15 mm. Incubation, which starts with the laying of the final egg, lasts for sixteen days and the nestling period for nineteen days. The young are dependent for about three weeks. The adults may attempt two nestings a year; certainly they re-nest after a failure.

FEEDING: They are obviously insect-eaters but no analysis of their food is available. They will certainly take items as large as blowflies and small moths, but the major part of their food appears to consist of

very small flying insects, such as midges. These are often gathered close
to the surface of water and in the evening. Usually they are day
feeders, but there is a recent description of the nesting of a pair who
fed their young by night with insects gathered from a well-lit nearby
filling station. (I.C.R.R.)

## TREE MARTIN *Cecropsis nigricans*

PLATE XIX

IDENTIFICATION: Length, 13.5 cm. *General colour above, dark
steel-blue; upper-tail coverts, dull white*; a line of dull rufous extends
across the forehead; chin and throat, white ringed with buff;
remainder of under-parts, dull, pale rufous, becoming almost white on
the centre breast and abdomen; bill, black; legs and feet, purplish-
black; iris, black. The sexes are similar.

It can be distinguished from the Welcome Swallow by the dull white
patch of the upper-tail coverts and the shallow fork of the tail; from
the Fairy Martin by the dark steel-blue colour of the crown of the head
which is rufous in the Fairy Martin.

VOICE: A quiet twittering is heard from circling flocks but the calls
are quiet and not distinctive.

DISTRIBUTION: It is found in New Guinea and some other northern
islands. In Australia it is a widespread species being found virtually all
over the continent and Tasmania but is most numerous in the south. It
is widespread in our area but its numbers in no way compare to those
in the inland. It has a pronounced preference for open country with
rather large, wide-spreading trees, particularly near water, and does
not penetrate the higher and wetter mountain forests.

There is a very well marked migration in our area. It arrives about
the second week of August and is fairly common in suitable habitats
until about the end of February. Stragglers remain as late as the end of
May in mild years. Although the migration is total in this region this is
not so elsewhere. At lower elevations in coastal New South Wales and
Victoria some individuals remain over the winter but the majority
migrate. In inland central New South Wales, however, any diminution
in local numbers in winter is small. In the far north of the Northern
Territory it is present at all times but the numbers increase during the
southern winter.

HABITS: The Tree Martin is usually in flocks, hawking for insects
between the trees and sometimes low over water. In our area the flocks
are small but in the inland to the west very large and quite spectacular
congregations of several thousand birds can be found over some of the

swamps and reedbeds at dusk prior to roosting. At night it roosts communally in reedbeds or hollow limbs.

BREEDING: In our area nests have been found in October and November. The nest is built in a hollow limb or a hole in a large tree and is seldom less than six metres from the ground. Occasionally the size of the entrance is reduced with mud. Several pairs sometimes use the one hollow. The nest itself is a shallow saucer of leaves and feathers. It has been reported from Western Australia that occasionally mud nests similar to those of the Welcome Swallow are built. The clutch is usually four to five. The eggs are white spotted with reddish-brown. They average 18 × 13 mm.

FEEDING: It feeds in the air on small insects. (H.J.F.)

## FAIRY MARTIN *Cecropsis ariel*

PLATE XIX

IDENTIFICATION: Length, 12 cm. *Head, chestnut*, with dark striations; upper back, blue-black; wings and tail, dark brown; *lower back, buffy-white* and conspicuous in flight; throat, sides of body, buff with dark striations; breast, white; under-wing, pale fawn; bill, black; legs and feet, black; iris, blackish-brown. The sexes are similar.

VOICE: The voice is a feeble twitter lacking the sweetness and variety of the Welcome Swallow's notes.

DISTRIBUTION: It is widely distributed throughout the Australian mainland but is only common in its preferred habitat of open country, particularly in the vicinity of lakes and streams. It is apparently only a rare visitor to Tasmania. In the southern parts of its range the Fairy Martin is only present during the summer months. Around Canberra the species first puts in an appearance in September although in some years odd birds have been seen as early as July. The bulk of the population moves out of the area by February but some birds may remain until April.

HABITS: They are usually seen in flocks hawking for insects low over the ground or water. The flight is similar to that of the other swallows, swift and erratic.

BREEDING: The local breeding season extends from October until early January. The Fairy Martin nests in colonies and constructs its mud nest against the wall or ceiling of a cave, building or culvert, the side of a hollow tree, a cliff-face or creek bank. The nests are strong and offer the nesting birds protection from all but the most determined of predators such as kingfishers, who have been recorded chipping holes into the sides of nests and consuming the contents. House Sparrows, Striated Pardalotes, and Zebra Finches sometimes take over and breed in Fairy Martin nests. Small bats may, on occasion, use them as roosts.

The nests are bottle shaped and built close together, sometimes in rows, but usually in clusters, and only the entrances of many of them are visible. Up to 1300 separate pieces of mud are required to complete one nest. The bottom may be lined with grass and feathers. They are variable in size, the bowl may be up to fifteen centimetres in diameter, the spout-like entrance thirteen millimetres in diameter and from ten to twenty centimetres long. Nests have been recorded as weighing between half and one kilogram.

The clutch size varies from four to six, usually four. The eggs are oval, dull white in colour, often lightly freckled yellowish or reddish-brown. The eggs measure about $17 \times 12$ mm. Both birds build the nest, brood the eggs and care for the young. Banding has shown that adults invariably return to the same area each year and that many of the young eventually take up residence in the colony in which they were born.

FEEDING: Fairy Martins, like other swallows, feed on insects caught on the wing. They usually cruise, hawking, over timber or swamps. (J.L.McK.)

## CUCKOO-SHRIKES

Cuckoo-shrikes have no close affinities to either cuckoos or shrikes. They are a separate family of birds with a mainly tropical distribution from Africa, through southern Asia and Malaysia to Australia and east to Samoa. They range in size from that of a sparrow to a pigeon and are usually coloured grey of various shades, although some members of the family, the minivets, are brightly coloured. They are all arboreal except for the Ground Cuckoo-shrike of inland Australia.

There are seventy-one species in the family and of these eight occur in Australia. These are know as cuckoo-shrikes, cicada-bird and cater-pillar-eaters, trillers, or peewee-larks. Four species occur in our region. The White-winged Triller and the Black-faced Cuckoo-shrike are common and breed regularly, while the Cicada-bird and the Little Cuckoo-shrike are rarely recorded and have not yet been reported breeding. A possible future addition to the list would be the Ground Cuckoo-shrike, a nomadic species which is not uncommon to the west and is liable to wander into our area at any time.

Family Campephagidae — Cuckoo-shrikes
BLACK-FACED CUCKOO-SHRIKE *Coracina novaehollandiae*
PLATE XXII

IDENTIFICATION: Length, 33 cm. General colour above, light grey; flight feathers, black with grey edgings; tail, black with distinct white tip; forehead, face and throat, black, grading to dark grey on the breast and through to white on the belly and under-tail coverts; bill, black; legs and feet, black; iris, dark brown. The sexes are alike.

Immatures have only a black mark extending from the bill through the eye to the ear coverts; the forehead is finely barred black and white and the throat grey; the under-parts are whitish.

VOICE: Two main calls are uttered, a pleasant rolling phrase usually when in flight, and another resembling "chereer-chereer" when at rest. A third, aggressive call is a harsh scolding note given when diving at an intruder near its nest.

DISTRIBUTION: It occurs in Australia, Tasmania, New Guinea and nearby islands. A recent survey showed that this species was recorded in more Australian district and bird lists than any other, which gives an idea of its wide ranging distribution. Around Canberra it is more often seen in savannah woodland and open forest rather than in the heavily timbered ranges.

HABITS: It is common and widely distributed during the period August to April when pairs or later family parties are usual. During winter, smaller numbers are seen in our area and the breeding territories are forsaken. There is some evidence of migration for large flocks containing a high percentage of immatures are seen in northern and central Australia during winter, when fewer birds, usually adults, are seen in southern Australia.

The flight is undulating with alternate gliding and flying movements and after alighting, the wings are always settled alternately with a flicking motion.

BREEDING: In our region the breeding season is October to January, most nests being found in the mature eucalypts of the savannah woodland country. The same tree, and the same nest site, may be used in successive seasons, presumably by the same individuals. They defend the nest vigorously against an intruder, diving steeply and only veering away at the last instant. The nest is shallow, saucer-shaped and invariably built on a horizontal forked branch, often a dead one, from six to twenty-five metres high. Materials used are small sticks and bark, always heavily bound together with cobweb. Both sexes build the nest,

215

brood the eggs and feed the young. Two or three eggs form a clutch, varying from blue-green to olive with spots of dark brown, red-brown and grey. They measure about 34 × 24 mm. The nestlings outgrow the nest well before they fledge and sit on it rather than in it, so it is not surprising that in windy weather they are sometimes found on the ground.

FEEDING: Black-faced Cuckoo-shrikes feed among the leaves of trees and shrubs as well as on the ground. They will also take flying insects. (G.S.C.)

## LITTLE CUCKOO-SHRIKE *Coracina papuensis*
PLATE XXII

IDENTIFICATION: Length, 28 cm. General colour above, pale-grey; flight feathers, black, edged with pale grey; tail, black tipped with white; a black band extends from the lores through the eye to the ear coverts; throat, white; breast, grey; belly and under-tail coverts, white; bill, legs and feet, black; iris, dark brown. The sexes are alike.

Immatures resemble the adult Black-faced Cuckoo-shrike and have the head, neck, throat and chest, black. Usually the feathers on the breast have a barred appearance but great variation occurs in the amount of barring and in the size of the frontal black area, which both diminish as the bird gets older.

VOICE: The two main calls are very different. One resembles the low rolling note of the black-faced species whereas the other is a shrill double whistling note with an upward inflection.

DISTRIBUTION: It occurs in northern Queensland south through New South Wales except the far west, throughout Victoria and west as far as Adelaide. It is a very occasional breeding visitor to the Australian Capital Territory. It is more plentiful in far north-eastern New South Wales and eastern Queensland than elsewhere.

HABITS: The Little Cuckoo-shrike seems to prefer more wooded areas than the black-faced species. However, its apparent rarity, combined with the difficulty of distinguishing it from juvenile Black-faced Cuckoo-shrikes results in a lack of reliable field information. It is generally regarded as being nomadic but there is at least one record of the same nest tree having been used in successive seasons.

BREEDING: The breeding season in our area is August to December. The flat saucer-shaped nest looks just like a smaller version of that of the Black-faced Cuckoo-shrike and is built on the horizontal fork of a tree six to twenty-five metres from the ground. It is usually located near the extremity of a branch. The clutch consists of two or three eggs which are only distinguishable from those of the black-faced species by their smaller size, averaging 30 × 22 mm.

FEEDING: The main diet is insects, obtained both in the leafy canopy and on the wing; seeds and berries are also eaten. (G.S.C.)

## CICADA-BIRD *Coracina tenuirostris*

PLATE XXXV

IDENTIFICATION: Male, length 27 cm. General colour, dark grey with flight feathers black, edged with grey; tail, black; black on the lores, cheeks and ear coverts; bill, legs and feet, black; iris, dark brown. The female is smaller; general colour above, greyish-brown with paler scalloping on the rump; wings, brown, the feathers all with paler edgings; tail, brown tipped buff; clear buff eyebrow contrasts with blackish lores and ear coverts; entire under-parts creamy-buff with darker markings on each feather.

VOICE: Cicada-birds are more often heard than seen. The loud cicada-like trilling call of the male as he sings high in a forest tree can often be heard up to 800 metres away; no doubt it is accentuated by the resonant atmosphere of the habitat, the heavily timbered mountain ranges. The call resembles "keee-keee-keee" repeated about ten times.

DISTRIBUTION: The range is chiefly coastal, from the Kimberleys, north Western Australia, to the east coast and south to near Melbourne. It also occurs in the Moluccas, New Guinea and the Solomon Islands. In northern Australia it prefers thickly wooded areas such as paperbark swamps and monsoon forest, but in south-east Australia it prefers the tallest timber in the mountain ranges and deeply dissected coastal country. Near Canberra, it has only been recorded occasionally on the lowlands and more often in the high ranges where it probably breeds. Nests are found occasionally farther south in Victoria. In southern Australia, Cicada-birds are strongly migratory arriving in October and departing in March. The first indication of their presence is always given by the loud, repetitive calling of the male.

HABITS: They are quite difficult to observe, keeping to the tops of the highest forest trees, generally high up near the crest of a ridge. Here they forage among the leaves and build their nests. They are very aggressive, driving other species of birds away from the nesting area as well as defending the nest vigorously against any human intruder.

BREEDING: Like the cuckoo-shrikes the Cicada-bird builds its nest on a horizontal fork, usually of a rough-barked tree at heights ranging upwards from ten metres. It is a very small nest compared to the size of the bird and measures only about eight centimetres in diameter. It is built of fine plant stems, lichen, moss, or *Casuarina* stems, bound well with spider's web and camouflaged with lichens on the outside. The single egg sits on the nest rather than in it. The ground colour of the egg varies from pale blue to green and it is heavily spotted and blotched all over with brown and grey markings. It measures about $31 \times 22$ mm.

FEEDING: The food consists of insects and their larvae taken in the tree canopy. (G.S.C.)

## WHITE-WINGED TRILLER *Lalage sueurii*
PLATE XXII

IDENTIFICATION: Length, 18 cm. Male: crown, nape and back, glossy black; *wings, black with white "shoulders"*; tail, black, tipped white; rump, grey; sides of neck and face, throat and under-parts, pure white; bill, legs and feet, black; iris, dark brown. The male wears an eclipse plumage in winter in which the black on the head and back is replaced with brown, but this phase is not seen in our area as the birds do not assume it until after they have migrated northwards. The female is a very inconspicuous bird when compared to the male. Upper-parts, brown, including wings and tail; a dull whitish eye-brow surmounting a darker mark in front of and behind the eye; breast, brownish; throat and remainder of under-parts, dull white; bill, dark brown, paler at the base of the lower mandible; legs and feet, grey-black; iris, dark brown. No colour changes occur in the female.

VOICE: Male White-winged Trillers have a loud repetitive "song" usually uttered in a short flight from the top of one tree to another, or after alighting. The most common call is a quick "oo-eee, oo-eee" rapidly repeated many times.

DISTRIBUTION: It extends through New Guinea, Timor and Australia, including Tasmania (rarely). The preferred habitat is savannah woodland and open shrubby areas. It is rarely seen in heavy forest country and in south-eastern Australia is more often seen in inland areas than near the coast. Trillers are migratory but their numbers vary greatly from year to year. They depart for northern Australia in February and are completely absent in the south during the winter. They usually arrive in our region in mid-October and quickly set about nesting activities.

218

HABITS: At all times the male is a conspicuous bird, flying around the territory singing loudly and chasing intruding males. Several pairs of trillers can often be found nesting in close proximity but the reason for this communal nesting is not clear.

BREEDING: The breeding season around Canberra is from October to February. Both sexes help to build the nest but the male often does more than his fair share, and advertises the fact by singing from the nest site. The nest is usually built in a fork at the extremity of a sloping or horizontal branch of a tree at heights from five to about fifteen metres. Sometimes it is closer to the ground in a shrub, but again on a sloping or horizontal fork as is the habit of all the other Australian members of the family Campephagidae. It is a shallow saucer-shaped structure about eight centimetres in diameter and built of fine rootlets and grasses liberally bound with spider's web. The clutch consists of two or three eggs which are blue to green in ground colour, blotched and streaked with reddish and chestnut markings. They average $21 \times 15$ mm. Both sexes brood the eggs which hatch in about fourteen days and they also co-operate in feeding the young.

FEEDING: Insects are the main food. Most of the feeding is done on or close to the ground, in shrubs or amongst fallen dead timber. In these situations the male is very conspicuous as he hops along but the female is well camouflaged and always difficult to find. (G.S.C.)

# THRUSHES, FLYCATCHERS AND ALLIES

The thrushes, flycatchers, robins, whistlers, shrike-thrushes, shrike-tits, fantails and monarch flycatchers were formerly placed in six different families, but recent studies indicate that the members of this large and seemingly varied assemblage have much in common and are best classified in a single family. Most species can be grouped into readily distinguished units and some of these are given subfamily names in taxonomic classifications. Thus the thrushes constitute the subfamily Turdinae and the typical flycatchers, including the Australian robins, make up the Muscicapinae. Current thought is to include also in this subfamily, the whistlers, shrike-thrushes and related birds, although these are sometimes separated into another subfamily, the Pachycephalinae. The fantails are placed in the Rhipidurinae and the monarch flycatchers in the Monarchinae. It is emphasised, however, that the classification of this family is under active study and the status of the various groups may change yet again in future.

The family is a large and successful one found on all continents and many oceanic islands. The predominant food taken is insects and other

219

invertebrates, although some species supplement their diet with small fruits and other plant food. Different groups of species are adapted to obtaining their insect food in a variety of different ways.

Thrushes are one of the most widespread groups of birds. Some are brightly coloured and others are plain or even solid black. They are typically plump, active birds with comparatively long slender legs and bills. Most of them spend much time on the ground and gather their food there. The young of some have mottled plumage. No doubt this enables them to be less conspicuous among ground litter and so escape predators. Australia has only one native thrush, the range of which extends through Asia to Europe. Two others, the Blackbird and the Song Thrush *Turdus philomelos* have been introduced from Europe. The Blackbird is a common species in urban parts of our area but the Song Thrush, which was deliberately introduced from New Zealand into Canberra about 1935 in an effort to control introduced garden snails, has not become established. In parts of southern Australia where it has become established it is mainly restricted to urban and highly developed agricultural districts.

The term "flycatcher" is a very loose one and covers a great number of birds including the "fantails" and others. Originally "flycatcher" was used to cover small European songbirds with short, broad bills that live by catching insects in the air, usually by flying after them from a vantage point. It has now come to include a very large group of more diversified birds that are distributed widely, particularly in the tropics. In Australia although a few retain the "flycatcher" habit most are birds of the trees and undergrowth that secure their food on the ground or in foliage. Many, because of a supposed resemblance to European birds familiar to the early settlers, were dubbed "robin" and the name has persisted. There are over 150 species in this group and of these twenty-one are found in Australia; eight are found in our area, most of which are known as robins.

The whistlers, shrike-thrushes, Shrike-tit and Crested Bellbird form a closely related group. They are undoubtedly of Australian origin and are confined to this continent, to South-east Asia and some Pacific islands. There are about forty-five species in the group. The genus *Pachycephala* "thickheads", is the most numerous and widely distributed. All members of the group have robust bodies and powerful bills, all are insectivorous and two have distinct crests. Most live in tall timber but in Australia there are several that live on the ground, or near it, in low arid scrubs. The calls are all melodious and loud, and, in many, the female calls immediately after the male so that the two sound as one. It is hard to travel anywhere in Australia without hearing one or other of the group.

In our area the Golden Whistler, Rufous Whistler and the Grey

Shrike-thrush are very common, while the Olive Whistler and Shrike-tit are less common residents.

Fantails are perky birds and are nearly always tame and confiding. They often live close to man and follow him about in the bush. They have short rounded wings that often droop, and long tails that are usually cocked up and partly fanned. They are very restless and flit from branch to branch and bush to bush more or less continuously. They are all insectivorous and control themselves in the air with remarkable agility when chasing flying insects. The nests are very neat cups usually with a distinct tail of fibres below. The group contains about forty species and is distributed throughout Australia and New Zealand to South-east Asia. There are numerous species in the tropics north of Australia but in this country there are only four, and of these three are moderately common in our area.

The Monarch Flycatchers are as a rule less active than fantails; they prefer to gather their insect food from leaves and twigs rather than to chase it through the air. As it happens, however, those that occur in our area differ in this respect and collect most of their food by darting after it. They typically sit on tree branches, stumps and fences with the wings slightly drooping and the tail hanging downward whilst waiting. Many of the group are colourful and some African species are adorned with long ornamental tails. In most the sexes are quite different in colour.

They are distributed throughout Africa south of the Sahara, eastern Asia and thence south to northern and eastern Australia. There are about ninety-two species in this group and of these twelve occur in Australia; four are found in the area discussed in this book.

Family Muscicapidae — Thrushes, Flycatchers and allies
## BLACKBIRD *Turdus merula*
PLATE XXIII

IDENTIFICATION: Length, 26 cm. *Whole bird, deep, sooty black; bill, orange*; legs and feet, dark brown; iris, dark brown; skin of eye, orange. *Female is rufous-brown above*, lighter below with dark mottling; bill, brownish-yellow; legs and feet, brown. Juveniles are similar to females but are more rufous with pronounced mottling below and upper-parts streaked rufous.

VOICE: It has a low "tchook, tchook, tchook" when disturbed but not seriously alarmèd. When startled it flies off giving a sudden shrill screaming chatter. A persistent "chick-chick-chick" is used when going to roost and also when scolding predators. Blackbirds also have a high-pitched aggressive call and a similar but lower-pitched distress call. The song is loud and clear, of a rich fluty quality in which the notes

221

merge into a continuous short warble, usually delivered from a tree or building. Occasionally while in song a harsh chuckle may be given or an imitation of another bird's call incorporated.

DISTRIBUTION: It occurs from Europe, south to north-western Africa, eastward to central Asia and southern China. It was introduced into Australia and New Zealand and self-introduced to outlying islands. In Australia it is common throughout most of Tasmania, Victoria and south-eastern South Australia and less common but gradually increasing and extending its range into southern New South Wales. It was first recorded in Canberra in August, 1949 and has now become a common resident in the older suburban areas and has spread to Queanbeyan, New South Wales, and the Brindabella Range. A small population has been present at Goulburn for many years and it is possible that the Canberra birds originated from there. It still has plenty of scope for population increase as most of the Canberra suburbs at present lack established bushes and shrubs for nesting sites, and even in the older suburban areas, the population is nowhere as dense as it is in the vicinity of Melbourne.

HABITS: On the ground the Blackbird moves with a combination of running and quick hops; it typically advances a few metres and then pauses. Its flight pattern over short distances is low and weak and over long distances is undulating and direct. As the Blackbird is strongly territorial it does not occur in groups though numbers may roost together in shrubberies, plantations or thickets.

BREEDING: Around Canberra the breeding season extends from early September to late January during which a pair may produce two or three broods. Pair bond usually lasts until the death of one of the partners. The female usually selects the nest site, builds the nest and incubates the eggs. Both parents feed the young. The nest is cup-shaped and built of dry grasses, stalks and other vegetable matter, plastered on the inside with mud or muddy leaves and lined with fine grass, thin dead stems or rootlets. If the first brood is successfully reared the nest may be patched up and relined for the second and third broods. The only species in our region with a similar nest is the Ground Thrush whose nest is bulkier and invariably adorned externally with mosses and lichens, and is not found in gardens.

The clutch size is usually two but can be up to five. The eggs are bluish-green, freckled or streaked red-brown or grey. They measure about $24 \times 19$ mm. The incubation period varies from thirteen to fifteen days, and the young stay in the nest from twelve to fifteen days.

FEEDING: Blackbirds eat a great variety of food. Earthworms are an important food item and are captured by a sudden jab into a garden bed or lawn. In summer when earthworms are less plentiful and the ground is much harder, fruit such as pears, peaches, apricots, apples, grapes, strawberries and blackberries feature in their diet to the concern of many back-yard fruit growers. Many other concealed food items, mostly inactive invertebrates, are extracted out of leaf litter, dug up from the soil or taken from rough pasture. Caterpillars and adult insects living above the ground are taken during late spring and summer and form the major part of the diet of the young. They also eat plants and grain and refuse. (J.L.McK.)

## AUSTRALIAN GROUND THRUSH *Zoothera dauma*

PLATE XXIII

IDENTIFICATION: Length, 29 cm. *General colour above, olive-brown, each feather having a black crescent shaped mark at the tip*; wing coverts, dark brown tipped with dull white; quills, brown; tail, olive-brown with the outer feathers tipped with white; under-parts, white with most feathers having a black crescent shaped marking at the tip; bill, dark brown with the base of the lower mandible yellowish-brown; legs and feet, pale, fleshy-brown; iris, blackish-brown. The sexes are similar.

VOICE: This is a very quiet species but it has a very melodic long, drawn out whistle, heard in the warmer months at the first light of dawn and sometimes on dull days. In spring it is one of the first birds to call in the forest and the song usually ceases before many other species have commenced calling. The song is loud and carries well.

DISTRIBUTION: It has usually been thought that this is a distinctive Australian species but it is now accepted that it is a race or subspecies of a thrush with a very wide distribution in Siberia and east Asia generally, Malaysia, Indonesia, the Philippines and parts of Polynesia. Many of the subspecies are very different in colour and size to the Australian bird.

The Australian race of this widespread species occurs down the coastal and mountain areas of the east coast, from northern Queensland to Victoria and south-eastern South Australia to as far as the Mount Lofty Ranges and Kangaroo Island. It also occurs in Tasmania. Its preferred habitat is the dense brushes and denser coastal scrubs. Around Canberra it is most common in the wet gullies and wet sclerophyll forests of the ranges. It is a fairly common bird in the ranges, and is found there at all seasons but it is nomadic or an altitudinal migrant in winter and is occasionally reported away from the wetter forests in scrub country well inland.

HABITS: The Ground Thrush is quiet in its actions as well as in voice. It is a bird of the shrub level of the forests and is seldom seen far from the ground except in really densely overgrown wet gullies. It is not easily alarmed and if approached quietly will often remain on the ground within a short distance of the observer, but it is not nearly so inquisitive as the Grey Shrike-thrush. When disturbed it flies low and softly for only a short distance before it alights and runs to dense cover.

BREEDING: In the mountains the breeding season is from August to November. The nest is a large cup-shaped structure, rather untidily built of strips of bark, rootlets and pieces of green moss and lichen. It is placed in a vertical, multiple fork of a shrub or a small tree, usually within two metres of the ground but in denser gullies, it may be placed at any height within the shrub level. Two or three eggs are laid. They vary in ground colour very considerably, from pale blue to buff or a stone colour with reddish-brown freckles or blotches. They measure about 37 × 23 mm.

FEEDING: This species takes a variety of small animal foods, chiefly insects and worms which are found on the ground in the moist gullies. (H.J.F.)

## JACKY WINTER *Microeca leucophaea*

PLATE XXV

IDENTIFICATION: Length, 13.5 cm. *General colour above, ashy-brown* with lighter edgings to the primaries and secondaries; there are *two white outer tail feathers*; under-parts, white with a pale brown wash on breast; bill, dark brown; legs and feet, brown; iris, brown. The sexes are similar. It could be mistaken for a female robin but is distinguished by the absence of wing markings.

VOICE: It has a variety of calls. One is a pretty and melodious song which carries well in the open forest. This is interspersed with a rapidly repeated "peter-peter-peter-peter" with a downward inflection.

DISTRIBUTION: It occurs throughout Australia and in southern New Guinea wherever there is open forest. Only wet sclerophyll and rain forest and the extreme dry country of the interior are avoided. The Jacky Winter is a breeding species on the Southern Tablelands but it is never numerous. It is found throughout the more open areas and does not occur in the denser forests of the ranges. It seems very likely that its movements are of a local nomadic nature only.

HABITS: This bird usually perches on stumps, fence-posts and dead branches. It often sways its tail sideways when perched. The white tail feathers are conspicuous in flight. It is usually in pairs and only occasionally in small groups.

BREEDING: The breeding season in our area is from late October to December but on the New South Wales coast it begins in August. The nest, five centimetres in diameter, is one of the tiniest constructed by Australian birds. It is a rather flat open cup, usually placed in the fork of a branch, and is constructed of bark and grasses bound with much cobweb. Pieces of bark are often worked into the outer surface and this, its siting and size make it difficult to find. It is placed between one to twenty metres from the ground but is usually between five to eight metres.

Two, sometimes three, eggs are laid. They average 20 × 14 mm and are of a pale greenish-blue ground colour freckled and blotched with purplish-brown. At times the markings are all over the egg while, at others, they form a zone at the larger end.

FEEDING: It takes a variety of insect foods both on the wing and on the ground. (S.J.W.)

## SCARLET ROBIN *Petroica multicolor*
PLATE XXIV

IDENTIFICATION: Length, 13 cm. Male: *black above* with prominent white markings on the wings, on the forehead and white outer tail feathers; *throat, black; breast, scarlet*; abdomen, flanks and under-tail coverts, white; bill, black; legs and feet, black; iris, hazel.

The female is brown above with *buffy-white wing and forehead markings*, the forehead spot is smaller than that of the male; *the breast is strongly washed with scarlet*, the throat and chin are greyish-white; remainder of under-parts dull white to pale brown.

Juvenile birds have mottled brown plumage particularly on the head and back. Immature birds are like the female but when very young the breast colour is lacking.

VOICE: The main call is a trilling, low, cheery whistle heard mostly in spring. There are also sharp repeated double calls on the one note and single clicking notes.

DISTRIBUTION: The range of the Scarlet Robin extends from the Darling Downs in Queensland through New South Wales from the coast across the Dividing Range to the limits of the western slopes, through much of Victoria to the Flinders Ranges in South Australia,

Yorke Peninsula, Eyre Peninsula and Kangaroo Island. It is common in Tasmania and the Bass Strait islands and there is an isolated race in the south-west of Western Australia. Several other races occur in the islands of the south-west Pacific. It is a bird of the open forests but in summer it retires to the denser forests at low altitudes. It can often be seen on the lower slopes of the hills surrounding Canberra, and by Lake George. This species is thinly distributed in the Capital Territory but, except in summer, an odd pair will usually be found on any walk in suitable habitat. In the cooler months, its numbers in the valleys rise remarkably indicating a movement of some distance but, apart from the fact that it moves between dense forest, open forest and grassland, the exact nature of its movements is not known. North-south migration appears unlikely in this area.

HABITS: Scarlet Robins move very quietly around the forest and woodland in pairs. When foraging they perch on a low vantage point, quite still except for an occasional quick flicking of the tail. They flit suddenly to the ground to seize the prey and return to another vantage point to repeat the process.

BREEDING: The breeding season in our area extends from September to November but elsewhere it is from July to December. The nest, which is constructed by the female, is an open cup-shaped structure of thin strips of bark, mosses and grasses securely woven together with cobweb and thickly lined with wool, feathers, hair or fur. The rim is thick and rounded and the exterior is lightly coated with pieces of bark and lichen. It is placed up to thirteen metres from the ground but is usually low; it may be in the fork of a tree, on a horizontal branch, between the trunk and loose bark or inside the hollow trunk of a tree. The outside of the nest is decorated to match the environment so the appearance can vary considerably.

The usual clutch is three eggs which are from pale green or bluish-white to dull brownish-white and are very thickly spotted at the larger end and often all over. The eggs average 17 × 14 mm. The incubation period is fifteen days and the nestling period sixteen to eighteen days.

FEEDING: It collects much of its food from the grass and various small insects, grubs and worms are taken. (S.J.W.)

## RED-CAPPED ROBIN *Petroica goodenovii*
PLATE XXIV

IDENTIFICATION: Length, 12 cm. Male: *dull black to blackish-brown above* with white markings on the wings and on the tail; *cap*, which is much larger than that of the other four "red" robins, *scarlet as is the breast*; remainder of the under-parts, white. In some male birds there is a wash of red on the black of the throat; bill, black; legs and feet, black; iris, dark brown.

Female: *dull brown above* with pale buff wing markings; the *cap is dull reddish-brown* but this is not very conspicuous in the field; *under-parts, brownish-white.*

On leaving the nest, the young are mottled brown, particularly on the upper-parts. The immature male resembles the adult female but has some breast feathers washed with red. Immature females have a buff coloured cap.

VOICE: One call resembles the ticking of a clock while another is a definite little song. Generally the calls are feeble and insect-like in tone; but this can be said of all our "red-breasted" robins.

DISTRIBUTION: Its range is virtually the whole of the mainland of Australia except the wetter forests. It is mainly a bird of the open forest of the inland, and while it prefers certain trees in some places, its preference varies in different parts of its habitat. It reaches the coast in some places but is rare east of the Divide. It is a rare bird in the Southern Tablelands but appears to be increasing in numbers. Several recent records were on the outskirts of the city. There have been several sightings in the Brindabella Range at 1200 metres, in November, 1965, the summer of 1967–68 and February and March 1981; surprising records for the species which is not normally found at higher levels nor in wet sclerophyll forest. Some movement is evident within its large range. It appears that in the non-breeding season it becomes somewhat nomadic, and occurs well beyond its breeding range but these appearances are sporadic.

HABITS: It is very similar in its general behaviour to the Scarlet Robin.

BREEDING: Generally in eastern Australia the breeding season is an extended one from July to December. Local records are in spring only. The nest is a small structure of shreds of bark and grasses bound together by cobwebs and lined with animal material including occasional feathers. Externally it blends into its surroundings and is decorated with pieces of lichen. The situation used includes upright forks, the tops of horizontal branches and places where several thin branches join. The nest is usually from two to six metres from the ground.

Two, occasionally three, eggs are laid. They measure about 17 × 13 mm and the colour varies from bluish-white to grey-green with spots of brownish shades chiefly at the larger end. The incubation period is about twelve days.

FEEDING: It feeds on insects, taken in flight, in trees and on the ground. (S.J.W.)

## FLAME ROBIN *Petroica phoenicea*

PLATE XXIV

IDENTIFICATION: Length, 13 cm. Male: *general colour above, greyish-black*; there are white markings on the wing, (larger than in the Scarlet Robin), tail and forehead (smaller than in the Scarlet Robin); lower portion of the abdomen and the lower-tail coverts, white and the remainder of the *under-parts, including throat, a vivid orange-scarlet*; bill, black; legs and feet, black; iris, brownish-black.

Female: brown above with pale buff markings on the wings and forehead; under-parts, brownish-white to brown, palest on the abdomen. *Old females have a faint, often irregular, wash of scarlet on the breast.*

Juvenile birds are mottled in shades of brown on the upper-parts. Immature birds resemble the adult female and as there are many records of breeding by two birds in "female" plumage, it appears that male plumage is assumed very slowly.

VOICE: The call is a quiet, fairly long one for a robin, a slightly descending trill which, with some imagination, has been interpreted as "you may come, if you will, to the sea". That sentence at least gives the timing and inflection. The "red-breasted" robins do not have loud notes but this is a fairly penetrating call.

DISTRIBUTION: It ranges through the Dividing Range from about the Queensland border to South Australia where it reaches as far as Kangaroo Island, Adelaide and Yorke Peninsula. It is very common in Tasmania and on the islands of Bass Strait. It is accepted that some Tasmanian birds cross Bass Strait each autumn though this has yet to be proved. Certainly it spreads throughout Victoria, southern New South Wales and across much of the south-east of South Australia, where it is not known to breed, each autumn and winter. It is rare in northern New South Wales.

As an altitudinal migrant from the mountain tops, through the denser forests to the open plains, the species can at times be found in all areas throughout the Southern Tablelands. In winter it is common in parkland about Canberra and on the lower slopes of the surrounding hills and at this time it is very widely distributed in the open country but is not present in the ranges.

A few birds breed near Canberra, beginning in August when others are already back in the ranges, but by the beginning of summer all have left for the higher country. In the Brindabella Ranges it breeds at all altitudes and in the warmer months it is abundant about the open places above 1200 metres.

HABITS: This species is well known for its habit of appearing in the colder months in open grasslands, ploughed paddocks and parkland when the orange-scarlet breast of the male is conspicuous as the bird perches on wires, fence posts or plant stems in its search for food.

BREEDING: The breeding season in our area is from mid-August to December and possibly later on the extreme heights of the ranges. Elsewhere it breeds from September to January. The nest is, by comparison with that of the Scarlet Robin, a bulky structure of fine strips of bark and grasses thickly coated with dry mosses and cobwebs. The very neat inside is lined with hair, fur or plant down. The nest always merges well into its surroundings. A variety of sites may be used such as a charred treetrunk or in a steep cutting beside a road, a grassy wall, creek bank, upturned roots, rafters of a shed, in the end of a hollow log, a tree fork or behind projecting bark. High nests are unusual.

Usually three eggs are laid, measuring 17 × 13 mm. The colour is pale bluish or greenish-white and there is a fine spotting or blotching of shades of brown, sometimes towards the larger end.

FEEDING: The Flame Robin takes a variety of small insects such as aphids but feeds on worms and insect larvae from the ground as well. (S.J.W.)

## PINK ROBIN *Petroica rodinogaster*

PLATE XXIV

IDENTIFICATION: Length, 10.5 cm. Male: general colour above, *slaty-black with a blackish-brown tail; there are no white outer tail feathers* and this feature distinguishes it from the Rose Robin; the white forehead spot is very small; *under-parts, rose-pink*, except for white under-tail coverts; bill, black-brown; legs and feet, black-brown; iris, blackish. Female: *olive-brown above and pale brown below*; there is no wash of red on the breast as there is in the Rose Robin; *tail, brown without white markings*; wing markings are rich buff.

Juvenile birds are mottled brown and immature males resemble the female.

VOICE: The call note is a quiet "tick tick" and there is also a pleasant but very quiet warble. It is virtually silent during the winter visits to the Brindabella Ranges.

DISTRIBUTION: This is a bird of the damp fern gullies of the wet sclerophyll forests of Tasmania and southern Victoria and was unknown in New South Wales and the Australian Capital Territory until it was found in the Brindabella Ranges in the winter of 1962. Since then it has been seen each winter in the ranges and as far as the National Botanic Gardens in Canberra and Lake George.

In the breeding season it has been reported from Tasmania and the wetter forest gullies of Victoria only. In winter numbers of the species are reported to cross Bass Strait to Victoria where it is found occasionally in open forest country, even to the north of the Divide.

As there are no breeding records from our area the origin of the birds near Canberra is a puzzle. The species has been reported in the Snowy River Valley to the north of Orbost, Victoria, in late February and March and breeding occurs in southern Victoria and Tasmania; it is possible that our birds originate from one of these areas. The winter population is a very small one but banding has shown a remarkable constancy in return to this non-breeding habitat and it is possible that these birds are from an unknown local breeding place.

While the Rose and Pink Robins have been reported as breeding together in the same gullies of the Otway Ranges in southern Victoria, in our area one species virtually replaces the other. The Pink Robin occurs from April to August, with one record in October; the Rose Robin is present from August to April, with one record in July.

HABITS: Pink Robins are very quiet and unobtrusive and in the breeding season are not easy to see in their dense haunts. They spend much of their time in the darker parts of the forest, flitting quickly from tree to tree and occasionally dropping to the ground or a log to seize their prey.

BREEDING: The breeding season in Tasmania is in the period October to January. The nest is similar to that of other red-breasted robins. It is a small cup built of moss, lichen and cobweb, lined with fine rootlets and placed in a low bush or tree in a moist gully. Three or four eggs, measuring 19 × 14 mm are laid. The ground colour is greenish-white with minute dots and spots of brown, purple or umber forming a ring at the larger end.

FEEDING: The species appears to feed exclusively on small insects taken from the ground or low in the undergrowth of the forest. (S.J.W.)

## ROSE ROBIN *Petroica rosea*

PLATE XXIV

IDENTIFICATION: Length, 10 cm. Male: *dark, slaty-grey upper-*

*parts* with blackish-brown wings and tail and *prominent white markings on the outer tail feathers*; white forehead spot is small; *breast, rose-red*; abdomen and under-tail coverts, white; the coloured breast area is larger in the male Pink Robin; bill, brown; legs and feet, brown; iris, dark brown.

Female: *dark ashy-brown* with dull greyish-white under-parts and a *faint rose-pink wash on the breast; the wing markings are dull cream* as is the forehead mark; *the white markings in the brown tail* are the chief means of identification, as they are in the male.

Juvenile birds are mottled brown and immature males resemble the female.

VOICE: The call is a pleasant and insect-like trill which is repeated frequently. Three quick notes are followed by three slightly slower ones, the last two very slightly higher in tone, making it somewhat plaintive. This call is given very frequently and is heard throughout the breeding season. The bird becomes much quieter in early autumn.

DISTRIBUTION: The species occurs in Queensland, New South Wales and Victoria from the ranges to the coast, occasionally extending beyond the Divide where suitable habitat exists. In this region it is a migrant and may be seen on passage in open forest country in spring or autumn. Primarily, however, it is a bird of the dense scrub of the moist mountain gullies and is numerous in the ranges between August and April. There is one winter record from our area and there are reports of occasional winter sightings in Victoria. In central coastal areas of New South Wales a few birds are often seen in winter in open forest country. In Queensland and in northern New South Wales it regularly moves into the more open country in winter in quite large numbers.

It breeds at different elevations throughout its range. In Queensland it has been reported to breed above 600 metres whereas along the southern areas of New South Wales and in Victoria it breeds at low altitudes as well as in the ranges. Its breeding at high altitudes in Queensland coupled with appearances near the coast in winter support the view that it is a vertical migrant there, though considerable north–south movement, as of our Canberra birds, is also evident. The regular return of significant numbers of individuals has been shown by banding in the Brindabella Ranges but the wintering area of these breeding birds is as yet unknown.

HABITS: Rose Robins have similar habits to Pink Robins but are more often seen on the edges of the wetter gullies, where the broad-leafed trees merge into the wet sclerophyll forest.

231

BREEDING: The breeding season is from October to January and appears fairly constant throughout the breeding range. The nest is a small cup-shaped structure of moss and cobweb, quite thick in relation to its size, and with a well rounded rim. It is smaller than that of the Pink Robin. It is always decorated on the outside with lichen and is built on a horizontal fork of a branch which carries a fair amount of lichen. The nest is lined with plant down or fur. The nest is often reported at a height of ten metres or more but around Canberra nests are often only a metre or so from the ground, well down towards the bottom of a moist gully.

The eggs are a faint bluish or greenish-grey and are minutely dotted or spotted in deep brown shades and measure 18 × 13 mm.

FEEDING: This is another insectivorous species and it appears to find its food in the lower strata of the vegetation of the gullies, or on the ground. (S.J.W.)

## HOODED ROBIN *Melanodryas cucullata*

PLATE XXIV

IDENTIFICATION: Length, 16.5 cm. Male: *a completely black hood* extending well down on the breast, *black wings with conspicuous white markings and white under-parts*; the scapulars are also white; bill, black; legs and feet, black; iris, dark brown. Female: *brownish-grey above* and pale brownish-grey below; *wing and tail markings, similar to those of the male* but there are small white markings on the tips of the tail and the white scapular markings of the male are lacking.

The immature male is similar to the female but has the upper-parts more strongly washed with grey. The chin, throat and fore neck are dull white mottled with dark brown.

VOICE: The main call is a rather feeble one; a fairly high-pitched call, on a slightly descending scale, with trilled notes. It also has a single, low, unmusical note. It calls at night and is often heard as the first light of dawn appears.

DISTRIBUTION: The Hooded Robin is found throughout Australia except the extreme north. It avoids the dense, wet forests but is widely distributed inland from the Dividing Range and through dry savannah and mulga areas around the periphery of the continent. It occasionally reaches the more coastal places in the east. The Hooded Robin is found in small numbers throughout the district wherever suitable habitat exists. Its favoured areas are the edges of open forest country and places where dead trees and stumps remain. It appears to be mainly sedentary but is more numerous in winter.

HABITS: This is a quiet and somewhat inconspicuous species despite the strong contrasts of the male plumage. It likes to sit quietly on the branches of dead trees, on fence posts and particularly on dead stumps from which it flies down to feed. It feigns injury in protecting nest and young in an endeavour to lead the intruder away from the nesting area.

BREEDING: The breeding season around Canberra is from early September to the end of December. An open cup-shaped structure is constructed in a more or less horizontal fork often close to the ground but occasionally up to six metres. It is usually inconspicuous and is often made externally to blend into the surroundings. Strips of bark and grasses are used in the nest and a binding of cobwebs holds the materials together.

The eggs are from pale olive to apple-green sometimes clouded with rich shades of brown, particularly on the larger end. Two, or occasionally three, eggs are laid. They measure 20 × 15 mm.

FEEDING: Insects and spiders are the main foods. These are usually procured on the ground. (S.J.W.)

## YELLOW ROBIN *Eopsaltria australis*

PLATE XXIV

IDENTIFICATION: Length, 16.5 cm. *General colour above, dark grey* with greyish-white on the chin and upper-part of the throat, the tail is washed with olive, *the upper-tail coverts are a bright yellow-green*; remainder of the *under-parts, bright yellow* washed lightly with olive on the flanks; bill, black; legs and feet, olive; iris, horn. The female is similar except that the markings are not quite so bright. It is not possible to distinguish the sex of live birds with certainty. Juveniles are pale rufous-brown above and below, the feathers on the upper-parts having prominent white or brownish-white shafts.

VOICE: This is one of the first birds to call of a morning in the forests. Its main call is a rather loud, prolonged piping on the one note, rather slower than that of the White-throated Tree-creeper and of a lower tone. This call is heard at all seasons but is heard less in the non-breeding period.

DISTRIBUTION: The Yellow Robin ranges from the extreme south-eastern corner of South Australia to northern Queensland. It extends from the coast through the ranges and slopes to the edge of the dry inland plains. In the southern areas of its range, that is about Dorrigo, New South Wales, southwards, the rump is yellow-green but in the

233

northern races, occurring in northern New South Wales and Queensland, the rump is of similar colour to the breast.

This bird is found throughout this district wherever there is forest country with some undergrowth. It is quite common throughout the ranges. It is regarded as a rather sedentary species though some local movement occurs.

HABITS: It is a fearless bird which can be approached closely without it becoming alarmed. It is inquisitive and will often perch on the bark of a vertical trunk or on a low branch while it inspects an intruder.

BREEDING: The breeding season in our area extends from September to January. Elsewhere it commences as early as July. The nest is beautifully moulded of thin strips of bark and grasses with some cobweb binding and the outside is decorated with pieces of lichen and long, pendant strips of bark which hang below the nest proper. It is usually placed in an upright or horizontal fork often as low as one metre from the ground but occasionally as high as ten metres. Two to eight eggs form the clutch, but most commonly three. The eggs are pale green to bluish-green spotted and blotched with reddish-brown. They measure about 23 × 18 mm.

FEEDING: Its food is insects secured on the ground, from the foliage and occasionally in the air. (S.J.W.)

## GREY FANTAIL *Rhipidura fuliginosa*

PLATE XXV

IDENTIFICATION: Length, 16 cm. General colour *above, greyish-brown* with two small white bars on the wings; *tail, long, outer feathers white*; a conspicuous line of white over the eye and another over the ear coverts; throat, white with a narrow black band at its base; underparts, buff; bill, black; legs and feet, brownish-black; iris, black. The sexes are similar. Immature birds are duller than adults; the white markings on the wings and head are buff; not white.

VOICE: The Grey Fantail has a quickly uttered "chip chip" heard throughout the year. It also has a high-pitched, very melodious, upward soaring song which is reminiscent of the tone of a violin. This is one of the more beautiful bird songs and appears to be a song of the breeding season.

DISTRIBUTION: It occurs virtually around the whole margin of the continent and in Tasmania, New Zealand, New Caledonia and New Hebrides. A small population extends to the ranges of central

234

Australia. In the east its breeding range extends from the coast to about the western limit of the slopes of the Divide, while winter movements take it very much farther west.

It is a common breeding species throughout our area and is found wherever there are a few trees with some scrubby undergrowth. In the ranges it is common from mid-September to April but very few remain at the high levels over winter. About Canberra it appears to become nomadic after breeding for breeding areas on the nearby hills are deserted by mid-summer in dry years but this has not been observed in the ranges where it is also a common breeding species. It is quite common in the area over winter but the numbers are greatly reduced. This accords with its appearance between March and October throughout the south-western districts of New South Wales but the real nature of these movements is not known.

HABITS: This bird is rarely still. When perched it indulges in frequent sideways movements of the body and tail. In flight the ever open tail enables a variety of acrobatic movements and it never flies in a straight line for more than a few feet. Its acrobatic abilities are responsible for its popular name of "Cranky Fan" and are visible proof of its ability as a catcher of flying insects.

BREEDING: The breeding season in our area extends from September to January. The nest is a very beautiful one; an open cup with a long thin tail somewhat like a wine-glass with the base removed. It is constructed with thin shreds of bark and similar very fine plant material thickly bound on the outside with cobweb. Usually a horizontal fork is used as a nest site but sometimes more upright forks or just a straight, thin branch serves as a support. The nest is usually low, seldom being above six metres from the ground. It will desert the nest if it is too closely inspected before the eggs are laid but after egg laying it becomes most excited and will attack an intruder. Two or three, sometimes four, eggs, measuring about $16 \times 12$ mm, are laid. They are dull white or creamy-white and are minutely freckled or blotched with brown shadings.

FEEDING: Insects appear to be the only food and these are taken on the wing. This feeding habit is responsible for its distinctive manner of flight. (S.J.W.)

## RUFOUS FANTAIL *Rhipidura rufifrons*

PLATE XXV

IDENTIFICATION: Length, 16 cm. Upper-parts, brown tinged with rufous which becomes *orange-rufous on the lower back and tail*;

terminal half of the tail, blackish-brown; throat, white; lower throat, black; breast feathers are black edged with white; bill, brown; legs and feet, brown; iris, brown. The sexes are similar.

Juveniles are similar to adults but have more orange-rufous on the upper-parts; the under-parts are brownish-white with a rufous wash becoming dull brown on the lower breast.

VOICE: Its calls resemble those of the Grey Fantail in that it has a "chip" call, often given in flight, and a soaring melody but this is more shrill and not so rhythmical or melodious as that of the Grey Fantail.

DISTRIBUTION: The distribution is from the extreme north of Western Australia eastwards to the bottom of the Gulf of Carpentaria, and from Cape York to the Otway Ranges in Victoria. It is accidental in Tasmania and South Australia. It also occurs in the islands northwards to Guam, including the Celebes and the Solomon Islands. In the southern parts of its range it is entirely migratory but about Sydney and farther north odd birds may be found in winter but the full nature and extent of its movements are not known in detail. Throughout its range the habitat is similar; wet forests for breeding with migratory movement where necessary through dry forest country.

Its breeding habitat in our area is the moist gullies of the ranges where it is quite common from late October and November till the later half of March. On its migrations during March and early April and again in October and early November it may be found temporarily in quite dry country and there are usually a few about Canberra, at Lake George, New South Wales, and along the Murrumbidgee River, at these times. It appears likely that its movements occur during daylight at low levels.

HABITS: This species is acrobatic in its flight but is not nearly so skilled as the Grey Fantail. It tends to fly fairly directly but its marvellous control is demonstrated by its unerrring flight through dense shrubbery. As with the Grey Fantail, the tail is never closed.

BREEDING: The breeding season in our area is from November to January. The nest is similar to that of the Grey Fantail, but is not quite so neat and is constructed of slightly coarser material. Very occasionally the tail is absent or very short. The nest is placed on a thin horizontal fork at heights from one to ten metres from the ground, usually in the understorey of the forest.

Two, occasionally three, eggs are laid. They vary in ground colour from pale stone to buff and are minutely spotted on the larger end with yellowish- to reddish-brown and measure about 16 × 12 mm.

FEEDING: Most insect food is collected among the shrubs but some is taken on the wing although the bird does not venture into the open in its search for insects as does the Grey Fantail. Feeding seems to be confined to the lower levels of the forest and it is rarely seen above the shrub level. (S.J.W.)

## WILLY WAGTAIL *Rhipidura leucophrys*
PLATE XXV

IDENTIFICATION: Length, 20.5 cm. *Upper-parts and throat, black*; there is a conspicuous white eyebrow. The remainder of the under-parts are white; bill, black; legs and feet, black; iris, black. The sexes are similar. Immature birds have buff markings on the tips of the black feathers on the upper-parts. The black throat of this species readily distinguishes it from the Restless Flycatcher which has a white throat.

VOICE: The chief call resembles the phrase "sweet pretty creature" or "sweet pretty little creature"; it is a chatter of quick notes with the last two rather longer and is fairly musical. The alarm calls are metallic rasps or rattles. The species frequently calls at night, occasionally even on moonless nights.

DISTRIBUTION: The Willy Wagtail is widely distributed throughout Australia. It does not inhabit the denser forest areas or the open treeless plains of the interior but with these exceptions it is found throughout the mainland of Australia. It also occurs in New Guinea, the Solomon Islands and in other nearby island groups and is accidental in Tasmania. In our area it occurs in all open areas and is one of the first open forest country birds to find the new clearings in the denser forests.

HABITS: The bird is very well known and is found singly or in pairs in all situations. Its habit of perching on any handy vantage point to dart after insects and of accompanying and riding on stock, is familiar to all. It has adapted itself well to habitation and is often found around farm buildings, in parks and generally about the outskirts of towns. Its habit of constantly swaying its body and tail from side to side is responsible for its common name. Breeding birds are aggressive and have been seen to attack large birds such as the Wedge-tailed Eagle flying over their territory. Hawks, magpies, Kookaburras and other large species are driven off by continuous attacks.

BREEDING: The breeding season in our area is from October to January but elsewhere breeding begins in July or August. The nest is a

237

small neat structure of fine grasses, so tightly bound with cobweb that it appears white. It is placed on a horizontal branch in a variety of situations, usually low in open country; verandahs and sheds are also used as nest sites. It is often placed near water, frequently in the same tree as that of the Magpie Lark.

Several clutches may be laid in a season and sometimes the same nest is used for successive broods. Three or four eggs are laid. The ground colour varies from pale creamy-brown to yellowish-white. Spots of brown, grey or bluish-black shades are concentrated at the larger end and sometimes form a ring. They measure $20 \times 15$ mm. Incubation takes about thirteen days and the young remain in the nest for a similar period.

FEEDING: Its food is insects and spiders. It is often perched on the backs of sheep, horses and cows from where it takes insects disturbed by the movement of the animals. It also takes spiders and other insects from the outsides of buildings quite often well away from the nearest cover. Worms are also taken. (S.J.W.)

## BLACK-FACED FLYCATCHER *Monarcha melanopsis*
PLATE XXXVI

IDENTIFICATION: Length 18 cm. Upper parts dark ashy grey; face, lores and throat black; breast ash-grey; remainder of under-parts rufous; bill, blue-grey; tarsus and toes, dark slate-grey; iris, dark brown. The sexes are similar. Immature similar to adult but lacking black on facial areas and with black bill.

VOICE: A loud, clear whistle "Why-you, Wit-yew", the first part with an upward inflection, the latter descending. It also possesses the more familiar flycatcher "grating" and assorted whistles.

DISTRIBUTION: The bird inhabits rainforest, wet sclerophyll forests, fern gullies and dense mangroves from Cape York to the Gippsland district of Victoria. It is also found in southern New Guinea and nearby islands.

The species is very rarely recorded in the Canberra area, and the few records are of immatures probably migrating through in Autumn. It is, however, quite a common breeding species on the escarpment to the east of Canberra.

HABITS: In the southern part of its range the bird is migratory, arriving in nearby coastal areas in September and departing in March. The bird is usually seen singly or in pairs, generally in the more heavily vegetated fern gullies and dense scrubs. Quite often it is heard rather than seen.

BREEDING: The breeding season is October to January. The nest is a beautiful structure made of fine plant material and heavily decorated on the outside with green mosses and lichens. It is cup shaped and usually placed in the upright fork of a tree at heights to about ten metres from the ground. Two, sometimes three, eggs are laid. They are smooth, white to pale pink, and dotted on the larger end with purplish-red spots. They measure about 24 × 17 mm.

FEEDING: The Black-faced Flycatcher procures insects and other invertebrates from amongst the leafy branches of the lower canopy trees. It is not as active in the aerial "hawking" of insects as other members of the flycatcher family. (M.C.)

## LEADEN FLYCATCHER *Myiagra rubecula*
PLATE XXV

IDENTIFICATION: Length, 15 cm. Male: *general colour above, leaden grey* with black wings edged with leaden grey; neck, throat and upper breast, slightly darker than the head; *under-parts, white*; bill, leaden blue; legs and feet, black; iris, black.

The adult female is similar in colour to the male but the wings and tail are dull brownish-grey and in strong contrast; the *throat is dull orange-buff* gradually becoming dull white on the rest of the lower parts. Both have small crests which are erected slightly when the birds are excited.

This species may be confused with the Satin Flycatcher and identi fication points are given under the latter species.

VOICE: The Leaden Flycatcher has a very distinctive call, a fairly rapid "too-ee-too"; which carries well in the open forest. Another is slurred and ascending and sounds something like "pretty-pretty". Others are not melodious and can be likened to hissing or sucking sounds. A frog-like note is responsible for the title "Frog-bird" in some places. All these are calls of the breeding season.

DISTRIBUTION: Its range is from the north of Western Australia east to the Gulf of Carpentaria and from Cape York south through to the west of Melbourne. It is accidental to Tasmania and South Australia. Normally the western slopes of the Divide are the limit of its range but inland occurrences have been reported during migration. It is much more common in the ranges.

It is not abundant in our area but there are a few areas where it can be found each spring and summer. It is only found in open forest country, where the trees are large and close but where there is little undergrowth. Several pairs may nest in an area of about two and a half hectares and there may be two kilometres between these small colonies, even in apparently suitable habitat. Elsewhere in its range it is found in denser and wetter country.

There is a very well marked migratory movement in south-eastern Australia generally. It arrives here about the middle of October and leaves by the middle of April and there are no winter records. The extent and nature of the movement are not known but it appears to leave Victoria and southern New South Wales entirely each autumn. The southern race has been reported in Papua in winter.

HABITS: It is a bird of the higher levels of the open forest and although usually inconspicuous it attracts attention with its distinctive, often repeated calls. It flicks its tail vertically and rapidly on alighting.

BREEDING: The breeding season in our area extends from November to early January but is a little earlier on the coast. The nest is an open cup structure of fine strips of bark lined with fine rootlets. Bark flakes are used on the outside and there is much binding of the outer material by cobweb. In damp breeding places, lichen is used on the exterior which is always made to blend in with the surroundings. The nest is sited on a dead, horizontal branch with a live branch a few centimetres higher than the nest. High sites are preferred. Usually the nest is placed from fifteen to thirty metres from the ground.

Two or three eggs, measuring 18 × 14 mm, are laid. They vary in ground colour from white to bluish-white and are dotted and spotted around the centre or on the larger end in shades of brown.

FEEDING: Insects are taken in flight among the treetops but some insects and spiders are taken from the trees themselves. The bird rarely comes down from the treetops. (S.J.W.)

## SATIN FLYCATCHER *Myiagra cyanoleuca*
PLATE XXV

IDENTIFICATION: Length, 16 cm. *A darker, more shining and slightly larger version of the Leaden Flycatcher.* Both sexes have small crests which are slightly erected when the birds are excited. Male: *upper-parts, shiny, deep blue-black*, sometimes appearing greenish-black depending on light; wings, black edged with blue-black; neck, throat and upper breast, blue-black; remainder of the *under-parts, white*; bill, leaden-black; legs and feet, black; iris, black. Female: dull slaty-grey above with brownish-grey wings and tail; the feathers on the head are darker and more glossy. In strong contrast to the male the *throat and upper breast are orange-rufous* with the remainder of the under-parts white.

240

The Leaden and Satin Flycatchers can easily be confused but their habitat is very different and in the breeding season this is sufficient indication of the species in our area. The Satin breeds only in the ranges while the Leaden breeds in lightly timbered country but both are migratory and can, during these movements, be found in open country. The adult males are distinctive but the adult females are very similar in appearance. The breast colour varies in shade with individuals and perhaps age and the only good identification point is the colour of the head which is darker and more glossy in the Satin. Juveniles of the two species are indistinguishable in the field.

VOICE: The call is somewhat like that of the Leaden Flycatcher but is deeper. It is a rather loud, piping whistle: "chee-ee chee-ee".

DISTRIBUTION: It extends from south-east South Australia and Tasmania along the coast and near coastal districts to north Queensland, New Guinea and New Britain. In Australia it does not extend inland beyond the higher slopes of the Divide. It is a bird of the upper levels of the forest and is quite rare. The known breeding areas in the region are confined to the gullies and slopes of the Brindabella and Tidbinbilla Ranges where it breeds in small loose colonies. It prefers a higher and moister habitat than the Leaden Flycatcher.

It is completely migratory in the southern half of its range. It normally appears in September and leaves in late February. In the Brindabella Ranges it arrives in October. During winter it appears in New Guinea, New Britain and nearby islands and is fairly numerous in northern Queensland. In summer its stronghold is Tasmania though it breeds in small numbers throughout the high, moist, well timbered areas of the Dividing Range.

HABITS: Its general behaviour is very similar to that of the Leaden Flycatcher.

BREEDING: The breeding season is from November to January. The nest is an open cup formed of thin strips of bark bound together and secured to a branch with cobweb. It has a softer lining of rootlets or grass. A few pieces of lichen are sometimes used externally. The site is usually a thin dead branch under a live branch and this may be fifteen to twenty-five metres from the ground.

The eggs are white in ground colour or with a faint bluish or greenish tinge. They are spotted with brown or purplish-brown mostly at the larger end, and occasionally the markings form a ring. They measure about 19 × 15 mm.

241

FEEDING: Insects, often taken on the wing high in the forest canopy or closely above it, are the food of this species. (S.J.W.)

## RESTLESS FLYCATCHER *Myiagra inquieta*
PLATE XXV

IDENTIFICATION: Length, 21 cm. Male: *upper-parts, black*; head, back, and wing coverts, deep blue-black in good light; *throat, and under-parts, white*; bill, black; legs and feet, black; iris, brown. The adult female is similar to the adult male but there is a *wash of buff on the throat and breast*. The feathers of the crown can be erected into a small crest.

VOICE: One of its calls is most distinctive and apparently resembles the sound of scissors being sharpened on an old-fashioned sandstone wheel; hence the popular name, "Scissors Grinder". Other calls are loud, repeated single notes, "zooing" with an upwards inflection and a loud whistling double note.

DISTRIBUTION: It is widely distributed and there are three more or less isolated populations. The first is in the south-west of Western Australia; the second occurs across the north of Australia; the third is found from about Mackay, Queensland, to Eyre Peninsula. In the east it extends from the coast inland to the limit of savannah woodland country and it is fairly common in such places. In our area it is not a common bird though it is widely distributed in open forest country.

HABITS: Usually seen singly it is distinctive among our smaller birds in that it can hover with a peculiar wing action, for a considerable time, thirty to sixty centimetres above the ground while it searches for food. The "scissors grinder" call is given while it hovers. Like the Willy Wagtail it is often seen around farm buildings and the outskirts of towns.

BREEDING: November and December is the breeding season in our area but elsewhere in the east it may commence in August and extend to January. The nest is a neat cup-shaped structure usually of thin strips of bark and grasses bound liberally with cobweb and with a lining of hair or fur. A little lichen is used externally. It is usually placed on top of a dead fork in a thin horizontal branch; but sometimes the fork is nearly vertical. The nest is always sited on the outside of a tree at heights up to twenty metres from the ground. Usually, four eggs, though sometimes three, are laid. They measure about 19 × 15 mm and the colour varies from dull white to buff. They are marked with purplish to brown spots often forming a band or zone about the larger end.

FEEDING: Flies, moths and other insects are taken on the ground and occasionally in the air. (S.J.W.)

## GOLDEN WHISTLER *Pachycephala pectoralis*

PLATE XXVIII

IDENTIFICATION: Length, 18 cm. Male: general colour above, olive-green with yellow band on neck; flight feathers, black with olive-green wash on secondaries; tail, black; head, black; *chin and throat, white; upper breast, a black bar; remainder of under-parts, yellow*; bill, black; legs, slate-grey; iris, red. Female: general colour above, greyish-brown often tinged with olive on wings and tail coverts; throat, mottled greyish-white; breast, grey; abdomen, whitish.

Juveniles are completely rufous except for grey flight feathers and rufous brown edges to the secondaries; at one year they resemble adult females and the male does not assume full colour until about three years of age. There are several races in Australia that differ slightly in plumage.

VOICE: It has a loud melodious whistle in spring and summer, and a long single whistle with upward inflection "sweeee", in autumn and winter. It often calls immediately after thunder or a loud noise.

DISTRIBUTION: The Golden Whistler has a wide distribution from the Philippines to southern Australia and from the Moluccas to the western Pacific. In Australia it extends, with a few gaps, around the periphery of the continent. It is mainly a bird of the coastal forests and the ranges but also extends inland into mallee and other arid scrublands. In our area it is usually found in tall forest and moist gullies of the ranges during the breeding season but at other times moves throughout the whole region. There is apparently considerable movement; birds in female plumage appear in the dry open forest around Canberra in February and adult males in May, but by October or November all have returned to the mountains. This altitudinal migration cannot involve the whole population as some birds overwinter in the ranges. Many individuals return to the same breeding place each year.

HABITS: Although brightly coloured, male Golden Whistlers are not conspicuous, especially when in tall timber. They fly softly through the undergrowth and make little sound except in the breeding season. They are usually seen as solitary birds and are never in groups.

BREEDING: The breeding season is October to January; most breed in the mountains but there are also records from lower country near

243

Canberra. The nest is open and cup-shaped, built of fine sticks and lined with fine rootlets and grass. It is placed usually in an upright fork in the dense understorey of shrubbery below five metres. The clutch size is two or three. The eggs are cream or buff-white freckled and blotched with brown, the markings form a zone at the larger end. They measure about $23 \times 17$ mm.

FEEDING: Golden Whistlers secure insects and some berries and feed among the leaves and twigs of trees and bushes. (S.J.W.)

## RUFOUS WHISTLER *Pachycephala rufiventris*
PLATE XXVIII

IDENTIFICATION: Length, 17.5 cm. Male: general colour above, grey; crown, grey; face, black, the colour extending to form a *prominent black band across chest; chin and throat, white; under-parts, rufous brown*; bill, black; legs and feet, dark grey; iris, reddish-brown. Female: general colour above, brownish-grey; chin, cheeks and throat, dull white streaked with blackish-brown; remainder of under-parts, buff distinctly streaked with blackish-brown.

Immature birds of both sexes resemble the female but the upper-parts have a greenish tone; bill, horn with grey tip; throat, streaked with blackish-brown and darker than in female. It is probable that males assume adult plumage at two to three years of age.

VOICE: It has a loud ringing "e-chong-chick" with the accent heavily on the middle note; the "chick" may be from the female. Another call may be rendered "joey-joey-joey" repeated rapidly.

DISTRIBUTION: The Rufous Whistler is found throughout Australia, excluding Tasmania, and extends to the Sulu Islands, New Guinea and the Moluccas and to New Caledonia in the east. In the north it is apparently sedentary but in southern Australia it is migratory. Although a few remain on the Southern Tablelands throughout the winter, most leave the area in early April and begin to return in September. Many banded individuals return to the same breeding place in successive years. Although commonly regarded as a bird of open forest and the dry inland scrubs, in this district it also breeds throughout the moist gullies of the ranges.

HABITS: Although less colourful, the Rufous Whistler is much more obvious than the Golden Whistler and is seen in gardens, countryside and forests. Usually the males are solitary but females and juveniles occur in groups of three or four.

BREEDING: It breeds in the period October to January. The nest is fragile, cup-shaped and built of thin twigs, grasses and rootlets lined with finer grass; the eggs can sometimes be seen through it. The nest is built in a slender upright fork up to ten metres from the ground. The clutch size is two or three eggs. The eggs are olive or olive-brown and measure about $22 \times 17$ mm. Both sexes incubate the eggs and brood and the young leave the nest at about fifteen days.

FEEDING: It is usually seen feeding in leaves and twigs, high in forest trees where it secures insects. (S.J.W.)

## OLIVE WHISTLER *Pachycephala olivacea*

PLATE XXVIII

IDENTIFICATION: Length, 20.5 cm. Male: general colour above, olive-brown; head, dark grey; *chin and throat, whitish flecked with grey and below this a grey band; under-parts, reddish-brown*; bill, dark brown; legs and feet, flesh-grey; iris, red-brown. The female is similar but there is no grey band on the breast and the head has an olive-brown wash. Immatures have narrow, pointed tail feathers and rufous edging to the feathers of the wing coverts; the crown is paler than in adults and the bill is horn coloured.

VOICE: A very distinctive whistle of four notes with a heavy accent on the second and the last two notes descending is the territorial call. It also has a long drawn mournful whistle with downward inflection. It does not call in the period March to August.

DISTRIBUTION: It ranges through the high country of southern Queensland and northern New South Wales, through eastern and southern Victoria to south-east South Australia and to Tasmania where it is common. It is widely but sparingly distributed in the Brindabella Ranges, and is present there at all seasons. There is at least some evidence of a partial altitudinal migration with some birds moving down to lower elevations in winter.

HABITS: It lives in dense scrubs and undergrowth and is usually seen travelling through the bushes, hopping from twig to twig and flitting from bush to bush low down. It travels considerable distances without flying more than a few metres at a time. Like other whistlers it crouches on the nest when disturbed brooding and can be approached very closely; at other times it is shy.

BREEDING: The breeding season in our area is in the period November to January; elsewhere it begins in September. The nest is a large but compact open cup of thin twigs, bark, dead leaves and grass placed in an upright fork up to six metres from the ground. The clutch size is three or four eggs. The eggs are buff in colour dotted and blotched with umber markings—chiefly at the larger end where they form a zone. They measure about $29 \times 19$ mm.

FEEDING: As with other whistlers, it feeds mainly on insects and their larvae collected from the foliage and bark but some are taken on the ground. (S.J.W.)

## GREY SHRIKE-THRUSH *Colluricincla harmonica*

PLATE XXVIII

IDENTIFICATION: Length, 24 cm. General colour above, *grey with umber on the scapulars and upper back; lores, chin, throat, dull white*; breast, ashy-grey; abdomen and under-tail coverts, dull white; bill, blackish-brown; legs and feet, greenish-grey; iris, dark brown. The sexes are similar but females have less white on the throat which is lightly streaked black. Juvenile birds have the upper-parts grey-brown with a distinct olive tinge and there is a pale rufous ring around the eye and a stripe over it; under-parts, grey-white; breast, white, brown streaked; abdomen, white. The lores and throat are not conspicuously white. Immature birds have less distinct streaking on the breast; the last immature feature lost is the rufous eyestripe.

VOICE: The calls are numerous and musical, clear and penetrating. Most are of several notes and end in a high clear whistle. In winter there is a single, long "chong" with a downward inflection. The alarm note is harsh and loud. The calls of the Grey Shrike-thrush are a very common component in the repertoire of the lyrebird.

DISTRIBUTION: The Grey Shrike-thrush extends throughout eastern and south-eastern Australia from Cape York to Spencer's Gulf and to Tasmania. It extends inland to the driest scrubs and throughout its range is found in all habitats that have some bushes. On the Southern Tablelands it is found in city parks and gardens, agricultural land where some trees remain, and throughout the ranges. In the ranges the numbers decline during winter suggesting at least some altitudinal migration, but in the main the bird is sedentary.

HABITS: It is one of the most ubiquitous and inquisitive birds in the forest. It bounds rapidly up or flies silently to nearby bushes to watch observers. Its favourite gait is a very rapid hopping interspersed with short flights across open spaces.

BREEDING: Nests are found in the period September to January. The nest is bulky, about fifteen to twenty centimetres in diameter, built of strips of bark, roots, twigs and grass and lined with finer material. It is usually placed lower than five metres from the ground; a favourite site is among regrowth twigs low in a damaged *Eucalyptus*. Nests are also placed in low bushes, hollows in stumps, broken branches, sometimes on the ground or on the bank of a gully. Two to four, but more usually three, eggs may be laid. The eggs vary greatly in colour; the ground colour is pale greyish or buff-white and they are blotched sparingly all over with olive or brownish-black. They are often more heavily marked at the larger end. They measure about $28 \times 22$ mm.

FEEDING: Most feeding is done on the ground, the bird hopping swiftly from place to place, usually where the soil is moist or leaf litter is thick. The main foods are insects, spiders and worms but elsewhere it has been reported to attack eggs and nestlings of smaller birds, small marsupials and frogs. (S.J.W.)

## SHRIKE-TIT *Falcunculus frontatus*

PLATE XXVIII

IDENTIFICATION: Length, 19 cm. Male: upper-parts, greenish-olive with white tip to tail; wings, blackish-brown; *head, throat, neck and prominent crest, black except for broad white band* above eye extending to nape and another from bill below eye; under-parts, bright yellow with greenish tinge; bill, black; legs and feet, blue-grey; iris, brown. Females differ in that the chin is grey and the throat greenish-olive. Juveniles have a yellow throat and cinnamon brown back. Immatures are similar to adults but are smaller, have browner wings and brownish-black bill with a white cutting edge.

VOICE: The identity call is a plaintive, quiet "oo-ee-oo" with the second note of higher pitch and emphasis; it is repeated several times. There is also a double note that resembles a finch but is harsher. The calls are very quiet and unobtrusive and easily missed.

DISTRIBUTION: Three sub-species of shrike-tit are recognised. The western form has a white abdomen and the northern is smaller and brighter in colour. The race in this district extends from about Cairns, Queensland, through New South Wales, Victoria and eastern South Australia. It is most numerous in the forests of the coast, ranges and tablelands but extends inland along treelined watercourses. On the Southern Tablelands it is found in small numbers in the hills near Canberra, the ranges, and throughout the area generally. It favours the tallest timber available.

HABITS: It is usually only found by deliberate search. It spends most of its time high in the timber searching the foliage, twigs and bark for food and can be very inconspicuous. The flight is very strong and rapid and it is only glimpsed as it darts from one tree head to another.

BREEDING: The breeding season in our area is from October to January but on the more salubrious coast eighty kilometres away it begins in August. The nest is tightly woven about a few vertical twigs and is a compact deep cup of fine twigs and bark often decorated with lichen and bound with cobweb; the gum tips above the nest are always nipped off, perhaps to reduce wind resistance. It is always located in the top of a tree, usually a large *Eucalyptus* ten to twenty metres from the ground.

The clutch is two or three and the eggs are white with dots and small spots of pale brown, slate or black, often forming a zone near the larger end. They measure about 28 × 17 mm.

FEEDING: They feed entirely in trees on insects. The heavy, powerful bill is used to strip off bark, to wrench insect casings from twigs and to tear open webs and insect galls. (S.J.W.)

Family Orthonychidae — Quail-thrushes, Whipbirds and allies
This small family of 10 species is confined to Australia and New Guinea. The Australian forms are the log runners, whipbirds, quail-thrushes and wedgebills. They are ground birds and different species may be found in all habitats from dense coastal forests to the inland deserts. They live on insects and other invertebrates taken on the ground.

Two are found in our area, a quail-thrush and a whipbird.

## SPOTTED QUAIL-THRUSH *Cinclosoma punctatum*
PLATE XXIII

IDENTIFICATION: Length, 28 cm. Male: upper-parts, mottled brown and black; shoulders, black spotted with white; central two tail feathers, brown, the remainder black, broadly tipped with white showing a *distinct white (terminal) band on tail* in flight; a distinct white patch on each cheek; throat, black; upper breast, grey above, *a narrow black band across the breast*; remainder of under-parts, white with distinct black spotting on flanks; bill, black; feet, pale flesh; iris, pale grey.

The female is duller than the male and lacks the black on the shoulders and throat. The eyebrow and cheek patch are buff instead of white and the black band on the breast is lacking.

VOICE: There are two calls. The contact call is that most commonly heard. It is of extremely high frequency (close to the limit of human hearing) and is audible only from a distance of less than thirty-five metres and is then quite difficult for the observer to determine its direction. It is best described as a high-pitched whistle, a monotone of two or three seconds duration repeated as many as four times. The second call is given by the male in the breeding season and is a double whistle like "fee-oo, fee-oo", the two notes being approximately an octave apart. The call is repeated about a dozen times from a vantage point, usually the low branch of a tree or a stump.

DISTRIBUTION: It extends from southern Queensland throughout the country generally east of the Great Dividing Range to Melbourne and through to the Mount Lofty Ranges near Adelaide. It also occurs in Tasmania. In our region it is most abundant in the sclerophyll forest of the ranges but also occurs in isolated patches of woodland left on the dry, stony ridges in farming country. It is found up to 1500 metres.

HABITS: Spotted Quail-thrushes are mainly terrestrial and spend their time foraging among litter in the drier parts of forests and woodlands, often on steep slopes and ridges. They occur in pairs or family parties, depending on the time of year and are quite sedentary, remaining in the territory the year round. They are infrequently seen and are very shy. When flushed they fly with a whirr of wings low over the shrub layer and rarely go more than seventy metres. On settling they run quickly across the ground and are difficult to locate.

BREEDING: In the region the breeding season is August to January. The nest is a small cup-shaped structure about fifteen centimetres in diameter, loosely built of bark, grass and leaves placed in a small depression in the ground. It is nearly always situated on sloping ground on the low side of a solid object such as rock, grass-tree, log, or the base of a tree and is often sheltered by ferns. The eggs, two or three to a clutch, are elongate oval in shape, dull white or cream spotted and blotched with shades of rich brown and blue-grey markings. They measure about 32 × 23 mm. Both male and female feed the nestlings.

FEEDING: The food consists of insects and their larvae procured among the debris of the forest floor. (G.S.C.)

## EASTERN WHIPBIRD *Psophodes olivaceus*

PLATE XXVIII

IDENTIFICATION: Length, 27 cm. General colour above, *dark olive-green*; head, black; there is a *prominent crest; cheeks and side of throat, white*; centre of throat and breast, black; under-parts, ashy-brown with an olive wash except for abdomen and breast which are white-flecked; bill, black; legs and feet, red-brown; iris, brown. The sexes are similar. The white markings on throat and breast appear at one year of age.

VOICE: The call is a loud, penetrating "whip-crack" which begins as a low whistle only heard from near at hand, and rapidly increases in volume. The crack is followed immediately by "choo-choo" provided by the female. There are also a number of harsh scolding calls uttered in alarm and soft clucks when feeding.

DISTRIBUTION: It has a coastal and mountain distribution from Cairns, Queensland, to the Dandenongs, Victoria. It is most common in rain-forest but also is found in moist gullies and even in the denser heaths. In the Southern Tablelands it is very sparingly distributed in moist gullies of the ranges. It was known to be present near Canberra, for lyrebirds imitated its distinctive call, some years before the bird itself was seen or heard.

HABITS: Whipbirds are very active but secretive, spending most of their time on the ground or lowest layers of the undergrowth and moving mainly by hopping rapidly. They have very weak powers of flight. They are seldom seen unless the observer is prepared to sit and wait for them to come close, as they often do—being quite inquisitive. They are strongly territorial and can always be found in the same locality.

BREEDING: Nests are found in the period October to January but mainly in November and December. The nest is a bulky but shallow cup about twenty centimetres in diameter and seven to ten centimetres deep; the cavity for the eggs is seven centimetres wide and five centimetres deep. It is built of quite long twigs loosely woven and is lined with very fine rootlets. The nest is always placed low in the densest undergrowth; they are sometimes less than sixty centimetres from the ground and rarely above three and a half metres. The clutch is two or rarely three. The eggs are pale blue, spotted and blotched with reddish-brown or grey. They measure $28 \times 20$ mm.

FEEDING: The birds feed mainly on the ground but do not ignore bushes. The food is entirely animal—insects, larvae and small worms. (S.J.W.)

# BABBLERS

The babblers and their relatives constitute a large family of over 250 species found in the forests and woodlands of Africa, southern and eastern Asia, and through Indonesia to Australia. They are very diversified in shape and size and some of them are brightly coloured. Only four species are found in Australia. They are attractive birds clad in various mixtures of black, grey, white and brown. Babblers live permanently in small social groups that hold territories in the lower layers of open forest or in low scrubs. They are very active birds constantly on the move and keep up a continuous chatter among themselves, hence their common name. Their food consists of insects and other small invertebrates collected on the ground or on low vegetation.

Two species formerly occurred in our area but now seem to have disappeared.

### Family Timaliidae — Babblers
## GREY-CROWNED BABBLER *Pomatostomus temporalis*
PLATE XXIII

IDENTIFICATION: Length, 28 cm. General colour above, shading from grey on the head through dark brown on the lower back and rump to brown-black on the tail, the latter being tipped with white; wings, dark brown; a broad white stripe extends from the upper bill over the eye to the nape and below this a dark brown stripe runs from the bill through the eye to the side of the neck; cheeks, throat, neck and centre breast, white; *sides of breast, rufous, shading to brown on the abdomen*, flanks and under-tail coverts; bill, thin, curved downwards, dark brown; legs, blackish; iris, yellow in adults.

VOICE: These birds keep up an endless chattering among themselves which defies description in words. The alarm note, however, is a very loud, distinctive "yahoo" repeated several times.

DISTRIBUTION: The Grey-crowned Babbler ranges over most of Australia, except south-west Western Australia, south-east Victoria, and the New South Wales south coast. It is mainly an inland species but extends to the coast in many places. It also occurs in New Guinea. In our area it is unusual but there has been one small resident flock for some years and doubtless other small colonies exist elsewhere. Prior to 1950, several colonies existed between Red Hill and Tuggeranong but these have not been recently reported. Shrubland is their optimum habitat and their numbers have probably been severely reduced by clean-clearing, and sowing to pasture, of woodland.

HABITS: Babblers are another example of extreme sociability so often found among Australian birds. They are usually in groups of five to ten, even when nesting, and study has shown that most of these associations consist of a pair and the progeny of several years. The bulky,

251

domed nests described below endure for several years and are used for roosting in at night. The groups forage mainly on the ground on short pasture, flying up into trees when alarmed and there hopping about and chattering in a way very similar to Apostle Birds, who often share the same habitat. When a member of the group finds food the others rush to join in and the noise increases. The birds run on the ground and do not hop. They rake litter with their bills but never with their feet. Babblers can fly strongly but usually do not keep it up for long before heading for cover and landing.

BREEDING: They are mainly spring breeders but eggs have been recorded as early as April and May. The bulky twig nest may exceed twenty-five centimetres in diameter; the outer framework is made of interlaced sticks about half a centimetre in diameter, and where African Boxthorn occurs, spiny dead twigs from this shrub are extensively used, making investigation painful and difficult. The entrance is often overhung by a porch making it hard to locate.

Nests are usually three to ten metres from the ground, in a bushy sapling or shrubby tree. The nest remains for several years and there are generally several in close proximity. Building is done by several, if not all group members and is an occasion for general social excitement; it may take place at any time of the year and it is not known if old nests are re-used for nesting or only for roosting (they are frequently used by other species for both roosting and nesting).

It appears that, like the White-winged Chough and the Apostle Bird, sometimes more than one female will lay in the same nest, but the roles of group members during nesting is not known nor are the incubation and nestling periods. The eggs of *Pomatostomus* babblers are very strikingly marked with a scribbling of fine black or dark brown lines on a brown or dark grey background. Three to five eggs form the normal clutch and the size of an average egg is 28 × 19 mm.

FEEDING: These birds appear to be entirely insectivorous. (I.C.R.R.)

WHITE-BROWED BABBLER *Pomatostomus superciliosus*
PLATE XXIII
IDENTIFICATION: Length, 20 cm. This bird is similar to the Grey-crowned Babbler and although, in the hand, it is *obviously smaller*, this is not so easy to gauge in the field if only one species is encountered. *The brown (not grey) crown and more extensive white area on the abdomen* are diagnostic.

DISTRIBUTION: The White-browed Babbler has a more restricted distribution than the Grey-crowned Babbler and is confined to the

252

southern half of the continent. It is also absent in the extreme south-west and south-east. No babblers reach Tasmania. It was reported around Canberra by Charles Barrett in 1922 and, until at least 1950, a group existed near Mount Stromlo, Australian Capital Territory, perhaps a remnant of an earlier invasion.

VOICE, HABITS, BREEDING: Its general biology is very similar to that of the Grey-crowned Babbler but the eggs are a little smaller, 24 × 17 mm. (I.C.R.R.)

# WARBLERS, WRENS AND THORNBILLS

This section contains representatives of four families of small to very small songbirds, the Old World warblers, the blue wren group, the thornbills and allies, and the chats, that are considered together for convenience. They were formerly believed to be closely related but only the blue wren and thornbill groups could now be so described.

The other two families are more distant from these two and from each other. The nearest relatives of the chats are the honeyeaters.

## Family Sylviidae — Old World Warblers

The term is used to separate a large number of small songbirds from a group of superficially similar small birds found in Australia, sometimes called the Australian warblers, and from another group in America, the wood warblers. There are over 350 species in the Old World group. They are mainly small, inconspicuous insectivorous birds, but many have beautiful songs. They are widely distributed in all continents except the Americas, and particularly in Africa. There are not many species in Australia, their place being taken by other warbler-like birds. We have nine species of which five have been seen in the area covered by this book.

## CISTICOLA *Cisticola exilis*

PLATE XXII

IDENTIFICATION: Length, 9–11.5 cm. Male: in breeding season: *crown, golden brown*; rump, a little lighter; wings, brown; *back, light brown heavily streaked with black*; under-parts, buffy-white; bill, dark brown; legs and feet, buff-brown; iris, light brown. In the winter the head of the male becomes brown striped with black and the tail becomes noticeably longer. Females resemble males in winter plumage. Immature birds have a lemon-yellow wash on all plumage.

VOICE: The commonest sound heard is the call of the male as he flies above the breeding territory; it occupies a full second. There are two notes, a long drawn-out "buzz" or "zipp" followed by a short deep liquid "plook", or "tweet". Often the second note is repeated. In the grass the birds have a harsh excited chatter.

DISTRIBUTION: There are a great number of cisticolas, mainly in the tropics and Southern Hemisphere, but particularly in Africa which has over forty kinds. There are two in Australia, a tropical species that just touches the north of the continent, and the one discussed here. The latter is distributed through China, India, Malaysia, and Indonesia and across northern Australia and down the east coast to south-east South Australia and north-east Tasmania. In Australia it is almost entirely restricted to coastal districts but small numbers are found further inland in a few places, particularly in the north. A few are usually to be found around Canberra. Its habitat is thick, wet grassland as on the edge of swamps and streams but it is also very common in cornfields of the New South Wales coast and in rice fields in northern Australia. There is no convincing evidence of much movement either on the tablelands or the coast and it is probably sedentary.

HABITS: In the non-breeding season they are not obvious and confine themselves to the thickest of cover and, being relatively silent, can be very easily overlooked. In the summer breeding season, however, the males, particularly, become very obvious and are seen fussing about the corn stalks and grass, chattering excitedly with the small crest raised, or flying around over the nest site with a jerky flight uttering the loud liquid call note. After several circuits they dive suddenly back into the grass.

BREEDING: In the tropics the breeding season is in the late wet season, January to March, but in southern Australia it begins earlier, in October; there is a good deal of evidence that the abundance of tall, thick cover has much to do with the timing of the breeding season. In our region nests are found from January to March. The nest is a small, dome-shaped structure about ten centimetres high and five to seven centimetres wide, built of very fine grasses and plant down, and placed in a dense overgrown bush or tussock of tall grass. The leaves of the bushes or grass are often stitched into the construction of the nest with cobwebs or fine wood fibres. It is lined with plant down. The clutch size is three or four, occasionally five. The eggs are pale blue and blotched and spotted with reddish chestnut. They measure about 18 × 12 mm. There is some evidence that the males are polygamous.

FEEDING: It feeds on small grasshoppers, moths, and beetles and other insects mostly caught among the grass stems or just above the cover. (H.J.F.)

## LITTLE GRASS-BIRD *Megalurus gramineus*
PLATE XXII

IDENTIFICATION: Length, 16.5 cm. General colour above *fulvous brown streaked with black*; tail, black; under-parts, dull white except for throat and breast which are spotted and streaked with black; there is a pale line above the eye; bill, brown; legs and feet, brown; iris, brown. The sexes are similar.

VOICE: Its sad but penetrating whistle has been well described as "pee-pee-ee". In the breeding season it is uttered incessantly. It also has a harsh, excited chatter. In inland New South Wales they become very vocal in August. A characteristic call can be written as "quartz quartz".

DISTRIBUTION: Widely distributed in eastern and south-west Australia. In the east it extends from north Queensland and New Guinea through to Eyre Peninsula in South Australia. It also occurs in Tasmania. It is found on the coast, throughout the tablelands and the interior of the eastern States, particularly New South Wales and southern Queensland where it is very numerous in the cumbungi, lignum and cane grass swamps. On the coast it seems to be fairly sedentary but inland, although it does choose the most permanent swamps, it is sometimes forced out of them by prolonged dry weather and makes local movements to some of the rivers. In our area it is resident in small numbers.

HABITS: It is one of the most secretive birds and spends its time low down in the densest cover. Even though the swamp can be ringing with the calls of hundreds of them they are almost impossible to see as they flit from one bush to another ahead of the observer and fall quiet as he approaches. In long grass they pop up momentarily and then dart down again before the eyes can be focused. Its flight seems very feeble but they do travel considerable distances from swamp to swamp.

BREEDING: Most nests are found in the period September to December but on the New South Wales coast they have been found breeding in most months of the year. The nest is a deep cup, not unlike that of the Reed Warbler, but smaller and less robust. It is built of coarse grasses and sedges and bound into upright grass stems or in cane grass or lignum. Sometimes they are partly covered at the top.

The clutch size is usually three, but occasionally four or five eggs are found. They are white or pink and are covered and almost obscured with reddish-purple spots. They measure about 18 × 14 mm.

255

FEEDING: It feeds among the dense grass, lignum, or cane grass, and on the ground on insects and small animals. Tiny shells have also been found in some specimens. (H.J.F.)

## REED WARBLER *Acrocephalus stentoreus*
PLATE XXVII

IDENTIFICATION: Length, 18 cm. Male: upper-parts, brown, slightly tinged with olive; rump and upper-tail coverts, dull fawn; there is a dull white line over the eye; under-parts, buffy-white becoming light fawn on the flanks; bill, long and thin, horn; legs and feet, grey; iris, dark brown. The adult female is similar to the male, but is slightly smaller.

VOICE: The typical call in the breeding season is loud and pleasant but not really musical and is rather mechanical in its regularity; a very distinctive call not readily confused with other calls in the typical habitat.

DISTRIBUTION: It occurs throughout mainland Australia and northern Tasmania, wherever suitable habitat exists and also in New Guinea and islands to the north. Most records from Canberra are between late September and late April. It is regarded as migratory throughout the southern part of its range though in warm districts a few are known to remain over winter. The nature and extent of the migratory movements are not known. In suitable habitat the species is usually abundant though most observers do not realise this. It is to be found in most freshwater localities where there are reeds and in the Australian Capital Territory in the willows and reedbeds along the Molonglo River and around Lake Burley Griffin.

HABITS: Living in dense reedbeds, it is more often heard than seen and the song is usually the only proof of its presence. When it is seen it is usually clinging to reeds or darting from one clump to another. In winter it is rather quiet and therefore difficult to identify. For this reason it may be more numerous in its southern distribution in winter than is realised.

BREEDING: Birds in our region breed from November to January though this period is shorter than in other parts of New South Wales where breeding from September to February has been reported. The nest is neatly constructed of the soft paper-like sheaths of reeds and decaying water weeds firmly woven around the stems of a few reeds. Sometimes it is built in the outer and lower branches of willows just a few centimetres over water. Usually the rim is slightly narrowed; this could assist in preventing eggs or young being thrown out by wind. It is lined with finer vegetable material but sometimes a few light coloured feathers are also used. Three or four eggs are laid. The ground colour varies considerably from bluish-white or greyish-white to pale yellowish-brown. They are spotted and blotched with reddish-brown and lavender and measure about 20 × 15 mm.

FEEDING: The food is the many forms of insect life found about the reedbeds and water generally. (S.J.W.)

## BROWN SONG-LARK *Cinclorhamphus cruralis*
PLATE XXVII

IDENTIFICATION: Length, male 25 cm. Female 18.5 cm. Male: general colour above, dark brown with the feathers narrowly edged with pale brown; the area in front of and below the eye is black; the *chin and throat are blackish-brown* and the remainder of the underparts, dusky-brown; *the tail is always cocked*; bill, black; legs and feet, brown; iris, brown. The male is considerably larger than the female, an unusual situation among Australian song-birds. Female: lighter and brighter in colour than the male; the feathers of the upper-parts are broadly edged with dull reddish-brown; the lores and the distinct line over the eye are buff; the throat is dull white and the remainder of the under-parts, pale brown with irregular darker centres to the feathers.

Young birds resemble the female. The period required for the development of adult male plumage is not known.

VOICE: The call, which is loud, melodious, but rather harsh and mechanical, has been likened to a rusty axle. It can be written as "pitchy pee-ee, pitchy pee-ee" and variations. It is often given while gliding from a high perch though it also calls from fence posts.

DISTRIBUTION: It occurs throughout mainland Australia, except the north-west, wherever there is suitable habitat. The Brown Songlark is a bird of open grassy areas and is most abundant in the dry inland, in grazing country, away from cultivation. In southern Australia it is migratory, arriving about September and leaving, after breeding, about February. Although it is not common in our region, it has been reported regularly in most summers in grasslands both in the Australian Capital Territory and in nearby parts of New South Wales.

HABITS: It usually occurs singly or in pairs, on the ground, a post or low bush. The tail of the male is always cocked nearly vertically. When on the ground it hops very rapidly. It frequently flies high and glides down with imperceptible movement of the wings, often from a high perch.

BREEDING: There is at least some evidence that the males are polygamous but this has not been proved. It has not been reported breeding in the Southern Tablelands though there is little doubt that it would do so. The normal season in inland New South Wales is from September to January but most nests have been found in September and October. However in the inland in wet seasons it can breed in winter. The nest is built on the ground generally in the shelter of a clump of grass or a low shrub. It is usually placed in a slight depression probably scratched out by the birds. It is cup-shaped and is composed of coarse grasses with a softer inner lining. There are three or four eggs in the clutch, coloured salmon-pink ground with pinkish-red specklings all over; they measure about 23 × 17 mm.

FEEDING: Food is usually found on the ground and consists chiefly of insects, including beetles and caterpillars. A little seed is taken. (S.J.W.)

## RUFOUS SONG-LARK *Cinclorhamphus mathewsi*
PLATE XXVII

IDENTIFICATION: Length male 19.5 cm, female 16.5 cm. Male: dark brown above with each feather margined with dull reddish-brown; *rump and upper-tail coverts, light rufous*; there is a dull white eye stripe; chin and throat, dull white; remainder of the under-parts, dull white tinged with buff; bill, dark brown; legs and feet, light brown; iris, brown.

The *male is considerably larger than the female* in this species and the Brown Song-lark; in most Australian passerines the sexes are of similar size.

VOICE: The breeding male defends his territory by singing constantly in flight from tree to tree. The defence call is a very loud song of half a dozen notes, musical but harsh because of its volume. As the male flies over the brooding female she usually responds with a quiet twitter. A rather strident two-note call is also given when perched. It can be written as "witchy weedle". The female has a double note call usually given before she returns to the nest. All these are calls of the breeding season. At other seasons the bird is very inconspicuous and quiet and may be easily overlooked.

DISTRIBUTION: The Rufous Song-lark is a bird of open forest, typically of grazing country with a fair number of eucalypts but little

258

undergrowth. The bird is found in suitable habitat over most of mainland Australia except the Cape York area and is migratory in the southern areas. It is fairly common on the Southern Tablelands, appearing in early October and remaining until late April, but its occurrence around Canberra could be over a longer period as it is a difficult species to find and identify during the non-breeding season when the bird is often silent. Numbers vary considerably from season to season and the date of arrival also appears to vary.

HABITS: Like the Brown Song-lark it habitually perches on stumps and low bushes and male birds aggressively pursue other males which intrude into their territory. This show of aggression with its accompanying song is sufficient to repel the intruder. The male has a talent for finding a feeding female away from the nest and when this happens a rapid zig-zag chase ensues; this behaviour is a regular aspect of the breeding season. Females in flight approach the nest by alighting some metres away; never beside the nest.

BREEDING: Breeding in our region has been recorded from November to January. It is generally regarded as polygamous and a male has been reported as mating with three females. The open, cup-shaped nest is placed on the ground in a slight depression under a tuft of grass or a shrub and is composed of coarse grass stems with lining of finer materials. Three or four eggs are laid. The ground colour of the eggs is white to faint reddish- or purplish-white and they are heavily speckled, particularly on the larger end, with reddish- or red-brown markings. They measure $22 \times 15$ mm.

FOOD: This species is mainly insectivorous and its food is taken on the ground. (S.J.W.)

Family Maluridae — Blue Wren and Emu-wren
This is a small family of 26 species confined to Australia and New Guinea, and containing the emu-wrens, grass-wrens and the blue wren group. All are very small birds with long cocked-up tails. They mostly frequent low shrubs and live on insects, although some grass-wrens of the arid country also eat seeds. A blue wren and an emu-wren occur in our area.

### SUPERB BLUE WREN *Malurus cyaneus*
PLATE XXVII
IDENTIFICATION: Length, 16.5 cm. Male in breeding plumage: a pale *iridescent blue crown, behind the ear, and on the upper back;* wings, grey-brown; *hind neck, lower back, tail, and throat, black;*

chest, black, sometimes shading to deep blue; the remainder of the under-parts, creamy white; bill and legs, black. After breeding most males revert to an "eclipse" plumage similar to that of the female, *but the bill is black*, the tail remains blue, the lores, pale flesh and the legs black. The time that the eclipse plumage is worn varies with age; very old males retain their breeding plumage throughout the year. In the adult female the upper-parts are brown with a slight reddish tinge; *lores and area about the eye are orange-brown*; tail, brown with a greenish wash; under-parts are creamy white; *the bill and legs, orange-brown*. The juvenile plumage, during the first four months or so, is very similar to that of the adult female; after this young males acquire blue tails and later, in the spring, full breeding plumage.

VOICE: The song is loud and characteristic; a rapid series of notes on the one level followed by a trill of surprising volume; this serves the function of advertisement, defence of territory, maintenance of the pair bond, and the cohesion of the family group. Females give a similar call but not so frequently as the males. Other calls include the "brooding purr", "threat call", a low churring call, and "feeding-young call".

HABITS: Single birds are rarely seen; usually small family parties are encountered with one and sometimes more birds in the adult male breeding plumage. The dominant male of each family group will aggressively defend the territory (0.5–1 ha) throughout the year. On the ground they progress by a series of rapid hops, and most of their food is gathered in this way. They can fly strongly for short distances. A distraction display (aptly termed "rodent run", because the bird appears like a small mammal running from the intruder) by male and female occurs. This display can be provoked by the alarm call of nestlings or fledglings, or the presence near the nest of an intruder (e.g. man or snake).

DISTRIBUTION: This species ranges from the Eyre Peninsula, in South Australia, to Springsure, in Queensland, extending inland from the coast up to 500 kilometres where it occurs near river frontages along the Murray, Lachlan, and Macquarie systems. It also occurs in Tasmania and the Bass Strait islands.

The Superb Blue Wren is a bird of open forests and scrubland wherever shrubby cover and open spaces for feeding occur. It is a vigorous coloniser and the clearing of forests and the creation of shrubby parks and gardens has probably extended its available habitat. Common about Canberra and the Southern Tablelands generally, it is the only species of "blue" wren found in the area.

BREEDING: About Canberra, breeding may extend from September to March with several clutches being laid. However, few clutches are laid after January. In coastal areas breeding starts as early as July and nests may be found until May.

The nest is a small domed structure made of grass with a lining of softer materials, such as wool or feathers. The entrance is in one side and the nest is usually placed about one metre from the ground in a bush or grass tussock. More rarely, nests up to six metres have been reported. Incubation takes about fourteen days and the young remain in the nest for twelve days after which they spend a week in dense cover before joining the foraging group; parents and supernumerary males feed the nestlings for a month. By the time the young are independent the female is usually sitting on a new clutch. Young from earlier nests may help to feed the later broods. The normal clutch is three, but four eggs are quite common. The eggs are white to reddish-white with reddish-brown markings, mainly at the blunt end. The eggs measure 15–18 × 11–14 mm.

Parasitism by both Horsfield and Golden Bronze Cuckoos has been recorded in the area.

FEEDING: The species is very largely insectivorous but it occasionally takes items of vegetable matter such as tiny seeds. Ants and shield-bugs are the commonest food items but most small insects are also devoured. (I.C.R.R.)

## SOUTHERN EMU-WREN *Stipiturus malachurus*
PLATE XXXVI

IDENTIFICATION: Length, 18 cm. Male: general colour above, brown streaked with black; crown of head, rufous; there is a light blue eye-brow; tail, brown, the six feathers very long, 10 cm, with very loose webs; *chin, throat, and fore neck light blue*, remainder of underside brown; bill, blackish-brown; legs, olive-brown; iris, dark brown. Females resemble males but the crown is brown, streaked black; she also lacks the light blue on eyebrow, throat, chin, and fore neck. Young birds are similar to females but are less distinctly streaked with black and the tail is shorter.

VOICE: The voice is a low, quite musical whistle or trill, not unlike that of the Superb Blue Wren, but higher pitched. It also has chattering alarm notes.

DISTRIBUTION: It extends from southern Queensland to the vicinity of Adelaide, South Australia, and to the south-west corner of Western Australia. It also occurs in Tasmania. Throughout this range it is mainly coastal and prefers heathlands, swampy grasslands and vegetated sand dunes. It does extend inland to the foothills of the south-eastern highlands and, although none have been seen on the Southern Tablelands, suitable habitats exist and it is included for it occurs just a few kilometres to the east of the region. In Victoria it has penetrated mountain gullies and has been collected at 300 metres.

HABITS: It is a very shy bird keeping to thick, often prickly, cover. It hops through the bushes ahead of the observer or runs from bush to bush like a mouse. When it does fly the flight is weak and the tail streams out behind. It seldom goes far before dropping into the grass or darting into a bush. When undisturbed it climbs to the tops of bushes and grass stalks with great agility. It is usually found in small parties.

BREEDING: Apparently in south-coastal New South Wales it breeds in the period August to December. The nest is a small dome-shaped structure fifteen centimetres high by eight centimetres wide with a small side entrance. It is built of dried grasses and is lined with finer grass. It is usually built in a very dense bush or tussock, twenty-five centimetres from the ground. The clutch size is usually three but sometimes four; the eggs measure about $17 \times 12$ mm and are white or slightly pink and covered with spots and freckles of brownish-red, particularly at the larger end.

FEEDING: The food is small insects gathered from plants or occasionally chased across the ground. (H.J.F.)

### Family Acanthizidae — Australian Warblers, Thornbills and Scrub-wrens

This family of Australian origin is found also in New Guinea and New Zealand. It contains about 67 species of small or very small insectivorous songbirds. They are found in all habitats from rainforest to desert. Some live in low shrubbery while others frequent treetops and outer foliage. Most of them have pleasant warbling or twittering songs. Eighteen species are found in our region.

## WHITE-THROATED WARBLER *Gerygone olivacea*

PLATE XXVI

IDENTIFICATION: Length, 11 cm. Upper-parts pale ashy-brown washed with olive; wings and tail, dark brown, the tail having a white band at the base and spots at the tips; cheeks and *throat, white; underparts, bright yellow*; bill, black; legs and feet, brown; iris, red. The sexes are similar. Juvenile birds are similar to the adults except that the markings of the throat and cheeks are yellow (not white).

VOICE: The call is a distinctive and beautiful warble; a song of descending notes which is unusual among our birds. The main song also ends in a double call with a strong downwards inflection. The call is uttered very frequently in spring and early summer but less and often incompletely during the autumn. An alarm call of a soft chattering note is given when an intruder is near the nest.

DISTRIBUTION: The White-throated Warbler occurs from Derby, Western Australia, across northern Australia and down the eastern coast through Queensland and New South Wales to northern Victoria with accidental occurrences farther south in Victoria and in south-eastern South Australia. It extends inland to the lower western slopes of the Divide. It is a bird of the open forest country though there is a record of it in the ranges. The species is migratory and arrives on the Southern Tablelands at the beginning of October and many have gone by April. Stragglers remain till late May but there are no winter records in the region. Odd birds are found about Sydney in winter but farther south it is totally migratory. The extent of migratory movements involved is unknown. It can be found, in season, wherever a few trees remain and it is a fairly common breeding species.

HABITS: Being very small and inconspicuous and usually in the top foliage of tall trees it is not often seen without careful search, despite its penetrating call notes. It is solitary, and is found busily searching the leaves for insect food. It is a bird of the outer foliage, and viewed from underneath, as it is usually seen, its bright yellow under-parts and small size are diagnostic.

BREEDING: The breeding season in this region extends from November to late January. The nest is up to twenty-five centimetres long, pendant and domed with a hooded entrance and a long tail with the tail more than half the total length. Long, thin strips of bark, grasses, and cobweb are used in the construction and there is a lining of feathers or hair. String or threads are occasionally worked in. It is placed in varying heights up to sixteen metres from the ground, usually in the outer foliage of a eucalypt, but occasionally in a shrub. Three, or sometimes two eggs are laid. These are white or reddish-white and are heavily dotted and spotted dull red or purplish-red predominantly at the larger end where a zone is sometimes formed. They measure about 18 × 12 mm.

FEEDING: Insect material taken in the outer foliage of the trees is the main food. The ability of this tiny bird to handle a medium-sized moth is an amazing sight, but generally the food is small insects. (S.J.W.)

## WESTERN WARBLER *Gerygone fusca*

PLATE XXVI

IDENTIFICATION: Length, 10.5 cm. General colour above, grey, darker on the wings and tail; tail, white at the base, dark grey towards the end with spots of white at the tip; *under-parts are a very pale greyish-white*; bill, black; legs and feet, black; iris, red. The sexes are similar.

VOICE: The call is similar to that of the White-throated Warbler but slower and more plaintive and gives the impression of being un-finished. It is a descending warble but usually lacks the double call at the end given by the White-throated Warbler. During the breeding season the call is repeated frequently; it is not often heard in the non-breeding season, and because of this the bird is difficult to find and identify. The popular name "Sleepy Dick" used in some districts relates to the call.

DISTRIBUTION: The Western Warbler has three apparently isolated populations. In the east it occurs inland from southern Queensland through New South Wales to northern Victoria. It reaches the coastal regions only in the Hunter River Valley, New South Wales. It occurs in the ranges of central Australia and is also found in Western Australia from the south coast to the Kimberley Division. Some nomadic move-ment occurs in the east in the non-breeding season but the nature of this is not yet known. It is a rare breeding species near Canberra. So far it has been seen there between September and April only. All observations of the bird have been in open forest, often more open than that favoured by the White-throated Warbler.

HABITS: Its habits are very similar to those of the White-throated Warbler.

BREEDING: Breeding records from Canberra are in November and December. Elsewhere the season is from October to January. The nest resembles that of the White-throated Warbler being a pendant, domed structure with a slightly hooded entrance and a long tail below. It is slightly smaller than that of the White-throated Warbler; it has less tail and more cobweb on the outside giving a greyer appearance. It is not so neatly constructed, particularly about the tail. The materials used are strips of bark, fine grasses and cobweb with a lining of finer grasses and feathers. Generally the nest is placed in the outer foliage of a eucalypt, often a sapling, at heights ranging from three to eight metres.

Three eggs, occasionally two, are laid. The ground colour of fleshy-white is dotted and spotted with dull pinkish-red, chiefly at the larger end where a well-defined zone is formed. They measure about 16 × 12 mm.

FEEDING: The food is small insects usually taken in the outer foliage of eucalypts. (S.J.W.)

## BROWN WARBLER *Gerygone mouki*

PLATE XXXVI

IDENTIFICATION: Length 10 cm. A plain, rather drab little warbler. Head and upper parts deep olive brown, wings slightly greyer; *distinct white eyebrow* with indistinct white eye ring; under-parts pale cream-brown, faintly tinged with rufous; tail, rich grey, tipped with broad black band and with *distinct white spot at tip of all feathers except central pair*; bill, black; legs and feet, dark olive-grey to black; iris, rich brick-red. The sexes are similar. Juveniles like adults but the eye is browner.

VOICE: During the summer the call is a three or four syllable "What-is-it" or "Witch-itch-is-it". The bird calls incessantly throughout the day. During the winter the call appears to be abbreviated to "Witch-it; Witch-it". At all times the call has an insect-like buzzing quality. Unlike its two relatives in the local area, the Brown Warbler does not possess a melodious song.

DISTRIBUTION: Three separate and isolated populations occur in Australia. The first is from about the Atherton Tableland to near Mount Spec; the second around Mackay. By far the greatest distribution is from the Brisbane area to eastern Gippsland in Victoria. Cool rainforests and wet sclerophyll forests are the preferred habitats but it can occasionally be found in mangroves and dry forest.

In our region it is common on the coastal ranges but is a rare vagrant further inland. It was first recorded on the western escarpment of Lake George in May 1978 when a single bird was seen in dry, but dense, sclerophyll forest. More recently, in the early winter of 1980, as many as six birds were recorded in the "rainforest gully" of the National Botanic Gardens, Canberra.

HABITS: A very active little bird, it is generally encountered in pairs or, during winter, in small loose flocks. In the southern parts of its range it is probably partially nomadic and these nomadic movements could explain the species' occurrence in the Canberra region.

Like the Black-faced Flycatcher, the Brown Warbler is a common breeding species on the coastal escarpment.

265

BREEDING: The breeding season in south-eastern Australia is from September to February. The nest is a small dome-shaped structure with a long tail and a hooded side entrance. It is composed of fine bark, grasses and rootlets, lined with soft plant material and feathers and bound together with cobweb. Some lichen is used to decorate the outside. Usually it is suspended from a thin vine or fine leafy twig, quite often near water, at heights up to 15 metres.

Two or three pinkish-white eggs, dotted and blotched on the larger end with purplish-red, are laid. They measure about $17 \times 12$ mm.

The Brown Warbler is often parasitised by the Golden Bronze Cuckoo.

FEEDING: Insects and other invertebrates taken from the outer foliage form the bulk of the diet. They are usually taken while the bird is hovering with rapid wing beats. Sometimes it will employ a fly-catcher technique and dart out to take a flying insect in the air. (M.C.)

## STRIATED THORNBILL *Acanthiza lineata*
PLATE XXVI

IDENTIFICATION: Length, 10.25 cm. *General colour above, dull olive*; wings, brown edged with olive; tail, a black subterminal band; *head, olive-brown with a streaked appearance*; face and ear coverts, white with darker edges to the feathers, and these markings continue the effect of streaks running back from the bill; chin, throat and upper breast, dull creamy-white with black edgings to the feathers, giving an irregularly marked effect; remainder of the *under-parts, yellowish-white*; bill, dark brown; legs and feet, greyish-brown; iris, grey. The sexes and juveniles are similar.

This species is difficult to distinguish from the Brown Thornbill and both often occur together. In our area the Striated Thornbill is usually a bird of the high outer foliage and the Brown Thornbill a bird of the scrub level, but this guide is not always reliable. The two species can be distinguished by their basic colours and by the markings of the heads. The Striated Thornbill has a greenish appearance above and is yellowish below. The Brown Thornbill is dark brown above with dull white under-parts. The conspicuous streakings of the head and face of the Striated Thornbill run backwards from the bill, whereas on the Brown Thornbill they run across the forehead. The calls are very distinctive.

VOICE: The normal call of the Striated Thornbill is a single note, "Zip", but sometimes this is repeated several times. Small flocks collectively give a quiet but animated rapid twittering on a pleasant, but not musical, note. In spring it also gives a very quiet, high trill, but one must be very close to the bird to hear it.

266

DISTRIBUTION: It extends from Charleville, Queensland, and a little north of Brisbane, through New South Wales and Victoria (except the north-west) and coastal south-east South Australia to the Mt Lofty Ranges and Kangaroo Island. It is essentially a forest-frequenting species of the east and south-east of the continent extending from the coast to the western slopes and slightly into the red gum fringes to the inland rivers. In our area it is a common species wherever there are trees in habitats varying from the dense, damp forests of the ranges to the open, dry forests. Banding data indicate that it is a sedentary species, with breeding birds remaining in the area from year to year.

HABITS: For most of the year small flocks are seen feeding through the tops of the trees, twittering quietly on the one note as they go. It is unusual to see a lone Striated Thornbill.

BREEDING: The breeding season in the region extends from early September to the end of the year, but it begins in July in coastal areas. The nest is a small domed one suspended by its top and with a high, hooded entrance; it is smaller and neater than the nests of the other common thornbills. It is usually placed less than ten metres high in the outer pendant branches of a tree or sapling. Thin strips of bark and grasses are used in the nest and these are lightly bound with cobweb. There is a lining of feathers, fur or other soft material. Three eggs are laid. The ground colour of the eggs is from pinkish-white to pale creamy-buff and they are more or less zoned at the larger end with pinkish-red to reddish-brown spots and freckles, with a few marks of similar shades over the remainder of the shell. They measure about 19 × 12 mm.

FEEDING: The Striated Thornbill is completely insectivorous, taking most of its food high in the outer foliage of eucalypts, sometimes hovering. Feeding flocks are very active, calling continuously as they work their way through the trees. Such flocks may be seen at most times of the year but particularly in the non-breeding season. (S.J.W.)

## LITTLE THORNBILL *Acanthiza nana*

PLATE XXVI

IDENTIFICATION: Length, 10 cm. *General colour above, dull olive-green* with dull brown primaries edged with olive-yellow; tail has a black subterminal band; ear coverts, dull olive-green with white shaft streaks; *under-parts, yellow,* washed with buff on the chin and throat and with olive-green on the flanks; bill, dark brown, pale grey underneath; legs and feet, greyish-black; iris, yellowish-white. The sexes are

267

similar. This species may be confused with the Brown Weebill, but the short blunt bill of the latter is distinctive. Both birds call frequently at all seasons and the calls readily identify the species.

VOICE: The call is a quiet "tiz tiz" uttered constantly while the bird is feeding, and heard in all seasons.

HABITS: It is usually found feeding in *Acacia*, chiefly the Cootamundra Wattle; few other small birds favour this tree. They are nearly always seen singly or in twos and threes; they do not form large feeding flocks.

DISTRIBUTION: This species covers a wide area of eastern Australia. It extends from northern Queensland down the eastern coast and across southern Queensland; it covers all of New South Wales and Victoria and extends into South Australia as far as the head of Spencer's Gulf and the Flinders Ranges. It is a rare bird and reports are usually from the suburbs of Canberra, though a few birds have been netted and banded among the *Acacia* on the western shore of Lake George. Though records are sporadic it appears to be present in small numbers, in suitable habitat, at all seasons, and seems to be sedentary.

BREEDING: There are few data on breeding in the region, the first nest having been found only in January 1981. Elsewhere the season is from August to December. The nest is a very small domed structure with an entrance near the top. Strips of bark fibre and fine grasses are the main materials used and these are bound with cobweb. The outside is often partly covered with spiders' egg sacs and mosses and the inside is lined with feathers or fur. It is built high in the outer branches of a tree or sapling between three to ten metres from the ground.

Three eggs are the usual clutch but two or four may be laid. The eggs are dull white with heavy freckles of purplish-red and a few lilac spots. They measure about 18 × 12 mm.

FEEDING: Not many species of birds feed on the Cootamundra Wattle, but about Canberra the Little Thornbill seems to feed almost exclusively in that tree. Insects of various forms taken among wattles and *Casuarina* appear to form the diet. (S.J.W.)

## BROWN THORNBILL *Acanthiza pusilla*

PLATE XXVI

IDENTIFICATION: Length, 11 cm. *General colour above, brown* washed with dull olive-green; tail has a black subterminal bar and pale brown tips to the feathers; forehead feathers have dull rufous edges to the feathers giving a *scalloped effect across the forehead*; under-parts, dull white becoming slightly yellowish-brown on the flanks; throat and upper breast, streaked with black; bill, black; legs and feet, dark brown; iris, bright red. The sexes are similar. The juvenile has only a small amount of indistinct scalloping on the forehead, the breast is buff-grey and the streaking of the breast is faint compared with that of the adult. The iris is chestnut-brown with a grey outer ring. Compare with identification note on Striated Thornbill.

VOICE: The call is a pleasing, musical chatter. The usual call is three rapid notes down the scale with a higher and longer note ending the song. Many variations are heard. All birds handled have indulged in a pleasant but extremely quiet mimicry sub-song. This often includes imitations of the chatter of a flock of Crimson Rosellas.

DISTRIBUTION: The Brown Thornbill occurs in south-eastern Australia, from central Queensland north of the Tropic, to the region of Adelaide, South Australia, and in Tasmania. It is common in most of this range.

It is common throughout our area wherever there are trees with a few shrubs. It is a bird of the scrub level of the forests both in the ranges and on the tablelands generally.

Banding has shown that birds of the Canberra area are in the main sedentary, though there is some as yet undetermined movement of juveniles.

HABITS: Brown Thornbills do not form flocks. Single birds or, less usually, pairs can be found feeding in the shrub level. Individuals are sometimes seen at higher levels but this is unusual. Its four-note call is not given as frequently as are the calls of the other thornbills.

BREEDING: Nests have been found from early September to the end of December, but in some areas it begins to breed as early as June. The nest is a domed structure with an entrance near the top; it is larger and more untidy than the nests of the Striated or Little Thornbills, and is also distinguished by being close to the ground. It is found among bracken, under the edge of a tussock, under grass on the side of a bank or in a low plant. In construction, shreds of bark, rather coarse grasses and pieces of bracken fern with a little cobweb are used. There is a lining of finer material and feather or fur. Usually three eggs are laid. The ground colour is white, occasionally tinged pale buff, and finely freckled with a few markings of dull red or reddish-brown, mostly at the larger end. They measure about 16 × 12 mm.

FEEDING: This is another insect-eating species. The local birds obtain their food chiefly in the shrub level of the forest. (S.J.W.)

## CHESTNUT-TAILED THORNBILL *Acanthiza uropygialis*
PLATE XXVI

IDENTIFICATION: Length 9 cm. *General colour above, greyish-brown*; wings, dusky-brown; *rump, rich chestnut*; tail, black, slightly tipped with white; under-parts, dull greyish-white. On the forehead the blackish-brown feathers have dull white tips giving a scalloped effect similar to that noted in the Brown and the Buff-tailed Thornbills. About the eye and ear coverts the brown feathers are tipped white giving a mottled appearance; bill, dark brown; legs and feet, blackish; iris, dull white. The sexes are similar.

VOICE: The song is quite a long animated one and appears to be given at all seasons, but particularly in spring. When feeding in flocks in the non-breeding season, a quiet and rather constant twitter of single notes is heard and presumably this is a contact call.

DISTRIBUTION: The Chestnut-tailed Thornbill is not found in the north-west of Western Australia or the northern halves of the Northern Territory or Queensland, but covers most of the remainder of the continent, particularly the inland part below the Tropic of Capricorn. It does not occur east of the Divide. The normal distribution is to the west of our area but it is one of several inland species which can be expected to appear on the tablelands of New South Wales during drought years in the inland. There is only one record from Canberra; two birds appeared in August 1961 and remained there for several days.

Its habitat is the dry scrub country of the inland but it appears to avoid the red-gum country of the Murray-Darling River systems.

HABITS: In its main range, where it is usually very common, feeding flocks of up to ten birds are seen, particularly in the non-breeding season. These are usually on the ground or in the low scrub levels.

BREEDING: There are no breeding records from our area. In inland New South Wales it breeds from August to December. Usually the nest is placed in the hollow spout of a dead tree but a variety of other situations, such as behind loose bark or in a hollow in a fence post, are used. Most nests are from one to six metres above the ground but they have also been reported high in dead trees. The nest is domed with a side entrance and is constructed of grasses and bark strips bound with cobwebs. There is usually an ample lining of fur, hair, or feathers.

Three eggs of flesh-white colour are laid. These are minutely freckled all over with reddish-brown, particularly at the larger end where a zone is usually formed. They measure about 17 × 13 mm.

FEEDING: This is an insectivorous species which seeks its food at all levels of the scrub. (S.J.W.)

## BUFF-TAILED THORNBILL *Acanthiza reguloides*

PLATE XXVI

IDENTIFICATION: Length 11 cm. General colour above, *olive-brown* with dusky-brown wings; *upper-tail coverts, dull buff*; tail, blackish-brown with pale brown tips; forehead, brown with lighter margins to the feathers giving a scalloped effect resembling that noted in the Brown and Chestnut-tailed Thornbills; *under-parts, buffy-yellow*; bill, dark brown, paler under; legs and feet, grey; iris, pale bluish-grey. The sexes are similar but fledglings are brighter in colour than the adults.

VOICE: The calls appear more limited than in some of the other thornbills. The chief call, which is quite diagnostic and is given at all seasons, is an animated, rapid rattle on two alternating notes. A few quiet, lower notes are given at times also.

DISTRIBUTION: The range extends from the coast to the western slopes of the Divide from Herberton, Queensland, through New South Wales, where it extends to the Riverina district, Victoria, and to the Mount Lofty Ranges in South Australia. This is a bird of the dry open forest country and it does not penetrate the wetter forests of the ranges. It is found along gullies, creeks, and rivers and wherever trees remain. It appears to be sedentary and no movements have been observed.

HABITS: Single birds, pairs, or family parties are usually noted feeding in the lower levels of the forest. It is often seen on the ground.

BREEDING: In our area it is an early breeder and nests are built in the last half of August. The season can, in a good year, continue to mid-January, but ends much earlier in a dry year. The nest is a domed, fairly roughly built structure of grasses and occasional bark strips, often bound with a few cobwebs and liberally lined with feathers, fur, hair, or plant down. It is sometimes built on the ground under a clump of grass but most nests are between one and three metres from the ground. An alternative common name of Bark Tit arises from its habit of building the nest behind loose bark on the trunk of a tree. This appears to be a favoured site though holes in trees are used also. Four,

271

but sometimes three eggs are laid. These are white to fleshy-white with small freckles and larger spots of a pale red to rich red-brown colour. At times these form a zone at the larger end. The eggs measure about 16 × 12 mm. Incubation lasts about twelve days.

FEEDING: This insect eater feeds on the ground as well as in the lower branches of trees. (S.J.W.)

## YELLOW-TAILED THORNBILL *Acanthiza chrysorrhoa*
PLATE XXVI

IDENTIFICATION: Length, 11.5 cm. Male: *upper-parts, brown* with an olive wash and the quills are dark brown; *rump, bright yellow* which is very obvious in sunlight; tail, black; forehead, blackish and the area about the eye and the ear coverts is whitish; there is white on the chin and throat; under-parts, yellowish-white; bill, black; legs and feet, greyish-black; iris, greyish-white. The sexes are similar.

VOICE: The Yellow-tailed Thornbill has a greater variety of calls than the other thornbills in our area. In flight they give a short, sharp "zip" note. A very pleasant song of a rapid and animated nature is given throughout the year and this seems to be a contact call as other birds tend to move to the caller.

DISTRIBUTION: The species ranges over almost the whole of Australia south of the Tropic of Capricorn, including Tasmania, and there is another population just south of the Gulf of Carpentaria. Open forest country is favoured in our area and as it does not penetrate dense forests, either wet or dry, it is not found in the higher ranges.

HABITS: It is found in pairs or small flocks; these are probably family groups and tend to remain together for long periods. Pairs of birds banded together have been trapped together one and two years later. The flocks do not completely break up even in the breeding season but in winter the species tends to congregate with other small birds in foraging for food. It forages a lot on the ground and small feeding flocks are a common sight in Canberra gardens. It is seldom found far from trees and favours park-like areas. When disturbed the yellow rump is most conspicuous as the bird flies away and the animated calling on alighting is a good guide to identification.

BREEDING: The species is one of the earliest in our area to commence breeding and nests have been noted from July to December. The bulky, domed pendant nest is built by both birds. It is usually in the dense, outer foliage of a tree or shrub and is usually rather well hidden.

Low sites are commonest, often only one metre from the ground, and most are below six metres. The nest chamber is low in the structure and the hooded, inconspicuous side entrance is also low. A peculiar open cup, resembling a false nest, is usually built on the top. Grasses are the chief building material but cobwebs, wool, spiders' egg sacs and plant stems are all used, and the lining is of finer grasses, feathers, fur, or wool.

Up to four clutches in the same nest in the one season have been reported. The incubation is carried out by the female who is not fed by the male but both birds feed the nestlings. Individuals from earlier broods sometimes assist with the latter task. Three is the normal clutch but four eggs are laid occasionally. The rather transparent egg is pale flesh colour and measures about 18 × 13 mm. Occasionally they are marked on the larger end with minute dots of dull red or reddish-brown.

Incubation takes eighteen to twenty days and the fledgling period lasts a further seventeen to nineteen days. Both these periods are rather long for a bird of this size.

FEEDING: Insects taken on the ground appear to be the chief food though some insects are also taken in the lower parts of trees and in shrubs. (S.J.W.)

## WHITE-BROWED SCRUB-WREN *Sericornis frontalis*

PLATE XXVII

IDENTIFICATION: Length, 12 cm. Male: *general colour above, dark brown*, upper-parts, with a faint olive wash and a deep rufous wash on the upper-tail coverts; tail, brown with a subterminal black band; lores, black; there is a *conspicuous white streak over the eye* and a black area below the eye; throat, yellowish-white with blackish-brown streaks; under-parts, pale, dull yellow becoming brown on the flanks; bill, black; legs and feet, light, dull brown; iris, dull buff. In the adult female the dull white line over the eye is narrower and not so well defined as in the male. The lores are dusky-brown (not black). The throat is only slightly streaked and the tail bar not so well defined.

In young birds there is no tail bar and the bar over the eye is missing, but otherwise they resemble females. Adult plumage is assumed at three months.

VOICE: The calls are varied but all are harsh, rather loud and un-musical. During the breeding season a prolonged, repeated "whee-oo whee-oo" is heard; a mechanical, rapid call. Harsh, scolding alarm calls are of four or five notes, the first and last being the longest.

273

DISTRIBUTION: The White-browed Scrub-wren occurs from the Atherton Tableland, north Queensland around the coast and ranges, to the Shark Bay district, Western Australia. It is also found in Tasmania and the Bass Strait Islands and other islands off the coast. Its range extends to the inland where suitable scrub exists, e.g. to the eastern Riverina district of New South Wales. On the Southern Tablelands it is found wherever trees and low undergrowth remain. A few are seen in Canberra gardens and it occurs along all the streams in the Brindabella and other ranges where it is probably the most common bird. No seasonal altitudinal movement has been proved though numbers have been observed to drop in the ranges in winter. Movement so far recorded appears to be a random disperal of individuals, particularly of juveniles.

HABITS: The bird is rarely seen higher than five metres from the ground. Its strong legs and feet are adapted to hopping on the ground and in the shrub level in its search for food. With the Pilot Bird, it occasionally follows the feeding lyrebird, picking up small insect material.

BREEDING: The breeding season is later in the high country than on the coast where it begins in July; in our area it extends from September to January. The nest is a domed structure with a rounded side entrance usually placed on the ground under the edge of a tussock, among debris or ferns, or on the edge of a bank. Occasionally it is found up to three metres high in rather dense shrubbery. Grasses, leaves, and fine twigs are the main items used. There is always an ample lining of fur, hair, feathers or other soft material. Three eggs is the usual clutch. The ground colour is off-white or greyish, sometimes with a faint purplish tone. There are a few freckles of shades a little darker than the ground colour and a zone of dull purplish-brown at the large end. They measure about 19 × 14 mm.

FEEDING: The species appears to be entirely insectivorous and food is taken on the ground or in the low scrub levels of the forests. (S.J.W.)

## LARGE-BILLED SCRUB-WREN *Sericornis magnirostris*
PLATE XXXVI

IDENTIFICATION: Length, 12 cm. *General colour above dull olive-green*; feathers of the wing coverts edged with lighter yellowish white; tail and upper-tail coverts, brown; head, olive-brown with rufous wash on forehead; face, yellowish-brown; *chin and throat, dull white*; under-parts, dull white with olive tinge; bill, black; legs and feet, pink with brown tinge; iris, yellow brown. The sexes are similar.

VOICE: The voice is similar to that of other scrub-wrens, consisting of quite loud, harsh, chattering notes.

DISTRIBUTION: It extends from at least as far north as Cooktown, north Queensland, through New South Wales and Victoria to the eastern edge of the Dandenongs. Its distribution is mainly coastal but it does extend into the slopes of the mountains and penetrates some of the gullies to high altitudes. It has not yet been seen on the Southern Tablelands but exists just a few kilometres to the east of the scarp near Braidwood, New South Wales. It has been recorded, although rarely, at over 600 metres in eastern Victoria. The habitat preferred is dense rainforest, typically the wetter parts where mosses and lichens are abundant on the trees. This habitat occurs in the wetter gullies of the Brindabella and Tidbinbilla Ranges and the bird might be recorded there ultimately.

HABITS: It is most commonly seen in the lower levels of the rainforest, up to ten metres from the ground and sometimes in the taller trees. This is quite distinct from the other scrub-wrens which are usually on the ground or in the undergrowth. It does visit these habitats however, usually in small groups that mingle with other small birds travelling through the lower stages of the forest.

BREEDING: On the coast of southern New South Wales it apparently breeds in the period August to January. The nest is more or less oval, about twenty centimetres high and ten centimetres wide, with a side entrance that is often slightly hooded. It is built of fine rootlets, lichens, and leaf skeletons and is lined with fine material and some feathers. In northern New South Wales it is usually built in a thicket of lawyer vines or in a dense bush. It often dispenses with building a new nest and renovates an old one of the Yellow-throated Scrub-wren. The clutch size is three or four and the eggs are white with a bluish tinge and are freckled and blotched with dark brown or purple, particularly at the larger end. They measure about $19 \times 14$ mm.

FEEDING: They feed among the low trees and undergrowth and on the ground on insects and other small animals. (H.J.F.)

## YELLOW-THROATED SCRUB-WREN *Sericornis citreogularis*

PLATE XXXVI

IDENTIFICATION: Length 12–15 cm. Male: *General colour above, olive-brown*, with a brown tone on the crown; rump rich brown, upper tail dark brown; lores, to ear coverts, glossy black; eyebrow white to yellow above the ear coverts; chin, white; throat and upper breast, bright yellow; belly, white and sides of breast and the flanks warm brown; bill, black; legs and feet, dull flesh colour; iris, reddish-brown. Female similar to the male but the distinctive facial marking is dull olive-green in the female.

In immatures the upper-parts are mottled with brown; the throat is yellow and the under-parts fawn.

VOICE: Loud chatter of rather harsh notes and also whistling notes of a melodious tone. The species is an accomplished mimic and calls during the breeding season are a mixture of its own and those of other local birds, given as it moves over the ground and through low vegetation.

DISTRIBUTION: From Cooktown to about Mount Spec in Queensland and from about Gympie to Mount Dromedary, New South Wales. Generally it is found in rainforests along the coast and in nearby ranges but it remains in scrub, particularly in damp places, long after the rainforest itself has been cleared. In our area in some moist places it comes well over the coastal divide but it is never very far from the rainforests of the coastal mountains.

HABITS: This is a ground-dweller with the typically strong feet and legs of a bird of this habitat. It is often seen in the low scrub of the forest but very seldom above the eye level of the observer.

BREEDING: The breeding season is long with active nests reported between August and March. The nest is a large untidy structure of vegetable material — often suspended over a stream — and in these circumstances one could mistake it for flood debris. It can be a metre in length with a long, loose tail. The nest chamber is usually towards the top of the mass and usually the side entrance is disguised by overhanging fibres. The two or three eggs vary in colour from a brownish-pink to chocolate brown with markings in diffused zones near the larger end. The eggs measure about $26 \times 19$ mm.

FEEDING: This species gleans its food, insects and other small animals, among the litter of the forest floor. (S.J.W.)

## HEATH-WREN *Sericornis pyrrhopygius*
PLATE XXXVI

IDENTIFICATION: Length, 15 cm. Male: general colour above, brown with an olive tinge; *upper-tail coverts, pale chestnut*; tail has a white subterminal bar and light tip; there is a *light line over the eye*;

under-parts dull white, each feather with blackish streak; under-tail coverts chestnut; bill, dark brown; legs and feet, flesh; iris, hazel. The female is similar but the under-parts are pale buff and less distinctly streaked, with the centre of abdomen dull white.

VOICE: It has a very musical warble with which is mixed an appreciable amount of mimicry of other small birds. It usually sings from a low bush and darts to cover on completion but has been seen singing on the ground. The female has a similar but less melodious song. There is also a sharp alarm note and a rapid chatter.

DISTRIBUTION: It is distributed from southern Queensland to south-east South Australia. It is mainly coastal in distribution but does extend inland to the slopes and mountains in a few places. The inland slopes and plains are occupied by another species, the Shy Heath-wren *S. cautus*. It has now been recorded in the Australian Capital Territory and the highlands of New South Wales, and also occurs in the mountains of north-eastern Victoria. It prefers dense undergrowth of forests and heathlands as habitat.

HABITS: It can fly well when it must but prefers to hop and is usually seen on the ground hopping about with upright tail or making very low short flights across open spaces. When moving rapidly it seems to bounce along the ground like a small brown ball. They travel in little lively excitable groups; these gatherings even occur in the breeding season. They are occasionally seen on low bushes but then, when disturbed, dart down close to the ground and make off.

BREEDING: The breeding season is in the spring and summer in Victoria but there is no record from our area. The nest is a small, domed structure, built of grass and bark as well as some small twigs and has a small entrance near the top that often has a small, rudimentary spout or platform. It is usually lined with feathers. The nest is placed in a low thick bush, often only a few centimetres, and seldom more than 25 cm, from the ground. The clutch size is usually three; the eggs measure 19 × 15 mm and are white with a pink tinge or darker to light reddish and are spotted and blotched with brown, often forming a zone at the larger end.

FEEDING: They feed entirely on the ground on small insects. (H.J.F.)

## SPECKLED WARBLER *Sericornis sagittatus*
PLATE XXVII

IDENTIFICATION: Length 12.5 cm. Male: General colour above,

*dull olive-brown streaked with dark brown*; primaries brown with white edges; a whitish stripe above the eye bordered above by a black line extending from the lores to the side of the nape; this line may be partly hidden by the crown feathers; tail tipped with white; *under-parts, white washed with olive-yellow and with heavy black streaks*; bill brownish; legs and feet brown; iris dark brown. Female: similar to male but white stripe above eye bordered above by a reddish-brown line from the lores to the side of the nape; this may at times be partly hidden by the crown feathers.

VOICE: The Speckled Warbler has two main calls. The chief one is a harsh, rapid, rattling sound; in spring it gives a quiet song of a few ascending notes. It is also a competent mimic of other birds.

DISTRIBUTION: It is found in south-eastern Queensland and the eastern half of New South Wales and over much of Victoria. South Australian records await confirmation. In New South Wales it extends from the coast across the Divide to the edge of plains country. Open forest with some scrub is the preferred habitat. The bird is often encountered on stony hillsides with very sparse timber and scrub. It does not penetrate forest areas where grass is entirely replaced by shrubs. Banding data indicate that it is quite sedentary as individuals are frequently retrapped at the banding place. It is not a common bird in our area but appears well distributed in small numbers wherever the habitat is suitable.

HABITS: They move about in pairs or small groups and are usually found on the ground feeding. It is often in the company of thornbills and other small ground-living birds. When disturbed, or when displaying, it sits in low trees but the ground is its true home.

BREEDING: The breeding season in our area commences in late August and continues to December. Autumn breeding has been reported elsewhere in New South Wales. The nest is always placed on the ground in a small depression at the base of the shrub, in or under a tussock. It is a domed structure of grasses and fine pieces of bark with a sparse lining of fine plant materials, fur or feathers. Usually three, but occasionally four eggs are laid. They are bright chocolate red, sometimes with a deeper shading at the larger end. The egg is a rounded oval in form, rather broader than most eggs of this size; it measures about 17 × 15 mm. The species is one of the few hosts of the Black-eared Cuckoo, which lays an egg of the same distinctive colour.

FEEDING: It appears that it is insectivorous obtaining most of its food on the ground or in low shrubs, but a small amount of seed is also eaten. (S.J.W.)

## BROWN WEEBILL *Smicrornis brevirostris*

PLATE XXVI

IDENTIFICATION: Length, 9 cm. *This is one of our smallest birds.* General colour above, dull olive-brown; wings, brown edged with dull olive; tail, brown with a black subterminal bar and white tips to the feathers; there is a pale rufous area about the eye and ear coverts; *under-parts are yellowish buff* becoming dull olive-yellow on the abdomen; bill, dull brown; legs, brown-grey; feet, flesh-brown; iris, straw-white. The sexes are similar.

The white tip to the tail, the short, blunt bill, and the calls distinguish this from similar species such as the Little Thornbill with which it may be confused.

VOICE: The call is very distinctive and is generally much more animated and varied than those of other similar sized species. The chief call is a rapid, clear whistle of several notes, clearer and louder than those of the thornbills. This has been rendered in words as "winnie weildt" and "pee-pee p'wee-weep". It also has a variety of rather harsh, low, unmusical "contact" calls.

DISTRIBUTION: The Brown Weebill is distributed widely throughout Australia. It favours savannah and mallee country and is probably the commonest bird in the latter areas. It avoids both the heavily forested country of the coast and the Divide, and the arid treeless plains of the interior. The species varies considerably; local birds are brownish, those of the broad belt east and west across the continent are rather pallid, while northern birds are yellowish. The local form ranges across south-eastern Australia from the Bunya Mountains in southern Queensland across New South Wales, Victoria, and South Australia to Eyre Peninsula, with a paler race in the mallee country.

It is a bird of the open forest and is not found in the more dense and moist forests of the ranges. It is fairly numerous in all suitable habitats of the Southern Tablelands and is frequently heard, if not always seen, in the immediate vicinity of Canberra. It is regarded as sedentary.

HABITS: It occurs in small groups usually high in the foliage. It is constantly moving among the leaves and may often be seen feeding during the middle of the day. This habit and its constant calling, even in winter, attract the observer's attention. The Brown Weebill can often be identified by its habit of hovering to pick some small items of

279

food from the outer foliage of a eucalypt, a habit it shares with the Striated Thornbill.

BREEDING: The main nesting season is from October to December but many nests are found at other times. The nest is a small, domed structure with a tiny spout-like opening near the top. Materials vary, but thin grass stems are usual and these are well bound with cobweb. Sometimes there is a finer lining including feathers. The nest is usually placed in the outer foliage of a small tree.

Two or three eggs are laid and these are of a creamy-buff to buffy-white colour with tiny buffy-brown or purplish-brown markings, liberally distributed all over the shell and occasionally making a zone at the larger end. They measure about $15 \times 12$ mm.

FEEDING: A remarkable variety of tiny animal foods have been recorded including aphids, leaf-hoppers, scale insects, jassids, weevils, leaf-beetles, ants and spiders. It takes food exclusively from the outer foliage of eucalypts. (S.J.W.)

## WHITEFACE *Aphelocephala leucopsis*

PLATE XXVI

IDENTIFICATION: Length, 13 cm. Adult male: general colour above, brown; tail, blackish-brown, tipped with white on the outer feathers; *lores and forehead, white*; under-parts, dull white, washed with dull brown; bill, black; legs and feet, brownish-black; iris, yellowish-white. The sexes are similar.

VOICE: The main call is a short, quiet, musical one of a few notes. In winter when it often associates in small feeding flocks with other species such as the Yellow-tailed Thornbill, it gives a rapidly repeated musical high-pitched call on the one note.

DISTRIBUTION: It is distributed in three races over the continent south of the Tropic of Capricorn. The local race occurs from the Bunya Mountains in Queensland across southern Queensland and the inland portions of New South Wales, Victoria, and South Australia to Eyre Peninsula. It occurs chiefly on the inland side of the Divide in New South Wales but reaches the coast in a few places. It is not an abundant bird, but is widely distributed in small numbers. It is occasionally seen in open grassland quite close to Canberra and appears to favour paddocks with fallen dead timber and a few living trees.

HABITS: It is nearly always seen very actively hopping on the ground, usually in open country where the grass is relatively short. It feeds in small flocks for much of the year. It is quiet, appears relatively unafraid, and is often seen near farm buildings.

BREEDING: The breeding season in this region is from September to January. The nest is a loosely constructed, large, domed structure of bark strips, grasses and roots, lined with feathers, fur and other soft materials. The site varies but the most usual is in a cavity in a dead tree or fence post. Occasionally it is placed in a dense shrub and sometimes in a cavity in a bank. Nests have been seen in a variety of peculiar locations about farm buildings. The nest is usually within three metres of the ground. Three to five eggs are laid. The dull white to pale buff ground colour is usually all but obscured by the heavy spots and freckles of pale brown to chocolate brown. They measure $16 \times 12$ mm.

FEEDING: Small insects are the major items of diet but small seeds are also taken extensively. It appears to be almost exclusively a ground feeder. (S.J.W.)

## ROCK WARBLER *Origma solitaria*

PLATE XXXVI

IDENTIFICATION: Length, 14 cm. *Upper-parts dull dark brown* with the rump tinged rufous; tail, dull black; ear coverts and feathers around the eye, rufous-brown; throat, greyish-white; remainder of *under-parts rufous*; bill, dark brown or black; legs and feet, dark brown; iris, red-brown. The sexes are similar.

VOICE: A loud, melancholy, repeated double-syllable call is given and there is a rasping note which is probably a contact call.

DISTRIBUTION: This is the only species confined to New South Wales. Its distribution is a patchy one in central eastern parts of the State from Scone in the north to Pigeon House Mountain in the south and as far west as Jenolan Caves. It is always associated with rough country with sandstone and limestone. Until recently it was regarded as endemic to the Hawkesbury sandstone area but it is now known to occur on rocky outcrops on Badja Mountain, 80 km south of Braidwood, New South Wales. It is a sedentary species.

HABITS: Normally this species is seen hopping rapidly about stone outcrops and escarpments and its movements usually draw the observer's attention. At times it moves through low branches of trees and shrubs. There is a rather constant sideways flicking of the tail.

281

BREEDING: Active nests are found from August to December. The nest is a hanging globular structure of vegetable material — roots, bark, moss and grasses bound with cobweb, with finer materials and a few feathers as lining and with a side entrance. Typically the nest is attached to overhanging rocks, cave roofs, etc. but a variety of other similar overhanging sites have been reported. The eggs are usually white but sometimes there is a fine dusting of dark markings. The normal clutch is three eggs. They measure about 20 × 15 mm.

FEEDING: Largely insectivorous, finding its food on the underside of overhanging rocks, rock faces and sometimes along road margins. Some vegetable material is also taken. (S.J.W.)

## PILOT BIRD *Pycnoptilus floccosus*
PLATE XXVII

IDENTIFICATION: Length, 16.5 cm. *General colour above, brown with a rufous wash* more pronounced on the upper-tail coverts; *breast deep rufous* with brown centres to the feathers giving a rich mottled appearance; bill, brown; legs and feet, black; iris, red. The sexes are similar.

VOICE: The call is very loud and melodious; it carries well in forest country and resembles the words "guinea a week". The call is given in all seasons but the bird is rather quiet in the winter months, being more often seen than heard.

DISTRIBUTION: The species has a restricted range through the wet forest country of the south-east of the continent only. It occurs from the Blue Mountains and Port Hacking southward into Victoria as far as the Dandenong Ranges. The Pilot Bird is an inhabitant of the moist gullies and wet forests and likes country similar to that favoured by the Superb Lyrebird. It occurs throughout the ranges but not above the levels where good timber grows. Visual and banding evidence indicate that the birds are not as numerous in winter in the ranges as they are at other seasons but it is likely that any movement of individuals is of a local, altitudinal nature only.

HABITS: This species is rather fearless and if one is quiet it is easily observed as it hops about on paths, in clearings or through the under-growth. It is a bird of the lowest levels of the forest, obviously fitted more to hopping than to flight, and it rarely moves more than two metres up from the ground, and seldom flies except when harried. The tail is carried high and is usually fanned.

BREEDING: Nests have been found in the ranges in late September and breeding continues until December or January. The nest is a fairly bulky and rather untidy, domed structure, built on the ground among the litter of the forest floor or under a fern. It is made of bark strips, leaves and tree fern roots and resembles the litter among which it is placed. It is lined with fine bark fibre and feathers. There are two rather large, broad eggs, smoky-brown to dusky-grey, darker in the ground colour at the larger end. They measure about 27 × 20 mm.

FEEDING: Its diet is of insects, worms and some small berries. The name Pilot Bird refers to an assumption that it pilots the lyrebird but it seems that the reverse is true and that it feeds, with the White-browed Scrub-wren, on the smaller material uncovered by the Lyrebird in its scratching of the forest floor. (S.J.W.)

Family Ephthianuridae — Australian Chats
There are only five species in this endemic Australian family. They are small insectivorous birds that live in arid and seasonally dry, wooded parts of the country, and are associated with low, open shrubbery. Two, one uncommon, one a rare vagrant, visit our area.

## WHITE-FRONTED CHAT *Ephthianura albifrons*
PLATE XXVI

IDENTIFICATION: Length, 12 cm. Male: back, dull grey; wings, dark brown to blackish-brown; tail, dark brown with white spots on the ends of the tail feathers; *there is a broad black band on back of the head, across the lower neck and upper breast.* The rest of the head and under-parts are pure white; bill, black; legs and feet, black; iris, yellowish-buff. The adult female is a drab version of the male. Juveniles resemble the female but the upper-parts have a buff tinge.

VOICE: It has a low, metallic "tang". This call is not sharp; rather it is slow and fairly drawn out, somewhat resembling the call of a finch.

DISTRIBUTION: It extends from south-eastern Queensland, over most of New South Wales except the extreme north-west, across the south of South Australia and Western Australia, and as far north as Shark Bay. It is a bird of swamps, lake margins and damp places generally. On the coast of New South Wales it favours samphire and rush-covered margins of estuaries and lakes. It is not common on the Southern Tablelands but has been seen fairly frequently at all seasons at the swampy eastern end of Lake Burley Griffin and the shores of Lakes George and Bathurst.

HABITS: In the non-breeding season the White-fronted Chat forms small nomadic flocks which may be seen feeding on the ground generally not far from water. They fly with a rapid twisting flight, that is quite characteristic of chats generally.

BREEDING: The few breeding records from our area are in late spring and young birds have been seen in early summer. The breeding season elsewhere is an extended one, nests having been reported from July to March but September and October are the chief months. The nest is constructed near the ground in a shrub or in tall grass, generally in a damp location. It is cup-shaped and built of grass or fine twigs with fine rootlets and grasses, and occasionally hair, as a lining. Three, occasionally four, eggs are laid. The ground colour is faint pinkish-white, with fairly large spots of reddish- or purplish-brown, chiefly at the larger end. They measure about 20 × 14 mm.

FEEDING: Food is usually taken on the ground where insects, including ants, cockroaches, beetles, and similar foods are found. (S.J.W.)

## CRIMSON CHAT *Ephthianura tricolor*

IDENTIFICATION: Length, 11.5 cm. Male: general colour above, ashy-brown with the nape and back blackish-brown; primaries and secondaries narrowly edged with brownish-white; rump and upper-tail coverts, crimson; tail, dark brown with white tip; *crown, crimson*; throat, white; *under-parts, bright crimson* except for white abdomen and under-tail coverts; bill, blackish-brown; legs and feet, blackish-brown; iris, yellowish-white. The adult female is duller in colour than the male; the head is brown, the chest buff, but the rump is scarlet as in the male.

VOICE: There are several calls; a mournful territorial call of two syllables "tee-wheee"; a sweet shrill repeated whistle "sheee"; a flat call of a metallic "ting", somewhat resembling that of the White-fronted Chat; a low aggressive chatter in defence of territory; and a plaintive hissing used in a distraction display while nesting.

DISTRIBUTION: This is a bird of the inland. Normally it may be found anywhere in the inland west of the Divide from the Gulf of Carpentaria to northern Victoria and makes pronounced seasonal movements probably relating to a constant search for suitable habitat. These movements are primarily of a migratory nature but in the southern half of the continent its appearances are sporadic, and exceptionally good rainfall, with abundant growth of grass, can be expected to lead to a great influx of birds.

Drought induced irruptions of the species also occur occasionally throughout the range but its appearances in the south are less regular than in the north. During 1957, a drought year, it was found nesting near Canberra. During the drought of the early 1980s several birds were seen and photographed near Gunning. The Southern Tablelands are the extreme south-eastern extension of its range so far recorded.

HABITS: In the inland it is very sociable and is found in small groups or, after rain, large flocks, and many nests are found in the one area. It is very timid and flies swiftly with a twisting flight, usually rising from the ground or a very low bush.

BREEDING: The one breeding record near Canberra was in September. In eastern Australia it breeds from September to December but in the inland it breeds at any time that heavy rain falls. The nest is a cup-shaped structure of fine twigs and grasses with a lining of finer vegetable material. It is usually placed in the top of a low bush or clump of spinifex. The nests are often in loose colonies but each territory is strongly defended. The usual clutch is three eggs but occasionally four are laid. They are of a pale fleshy-white colour sparsely dotted and spotted with rich red to purplish-red all over. They measure about 17 × 13 mm.

FEEDING: Insects are taken on the ground, in low shrubs and in grass clumps. (S.J.W.)

# TREECREEPERS

The treecreepers and treerunners are another example of birds that, though not particularly closely related, have evolved in a convergent manner to produce forms that have rather similar life habits. In this grouping there are four separate families involved, the Certhiidae tree-creepers and Sittidae nuthatches that are restricted to the Northern Hemisphere, the Climacteridae Australian treecreepers, and the Neosittidae sittellas. All live by running up and over the bark of standing trees but there the similarity ceases and a certain amount of discussion continues on the exact relationships of the families to one another.

Family Climacteridae — Australian Treecreepers
This small family of birds is restricted to Australia except for one that extends into New Guinea. They are all rather similar in appearance

and general habits. They are all dark-coloured birds, 15–20 cm long, with a coloured wing bar and eyestripe and striped under-parts. The bill is slender and long and down-curved, and the legs and toes are very much elongated for clinging to vertical tree trunks. They run *up* trees not down, as do the sittellas.

They are distributed throughout the continent except in areas of grassland or treeless desert. Although there has been much discussion on the number of species there is now general agreement that there are seven.

There are three in our area, the Brown Treecreeper, the White-throated Treecreeper and the Red-browed Treecreeper. The presence of three very closely related and similar birds in the one district is of considerable interest. Although there is a slight separation, at least two are found together in most habitats. It would be of great interest to know the food habits of the birds in detail to learn how it is they do not compete with one another.

## BROWN TREECREEPER *Climacteris picumnus*
PLATE XXIII

IDENTIFICATION: Length, 18.5 cm. Male: *General colour above, dull brown* richer on the rump and upper-tail coverts; *flight feathers of the wings, crossed by a broad band of buff* which is a very conspicuous field mark when the bird is in flight, but is not visible when at rest; tail, brown with a black subterminal bar; crown, dull greyish-brown; there is a pale line above the eye; cheeks and throat, pale buff; there are *small black markings on the centre of the upper breast*; breast and abdomen, buffy-brown heavily streaked with white and black; under-tail coverts, white barred with blackish-brown; bill, greyish-black; legs and feet, dull grey; iris, blackish-brown.

The female can be distinguished from the male by faint reddish (not black) markings in the centre of the upper breast. Immature birds lack the heavy streaking of the under-parts of the adult; this is ill-defined. The sides of the breast and the under-tail coverts are rufous (not white with dark bars).

VOICE: The call is a sharp, loud, piercing, single note possibly repeated several times but these calls are irregularly spaced. The call is heard frequently at all seasons but particularly while the birds are breeding. The alarm call is a fairly loud rattle on the one note, much quieter than the normal call.

DISTRIBUTION: It is a bird of the south-eastern part of the continent extending from about Rockhampton in Queensland through New South Wales to the eastern parts of South Australia. It is generally uncommon in coastal areas but is abundant in many parts of its inland range. In our area it is found in open forests and partly cleared country. It appears to be sedentary; small parties have been sighted regularly in some areas over periods of several years.

HABITS: The habits of all three treecreepers are similar. With the large, strong claws they can cling to even very smooth, hard gum trees but seem to prefer rough bark. They move up the tree and are seldom seen head down. They spiral around the tree and larger limbs and jump forward, backwards and sideways with great agility and even run out along the underside of nearly horizontal limbs. The flight is strong but the birds prefer to fly from high in one tree to the base of the next and then run up the trunk. The wing beat is very rapid and gliding is frequent. The Brown Treecreeper is found on the ground, fence posts and fallen logs much more often than the White-throated and Red-browed Treecreepers.

BREEDING: Breeding, in this region, extends from early October to the end of January, but the breeding season starts as early as July in the warmer inland areas. Two, occasionally three, broods are reared in the one nest which may be re-lined and used again in later seasons. The usual nest site is a hole in the limb of a tree from one to five metres from the ground, sometimes up to fifteen metres, but a hollow in a stump or in a fence post is sometimes selected. The nest itself is a loose structure in the base of the hollow and is composed mainly of fur and feathers. Occasionally dried grasses are used. The normal clutch is three eggs which are of a pinkish-white ground colour almost covered with tiny spots of pinkish- and purplish-red. They measure about $21 \times 16$ mm.

FEEDING: Insects, spiders, etc., taken from the crevices of the bark of trees, both alive and dead, and also from the ground, are the food of this species. (S.J.W.)

## WHITE-THROATED TREECREEPER *Climacteris leucophaea*

PLATE XXIII

IDENTIFICATION: Length, 16.5 cm. Male: *General colour above, dull olive-brown with dark upper-tail coverts; flight feathers, dark brown crossed by a bar of pale fawn* which is conspicuous when the bird is in flight but is not visible at rest; tail, brownish-grey with a black subterminal bar; *throat and upper centre breast, white* while there is a conspicuous streaking of brown and white on the sides of the breast and flanks; under-tail coverts, white with bars of blackish-brown; bill, black; legs and feet, greyish-black; iris, blackish-brown.

The female is similar to the male but can be distinguished by having a conspicuous orange-red spot just below the ear coverts.

Immature birds have the rump and upper-tail coverts a rich rust-red and this appears to persist for the first few months of life only. Even a few rust-red feathers in this area denote a bird of the preceding breeding season.

VOICE: The chief call is a loud, rapid, piping note repeated up to about six times but occasionally during the breeding season this call may continue for some minutes. Over 400 repeated calls have been counted. Usually the first three notes are on a very slightly descending scale; so slight that it often appears as the one note. Rather more quiet and mellow warbling notes are heard in the breeding season only.

DISTRIBUTION: It extends from south-eastern Queensland through New South Wales and Victoria to south-east South Australia. In Tasmania it is rare. It generally extends from the coast to the extremity of the western slopes but does not go out onto the plains. It does, however, follow the Murray River inland and is found throughout Victoria except in the mallee regions of the north-west.

On the Southern Tablelands it seems to be sedentary and is a fairly common bird in all areas except the most open paddocks.

HABITS: The loud, repeated call is most conspicuous and draws immediate attention to the bird wherever it occurs. It is often in pairs. With the other treecreepers of this area it shares the habit of spiralling upwards around the trunks and thicker branches of the trees in its search for food. It is very active.

BREEDING: The nest site is a hollow in the trunk of a tree or the open spout of a broken hollow branch, generally in the upper levels of a rather large tree. The nest chamber is lined with strips of bark and occasionally with grass, and finished with hair, fur or feathers. One pair has nested in a large cavity behind a crevice in an old stone homestead. In this case the nest was a distinctly cup-shaped structure fifteen centimetres wide and four centimetres high overall, and had a bowl eight centimetres diameter by about one centimetre deep.

Three eggs are usually laid but sometimes there are only two. These are white, sparingly marked with reddish and purplish-brown. They measure about 21 × 16 mm.

FEEDING: The species is insectivorous and feeds as it spirals up the trees constantly searching the crevices of the bark. (S.J.W.)

# RED-BROWED TREECREEPER *Climacteris erythrops*
PLATE XXIII

IDENTIFICATION: Length, 15 cm. Male: Upper-parts, generally dull brown with dusky-grey rump and upper-tail coverts; flight feathers of the *wings, dull brown with a broad greyish-buff* bar; tail, dark grey with a blackish-brown subterminal bar; *lores, a broad stripe over the eye and the area below the eye are rusty-red*; chin and throat, dull white passing to greyish-brown on the upper breast; abdomen, dull buff; under-tail coverts, dull with indistinct black lines; bill, black; legs and feet, brownish-black; iris, brown.

In the adult female the lores and area above and below the eye are richer in colour than in the male and the feathers of the upper breast are rusty-red with a broad stripe of dull white (not plain greyish-brown). Immature birds lack the rusty-red markings about the eye; this is greyish-brown. The under-parts are greyish-brown and are not streaked.

VOICE: The call is a rapid chatter of notes of similar tone. By comparison with the main call of the White-throated Treecreeper the call is softer, lacks the piping quality and has a hissing tone.

DISTRIBUTION: It extends from south-eastern Queensland through coastal and mountain areas of eastern New South Wales and similar country in Victoria to as far as the central districts of that State. The species is well distributed in small numbers throughout the ranges. Elsewhere it is confined to heavily timbered and generally wetter areas and it does not appear to be a common species anywhere.

HABITS: It spends most of its time in the higher levels of the wetter forests. When flying between trees it usually lands at higher levels than the White-throated Treecreeper and then, like that species, spirals upwards in its search for food. Occasionally, but not often, it is noticed at low levels. The species appears to be sedentary.

BREEDING: Breeding was recorded in the Capital Territory for the first time in October 1981. Previously birds had been seen entering holes high in the forests, usually in dead trees. Elsewhere the breeding season is from August to January. The nest is made in the hollow of a tree up to thirteen metres, and probably even higher, from the ground; it is built of bark strips, fur scraps and plant down. Three eggs are laid which are purplish-red and measure about $22 \times 17$ mm.

FEEDING: This species is insectivorous and feeds as it spirals up the trunks and larger branches of the forest trees. (S.J.W.)

289

## Family Neosittidae — Sittellas

This is a small family of three species, one in Australia and two in New Guinea. They were formerly believed to be members of the Northern Hemisphere family Sittidae nuthatches. The apparently close resemblances between the sittellas and nuthatches are now known to be superficial and not a result of basic relationships. Sittellas are found in every part of Australia wherever there are sufficient trees to support them. The single Australian species is divided into several well-marked subspecies. These were formerly thought to be good species but they hybridise freely where they meet. Sittellas have many resemblances to treecreepers.

## ORANGE-WINGED SITTELLA *Daphoenositta chrysoptera*
PLATE XXIII

IDENTIFICATION: Length, 11.5 cm. Male: *general colour above, dusky greyish-brown* many of the feathers having conspicuous blackish-brown centres; rump, white; wing coverts, dark brown and the *flight feathers are also brown but are crossed with a broad band of rich rufous*; tail, blackish-brown; chin, cheeks and upper throat, white; remainder of *under-parts, dull white* with a few distinct brown streaks; bill, brown; legs and feet, yellow; iris, pale creamy-buff. The bill has a slight upwards curve. In the adult female the feathers of the head area are darker than in the male. Immature birds appear mottled on the head and back.

VOICE: The call is a quiet "chip" louder and more frequently given while in flight. When flying, several birds give a succession of single calls and this often draws attention to them.

DISTRIBUTION: The sittellas cover most of the continent where there are trees. The local subspecies, the Orange-winged Sittella, occurs from the extreme south-east of Queensland through New South Wales from the coast, through the mountains and slopes to about the edge of the western plains and through Victoria to the western edge of the central districts. It is a fairly common resident of open and dry forests throughout the area but it has not been reported from the wetter forests of the ranges.

HABITS: Unlike treecreepers which spiral upwards in the search for food, sittellas have a distinctive habit of spiralling down the trunks and main branches of trees. On horizontal branches they spiral along, going under and over as they move. They are very active little birds ceaselessly running on the trees and flying from one to the next. There is something butterfly-like about their short flights.

290

It is possible that family relationships occur in this species as it is most unusual to see single birds or pairs. They are always in groups of six to eight birds and more than two birds have been seen to feed young in the nest.

BREEDING: The breeding season in the region extends from early September to the latter half of December; elsewhere it breeds from August to January. The nest is a work of art and among the neatest built by Australian birds. It is usually sited on a dead, near vertical, forked stick high in the crown of a medium sized tree, is closely moulded to the branch and is made of bark and cobwebs and decorated on the outside with vertical strips of bark. In appearance it very closely resembles a broken, dead branch of a tree. Lower nests have been reported but in this region the nests are usually at least six and as high as twenty metres above the ground. The normal clutch is three eggs of a greyish-white colour with dark olive and slate coloured spots or blotches. They measure about $17 \times 12$ mm.

FEEDING: The species is entirely insectivorous and feeds as it spirals down the trees, probing in crevices of the bark. (S.J.W.)

# FLOWERPECKERS, PARDALOTES AND SILVEREYES

Some of the most widespread, attractive and well known small birds of Australia are included in the three families described here. The Silvereye is abundant nearly everywhere and in Canberra, in the winter, is one of the commonest small birds in the gardens as it searches the shrubs for winter berries, and in the spring as it searches the roses for aphids. The pardalotes are less obvious but no less numerous as they travel through the gums in parks and gardens and street plantings in lively troops. The continued growth of city gardens can be expected to help both groups provided their food is not removed or poisoned by over-zealous spraying of trees and shrubs. Most of them depend to a large extent on insects or ornamental berries.

## Family Dicaeidae—Flowerpeckers

The family of birds known as flowerpeckers is restricted to the Oriental and Australian regions. The fifty species are small, active birds that live among the foliage of trees, particularly the birds' food trees; those that have berries or are parasitised by mistletoe. They have short tails and relatively short, down-curved bills. The males are strikingly coloured, usually with patches of bright red contrasting with dark glossy backs and pale undersides.

291

The name flowerpecker is not in use in Australia but the name mistletoe-bird replaces it. The mistletoe birds live mainly on small berries
and many, including the sole Australian representative, are specialised
to feed almost exclusively on mistletoe berries. The flowerpeckers are
often classed as pests for spreading mistletoe. They build beautiful,
delicate, suspended nests.

## MISTLETOE-BIRD *Dicaeum hirundinaceum*

PLATE XXIX

IDENTIFICATION: Length, 10 cm. Male: *Upper-parts, gleaming
black* with blue metallic sheen; chin, *throat and under-tail, scarlet*;
breast, dull white with broad black streak down the centre; bill, legs
and feet, black; iris, buffy-brown. Female is dark ashy-brown above;
tail, black; under-parts, creamy-white; under-tail, pale scarlet; bill,
legs and feet, greyish-black; iris, buffy-brown. Juveniles resemble the
female but their bills are tinged red.

VOICE: Its calls are a high-pitched "wit-a, wita" or "per wit-a, per
wita" or other brisk variations of these. A single, sharp call is given in
flight. The Mistletoe-bird also has a warbling song and sometimes
incorporates mimicry of other birds' voices.

DISTRIBUTION: It is found throughout continental Australia and in
some of the islands of Indonesia. Its distribution in the continent is
determined by that of the numerous kinds of parasitic mistletoe on
which it depends very largely for food. Its absence from Tasmania is
perhaps explained by the absence of mistletoe in that State.

The range of habitat occupied by the Mistletoe-bird is very extensive. It is as equally at home in dense tropical rainforest as it is in the
mulga scrub of arid Central Australia, but then so are parasitic mistletoes.

The timing of nesting and the extent of nomadism of the Mistletoe-
bird are governed by the fruiting of mistletoes, an event that varies
with the species, the season and the locality. In the Capital Territory
and surrounding district the numbers of Mistletoe-birds vary considerably during the course of the year. They first appear along the Murrumbidgee River in early spring and leave the area about April by
which time the mistletoe fruiting season is completed.

HABITS: The long narrow wings are associated with strong and swift
flight, so that the little bird is usually seen moving very rapidly from
tree to tree and travels long distances. It is usually seen in pairs but
solitary males are very common. When feeding, it is in constant movement and indeed at any time is rarely still.

BREEDING: The breeding season in the region extends from October to January. The female usually builds the nest and incubates the eggs without any assistance from the male. Both sexes feed the young. The nest is very neat and pear-shaped and is usually suspended from a thin horizontal twig at heights from a metre to fifteen metres above the ground. It is made of plant down matted together with cobwebs and often partly covered with the dried remains of caterpillars, wattle blossoms or lichen. The nest is some seven centimetres in length and three to six centimetres wide. The entrance to the nest is a narrow slit-like opening at the side about four and a half centimetres long and one to two centimetres wide. The usual clutch size is three. The eggs are oval in shape, white in colour and measure about $17 \times 11$ mm. Incubation period is twelve days and the young remain in the nest for about fifteen days.

FEEDING: Their main food is the fruit of mistletoes and they are an important agent in their distribution. The muscular stomach or gizzard present in most birds has, in the Mistletoe-bird, practically disappeared and the whole digestive system has become an even duct enabling the large numbers of mistletoe-berries to pass quickly through the bird. Experiments have shown that mistletoe berries may be consumed and the seeds voided by a Mistletoe-bird within twenty-five minutes. The seeds of the mistletoe berries when voided are not harmed and are very sticky. If lodged on the branch of a suitable tree they remain there and usually germinate.

In addition to mistletoe berries, they eat the berries of a few other plants, including saltbush, box-thorn, privet, hawthorn and pepper trees. Insects are also eaten and, in fact, form the main food given to the nestlings during their first few days of life. (J.L.McK.)

### Family Pardalotidae — Pardalotes

This family of five species of small colourful birds with short bills and tails, is restricted to Australia. They feed on insects gleaned from the foliage and bark of trees. They build domed holes in trees or in tunnels that they drill into the earth for the purpose. There are two groups of pardalotes, one of birds spotted on the wings and heads and the other of birds with streaked crowns and white-striped wings. Two common species and a rare vagrant occur in the region.

### SPOTTED PARDALOTE *Pardalotus punctatus*
PLATE XXIX

IDENTIFICATION: Length, 9 cm. Male: forehead, crown, *wings and tail, black spotted with white*; back, greyish-brown spotted with buff; *base of upper-tail, chestnut-brown and crimson*; eyebrow, white; sides

293

of head, grey finely barred white; throat patch and base of under-tail, bright yellow; rest of under-parts, buffy-brown; bill, black; legs and feet, fleshy-brown; iris, grey. The female differs in being generally duller in colour; spots on the head, bright yellow; eyebrow, buff and ill-defined; base of upper-tail, brown and red; throat patch, whitish-buff; rest of under-parts, buffy-white. Juveniles are even duller than adult females; crown, greyish with pale dull yellow indistinct spots; eyebrow, very faint buffy-white; base of upper-tail, chestnut-brown.

VOICE: The two common calls of the Spotted Pardalote are a soft "pee-too" and a persistent, three-syllabled call that has been likened to the words "sleep baby", and is surprisingly loud and clear for such a small bird. The male has been noted giving a subdued chattering call when selecting the nest site.

DISTRIBUTION: It occurs in eastern Australia except Cape York Peninsula, south-eastern South Australia, south-western Western Australia and Tasmania. In this area it is distributed in all habitats during the breeding season but is especially abundant in the ranges. It seems, from local observation, that many birds leave our area during the winter months. As the species is not uncommon on the coast during winter it is likely that some of the highland Spotted Pardalotes move there.

HABITS: Pardalotes, in general, are birds of the outer foliage and are usually seen high in the tree tops busily searching the surface of every leaf and twig for tiny insects. The birds in the flock cover the whole tree and when they move flit one by one to the next tree head; the whole flock usually moves slowly but steadily through the tops of the forest. They are sometimes very difficult to detect in the tree tops, although their presence is shown by the incessant soft calling.
　　During the breeding season they are territorial and the birds are to be seen singly or in pairs. When the young leave the nest small family parties are formed which, with the advent of autumn, combine with other family groups into flocks of often up to several hundred birds.

BREEDING: The male seems to take the initiative in pair formation and in the selection of the nest site. They tend to return to the same nest site, or one close by, in successive years, and it has been seen with banded birds that males return to the last year's site far more frequently than do females. Both sexes excavate the nesting burrow, build the nest, incubate the eggs and tend the young. The breeding season extends from October to January.
　　The birds excavate a narrow nesting burrow some forty-five to

294

seventy centimetres in length, usually in the side of a creek bank or cliff. A chamber is dug at the end of the burrow to accommodate the substantial dome-shaped nest that is eight to fifteen centimetres in diameter. Fine bark fibre or grass comprise the bulk of the nesting material although sometimes feathers are used as a lining. On rare occasions tree-hollows are used as a nesting site.

The clutch size varies from three to five eggs, but is usually four. The eggs are pure white in colour, oval in shape and measure about 16 × 13 mm. The incubation period is fourteen to sixteen days.

FEEDING: Most of the food taken by Spotted Pardalotes is obtained from the outer foliage of trees, particularly gums. Scale insects are especially favoured but thrips, lerps, moths, caterpillars, small beetles, other insects and spiders are also eaten. (J.L.McK.)

## YELLOW-TAILED PARDALOTE *Pardalotus xanthopygus*

IDENTIFICATION: Length, 9 cm. This bird is very similar to the Spotted Pardalote except that the *base of the upper surface of the tail is golden yellow*.

VOICE: The calls are similar to those of the Spotted Pardalote, but the first syllable of the "sleep baby" call is lower pitched.

DISTRIBUTION: It occurs in south-western New South Wales, north-western Victoria, southern Western Australia and south-eastern South Australia. Vagrants have been reported from Melbourne and Canberra. The sole local record concerns a bird seen at close quarters by a reliable observer at Black Mountain, Canberra, in November, 1965. The Yellow-tailed Pardalote is the mallee representative of the Spotted Pardalote and is rarely recorded away from its mallee habitat. It does not appear to be nomadic or migratory as is the Spotted Pardalote but in view of its close similarity to the Spotted Pardalote, unsuspecting observers might mistake it for that species and hence the possibility exists that it may be a greater wanderer than previously suspected.

HABITS: They are similar to other pardalotes in their general behaviour.

BREEDING: In south-western New South Wales the breeding season extends from September to December. The nest and eggs are similar to those of the Spotted Pardalote except that the Yellow-tailed Pardalote usually excavates a tunnel sloping downwards on fairly level ground.

The nest burrow is often situated in the shade of a mallee eucalypt.

FEEDING: The species feeds on scale insects, other small insects and spiders. (J.L.McK.)

## STRIATED PARDALOTE *Pardalotus striatus*

PLATE XXIX

IDENTIFICATION: Length, 11 cm. *Crown of the head, black distinctly streaked with white*; upper-parts, olive-grey, more brownish on the lower back; tail, black slightly tipped white; eyebrow stripe, yellow changing abruptly to white beyond the eye; small ear patch, black streaked white; cheeks, white; chin and throat, bright yellow; rest of under-parts, buff and white; wings, black with a small *orange or red spot near shoulder of wing*; there is a *narrow white wing stripe*; bill, black; legs and feet, blackish-brown; iris, brownish-olive. The sexes are similar. Young birds which have just left the nest have the crown and the head olive-grey.

The above description is of the eastern form, the common breeding one in the region. The Tasmanian form, which has a *yellow wing spot*, also occurs here. The western form is observed in the region on occasions. It has an orange or red wing spot and a *broad white wing stripe*.

VOICE: The commonest notes are a constant series of sharp "pick-it-up" and loud "chip-chip" calls. A long trilling call and a soft "cheeoo" are also part of the vocabulary of this species.

DISTRIBUTION: The Striated Pardalote is Australia-wide in distribution. The eastern form occurs in coastal south-eastern Australia inland to the Dividing Range as far north as south-eastern Queensland. It is the common form in the region. The Tasmanian form winters in mainland south-eastern Australia. It is common in winter in our region, arriving about May and departing by early August. The western form has a broad distribution from Western Australia through southern central and South Australia and inland New South Wales. It is occasionally seen in our region, perhaps more frequently during winter months when possibly migrant birds from other districts move into our area.

The Striated Pardalote is a bird of the *Eucalyptus* woodland, and is commonly seen in eucalypts in parks and gardens.

HABITS: It is similar to other pardalotes in its general behaviour.

BREEDING: The breeding season extends from about August to

January. The nest is situated either in the hollow limb of a tree or at the end of a narrow tunnel in the side of a creek, cliff or bank. The nests are made of bark fibres, grasses and rootlets and may be cup-shaped, partly domed or domed. They are sometimes lined with feathers. The clutch size varies from three to five, and the eggs are white in colour, oval in shape and measure about $19 \times 15$ mm.

FEEDING: The food consists mainly of small tree-frequenting insects captured among the foliage of eucalypts. The following food items have been recorded: cicadas, psyllids, lerps, plant bugs, tree-frequenting grasshoppers, cockroaches, small beetles, weevils, thrips, flies, caterpillars, ants, native bees, chalcid wasps and various spiders. (J.L.McK.)

## Family Zosteropidae — Silvereyes

There are about eighty-five species of silvereyes; they are usually called "white-eyes" outside Australia. They are a remarkably homogeneous group of birds. They have slightly down-curved bills and brush tongues and are usually greenish or greyish in colour and all are distinguished by a prominent ring of white feathers around the eye. They extend throughout Africa, Asia and Australia. They are essentially tropical but an Australian species has established itself in New Zealand in recent times.

The silvereyes have been notoriously difficult to classify, as many populations are very variable.

## GREY-BREASTED SILVEREYE *Zosterops lateralis*

PLATE XXIX

IDENTIFICATION: Length, 10 cm. Head, *olive-green, with white ring around the eye*; back, greyish-olive; rump and tail, olive green; breast, grey; abdomen, grey with some brown wash; flanks, grey with some brown wash; bill, brown; legs and feet, brown; iris, brown. The sexes are similar but males are brighter. The amount of brown on the abdomen and flanks varies greatly. In Tasmania it is very prominent and the flanks can be described as chestnut; near Canberra they are almost pure grey; father north they are very pale in colour.

VOICE: The contact call is a thin, peevish sounding whistle, "psee". There is a soft and pleasant twittering song and a softer subsong that is said to include some mimicry of other birds. Groups call incessantly in flight with a sharp twitter.

DISTRIBUTION: Found in south-western Australia, through southern South Australia, to Cape York. It is mainly confined to the coastal

297

districts, ranges and inland slopes, but in the south-east follows the main river systems with their timber fringe and so is found throughout Victoria, inland New South Wales and south-west Queensland. It is abundant in Tasmania. In our area it is common wherever there are trees.

Its movements are not completely understood, but banding has shown that Tasmanian birds arrive in eastern Australia during the winter. Brown flanked birds, presumably from Tasmania, are common in our area during this period. Some, together with local birds, move further north. Numerous birds remain in Tasmania and this suggests that different populations are partial migrants.

HABITS: Silvereyes are very sociable little birds even in the breeding season and travel about in small groups. In winter they are in large flocks and are common throughout parks and gardens and bushland alike. They are usually seen busily searching the leaves and twigs of shrubs for insects. The flight is swift and direct, and the flocks are very noisy as they pass overhead.

BREEDING: The breeding season locally extends from November to January but most clutches are begun in November and early December. The nest is a very delicate but strong cup, usually of hair and grass bound firmly with cobwebs. It is relatively deep, over two centimetres, but only about five centimetres in diameter, and is suspended by its rim from a horizontal fork in a low bush. The clutch size is usually three but occasionally two or four. The eggs are a very delicate pale blue and average $17 \times 12$ mm. The incubation period is ten to twelve days and the young remain in the nest about thirteen days.

FEEDING: No detailed study of its food has been published but it is known that it feeds on insects, nectar and fruit. Insects are collected from twigs and leaves rather than from the air. The fruit eaten is varied and includes many native and introduced plants. Each winter the bird is very prominent in the city of Canberra feeding on the winter berries of *Crataegus*, *Pyracantha* and *Cotoneaster* in the public and household gardens. In autumn and summer it feeds on the berries of pepper trees and blackberries and causes a considerable nuisance in puncturing cultivated soft fruits allowing fungi to enter and cause rot. In horticultural districts beyond our area it causes considerable economic damage. (H.J.F.)

# HONEYEATERS

Honeyeaters are mainly confined to the Australasian region and there are about 170 species in the family.

Australia itself has sixty-six species, making it the largest family in the country, and New Guinea sixty-seven. Honeyeaters are distributed throughout the whole continent of Australia and have evolved to fill a very wide variety of habitats. Every district has honeyeaters and even the spinifex deserts support one. The remainder are distributed through the Pacific Islands and New Zealand. Twenty-three have been recorded in our area.

The most striking character of the family is the brush tongue, adapted to collect nectar from flowers. In many species the bill is also long and slender and sometimes curved so that the bottoms of tube-like flowers can be reached. Because of their feeding habit many honeyeaters are efficient pollinating agents and are very important pollinators of many indigenous tree and shrub families, e.g. Myrtaceae, Proteaceae and Epacridaceae.

All honeyeaters are arboreal and, although all eat nectar, some also feed on fruit and insects; a few are almost entirely insectivorous. They are mainly gregarious birds and live in small parties or sometimes large flocks. Many are migratory and the real extent of this phenomenon among the honeyeaters of south-eastern Australia has only recently been appreciated. Many other species are nomadic. In our area, the mass movements of migrating honeyeaters, as well as the sudden appearance of vagrants, are conspicuous features.

## Family Meliphagidae — Honeyeaters
## SCARLET HONEYEATER *Myzomela sanguinolenta*
PLATE XXXVI

IDENTIFICATION: Length, 11 cm. Male: *Head, breast and neck, rich shining scarlet*; feathers of the mantle, back, rump and upper-tail coverts, black, tipped with scarlet, giving an irregular marking of black and scarlet down the back; wings and tail, black; abdomen, dull greyish with a yellowish wash; bill, black; legs and feet, blackish; iris, black.

The female is *brown on the head and upper-parts*. The under-parts are brownish washed with white becoming paler on the abdomen and under-tail coverts. The bill is brown. Immature male birds resemble the female. The scarlet feathers first appear on the chin and sides of the head and down the centre of the back.

VOICE: The male has a clear, penetrating, tinkling, bell-like call while that of the female is less clear. The male has a more musical call than other honeyeaters and calls throughout the day during the breeding season but the female voice is rarely heard.

It is often seen feeding on the outer flowering twigs of trees and shrubs, singing as it does so, even in the heat of the day. The calls are similar to those of warblers.

299

DISTRIBUTION: The range of the Scarlet Honeyeater extends from the Atherton and Herberton Tablelands in northern Queensland through the ranges south to about Mackay then through the coastal and coastal range areas of Queensland, New South Wales and Victoria to the Gippsland lakes. It appears to follow the blossoming of nectar-producing trees and shrubs and is usually found in the vicinity of streams. In the southern areas of its range the species is migratory, moving north during winter.

The Scarlet Honeyeater is considered a rare bird in our area. It is occasionally seen feeding in flowering eucalypts and grevillias in suburban gardens. Normally it does not often move far from the eastern coast, though North reports that "stragglers were also obtained near Cootamundra", which is considerably further inland.

HABITS: It is a very active little bird and moves rapidly from bush to bush, though it seems to prefer to be under cover as much as possible.

BREEDING: The breeding season extends from August to January but there are no breeding records from the Southern Tablelands area. The nest is a frail open cup of very fine bark strips with a few cobwebs and is attached by the rim to the outer twigs of a tree or shrub up to ten metres from the ground. Two eggs are the normal clutch but occasionally three eggs are laid. The eggs are from pure white to buffy-white with spots of a faint purplish or reddish-brown or yellowish-brown entirely or largely confined to the larger end. They measure 15 × 12 mm.

The incubation period is eleven or twelve days and the young leave the nest after a similar period. The probability of triple brooding has been reported.

FEEDING: Its greatest love is nectar and it follows the blossoming of the various suitable trees and shrubs. Turpentine and *Melaleuca* are favoured. In the absence of nectar it also takes insects, which are sometimes caught on the wing in the manner of a flycatcher. (S.J.W.)

## PAINTED HONEYEATER *Grantiella picta*

PLATE XXXI

IDENTIFICATION: Length, 16 cm. Male: upper-parts, *deep brownish-black with a wash of bright yellow on wings and tail; under-parts, white* with some small blackish-brown streaks, particularly on the lower flanks; white markings in the under-tail are prominent; bill, fleshy-pink; legs and feet, dark grey; iris, dark hazel. The adult female is slightly smaller with the upper-parts smoky-black rather than brownish-black.

VOICE: The chief call is an easily distinguished, repeated "georgie", the first note being the lower. There is also a harsher double call in which the first note is the lower and this could be interpreted as "seeeee saw".

DISTRIBUTION: It is thinly distributed throughout its wide range through the inland from the MacArthur River in the Northern Territory, the Leichhardt River in north-western Queensland thence through the three eastern States to southern Victoria. It reaches the coast in a few areas, particularly about Sydney, where suitable habitat exists.

It is a rare bird throughout its range and its movements are erratic. It is thought that it returns to our area each year and breeds in the river she-oaks along the Murrumbidgee River, particularly in the large trees near Uriarra Crossing. In 1962–3 it was also seen for several weeks in open forest on the eastern slopes of Mount Ainslie. It is a strict migrant in the south and appears to return to the Murrumbidgee River in November each year, breed immediately and depart by February. In more northern areas its appearance is quite sporadic and tied to the fruiting of mistletoes.

HABITS: Apart from its resonant call it is not conspicuous and, as in this area, it frequents the upper parts of trees twenty to thirty metres high, its presence could be undetected. It is never far from trees bearing mistletoe fruits. In this area it is found occasionally in small groups where mistletoe is prevalent.

BREEDING: The breeding season in the region is from late November to early January. The nest is a frail, lace-like structure of she-oak stems and other vegetable material bound with cobwebs and suspended by its rim from the outer drooping branches of a she-oak usually six to twenty metres from the ground. The eggs can usually be seen from below. The clutch is two eggs of a salmon-pink colour, thickly spotted and freckled with darker shades of red at the larger end. The eggs measure 20 × 15 mm and the incubation time is fourteen to fifteen days.

FEEDING: The usual food is mistletoe fruits though it also takes nectar from mistletoe flowers. This limited food choice appears to account for its nomadic wanderings and to some degree its irregular appearances throughout its range. In this area, the fruiting mistletoes along the Murrumbidgee River appear regularly and the appearance of small numbers of the species here is more predictable than in other localities. (S.J.W.)

301

## REGENT HONEYEATER *Xanthomyza phrygia*
PLATE XXXI

IDENTIFICATION: Length, 20 cm. *Head and neck, black;* other feathers, black with yellow markings in varying shades except that the lower under-parts are yellowish-white; *the yellow markings of the wings and tail form brilliant patches* which are most conspicuous in flight; bill, black, but most birds in Canberra have yellow (juvenile) bills; legs and feet, brown; iris, red-brown. The sexes are similar.

VOICE: The main call, when perched, is a metallic but bell-like "clink clank" accompanied by a peculiar bowing of the head. In flight a clattering sound, which resembles the sound of the wings beating together, is heard.

DISTRIBUTION: Its distribution is from about Dalby in Queensland to South Australia. It extends from the coast to the western edges of the slopes of the ranges in New South Wales, through many areas of Victoria except mallee areas, and in South Australia, Kangaroo Island, the Mount Lofty Ranges, and about Adelaide.

In our area the species is rare. In recent years it has occurred regularly in small numbers from spring to autumn in the open woodland and drier forest areas. Throughout its range it appears to be highly nomadic.

HABITS: Although a large honeyeater, it blends well with the topmost foliage and the loud call is usually the first indication of its presence. It is wary and, if disturbed, flies swiftly for a considerable distance. In our area it is found in isolated pairs usually, but sometimes small groups concentrate in a flowering eucalypt.

BREEDING: Breeding in the region is late, in December and January, but elsewhere it can begin in August. The nest is a thick-walled, rounded, cup-like structure of fine grasses lined with shreds of bark and grasses. Occasionally down is also used. It is usually placed in a vertical fork of a tree from two to eight metres from the ground, and a favourite site is in thick growth such as a clump of mistletoe.

Normally two eggs are laid but there are records of three. They measure 24×18 mm and in colour are rich reddish-buff, darker towards the larger end with spots of purplish-red all over but chiefly at the larger end.

FEEDING: Nectar is the major food and the birds' nomadic wanderings are associated with the search for suitable flowering trees and shrubs, chiefly *Eucalyptus, Banksia* and *Grevillea*. Insects and

302

native fruits are eaten. It also has some liking for ripening fruit crops. (S.J.W.)

## LEWIN HONEYEATER *Meliphaga lewinii*

PLATE XXX

IDENTIFICATION: Length, 18 cm. *General colour above, dull olive-green* with the wings and tail brighter; there is a blackish-grey wash on the forehead and black in front of the eye; ear coverts, grey; *side of the upper neck has a prominent patch of yellow*; the prominent gape and a line extending below the eye are straw-yellow; under-parts, olive-grey becoming dull olive-yellow on the abdomen; all under-parts are streaked; bill, black; legs and feet, light brown; iris, bluish-grey. The sexes are similar.

VOICE: The call is a series of fast, quavering, whistling notes which could also be described as rattle-like, on the one note. This appears to be a contact call and is given at all seasons.

DISTRIBUTION: Its northern limit is the Atherton Tablelands. It occurs throughout suitable habitat on the coast and nearby ranges of New South Wales into eastern Victoria. Its western limit is the Dandenong Ranges in Victoria. In the high country generally it is rarely seen. It occasionally wanders into this area from its more coastal breeding territory in autumn and winter but it is never found far from dense timber and thick shrub. Its favoured habitat is the dense coastal scrubs and the rainforest gullies of the adjacent ranges, always being found near the creeks. It may be fairly thickly distributed in such habitat but it does not extend to the drier slopes of the same areas. It is somewhat colonial in its habits and rather sedentary.

HABITS: This species is a bird of the scrub and is seldom seen far from dense cover. It is fearless, inquisitive and pugnacious and can be readily "squeaked" up to an observer. In the bush it is constantly on the move, darting into trees and shrubs and bouncing from limb to limb.

BREEDING: The species does not breed in the region but in its breeding range the season extends from August to March. It has been reported as double-brooded. The nest is fairly large and flimsy—a rather untidy structure suspended by its rim from thin, forked horizontal twigs of a tree up to six metres from the ground. Orange trees are often used as nest sites in areas north of Sydney. The nest is made of thin strips of bark, egg sacs of spiders and grasses or fine rootlets, the finer materials being used internally and the whole

303

interwoven with some spider's webbing. Pieces of paper and string are often used in the structure. The eggs are normally two or three in number, measuring 26 × 18 mm, fleshy-white in colour spotted with deep red on the larger end or occasionally all over.

FEEDING: The Lewin Honeyeater favours a diet of insects and native fruits rather than of nectar. It freely associates with fruit pigeons and orioles in the tops of rainforest fruit trees. In coastal New South Wales it is one of the few birds to eat lantana berries, and at times also attacks cultivated fruit crops. The young are fed on such animal foods as the soft parts of beetles and cicadas but are also given native fruits and berries. (S.J.W.)

### SINGING HONEYEATER *Lichenostomus virescens*
PLATE XXX

IDENTIFICATION: Length, 19 cm. General colour, light brownish-olive with light under-parts; *there is a prominent black line through the eye to the neck and below this are patches of yellow and of white*; crown of the head, greyish-brown; under-parts, yellowish-white merging into brownish-white with brown streaks on the lower areas; bill, black; legs and feet, blue-grey; iris, sepia.

VOICE: The calls are loud and resonant but "singing" is really a misnomer. The chief call is a repeated one of two notes with an upward inflection that has been rendered as "queek". It also has an animated buzz "terric" resembling the call of a bee-eater, and a sharp rippling alarm note.

DISTRIBUTION: It is a rare vagrant in our region but it occurs over much of the mainland of Australia except parts of Arnhem Land, Cape York, the heavy forest of south-west Western Australia and most of the coastal districts of the eastern States. In Victoria it is coastal from Port Phillip Bay westwards. It appears to be sedentary.

HABITS: It is one of the most pugnacious of honeyeaters, and attacks and drives other small birds, particularly other honeyeaters, from the tree in which it might be. It is also bold and inquisitive and quite tolerant of observers nearby.

BREEDING: No local breeding records are known. Elsewhere its normal breeding season is from August to December but in the inland and northern areas breeding appears tied to rainfall irrespective of the season. The nest is less neat than than of most honeyeaters. It is made of fairly coarse plant material woven together with cobweb and spider's egg sacs, and has a lining of softer and finer materials including wool and fur, when available. A horizontal fork of an outer branch is the usual site and nests are normally built less than four metres from the ground. The nest is suspended by its rim. Two or three eggs are laid and they average 22 × 16 mm and range in colour from fleshy-white to reddish-buff, distinctly darker at the larger end where there are a few tiny specks of chestnut or brown.

FEEDING: Nectar is a favourite food when available but it does not appear to travel much in search of it. Insects and native fruits are used also and it appears to have developed a liking for grapes. It has been seen destroying colonies of finches by eating the eggs. (S.J.W.)

## FUSCOUS HONEYEATER *Lichenostomus fuscus*
PLATE XXX

IDENTIFICATION: Length, 15 cm. Upper-parts, grey-brown tinged with olive; wings and tail, washed with yellow-olive; under-parts, greyish-brown lighter on the abdomen and under-tail coverts; *ear coverts, dark brown and behind is a tiny bright yellow plume*; bill, black; legs and feet, fleshy-grey; iris, black. The sexes are similar. Breeding adults have a black eye ring and gape but in non-breeding adults and juveniles these parts are yellow.

VOICE: A variety of calls is given. The chief one is a clear resounding call of which one interpretation is "out with the whip". Another call is a very rapid, rather unmusical trill on the one note. A single "chip" is often heard.

DISTRIBUTION: The Fuscous Honeyeater ranges from the Atherton Tablelands in northern Queensland through the Dividing Range, particularly its western slopes, to Victoria and the Mount Lofty Ranges in South Australia. It is not coastal except near Sydney and its southern limit is the outskirts of Melbourne. It is not found in the extreme south-east of New South Wales or in eastern Victoria. This bird belongs in somewhat open forest in areas of medium rainfall, and therefore, while it is abundant on the western slopes of the Divide, it does not extend to the drier plains or into the mallee.

While in other places it is reported to be sedentary and occasionally nomadic, in the Brindabella Range and about Canberra it assumes the unexpected role of a passage migrant in autumn and spring with a few individuals remaining over winter. Large scale migrations of Yellow-faced and White-naped Honeyeaters occur through the area in autumn and smaller numbers of Fuscous Honeyeaters are swept up in the general excitement. The Fuscous Honeyeaters moving with the other migrants include many with a yellow base to the bill and a yellow eye-ring.

HABITS: This species can be attracted to home gardens by the provision of suitable food — even bread crumbs. Occasionally it takes insects on the wing. It is a sociable species and is often seen in small flocks of half a dozen or so and readily adapts to living within towns and developed districts.

BREEDING: July to January is the breeding season. The nest of this species is one of the neatest of honeyeaters. It is suspended by its rim from a horizontal branch one metre or so above the ground. Fine strips of bark or grasses are used in the nest and these are bound together with cobweb, wool, etc., with a thin bottom lining of wool, down or similar material. The normal clutch is three eggs, occasionally two, and these are from a yellowish to salmon-buff colour with a few faint spots of a darker red shade. They measure about $20 \times 15$ mm.

The species breeds in the southern part of the Capital Territory in November to February.

FEEDING: The Fuscous Honeyeater loves nectar. They were numerous in Canberra in the spring of 1964 and were mostly confined to the Botanical Gardens where a variety of cultivated *Eucalyptus* and *Grevillea* were in flower. They also occur on stands of flowering *Grevillea juniperina* along the Murrumbidgee River. Insects are also taken in the absence of nectar. (S.J.W.)

## YELLOW-FACED HONEYEATER *Lichenostomus chrysops*
PLATE XXX

IDENTIFICATION: Length, 17 cm. General colour above, ashy-brown tinged olive; there is a *narrow bright yellow line below eye* from bill to ear with a *black line above and below it*; throat, greyish; breast, ashy-brown; abdomen, mottled dull white; bill, black; legs, bluish; iris, blue-grey. The sexes and immatures are similar.

VOICE: The calls in the breeding season are "chick-up chick-up" and a slow whistle of four notes on descending scale. In autumn a crisp "chip" and in spring a harsh "kheer" with downward inflection are heard.

DISTRIBUTION: It ranges from the Atherton Tablelands, Queensland, to the Mount Lofty and Flinders Ranges in South Australia. In New South Wales it extends from the coast to the edge of the inland plains and in Victoria it is widespread except in the north-west. It is distributed in all habitats in the breeding season but is most abundant in the ranges. It has a well marked migration and is very conspicuous moving through the area in autumn following well used routes along tree lines. Numbers remain during the winter but most begin to move out in late March and many thousands may pass a point in one day. Most movement is complete by mid-May. The return is in the period mid-August to November but is not so obvious as the autumn migration. Many individuals return to the area they had occupied in the previous summer. The migration is widespread in Victoria, the Capital Territory and coastal and southern New South Wales but has not been studied in detail.

HABITS: A very active and inquisitive bird, it is seen among bushes and flowering shrubs everywhere but is most spectacular during its northern movement when large flocks are seen moving overhead and through the towns and cities.

BREEDING: The breeding season locally is from late October to late February; on the coast from July to January. The nest is a neat, small cup eight centimetres in diameter and six centimetres deep, bound by its rim to a horizontal fork in the outer twigs of a tree or shrub, between one and six metres from the ground. It is built of fine grass and rootlets often decorated with lichen and bound with cobweb and, although the eggs can sometimes be seen through it, it is very strong.

The clutch is usually three, but sometimes two. The eggs are faint pink to yellow-buff and are spotted with red or purple-brown more densely towards the larger end. They measure 21 × 14 mm.

FEEDING: In autumn, winter and spring it gathers nectar from flowering *Eucalyptus, Banksia* and *Grevillea,* and occasionally attacks soft fruit. In winter it is largely insectivorous. (S.J.W.)

## WHITE-EARED HONEYEATER *Lichenostomus leucotis*
PLATE XXX

IDENTIFICATION: Length, 20 cm. Male: general bright olive-green colour above; crown, dark grey; *cheeks, throat and breast, black*; there is a conspicuous *white patch behind the eye*; breast, abdomen and under-tail coverts, olive-yellow edged with yellow; bill, black; legs and feet, grey; iris, black.

The adult female is similar to the male, though smaller, and the black feathers do not extend as far down the breast as they do in the male. Juveniles have an olive-green instead of a grey crown and early in life the ear patch is cream, not white. The plumage is somewhat duller.

307

VOICE: It has a variety of calls. A loud, slow "chock, chock" on the one note is the most common and appears to be a contact call. Sometimes this is varied to a slow "chock, chock, chock" on a slightly descending scale and it also has a rather rapid call of three ascending notes which is usually repeated two or three times. The last call is low and more liquid.

DISTRIBUTION: Its northern limit is just south of the Tropic of Capricorn and its range then spreads through New South Wales south to the coast near Sydney and south-west through the inland and Victoria to the Murray River near the South Australian border, across to the top of Spencer's Gulf and Eyre Peninsula. It also occurs widely in Western Australia.

The White-eared Honeyeater uses a wide variety of habitats. It is often regarded as a bird of the mallee, coastal scrubs or open eucalypt forests but is widely distributed in the highlands and is common in the wet sclerophyll forests of the ranges. In these areas it is most abundant in spring and summer but remains in the mountains throughout the winter in smaller numbers. In the colder weather it becomes more numerous about Canberra and Lake George, generally being found in areas of fairly thick scrub and in gardens with native flora.

HABITS: It is one of the bolder and more inquisitive honeyeaters. It is a very active bird and when feeding is in constant movement from bush to bush, darting into the heart of each on arrival there.

BREEDING: The breeding season on the coast is from August to January but local evidence indicates a later starting date here. The nest is not so tidy as those of some other honeyeaters. It is suspended by its rim from several thin, more or less upright twigs and is made of bark and dried grasses bound with cobweb and egg sacs with a lining of softer material such as wool, down or fur. The nest is usually low and is usually within arm's reach. Two eggs or occasionally three are laid. They are from white to fleshy-white in colour and are minutely dotted on the larger end with chestnut-red to reddish-brown. They measure $21 \times 15$ mm.

FEEDING: The chief food is insects, including beetles, and native fruits. It takes nectar at times but does not seem to move about seeking it as many other honeyeaters do. It has been sometimes reported attacking cultivated fruits. (S.J.W.)

YELLOW-TUFTED HONEYEATER *Lichenostomus melanops*
PLATE XXX
IDENTIFICATION: Length, 19.5 cm. Head and nape, olive-green;

remainder of upper-parts, olive-brown to olive-yellow; lores and ear coverts, black; *throat and tuft of feathers behind the ear are bright yellow*; remainder of under-parts, brownish-yellow becoming dull-yellow on the abdomen and under-tail coverts; bill, black; legs and feet, grey; iris, chestnut. The sexes are similar.

VOICE: It has a variety of high-pitched notes which include a musical trill and several harsh notes.

DISTRIBUTION: Colonies and wandering individuals are found from the Tropic of Capricorn in Queensland southward through New South Wales, Victoria, except the north-west corner, and in South Australia near Naracoorte only. It extends from the coast to the edge of the inland plains. In the highlands it is found in scattered breeding colonies of up to 200 birds. A few visit Canberra gardens in winter.

HABITS: It is usually found in dense concentrations, or colonies, where it is resident. It is a very active bird that keeps to the shrubbery and outer foliage of trees. It noisily mobs predators when they appear. Some individuals are nomadic in winter.

BREEDING: The breeding season is a long one and nests have been reported from June to January. The usual nest is a loose, not very tidy structure of bark and coarse grass, bound with cobweb and egg sacs, and with some lining of softer plant or animal material. Usually it is suspended from twigs by the rim but sometimes it is in a fork and in rare cases, under tussocks on the ground. Occasionally it is built below creepers. It is often placed within arm's reach but occasionally much higher. The normal clutch is two, but sometimes three eggs are laid. They measure about $18 \times 12$ mm and are normally fleshy-buff, sometimes deeper at the larger end with spots and blotches of deeper reddish tones also at that end.

FEEDING: It is often seen searching under bark for insects which are the main food. It also takes insects on the wing. Nectar is taken when available, chiefly in winter and early spring. On occasions it attacks ripening fruit though this is not a normal feeding habit of the species. (S.J.W.)

WHITE-PLUMED HONEYEATER *Lichenostomus penicillatus*
PLATE XXX
IDENTIFICATION: Length, 17 cm. Crown and nape, olive-yellow; *upper-parts, light brown tinged with green*; wings and tail, deeper brown strongly tinged with olive-yellow; under-parts, pale brownish-white; there is a fairly conspicuous *line of white behind the ear coverts*;

309

bill, black; legs and feet, pale brown; iris, dark brown. The sexes are similar.

VOICE: The call is usually translated as "chick-o-wee" but it is often better rendered as "chick-a-bid-ee" with a fourth note. It has a variety of chatters and scolding notes as well.

DISTRIBUTION: This is one of Australia's best known and most widely distributed honeyeaters. It occurs throughout the greater part of the continent but is less numerous in Western Australia, where it is most common along the inland rivers, than in the east.

In our area it is a common bird, being widely distributed in all areas where trees remain, other than the mountain forests. It is usually a bird of the tree-tops in open forests but is found at all levels. It has been regarded as sedentary but it is now known that some movement takes place. A bird banded at Maryborough, Victoria, on 2 July 1961 was found dead at Maude, New South Wales, on 17 April 1963, a direct distance of 190 kilometres to the north.

HABITS: It spends most of its time among the foliage of mature eucalypts. It is seen in pairs or small parties and seldom in flocks, like many of the other honeyeaters. It is a noisy, active bird, quite fearless and has adapted to life in cities, parks and gardens in many places. It loves to bathe and is never very far from water.

BREEDING: In the eastern States the breeding season extends from June to February, but in the highlands from October to December. The nest is a neat structure of grasses with some binding of cobweb and a slight lining of softer vegetable or animal material. It is suspended by its rim from the outer twigs of a tree or shrub at various heights from one to twenty metres. The normal clutch is three eggs but occasionally two are laid. The colour varies between white, yellowish-buff and a light red with reddish-purple to reddish-chestnut markings all over but more often chiefly towards the larger end. They average 20 × 15 mm.

FEEDING: Winter movements appear to be associated with the search for food and any flowering *Eucalytus, Banksia* or *Grevillea* will be regularly visited each day by a few birds. Nectar is taken when available but in the normal habitat of the open forests this may not occur often. Insects are eaten in the absence of nectar. (S.J.W.)

## WHITE-NAPED HONEYEATER *Melithreptus lunatus*
PLATE XXXI

IDENTIFICATION: Length, 14 cm. Upper-parts, bright yellowish-olive; wings, grey with a strong olive wash; *head and nape, black*, except for a *white stripe across the nape*, and *bare skin around the eye appears red in the field but is orange; under-parts, white*; bill, black; legs and feet, grey-brown; iris, brown. The sexes are similar. Juveniles are duller generally. Traces of the juvenile plumage may last six months or a little more. The juvenile could be confused with the Brown-headed Honeyeater but the upper-parts are brighter green and the under-parts more cream than those of that bird.

VOICE: The most frequently heard is a double call; a rather peevish sound and can be imitated with the lips, by sucking. Quiet single notes, obviously contact calls, are given by birds on migration.

DISTRIBUTION: The White-naped Honeyeater has a wide distribution in the eastern States from south-eastern South Australia, through Victoria, the coastal hills and the ranges of New South Wales and the ranges of Queensland to the far north of that State. It also occurs in south-west Western Australia. It is a very common breeding bird in the south-east highlands and also breeds in the tall gums bordering Lake George. It is almost totally migratory, the only winter records being odd stragglers in the ranges or remaining near abundant nectar in public and suburban gardens.

The birds congregate in March and migrate with other honeyeaters in the last days of March or early April, depending on weather. A cool snap followed by clear days appears to start the movement. The White-naped Honeyeater forms only about ten per cent of the early flocks and when the migration ends about the third week of May the flocks are almost entirely of this species. The migration may be seen in the ranges, in Canberra suburbs, along the western shore of Lake George and in many other places. Migration takes place chiefly between 8.00 a.m. and noon and follows any suitable line of trees but does not occur on days of full overcast. On suitable days many thousands may pass a given point. The return movement is a drift of individuals and begins in mid-August and lasts into November. Many individuals return to their original location.

HABITS: Generally, the White-naped Honeyeater is a bird of the upper forest levels, and is frequently seen clinging to the outer branches of trees and shrubs, feeding in an inverted attitude. It is a sociable little bird usually seen in small groups.

BREEDING: The nest is typical of honeyeaters, rather frail and made of fine vegetable material and cobweb suspended by its rim from the outer foliage of a tree or sapling, generally three to fifteen metres from

311

the ground. The nesting season in this area extends from late October to mid-February. The breeding season is earlier and longer on the New South Wales coast. Two or three eggs are laid. The eggs are from a rich flesh to a yellowish-buff colour finely spotted with chestnut-red chiefly on the larger end. The markings frequently form a zone. They measure about 18 × 14 mm.

FEEDING: The White-naped Honeyeater is a nectar feeder while this food is available and takes insects at other times. On migration in spring, the species feeds on *Grevillea* of many species in the Canberra Botanical Gardens and suburban gardens, and occurs in large numbers on the stands of *Grevillea juniperina* along the Murrumbidgee River while the blossom lasts. (S.J.W.)

## BROWN-HEADED HONEYEATER *Melithreptus brevirostris*
PLATE XXXI

IDENTIFICATION: Length, 14 cm. *Head and nape, dull brown with a nape band of dull cream*; wings, dull brown; remainder of upper-parts, brown washed with dull greenish-olive; under-parts, dull creamy-brown; small patch of bare skin about the eye, greenish-blue in the winter, dull yellow in summer; bill, dark brown; legs and feet, reddish-brown; iris, brown. The sexes are similar. Juvenile birds have a general wash of olive-green instead of brown on the head and wings but lack the definition in the marking on the nape. They are brighter than the adults and the feet are a dull flesh-pink.

VOICE: The chief call is a quiet but sharp and unmusical "click" in various tones repeated individually by various birds of the group so that it appears to be a succession of calls from the one bird. This appears to be a contact call and is heard at all seasons.

DISTRIBUTION: Its reported northern limit is in the vicinity of the Tropic of Capricorn in Queensland and it occurs over most of New South Wales except the north-west, throughout Victoria, on King Island, on Kangaroo Island, through south-eastern and southern areas of South Australia to as far north as the Flinders Ranges and Ooldea and through the mallee and salmon gum areas of Western Australia as far north as Mullewa. It is essentially a bird of the drier country. The Brown-headed Honeyeater is resident near Canberra but is not abundant. Small parties are sometimes seen in open forest country which appears to be the preferred habitat though it is also often in the ranges. It is possible that the species is resident in the ranges but evidence of breeding there has not been found.

HABITS: The Brown-headed Honeyeater is usually found in small parties of up to ten birds and banding results indicate that they stay together with remarkable constancy. Such groups tend to feed over areas of five to eight square kilometres and this habit has given the species the reputation of being nomadic. It is a bird of the treetops and is usually seen high up among the foliage.

BREEDING: It has been recorded breeding near Canberra in December and mid-February. The nesting season commences in September in New South Wales. The nest is a neat structure of bark, grasses, cobwebs and hair suspended by the rim in the upper twigs of a sapling or tree usually from three to ten metres above the ground. It is thicker than that of the White-naped Honeyeater.

Two or three eggs are laid. They vary from fleshy-white to fleshy-buff and are dotted and spotted with reddish-chestnut or purplish-red. They measure about 16 × 13 mm.

FEEDING: Insects appear to form the staple diet but it is attracted by the nectar of flowering gums, *Banksia* and *Grevillea* when this is available. A few are always near these flowering shrubs in the Canberra Botanical Gardens but flowering shrubs do not cause a gathering of this species in winter as they do with the Eastern Spinebill. (S.J.W.)

## EASTERN SPINEBILL *Acanthorhynchus tenuirostris*

PLATE XXXI

IDENTIFICATION: Length, 16 cm. Male: there is a *crescent marking in black on each side of the neck* which enclose a white throat area with chestnut-brown in its centre; bill, long, slender and down-curved; under-parts, light chestnut-brown; back, brown; wings, black and grey; crown, lustrous black; tail, black except for white markings in the outer feathers. These white tail markings are prominent in flight; bill, black; legs and feet, black; iris, red.

The adult female is a somewhat duller version of the male and has a grey crown; not black as in the male. The juveniles have the upper-parts grey washed with olive and all under-parts dull fawn.

VOICE: The most typical call, heard at all seasons, is a succession of shrill musical piping notes, not varying in tone, uttered quite rapidly. It is higher-pitched and more rapid than that of the White-throated Treecreeper which it superficially resembles. A rapidly repeated call of four notes with the fourth note rather longer than the other three, appears to be a call of the breeding season only. The bird has an audible wing beat and at close quarters the distinctive sound of the rapid beating of the wings is sufficient for one to recognise the bird.

313

DISTRIBUTION: The northern limit of its range is the tablelands areas inland from Cooktown, Queensland, and it extends throughout the Dividing Range reaching the coast about Bundaberg, Queensland, and southward. It extends from the coast to the eastern and southern edges of the plains in New South Wales and Victoria respectively. In South Australia it occurs in the south-east and in the Mount Lofty Ranges and about Adelaide. It is also found in the Bass Strait islands and Tasmania.

Throughout much of our area it is widely distributed in small numbers. There is some seasonal movement to and from the higher country. Numbers increase in the ranges in spring and summer, in the lower areas and along the Murrumbidgee River in autumn and in suburban gardens throughout the autumn, winter and spring. It is to be found at all seasons in all the moister valleys of the tablelands and ranges.

HABITS: It is one of the most active of birds and is constantly on the move from bush to bush and from flower to flower. It darts into a bush, probes a flower or two and then darts off again. Sometimes it does not even settle but probes the flower while hovering before it.

BREEDING: In coastal New South Wales the breeding season extends from August to early February but it is not well established in our area. Two broods are often reared in a season.

The nest is a cup-shaped structure attached to twigs at the rim. It is made of bulkier fibres and grass, with a lining of feathers. The height from the ground is from one to five metres but is occasionally much higher. Usually two, but occasionally three, eggs are laid. They are fleshy-buff in colour and are spotted chestnut to rich reddish-brown towards the larger end. They measure 17 × 13 mm.

FEEDING: The Eastern Spinebill is a nectar feeder and its movements seem to be controlled by nectar availability. In winter it is most abundant in areas where *Banksia* and *Grevillea* provide ample food. Its love of nectar will often bring it into country and suburban gardens and it appears well adapted to withstand the spread of urban development. Some small insects are taken in the absence of nectar. (S.J.W.)

## TAWNY-CROWNED HONEYEATER *Phylidonyris melanops*

IDENTIFICATION: Length, 18 cm. Male: general colour above, ashy-brown faintly washed with olive; wings, dark brown with narrow yellowish margins to feathers: *crown, pale reddish-brown* and below this is a thin white line over the eye; there is *a prominent crescent marking below the eye to beyond the ear coverts and down the sides of the throat*; chin and throat, white; centre of the breast and abdomen, buffy-white; flanks, ashy-brown with a slight reddish wash; bill, black; legs and feet, light brown; iris, brown. The sexes are similar.

VOICE: The call is a simple but melodious one, rather clear and bell-like. Because of its habitat the call often is the first indication of the bird's presence. It often calls before dawn in spring.

DISTRIBUTION: The distribution covers the coastal areas of New South Wales, Victoria and south-east South Australia to Eyre Peninsula, with inland extensions to the latter two States, chiefly to mallee country. It is a rare bird in Tasmania and in Western Australia it extends across the south-west.

The Tawny-crowned Honeyeater is not normally in our area but it has turned up occasionally in the colder months in Canberra gardens, generally to feed on nectar-providing native plants in association with other Honeyeaters like the Fuscous, Yellow-faced, White-plumed and Eastern Spinebill. It is generally regarded as sedentary.

HABITS: It flies low, generally, and seen in this manner could be mistaken for a Pipit. Occasionally one will fly as high as forty-five metres, utter a few calls, then descend in a fluttering manner, presumably a territorial defence or courtship display.

BREEDING: There are no local breeding records but on the New South Wales coast the season is from July to February or longer in suitable conditions. The nest is an open, cup-shaped structure, rather untidy for a honeyeater, and is placed on or near the ground in a tussock or low bush. It is always under one metre from the ground. The nest is made of coarse strips of bark bound by a little cobweb and lined with grasses and plant down. It is attached by its rim but typically it rests between several upright stems of a small shrub.

Two eggs, or sometimes three, are laid. These are white with varying intensities of markings, and are usually spotted in shades of pale chestnut to deep red, often all over but usually at the larger end only. They measure about 21 × 14 mm.

FEEDING: It feeds on the nectar of the *Banksia* and *Grevillea* of the heathland and this is a staple diet in such areas but insects are eaten when nectar is not available. (S.J.W.)

### CRESCENT HONEYEATER *Phylidonyris pyrrhoptera*
PLATE XXXI

IDENTIFICATION: Length, 15.5 cm. Male: *general colour above, dull ashy-black* with blackish-brown on the wings and tail; there are *prominent patches of bright yellow on wings and tail*; tail has white markings visible chiefly from below; there is a narrow white line over the eye; under-parts are streaked dull grey except the upper breast area where there is *a broad black crescent on a dull white background*; bill, black; legs and feet, slate; iris, red.

The female is an olive-brown version of the male; upper-parts, olive-brown with dark brown wings and tail; the bright yellow wings and tail markings of the male are replaced by dull olive-yellow in the female; the white of the tail is not as clear as in the male; the eye stripe is very faint; under-parts are dull brown tinged with olive; the crescent is inconspicuous. Juveniles seem to resemble adults of the same sex but lack the crescent markings.

VOICE: The voice is very loud, somewhat harsh and mechanical. There are a variety of calls of which the "e-gypt" call, with the second note higher in tone and somewhat longer, is the best known. Most of the calls heard relate to breeding; in winter only a single note is given. Calls begin before first light in spring.

DISTRIBUTION: The Crescent Honeyeater is a southern species. It is most common in Tasmania and also occurs in the Kent group in Bass Strait. It is numerous in southern Victoria and New South Wales almost as far north as Newcastle and as far west as the limits of the Blue Mountains and the Brindabella Ranges. In South Australia it occurs on Kangaroo Island and along the south-eastern coastal strip to the Mount Lofty Ranges.

In this region it is a bird of wet sclerophyll forests, where the undergrowth is dense along the creeks. It is widely distributed but never very numerous. Banding has shown movements of only three to four kilometres but it is evident that more extensive cold season movements occur. The species is always to be found in the ranges but numbers decline in winter and at that time small numbers appear in Canberra gardens. In recent years it has become established as a breeding species in the National Botanic Gardens.

HABITS: Crescent Honeyeaters are sociable little birds and are usually seen in small groups but keep to the bush and are not so conspicuous or active as some other honeyeaters.

BREEDING: Elsewhere active nests may be found from July to January though in this part of its range, the evidence suggests a breeding season from October to January. The nest is hidden in low scrub or ferns and is seldom more than sixty centimetres from the ground. It is a rather rough structure for a honeyeater and is of bark, leaves and grass with slight binding of cobweb. The bottom of the inside is lined with softer plant or animal material including, at times, a few feathers. Three eggs is the normal clutch though two and four have been reported. The colour varies from pale salmon-pink to a faint reddish or fleshy-buff shade becoming darker at the larger end where they are marked with chestnut-brown to purplish-brown. The eggs measure 19 × 14 mm.

FEEDING: In its normal habitat of dense, moist scrub, insects appear to be its staple diet though its nomadic winter movements seem to relate to search for nectar. (S.J.W.)

## NEW HOLLAND HONEYEATER
### *Phylidonyris novaehollandiae*
PLATE XXXI

IDENTIFICATION: Length, 18 cm. *Upper-parts, black* becoming washed with brown on the wings, rump and tail; back, lightly streaked with white; conspicuous yellow markings in the wing are seen both at rest and in flight; *white markings occur on the cheeks, behind the ear coverts and above the eye*; tail, tipped with white and has inconspicuous yellow markings on the outer feathers towards the base of the tail; under-parts, white, heavily streaked with blackish-brown; bill, black; legs and feet, black; iris, white.

The White-cheeked Honeyeater *P. nigra* which occurs on the New South Wales coast is distinguished from the New Holland Honeyeater by a very conspicuous, large, white cheek patch and a brown iris. See also the Crescent Honeyeater.

VOICE: The spring call is sharp and high-pitched while its alarm note is a loud chatter.

DISTRIBUTION: The McPherson Range is the northern limit of its range and it occurs in New South Wales from the coast to just beyond the Dividing Range and through southern Victoria into South Australia to as far north as the head of Spencer's Gulf, on Eyre Peninsula and on Kangaroo Island. It also occurs throughout Tasmania, on Flinders Island and in south-western Western Australia.

The birds breed in large numbers in loose colonies along the Murrumbidgee River particularly in places where there is dense scrub along the valley and where the flowers of *Grevillea juniperina* provide abundant food in spring and early summer. After the breeding season the colonies break up and individuals or small flocks appear in various parts of the Brindabella Ranges. There are always a few birds in Canberra gardens during winter, particularly in the Botanical Gardens.

HABITS: It is a very active and noisy bird that darts swiftly from bush to bush, usually chattering loudly. It is not so inquisitive as many honey-eaters and moves into thick cover when disturbed. It is often seen perched above the general shrubbery on a vertical limb but darts out of sight when disturbed.

BREEDING: The species has been reported breeding on the New South Wales coast in all months of the year when conditions are favourable. It breeds there in most years in autumn and again in spring and early summer. In the Capital Territory the season begins in August and extends to January. The nest is roughly formed and is large for a honeyeater of its size. It is cup-shaped and usually placed in an upright fork and not suspended by its rim. Thin strips of bark, plant stalks and grasses are used with a finer lining of plant material. The nest is always placed in a low situation rarely above two metres in a dense shrub or low branch of a tree. Two or three eggs are laid. They are from a very pale buff to a pinkish shade with reddish or purplish markings, larger and more numerous at the thicker end. They measure $20 \times 15$ mm. The incubation time is fifteen days and the young remain in the nest for about sixteen days.

FEEDING: Both nectar and insects are taken. (S.J.W.)

## NOISY MINER *Manorina melanocephala*
PLATE XXXI

IDENTIFICATION: Length, 24 cm. Upper-parts, light greyish-brown, lighter at the back of the neck; there is a bright olive-yellow wash on part of the wing; tail, brown tipped with brownish-white; face, greyish-white; crown, dull black; blackish-grey markings about the eye, ear and sides of throat; under-parts, chiefly greyish-white with dusky-grey margins to the feathers, the lower under-parts are white; *legs, bill and bare skin behind the eye, bright yellow*; iris, brown. The sexes are similar.

VOICE: The main call is a repeated, single note; loud, fairly long and with a pronounced upward inflection. It is fairly harsh but not un-musical. Another call is a loud and rapidly repeated "wick-wick-wick-wick-wick". It is well described as garrulous.

DISTRIBUTION: Its northern limit is the Herberton Tablelands in Queensland and it extends through much of that State, throughout New South Wales except in the north-west and the extreme south-east, through most of Victoria and Tasmania, the area below the Murray in South Australia and almost to the head of Spencer's Gulf. In our area

318

it is most typical of grazing country where a few trees remain in the paddocks and where native shrubs have given way to pastures. It is also found in fairly open forest country. Some slight, local movement is evident as during several recent winters flocks have moved temporarily into open parkland in Canberra suburbs.

HABITS: It is often called "Soldier Bird" because of its habit of giving continual and vociferous warning of any intruder in its area and it will often follow a person for some distance, calling loudly all the time. If one is quiet it will often gradually descend to a low level, constantly peering from the tree at the intruder from a variety of acrobatic attitudes. When moving it often flies low to the ground from one tree to the next.

BREEDING: The breeding season in our area extends from September to December but in other areas it may extend from June to January. The nest is typically placed in a fairly conspicuous site in the outer twigs of a eucalypt or in an upright fork of a sapling. It is an open cup-shaped structure of up to eighteen centimetres in diameter and eleven centimetres in depth, composed externally of long thin twigs and coarse grasses with some binding of cobweb and lined with softer plant and animal material including wool. The nest site may vary from two to ten metres from the ground.

Three is the usual clutch but two or four eggs may be laid. The egg colour varies from white to pale reddish or creamy-buff with reddish-brown to purplish-red markings, sometimes chiefly at the larger end. They measure 28 × 20 mm.

FEEDING: Insects, including beetles and caterpillars, are the chief food but nectar is taken when the local eucalypts are in flower. It has been seen to take insects from under the bark of trees while perched, using the tail as a brace, as illustrated. In some fruit-growing areas it tends to attack grapes and soft fruits. (S.J.W.)

## LITTLE WATTLE-BIRD *Anthochaera chrysoptera*

IDENTIFICATION: Length, 30.5 cm. *General colour, dull grey-brown* with the head darker and the sides of the neck paler, and with a *shaft streak of white in each body feather*; tail, dark brown tipped with white; *wings, dark brown with a rufous patch* which is conspicuous in flight; bill, dark brown; legs and feet, slaty-black; iris, red-brown. The sexes are similar. Young birds are more brown than the adults with the white shaft markings of the plumage less distinct.

VOICE: The calls are varied but all are harsh, loud and unmusical. It also clatters its bill very rapidly and quite loudly.

DISTRIBUTION: The normal range is coastal, from Rockhampton, Queensland, through New South Wales, Victoria and South Australia as far as Yorke Peninsula and Kangaroo Island. It is also common throughout Tasmania and parts of Western Australia.

It is a bird of the coastal scrubs, particularly where *Banksia* is in flower. Its very occasional appearances in Canberra and at Lake George are in line with the sporadic appearance of individuals at other inland places beyond its normal range. It appears to move widely in the non-breeding season, apparently in search of nectar. It has been noted at flowering time feeding in all the species of *Banksia* which grow along the coast. The extent of the movements involved is not known.

HABITS: It is a very noisy and pugnacious bird on the coast and lives in flocks that rollick among the *Banksia*. In our area it tends to be seen as solitary vagrants moving among the bare bushes of winter gardens.

BREEDING: There are no local breeding records. Elsewhere it breeds from August to January and in Tasmania breeding extends to April. Two or three broods are reared in the one nest in the same season. The nest is a deep, saucer-shaped affair of thin twigs with a finer lining of soft bark or plant down and is placed in a forked branch of a *Banksia*, tea-tree or *Eucalyptus* sapling. The nest is usually quite low but may be up to ten metres high. One or two eggs are laid. They vary from reddish-buff to reddish-salmon in colour, and have irregularly shaped markings of chestnut-brown to purplish-red chiefly on the larger end where a zone is sometimes formed. They measure 29 × 21 mm.

FEEDING: Nectar is the main food and flowering coastal *Banksia* always seem to have a quota of Little Wattle-birds. Flies and other insects are also taken. (S.J.W.)

## RED WATTLE-BIRD *Anthochaera carunculata*
PLATE XXXI

IDENTIFICATION: Length, 35 cm. The largest mainland honey-eater. *Upper-parts, dark greyish-brown with white shaft streaks*; wing feathers and the upper-tail coverts have greyish-white margins; tail, blackish-brown tipped with white; under-parts, dark greyish-brown streaked with white except for the *abdomen area which is yellow*; there is a silver white cheek patch on the lores and below and behind the eye and a pendant pinkish-red wattle behind the cheeks, this appears to lengthen with age to nearly 2.5 cm; bill, black; legs and feet, brownish-grey; iris, red. The sexes are similar. Juvenile birds have no pendant wattle and the cheek patch is dark grey. It is probable that these feathers remain for a few months only. This species can be distinguished from the Little Wattle-bird by its larger size, the yellow not grey abdomen, the wattles, the silver cheek patch, by the grey-brown wings with white tips, and there is no rufous wing patch as in the Little Wattle-bird.

VOICE: The Red Wattle-bird has a variety of loud harsh unmusical calls. The most frequently heard is a fairly long note followed by two shorter ones. The calls are heard at all seasons, particularly when feeding, but more frequently in spring.

DISTRIBUTION: The northern limit of the species is the extreme south-east corner of Queensland. In New South Wales it extends from the coast to the western slopes of the Divide; in Victoria it is widely distributed and it extends back into New South Wales along the Murray between the Darling and Murrumbidgee Rivers; in South Australia it is found in the south east and to the head of Spencer's Gulf and in Eyre Peninsula; it also occurs in south-west Western Australia. In the highlands it is moderately common in open forest and wet sclerophyll forests. In winter it is found in parks and gardens of Canberra in greater numbers than at other seasons.

HABITS: This very noisy and pugnacious bird is usually seen in small groups in our area but winter visitors to gardens are usually solitary. It is very active and is seldom still.

BREEDING: The breeding season in the highlands extends from October to February, while elsewhere it is from July to January, some birds raising two broods. The nest is an open cup; a rather rough structure of thin twigs lined internally with soft fibrous plant material. Occasionally a few feathers or wool are used as lining. It is placed from one to twelve metres high but low nests are exceptional.

Two, occasionally three, eggs are laid and these are from a pale flesh colour to a pale reddish-buff or pale salmon-red with chestnut or purplish-red spots mostly at the larger end. They measure 31 × 22 mm.

FEEDING: Nectar is an important winter food and *Banksia* in particular is a great attraction. Insects are eaten and it has also been reported as attacking apricots, plums and grapes. (S.J.W.)

SPINY-CHEEKED HONEYEATER *Acanthagenys rufogularis*

IDENTIFICATION: Length, 24 cm. General colour above, including the crown, *dull brownish-grey*; rump and upper-tail covert feathers are yellowish with brown centres; *tail, black-brown tipped with white*; there is a black line below the eye and below this is a *line of pink flesh running from the bill*; the spine-like feathers of the cheek are white to yellow; chin and upper breast, rich rufous edged with brown; abdomen, yellow streaked with brown; bill is pink with a black tip; legs and feet, slate-grey; iris, bone. The sexes are similar.

VOICE: Its main call is a rather plaintive trilling one, a distinctive sound which is quite melodious. It also has some rather loud, single notes, often of a peculiar tone.

DISTRIBUTION: It inhabits most of mainland Australia with the exception of the extreme north and north-west, and the wet forests of the east and south-west. This is a bird of the inland and is very rarely recorded in the region. There are a few recent records. To some extent it is nomadic, as its appearances in some districts are seasonal, e.g., in central Victoria, but the nature of such movements is not known. In most places it is sedentary.

HABITS: In its inland mallee habitats it is a very inconspicuous bird usually found singly or in pairs in the low undergrowth. It has a quite spectacular display flight in which it flies vertically upwards for some distance and then flutters down, calling.

BREEDING: There are no breeding records from the highlands. In south-eastern Australia the season extends from July to December and is earliest in its more inland range. The nest is cup-shaped and composed of grasses, vines, rootlets, plant stalks and includes other material such as wool. The nest material is often worked in perpendicularly rather than horizontally. The nest is usually suspended from a horizontal fork or from a mistletoe, one to twelve metres from the ground. Low nests are common.

Usually two eggs are laid and the ground colour is from yellowish to creamy-brown, often darker at the larger end, there are some deep brown markings usually at the larger end. They measure about 25 × 18 mm.

FEEDING: Insects appear to be the main item of diet but native fruits and berries, including those of the mistletoe, are eaten. Nectar is used when available. (S.J.W.)

## BLUE-FACED HONEYEATER *Entomyzon cyanotis*

IDENTIFICATION: Length, 30 cm. Upper-parts, golden olive; tail has a white tip; crown, neck and ear coverts, black; there is *a large area of bare blue skin about the eye*, and there is a white nape band; under-parts are white except for a central area of grey from the chin to the breast; bill, black; legs and feet, brown-olive; iris, buff-yellow. The sexes are similar.

VOICE: The voice is usually a loud monotonous single note but it also scolds loudly when excited.

DISTRIBUTION: It occurs in the Aru Islands and New Guinea as well as in Australia. It is found across the better watered areas of the north of the continent and throughout Queensland except the far west. In New South Wales it is mainly coastal but extends inland in the south-west and into northern Victoria. It is accidental further south. In its southern range this is a bird of the inland river systems and it has not been recorded in the Southern Tablelands in recent years but Mathews included it in the list of birds in the Australian Capital Territory. It appears to be a sedentary species, but some movements have been re-ported from southern Queensland.

HABITS: In Northern Australia, where it is commonest, it is one of the most active and pugnacious of birds. It is constantly on the move, noisily flying from tree to tree and jumping from limb to limb. Usually it is in groups of six to eight particularly in paperbark forests.

BREEDING: There are no breeding records from the highlands. Else-where the chief breeding months are August and September but nests have been reported from June to January. The nest is very large with a bulky foundation of twigs up to half a metre in length with an open cup of finer grasses centrally placed. Often the twig foundation is lacking and the nest is formed only of bark strips and grasses. It some-times uses old nests of babblers, Magpie-larks and Noisy Friar-birds. The nest is usually from three to eight metres high but along the inland rivers higher nests are usual. Usually two, but occasionally three or more, eggs are laid. These range from fleshy-buff to rich salmon in colour, sparingly spotted with purplish-red to brown and measure 30 × 23 mm.

FEEDING: Nectar and insects are the principal items of food and native fruits and berries are also used. It is known to attack peaches, plums, apricots and bananas. (S.J.W.)

## NOISY FRIAR-BIRD *Philemon corniculatus*

PLATE XXXI

IDENTIFICATION: Length, 33 cm. General colour above, greyish-brown with a small white tip to the tail; *head, naked and black with a knob on the bill*; feathers of the neck and upper breast, unusually long, silvery-white and with narrow brown shaft streaks; lower breast, pale brown passing to white on the abdomen and under-tail coverts; bill, black; legs and feet, dark grey; iris, red. The sexes are similar.

VOICE: "Four-o-clock" is an often quoted rendering of a main call; this is of three, rather short, abrupt notes, the second being the highest. Many varied calls are given and most are rather loud and harsh. It is fairly quiet before its autumn migration and very noisy in spring.

DISTRIBUTION: It occurs in New Guinea and from North Queensland to Lakes Entrance in Victoria, from the coast to the limits of the western slopes of the Dividing Range and sometimes a little beyond. In Victoria it is a rare bird except in east Gippsland and the north-east of the State. In our area it is a bird of the rather dry, open forests. It is common about Canberra in the warmer months and occasionally birds appear in the ranges. In other parts of its range it is found in moister country. About Canberra it is migratory leaving in April and May and returning in late September to November. The winter quarters of these birds are not known. Occasional birds are seen in Canberra in winter. Elsewhere it is reported to be nomadic rather than migratory.

HABITS: It is a very noisy, peculiar-looking bird and very pugnacious to others. It is usually in flocks that congregate with raucous clamour at sources of food.

BREEDING: The breeding season in our area is late October to early January; elsewhere it is from August to January.
   The nest is a rather thin, large, very deep, open cup attached by its rim to an outer horizontal forked twig. Usually strips of bark and dry fine grass are used. One local nest was made entirely of wool from the body of a sheep immediately under the nest. The nest is sometimes quite low in the outer branches of a spreading eucalypt but usually it is high in the outermost twigs. The birds attack noisily when a nest is examined. Three or four eggs, measuring about $36 \times 23$ mm are laid. Their colour is rich salmon-red spotted and blotched with chestnut-red and dull purplish-grey.

FEEDING: The birds congregate in spring on *Grevillea juniperina* along the Murrumbidgee River and remain there, feeding noisily, for a few weeks before passing on to their breeding territories. Nectar provides a great attraction and some wandering probably relates to a search for flowering trees and shrubs. In December and January it has a great liking for Christmas beetles and often takes them on the wing. Other insects are also taken. Attacks on soft fruits have been reported at times but it has not been reported raiding gardens in the Canberra area. (S.J.W.)

## LITTLE FRIAR-BIRD *Philemon citreogularis*
PLATE XXXV

IDENTIFICATION: Length 25-28 cm. Above dark grey-brown; a narrow grey-white fringe on nape extends to sides of neck; chin and upper throat off-white; under-parts generally pale fawn-brown, slightly paler on lower abdomen; breast lightly flecked with white; facial skin, blue-black; bill, black; tarsus and toes, dark slate-grey; iris, grey-brown. It is the only friar-bird without a knob on the upper bill. The sexes are similar. Juvenile has yellow on throat and upper breast.

VOICE: A loud raucous "ar-koo" and "rockety cruk-shank" are the more familiar calls. When in a group, particularly when squabbling, it produces a variety of jumbled, muted notes.

DISTRIBUTION: Northern and eastern Australia to as far as the Murray Valley in South Australia. It appears to avoid the heavily vegetated coastal strip of eastern New South Wales. The species is also found in southern New Guinea.

The Australian Capital Territory appears to be the eastern boundary of this inland species' distribution. The bird was first recorded here in January 1968, with most records from mid 1968 onwards. These coincided with an influx of several other "western" species into south-eastern Australia, which diminished towards the end of 1971. Occasional birds are still recorded. Although considered migratory, records in the local area span the whole year.

HABITS: The Little Friar-bird is a bird of the open, dry sclerophyll woodlands. In the south the bird is migratory, arriving in early spring and leaving by mid autumn. It is often associated with watercourses and lakes, particularly where the Red Gum *Eucalyptus camaldulensis* occurs. Generally the bird is encountered in pairs or small flocks. It is very aggressive and will chase other species, regardless of size, from a favoured food source and especially from near the nest site.

BREEDING: In the southern half of its range the breeding season is September to March. The nest, made of fine bark, dry grasses and rootlets, is open and cup shaped. It is interwoven with spider web, insect cocoons and animal hair and lined with finer plant material and

325

hair. Usually it is placed in the outer leafy branches where it is suspended by its rim. The nest is often placed over water, at heights of up to 12 metres.

Two or three, rarely four, salmon-pink eggs, blotched and speckled with purplish-red and brown towards the larger end, are laid. The eggs measure about 28 × 20 mm.

There are no breeding records locally.

FEEDING: The Little Friar-bird feeds on nectar, insects and occasionally fruit. It will often take insects on the wing in the same manner as the Noisy Friar-bird. The birds will follow flowering trees, especially eucalypts in the south and melaleucas in the north. (M.C.)


# FINCHES

The Australian finches include some of the most beautiful small birds in the world. They have been favourites since the earliest days of settlement and some became aviary birds in Sydney within the first year or so. Since then they have been admired in the wild and in aviaries throughout the world so that some have become almost domesticated and rival the Budgerigar in this sphere.

Although the word "finch" is in universal use in Australia, the birds in this country are, more correctly, "grass-finches". The true "finches" are a group of birds restricted to Eurasia, Africa and the Americas. The grass-finches are now included in the Ploceidae with the "weaver-finches" of Africa and Asia. Several of these groups have been introduced to Australia and popular usage is to call them simply "finches".

### Family Ploceidae — Weaver- and Grass-finches

Weaver-finches and grass-finches are small, colourful birds that belong to a large family distributed in Africa, southern Asia and Australia, including islands in the Indian Ocean and western Polynesia. The family contains about 237 species of which eighteen are native to Australia. Two grass-finches from Asia, the Spice Finch and Black-headed Mannikin, have established themselves from aviary escapes. Two African weaver-finches were established but now appear to have disappeared. In our area four of the native species occur regularly and two as vagrants.

Grass-finches are social birds living and moving in flocks, in the case of the highland species small flocks, and during the breeding season the nests tend to be in loose colonies in areas of suitable nesting habitat. The unmated birds often remain in the same general area. Grass-finches tend to roost in close groups and many pack into old nests at night. They progress over the ground by hopping and most feed on the ground or in low bushes or grass.

The nests are all untidy domed structures with a funnel entrance. They are built of dried grass and lined with finer grasses and feathers. The eggs are always white. The incubation period is twelve to sixteen days. The birds have a very long pair bond, perhaps for life, and in the breeding season may rear several broods.

## RED-BROWED FINCH *Emblema temporalis*
PLATE XXXII

IDENTIFICATION: Length, 11.5 cm. General colour above, dull olive-yellow; rump, crimson; crown of head and nape, grey; face, light grey with a *broad crimson stripe extending from bill above the eye to the back of the head*; under-parts, grey; bill, red; legs and feet, pink; iris, reddish-brown. The sexes are similar. Juveniles are browner on the head, the crimson is much duller than in adults and the bill is black.

VOICE: The contact call is a piercing high-pitched "sseee-sseee" that is uttered incessantly. In courtship the song is a twitter derived from the contact call.

DISTRIBUTION: The Red-browed Finch is characteristic of the coast and ranges of eastern Australia from Cape York to south-east South Australia. The range does not extend inland much beyond Yass, New South Wales. Its preferred habitat is shrubbery or the forest edge where there is dense undergrowth; it occupies open grassland so long as dense bushes are present. In this district it is widely dispersed in picnic grounds, gardens, fields and forests but is particularly common along the edges of streams and roads in the mountains, where blackberries and other dense cover exists.

HABITS: They are usually found in small groups although in winter concentrations of one hundred or more occur. They are seen hopping across the ground or darting from bush to bush. The flight is strong but they prefer to hop and flit through the shrubbery rather than fly over it.

BREEDING: The nest is usually ten to fifteen centimetres in height and fifteen to twenty centimetres in length, excluding the funnel, and is usually placed in a thorny, dense bush. They are, however, sometimes in clumps of leaves or in a fork in more open trees. They are seldom more than two metres from the ground but have been seen up to six metres high. The clutch size is four to six but five is commonest. The eggs measure about $16 \times 12$ mm. Both parents share in incubation and roost in the nest at night.

The breeding season on the New South Wales coast is extended, nests having been found in every month except July and August but most are found in October and November. On the Southern Table-lands nests are found from early October through to April.

FEEDING: They usually feed on seeds and berries on the ground but are capable of securing these items from tall growing grass and bushes. They secure many insects from the foliage of bushes and small trees. (H.J.F.)

## BEAUTIFUL FIRETAIL *Emblema bella*
PLATE XXXII

IDENTIFICATION: Length, 11.5 cm. General colour above, olive-brown finely barred with darker brown; *rump, bright crimson*; face, olive-brown with *black around the eye*; chin, throat and breast, light grey with *fine blackish bars*; abdomen and under-tail, black; bill, red; legs and feet, pale pink; iris, hazel. The females only differ in having the abdomen barred like rest of the underside, not black as in the male.

VOICE: A penetrating, mournful, piping whistle "weeeeee" is the usual call heard but it also has a more rapid call of two or three high notes ending with a downward run "tee tee te te".

DISTRIBUTION: It is normally restricted to coastal districts from Newcastle, New South Wales to south-east South Australia, Kangaroo Island and Tasmania and, except in Tasmania, is nowhere very common. The record in this district is a solitary one. Its preferred habitat is dense shrubbery in moist gullies and on creek banks, in sheltered *Banksia* heathlands and also in more open forest provided there is some dense undergrowth.

HABITS: Beautiful Firetails are very secretive and are seldom seen except when flitting from one dense bush to another. They occur in pairs or small groups and are often on the ground from which they rise with a rapid whirr of the wings. Sometimes, however, they do not flush easily, preferring to crouch and hide among the grass stems or low plants. They move rapidly over the ground sometimes resembling "a small mouse running".

BREEDING: There is no breeding record from the highlands but it occurs in the period September to January on the New South Wales coast and in Tasmania. The nest is spherical, about fifteen centimetres in diameter and has a long entrance funnel, fifteen to eighteen centimetres long. It is neater and more solidly constructed than those of most finches; the walls can be two to four centimetres thick. The nest is usually built in a low tree or bush less than six metres high. The clutch size is four to seven and the eggs measure 18 × 12 mm.

FEEDING: They feed entirely on small seeds on the ground but also secure many insects from the foliage of bushes; it is thought that for a finch, relatively large quantities of insect food are taken but there has been no quantitative study of this. (H.J.F.)

## DIAMOND FIRETAIL *Emblema guttata*

PLATE XXXII

IDENTIFICATION: Length, 12.5 cm. General colour above, brown; *rump, bright crimson*; head, grey; *face and throat, white*; there is some black around the eye; there is a broad, black band across upper breast; remainder of under-parts, white; flanks, black with prominent white spots; bill, red; legs and feet, dark grey; iris, red. The sexes are similar.

VOICE: The call is long, drawn out and mournful. Of its two syllables the first rises slightly and the second declines, "twooo-warrt".

DISTRIBUTION: The range is from about the Dawson River, Queensland, to Eyre Peninsula, South Australia. It is mainly a bird of the tablelands but is common also on the coast and isolated groups occur in the semi-arid inland to as far west as Griffith, New South Wales. In the Southern Tablelands it is widely distributed in the more open country but is not common in the heavily forested mountains.

HABITS: The bird lives in flocks of twenty to thirty though smaller groups are also seen. They are usually on the ground or fences in open grassland with scattered timber but also sit in tall eucalypt trees where they are very inconspicuous indeed. They rise from the ground with a whirr and fly silently and swiftly away with an undulating flight; the crimson rump is very conspicuous. It can become quite tame and is found at times in the parks and gardens of Canberra city but then is usually in passage to coarser grasslands on its outskirts.

BREEDING: Near Sydney it breeds throughout most of the year but most nests are in the period August to January. Nests have been found in the highlands from early November to the end of January.
The nest is rather large, twenty centimetres or more in diameter with a funnel of fifteen to twenty centimetres in length. It quite often has an extra entrance, or perhaps escape hole, in the back. It is some-

times built in low shrubs but more commonly is in a fork or bunch of leaves in a *Eucalyptus* or *Casuarina* tree thirteen metres or more from the ground. Sometimes several birds' nests are built in the one tree. The clutch size is four to seven, commonly five, and the eggs measure about 18 × 13 mm.

FEEDING: They feed entirely on the ground on small grass seeds and insects. (H.J.F.)

## PLUM-HEADED FINCH *Aidemosyne modesta*

PLATE XXXII

IDENTIFICATION: Length, 11.5 cm. Male: general colour above, dark olive-brown; feathers of rump and upper-tail coverts barred with white; tail, black; wings, olive-brown with white bars; *crown of head and chin, deep claret red*; face, white; throat and breast, white barred with brown; abdomen, white; bill, black; legs and feet, brown; iris, dark brown. Females are considerably duller than males, they lack the claret spot on the chin and there is a white line above the eye. Immatures have no red on the head and under-parts have very few bars.

VOICE: Except when in large flocks the Plum-headed Finch is very silent. The identity call is a musical, bell-like "ting" that can be quite loud but the other sounds made are all very soft.

DISTRIBUTION: They are nowhere very abundant and the bird has a patchy distribution, mainly on the tablelands and inland slopes of the Dividing Range, from near Port Denison, Queensland, to central New South Wales. They are usually found in low-lying areas in coarse grasses interspersed with some trees. Those that visit the Canberra district occasionally are wanderers; a small flock spent several weeks at Uriarra in 1960. The Plum-headed Finch is one of the more nomadic of the grass-finches and small groups or flocks live for a period in the one place and then move a few kilometres away or disappear entirely. The movements are influenced by the weather.

In recent years occasional local records have been obtained of the introduced Spice Finch *Lonchura punctulata*, presumably aviary escapees. This species is superficially similar to the Plum-headed Finch and care should be taken with identification.

HABITS: They are usually in small groups but flocks of up to five hundred do occur in dry times. It is usually inconspicuous keeping to coarse long grasses and making little sound but flocks on the move can be noisy. It is remarkably tame in the wild.

BREEDING: The breeding season is usually between September and January but is influenced by the weather and can be much more extended. There is no local breeding record. The nest, one of the smallest of all grass-finches, is ten to fifteen centimetres long and about eight centimetres broad. It has a very small entrance hole, no entrance funnel and it is built of green grasses and is usually in tall grass or an overgrown low bush. The eggs measure about 17 × 12 mm and four to seven form the clutch.

FEEDING: Some seed is collected from the ground but Plum-headed Finches also ascend grass stems with great agility to secure the seed-heads. (H.J.F.)

## ZEBRA FINCH *Poephila guttata*

PLATE XXXII

IDENTIFICATION: Length, 10 cm. Male: general colour above, brownish-grey; crown of head and nape, grey; *face, bright chestnut*, there is a black mark extending downward from the eye and a white one from the bill; tail, black, barred with white; throat and breast, grey, prominently barred with black; abdomen, white; *flanks, chestnut with white spots*; bill, red; legs and feet, orange; iris, red. Females lack the chestnut on the face, and the throat, breast, abdomen and flanks are white. Immatures are similar to females but lack the black and white face markings and their bills are black.

VOICE: The contact call has been, very aptly, likened to the sound of a toy trumpet "tia tia" and there are several other sharp notes when feeding and flying. The courtship song is a musical series of trilling versions of the identity call.

DISTRIBUTION: The Zebra Finch is one of the most numerous and widespread birds in Australia. It does not occur in Tasmania but is found throughout most of the continent wherever the country is open without dense timber and where water is available. In general terms it is most abundant in the arid and semi-arid inland savannah, is less numerous in the forests of the inland slopes and avoids the dense forests of south-west Western Australia and the east coast, although it has invaded the coast wherever clearing has been extensive. It is not found on Cape York or in southern Victoria. In our area it is usually uncommon but its numbers vary tremendously according to the climate inland and, in times of drought, it appears in numbers and remains to breed although the population declines in successive years. Occasional single birds seen in Canberra may be aviary escapees.

331

HABITS: It is highly gregarious and occurs most commonly in flocks of fifty or more although in our area a group of this size is unusual. The flocks tend to remain fairly localised and, even in the breeding season, the birds associate with one another at feeding and sunning places in the vicinity of the nests. It is very active and noisy, the flocks keep up continuous chatter and twittering and there is a good deal of flying and chasing among the individuals in the group.

BREEDING: The breeding season is very much influenced by rainfall and, in the inland, is controlled by it; breeding begins almost immediately rain falls in sufficient quantity to germinate grasses, at any time of the year. Some birds begin building while the rain is still falling. In regions of more regular rainfall the breeding season is more regular. On the New South Wales coast it occurs during spring and in the tropics during the wet season. Near Canberra nests have been found in the period November to April. Several broods are reared in the one season. The nest is very untidy and loosely constructed of dry grass and any other material that is available and is lined with feathers, fur or wool. It is usually built in a thick bush but can be in a stump or a treehole or almost anywhere. The clutch size varies from two or eight but most pairs lay four or five. The first egg is often laid well before the nest is roofed over. The eggs vary in size from $14-16 \times 10-12$ mm. The young leave the nest at about twenty days of age.

FEEDING: Zebra finches feed almost entirely on the ground but jump up to secure higher seedheads. They frequently dart into the air to catch flying insects and feed the nestlings largely on this material. (H.J.F.)

## BANDED FINCH *Poephila bichenovii*

PLATE XXXII

IDENTIFICATION: Length, 10 cm. General colour above, pale brown; rump, white; upper wings, pale brown but terminal half black, finely spotted with white; face and under-parts, white, there *is a black line from the bill that extends over the eye and around the face and another black line across the upper breast*; under-tail, black; bill, blue-green; legs and feet, grey; eye, dark brown. Females are similar but perhaps a little duller.

VOICE: The call is not unlike that of the Zebra Finch but is higher-pitched, more drawn out and has a plaintive note.

DISTRIBUTION: It extends from Western Australia across the north of the continent and through eastern Australia to about the Victorian border. Two races occur in this extensive range, a black-rumped form in the north and a white-rumped form elsewhere. In New South Wales it straggles inland, as far as 640 kilometres but is most numerous on the Northern Tablelands and the north coast. On the Southern Table-lands it is not common although there are some colonies throughout the area.

HABITS: Banded Finches live in small groups; they remain very close together and favour areas with scattered bushes for cover, and short, soft grasses for food. They are very quiet and retiring and prefer to flit from cover to the ground or from one bush to another when crossing open space. Their powers of flight are weak. They are usually found feeding quietly on the ground. Banded Finches, more than other grass-finches, build roosting nests outside the breeding season and it is not uncommon to find six to eight birds huddled in such a nest at night.

BREEDING: In coastal New South Wales the main breeding season is in the spring but there is also considerable autumn nesting and a few nests might be found at any time. Nests have been found in our area in the period November to April. The nests are smaller than those of other grass-finches and are seldom more than ten centimetres in dia-meter, excluding a short entrance funnel. They are almost spherical and the walls are very thin. They are built of very fine grass stems. Often many nests are built in the one bush. The clutch varies from three to six but most nests contain four or five eggs. The eggs measure about 16 × 12 mm.

FEEDING: They feed on small seeds mainly collected from the ground but they also jump onto lodged grass and jump up to secure seedheads that are out of reach. They also secure great numbers of insects. (H.J.F.)

### Family Passeridae — Sparrows
The Passeridae is a small family of about 16 species found in Europe, Asia and Africa. Their relationships to other birds are unknown. They are mostly dull-coloured in various combinations of black, grey, white and brown. The association of the best-known species, the House Sparrow, with humans is very old and must have arisen almost as soon as humans began to lead a settled existence and make permanent buildings. Since the mid 19th century, two, the Tree Sparrow and the House Sparrow — have been introduced to the Americas and Austral-asia and are now widely dispersed there.

### HOUSE SPARROW *Passer domesticus*
PLATE XXXII
IDENTIFICATION: Length, 15 cm. Male: *upper-parts, brown*

333

*streaked with black*; crown, dark grey; throat, black; cheeks, greyish-white; wings, brown with white bar; bill, black; legs and feet, pale brown; iris, hazel. Adult females are duller and lack the black throat, grey on crown and rump, and distinct wing bar.

VOICE: A very noisy bird, the House Sparrow has a variety of chirping call notes. The commonest are a loud, penetrating "chee-up" and a harsh twitter.

DISTRIBUTION: This European bird was introduced to Australia in the 1850s and was carefully protected until it became established, in much the same misguided way as was the rabbit. In Australia it is now numerous nearly everywhere from central Queensland to South Australia. It has not yet reached the Northern Territory, and a few migrants that have followed the railway to Western Australia have been shot. In our area it is abundant in all urban and agricultural districts but has been unable to penetrate the forests and ranges.

HABITS: Everyone is familiar with the House Sparrow. It is gregarious, bold and perky and is seen in all situations bustling to and from nests or hopping rapidly in streets and yards. It is never seen away from human habitation.

BREEDING: Strangely, the breeding season has not been accurately recorded in this district but nests are very numerous in spring and summer. The nest is an untidy dome of straw or grass, or almost any rubbish, and has a side entrance; it usually measures twenty centimetres or more in diameter and is larger than the nests of grass-finches. It is sometimes built in bushes but more commonly is in the ceilings of buildings and crevices in them. The clutch size is three to five but sometimes six or seven. There are several successive broods. The eggs are very variable but are usually greyish-white speckled and blotched with brown or grey. They measure $22-25 \times 15-17$ mm. The incubation period is twelve to fourteen days and the young fledge in fifteen days.

FEEDING: It is mainly a ground feeder and eats seeds (in urban areas mainly waste grain and street refuse), some insects and fruit and buds as well as the edible parts of man's refuse. It also picks seeds and insect remains off the radiators and underparts of cars and other vehicles. (H.J.F.)

## TREE SPARROW *Passer montanus*

PLATE XXXII

IDENTIFICATION: Length, 14 cm. Both sexes resemble those of the House Sparrow but differ from it in being slightly smaller and trimmer.

There is a *black patch on the ear coverts and a chocolate, not grey, crown*; bill, black; legs and feet, brown; iris, dark brown. Juveniles are similar to adults.

VOICE: The notes are very similar to those of the House Sparrow but are more musical and higher pitched.

DISTRIBUTION: Introduced from Europe in the 1860s, the bird has become quite widely spread in Victoria but elsewhere is rare. There have been a few records in southern New South Wales and one in our area at Queanbeyan. In Britain it is less attached to man than is the House Sparrow but this is not yet obvious in Australia where it frequents towns and farms but has not managed to penetrate the bush.

HABITS: It is more retiring and shy than the House Sparrow but freely mingles with it and has very similar general behaviour.

BREEDING: The nest is very similar to that of the House Sparrow. In Britain the clutch is larger than that species, four to six or up to nine and the eggs are smaller, measuring $19-21 \times 13-15$ mm. They are also darker, more brown in general colour, with finer stippling and more glossy. Incubation period is twelve to fourteen days. Two broods are common and the young fledge in twelve to fourteen days.

FEEDING: Seeds and insects are procured on the ground. (H.J.F.)

### Family Fringillidae — Typical Finches

This family, that of the true "finches", is a moderately large one containing about 122 species, and is found in Europe, Asia, Africa, and North and South America. The chief food is seeds and the various groups of species have different kinds of bills for dealing with particular seeds. Extreme forms have heavy bills for cracking hard seeds, or are specialised for extracting the seeds from cones of conifers. The majority of species in all continents belong to the subfamily Carduelinae. This group includes some of the most accomplished songsters, the Canary, Linnet and Goldfinch. Two, the Goldfinch and Greenfinch, have been introduced to Australia.

There are many differences between these finches and the native grass-finches. The nest is cup-shaped, not vase-shaped and may be beautifully decorated. Many breed in loose colonies and the eggs are blue with reddish or brown marks, unlike the pure white eggs of the grass-finches.

### GOLDFINCH *Carduelis carduelis*

PLATE XXXII

IDENTIFICATION: Length, 12 cm. General colour above, tawny

335

brown; tail, black; forehead, chin and upper throat, crimson; back of head, black; *wings, black with conspicuous golden yellow band*; breast, brown; abdomen, white; bill, pinkish-white; legs and feet, flesh; iris, dark brown. The sexes are similar.

VOICE: The song is a pleasant liquid twitter uttered from a perch or in flight — it strongly resembles that of the canary. Contact call is an agitated "whit whit".

DISTRIBUTION: This European bird was introduced to Victoria and New South Wales in about 1863 and is now widespread in south-east Australia including Tasmania; isolated colonies also exist in Western Australia. It is common in our area in gardens and pasture lands, particularly when thistles are abundant. Throughout its range it is now thoroughly adapted to agricultural lands and towns where exotic conifers have been planted.

HABITS: The Goldfinch lives in small groups that, in winter, build up to one hundred or more birds but it is not as gregarious during the breeding season as are Australian grass-finches. It is usually found moving in its swift, undulating flight over open paddocks or, in the breeding season, twittering from the tops of tall coniferous trees. It is not commonly seen on the ground as it secures most of its food from growing plants.

BREEDING: The breeding season is in summer, mid-October to mid-January. The nest is a very neat, deep cup, built of fine rootlets and grasses bound with cobweb. It is usually lined with wool and thistle-down. The nest is usually placed in an exotic shrub or tree, and conifers are often used, between two and thirteen metres high. The clutch size, in inland New South Wales, is three to six.

The eggs are pale blue and are spotted with brown and reddish-brown particularly towards the larger end. The incubation time is twelve to thirteen days and the young fledge in about fourteen days.

FEEDING: Goldfinches do feed on the ground but more usually take the seed from standing plants, thistles being particularly favoured. The newly hatched young are fed entirely on small spiders although the adults eat mainly seed. (H.J.F.)

## GREENFINCH *Carduelis chloris*
PLATE XXXII

IDENTIFICATION: Length, 15 cm. *General colour above, olive-green*; rump and under-parts, yellow-green; patches on sides of tail and *wing primaries, bright yellow*; bill, whitish-flesh; legs and feet, flesh; iris, brown. Females are duller than males and are less streaked with dark brown above and below.

VOICE: A loud, rapid twitter, also a repeated short "cheu" or "chup". In the breeding season the male utters a persistent harsh "zzweeee", usually while perched at the top of a tree. The species also has a canary-like twittering song.

DISTRIBUTION: Europe and north-western Africa, eastward to the mountains of southern Russian Turkestan. Introduced into Australia and New Zealand. In Australia it is sparingly distributed throughout portions of Victoria, Tasmania, southern South Australia and south-eastern New South Wales. It is very uncommon in our area and was first recorded during January, 1961 in parkland in Canberra. Subsequently it has become established as a resident.

HABITS: The Greenfinch in Australia is found in places well supplied with exotic trees and bushes, such as suburban gardens and farm lands, particularly those with windbreaks of pines or box-thorn hedges. It rarely visits and never resides in native forest. The flight is slightly undulating with a few rapid wing beats alternating with a momentary closure of wings. The bird is inconspicuous and usually to be found in pairs or singly during the breeding season and in small flocks during autumn and winter.

BREEDING: There is no local information but in New South Wales and Victoria the breeding season extends from September to January. The nest is cup-shaped, composed of twigs sometimes mixed with animal hair and usually lined with feathers, rootlets or hair. It is placed in a shrub or hedge, occasionally in a taller tree. The clutch size is from four to six. The eggs vary in colour from dirty white to pale greenish-blue with spots or streaks of red-brown and pale violet. The eggs measure about $21 \times 15$ mm. Incubation is from thirteen to fourteen days and is done by the female alone. The young are fed by both sexes and leave the nest thirteen to fifteen days after hatching. It is not uncommon for a pair to produce two broods of young each season.

FEEDING: Apart from field observations of the Greenfinch eating box-thorn and *Cotoneaster* berries and the seeds of white clover, nothing is known of its food preferences in Australia. In Britain the species eats mainly seeds, particularly those of thistles, daisies, wire-weeds, docks and grasses. Animal food is not important except in the breeding season. (J.L.McK)

337

# STARLINGS

The starlings are a large family of some one hundred and ten species that are found, naturally, in all continents except the Americas, but several have been widely distributed over the world by man. The family is largely tropical and reaches its greatest development in Indonesia. Only one species reaches Australia, the Shining Starling *Aplonis metallica* which migrates into north Queensland from New Guinea and breeds each spring. Two others, the common European Starling *Sturnus vulgaris* and the Common Mynah *Acridotheres tristis*, have been introduced to the continent and are now widespread. The Mynah has remained in the cities but the Starling has now spread more widely.

Starlings are medium to large birds, generally eighteen to forty centimetres in length. They are usually solidly built, have strong legs and bill, and are usually black or brown in colour but frequently have brightly iridescent plumage. They are omnivorous. Many are arboreal but several spend much time on the ground hopping strongly. All are more or less gregarious and some nest in very large colonies.

Family Sturnidae — Starlings and Mynahs
## STARLING *Sturnus vulgaris*

PLATE XXXIII

IDENTIFICATION: Length, 20 cm. Male: general colour, *blackish with pronounced metallic reflections*; feathers of upper-parts tipped with buff and of under-parts tipped with white; reflections on crown and nape, green or purple, and on the breast, bronze-green; tail feathers and primaries, black brown; bill, yellow; legs and feet, reddish-brown; iris, dark brown. The sexes are similar but the female is duller, the metallic reflections not so bright and the iris is brown but usually has a pale inner or outer ring.

Juveniles are dark grey above and brownish-grey below; the feathers of the tail and wing coverts are edged with buff; bill, grey-brown; legs and feet, dark grey. In the first winter they resemble adults but the buff and white tips to the feathers are larger, giving the whole bird a spotted appearance; the forehead is buff.

VOICE: The usual sound heard is a grating "tcheerr", but musical whistles and clicking sounds are also made. The song is a throaty warble, sometimes including some mimicry.

DISTRIBUTION: Its natural range is in the Northern Hemisphere, across Europe from Norway and England to Russia and in winter it migrates to the Mediterranean region. It has been introduced to, and is very numerous in, several other countries including Australia and

North America. Introduced to Victoria in the 1850s it has spread widely and is now distributed through that State, Tasmania, New South Wales and to as far north as central Queensland; it extends west through South Australia to the edge of the Nullarbor Plain, but has not crossed it. It is found in all cities and towns within its range, is widespread throughout agricultural districts, and has invaded some thinly settled pastoral districts where it now lives in the bush. It is widely distributed in the Australian Capital Territory but has been unable to penetrate the wet sclerophyll forests of the ranges.

HABITS: It spends much time on the ground in groups and flocks where it walks about rapidly feeding; its quick jerky walk with body held fairly erect is very characteristic. It is very sociable and in autumn and winter gathers into large flocks which feed in the parks and grass-lands, perch along great lengths of telegraph lines and at dusk fly to communal roosts in noisy massed flocks.

BREEDING: The breeding season is in the period August to December. The nest is an untidy heap of grass, straw, wool and other rubbish; it is cup-shaped at the top and is lined with softer materials including feathers, wool and leaves. The birds tend to nest in colonies and the nests are built in the ceilings of houses, crevices in buildings, cracks in rocks, and in tree holes. It is thought that this very hardy and vigorous bird competes successfully with more desirable native species for tree holes. The clutch varies from three to nine but is usually four or five. The eggs are very pale blue in colour and measure about $30 \times 21$ mm. The incubation period is twelve to thirteen days and the young fledge in about twenty-one days. Several successive broods are reared.

FEEDING: The Starling is omnivorous and feeds on the ground or in trees and bushes. On the ground it walks briskly, prodding with the bill to secure worms and insects and in bushes and trees it collects insects from the leaves, swallows small fruit whole and punctures larger fruits. It is considered a serious pest of fruit. There has been no study of the food in this area. (H.J.F.)

## COMMON MYNAH *Acridotheres tristis*

PLATE XXXV

IDENTIFICATION: Length, 26 cm. General colour of upper-parts, chocolate brown; under-parts paler; head, black with green sheen; nape, sides of neck and upper breast, dark brown; white belly stripe; under-tail coverts, white; tail, dark brown with white tips; wings, chocolate brown with large white "bullseye", seen when in flight; large patch of yellow skin around eye; bill, tarsus and toes, golden yellow;

iris, yellow. The sexes are similar. Immatures similar to adults but duller in appearance.

VOICE: Loud and raucous, the commonest notes being likened to "kiki-kiki" or "o-kick, o-kick"; also numerous chatterings, scoldings and squeaks.

DISTRIBUTION: Introduced from South-east Asia where it is widespread. It has been liberated in South Africa, New Zealand and islands in the Indian and Pacific Oceans as well as Australia. The bird can now be found in many of the larger cities and towns of eastern and southern Australia where its range appears to be expanding.

First recorded from the local area in May 1968, when two birds were seen at Campbell, and July 1968 when one was seen near Yass. Around the Canberra district it has gained a good foothold, particularly in the older suburbs, but is now also well established in some newer suburbs.

In the early 1970s it was established that the Common Mynah was being imported and released into Canberra intentionally by a well-meaning, but misguided citizen. Whether all of the birds now resident originated from this source is not known.

HABITS: The species is also known as the Indian Mynah. Because of its fearless nature it is a conspicuous bird wherever it occurs. Usually it is found in pairs or scattered groups, feeding on the ground in a rather jaunty fashion, or perched on a pole or wires where it is constantly calling or chattering. At night, noisy, jostling groups form in roosting areas under bridges or in trees. Unlike its relative, the Common or European Starling, it has not reached pest proportions, but must cause concern because it competes with native hole-nesting species for breeding space.

BREEDING: The breeding season is from September to March. The nest is a loose, untidy affair of grass, leaves, feathers and man-made material placed in any convenient hole in a building or similar structure, in holes in trees or amongst thick vegetation such as palm trees. From three to six pale blue eggs, measuring $31 \times 22$ mm, form the clutch.

Breeding is regularly recorded in many areas around Canberra.

FEEDING: Being a scavenger, the bird is omnivorous. It feeds on the ground in parks and gardens, rubbish dumps and edges of roads wherever it can find insects, fruit and seeds. Around market gardening areas it can be a nuisance pulling up small seedlings. (M.C.)

# ORIOLES

This is a remarkably homogeneous family of only twenty-eight species that is mainly tropical in distribution. They range from Africa across Asia, the Philippines and Malaysia to Australia. There are four species in Australia; two are known as fig-birds and two as orioles. In each of these two groups one species is restricted to the tropics and the other has a wider distribution down the east coast. Of the two orioles the Yellow Oriole *Oriolus flavocinctus* is restricted to the north while the Olive-backed Oriole *O. sagittatus* extends to the southern coast and visits our area.

All members of the family are medium sized, quite robust birds with strong, slightly down-curved, pointed bills. The wings are long and pointed and the birds are very swift in flight. They are all exclusively arboreal and feed on insects and fruit.

Family Oriolidae — Orioles
## OLIVE-BACKED ORIOLE *Oriolus sagittatus*

PLATE XXII

IDENTIFICATION: Length, 28 cm. General colour above, dusky green streaked with black; upper side of tail, dark grey; flight feathers, dark grey; upper-wing coverts, tinged with buff; underside, white prominently streaked with black; underside of tail, dark grey, each feather tipped with white; bill, orange-brown; legs and feet, blackish-blue; iris, orange. The sexes are similar.

VOICE: The voice is a monotonous whistle of three very similar notes with little difference in inflection. During feeding it utters a number of squeaks and chatters.

DISTRIBUTION: It extends from the Kimberley region of Western Australia across the north and down the east coast and to as far west as Adelaide. It is mainly coastal in distribution but extends inland in some places, as in south-western New South Wales where it occasionally penetrates mallee scrub and the timbered fringes of the rivers, some six hundred kilometres from the coast.

It is uncommon locally but a few birds are seen in most summers in savannah woodland. It arrives in early September and moves away again in April; none seem to remain over winter. In the north its main habitats are the monsoon forests and rainforests where it feeds together with fruit pigeons in the treetops but it also moves along timbered watercourses and more open country. In the north of New South Wales and in the Northern Territory it is clearly nomadic following the fruiting of various trees, but in our area it has regular movements.

341

HABITS: They are entirely arboreal and are usually seen in thick scrub or shrubs but rarely close to the ground. Owing to the density of the cover and their colour they are usually very inconspicuous. However, they are very active birds when feeding and the flight is swift and direct, though silent. When flying across open spaces the flight is distinctly undulating. In some places it is regularly shot illegally for food, this act being justified by the shooters by the local name Cedar Pigeon.

BREEDING: The breeding season in this region is in the period November to January. The nest is a deep cup fifteen to eighteen centimetres across and twelve to fifteen centimetres deep. It is built of strips of bark with some leaves, cocoons, lichens, and grass. It is lined with fine grasses. The nest is suspended by its rim in an outermost pendulous branch of a *Eucalyptus* or *Casuarina*. It is usually in open forest and often near the edge of denser forest. The clutch size is three or four. The eggs are fairly oval and measure about 35 × 23 mm. In colour they are cream, spotted and blotched with grey, brown and chestnut.

FEEDING: It feeds in the trees and probably never takes food from the ground. In north-east New South Wales it feeds very largely on fruit, wild figs, white cedar berries, camphor laurel berries and inkweeds. There is little fruit in the forest in our area and although there has been no study of the food there seems little doubt that it feeds mainly on insects. (H.J.F.)

## MUD-NEST BUILDERS

Two families of birds are notable for the fact that their members build bowl-shaped nests of mud. They were formerly placed in a single family but they appear to have little in common other than the type of nest they build.

### Family Grallinidae — Magpie-larks
There are two species in the family, one in Australia and the other in New Guinea. The Australian species is common and widely distributed. Pairs hold territories during the breeding season but they live in large flocks at other times. The New Guinea form on the other hand is rare, and lives permanently in pairs only along mountain streams.

### MAGPIE-LARK *Grallina cyanoleuca*
PLATE XXXIV

IDENTIFICATION: Length, 30 cm. Male: head, throat, back, part of wings and the posterior half of the tail, black; face, white with broad black stripe through eye; base and tip of the tail, the lower breast, abdomen and part of the wings, white; legs, black; bill, whitish-grey; iris, pale yellow. The female differs in having the forehead and throat white and by lacking the white stripe over the eye. For about three months after fledging the young have a compromise plumage — they have the male's white eyebrow, and the female's white throat.

VOICE: The main song consists of five notes delivered as a duet by the pair. One bird utters the first two and the other follows with the second three notes so well in time that it sounds like a continuous piece.

DISTRIBUTION: It occurs throughout Australia wherever there is surface water. Its range has probably been extended greatly by the provision of stock-water since settlement. There are no breeding records for Tasmania but a few visitors have been recorded there. Locally it is very common.

HABITS: Magpie-larks are strong fliers although they spend most of their time feeding on the ground. Their favourite haunts are the margins of farm dams and, next to this, bitumen roads, where, in contrast to the Magpie, they seem to live a charmed life and are seldom struck by cars. Pairs mate for life and are strongly territorial, defending an area of from six to eight hectares against intruders. Usually the territory includes a dam or water frontage of some sort. They are one of the first species to fly up in defence of their territory if a predator intrudes; even Wedge-tailed Eagles have been seen to be attacked persistently. In the autumn the territories are generally abandoned and quite large flocks of Magpie-larks congregate and forage together, a flock of up to 500 being recorded in Western Australia, but a flock of one hundred is large near Canberra. These flocks are particularly conspicuous in the evening before they move to roost; by July the gatherings are smaller and rarer as the territories become occupied again.

Too frequently to be by chance, these and other species of black and white birds, e.g., White-winged Chough, Willie Wagtail, Restless Flycatcher, and White-winged Triller, nest in the same tree at the same, or overlapping, time. Very little interspecific quarrelling occurs even though the nests may be only three metres apart. Probably some benefit from communal defence is achieved; certainly the number of watchful eyes is increased presumably reducing the chance that stealthy nest predation would be successful.

BREEDING: In other parts of its range nesting may start as early as August but on the highlands few eggs are laid before October and eggs

343

may still be laid as late as January. Farther north eggs may be laid as late as March. The nest is a small bowl made of mud and fibre lined with hair or fine grasses. It is plastered to a horizontal branch which, though bare itself, is usually well shaded from above. The diameter of the nest-bowl is about fifteen centimetres and it may weigh one kilogram. Thirty-six local nests were, on average, twelve metres above the ground. As with other widely distributed species, the kind of tree used varies considerably; locally seventy per cent of nests are in eucalypts and seventeen per cent in willows. In harsher environments telephone poles and windmills may be used. Because wet mud is used in nest building it is not surprising that the nests are usually near water.

Three to five eggs are laid; they are white or pink with purplish-brown spots and blotches and average 29 × 21 mm in size. Both parents incubate and feed the young which do not remain dependent for much more than a month after leaving the nest so that in good (i.e. "wet") years several broods may be raised in a season.

FEEDING: The birds are chiefly insectivorous and gather most of their food along the shallow, muddy margins of water. In much of Australia this habitat is also occupied by the freshwater snail *Lymnea tomentosa*, which is the intermediate host for liver fluke — a serious parasitic pest of cattle and sheep. Magpie-larks eat a considerable number of these snails. (I.C.R.R.)

Family Corcoraciidae — Apostle Bird and White-winged Chough
Apostle Birds and White-winged Choughs, the only two species in the family, are sociable birds and are usually found in groups of from five to twenty. Both have "soft" plumage which has a "fluffy" appearance in the hand compared to the sleeked plumage of most passerine birds. They have markedly similar calls and displays. Both forage mainly on the ground and both communally build mud and fibre bowl nests. With both species the young persist with the parental group at least until maturity and often beyond this; there is no sexual dimorphism but both species change in eye colour with increasing age.

## WHITE-WINGED CHOUGH *Corcorax melanorhamphos*
PLATE XXXIV

IDENTIFICATION: Length, 47 cm. Entirely black except for a *white patch, the size of a tennis ball, extending over all ten primaries* of each wing. Bill, black, thin and markedly down-curved; legs, long and black; feet, black. The sexes are similar. Fledglings retain two lines of nestling down above each eye until they are eight to nine weeks old; eye colour varies from brown to red and its colour is a reliable indicator of age. In the first year the eye is brown, in the second, brown with an orange-brown margin, in the third year it is orange with a brown inner ring and when adult, orange with yellow inner ring or red with orange ring.

VOICE: Calls mainly consist of single and double pipes and whistles which serve as contact calls, mild "alerts" and alarm signals. The aggressive call is a throaty "cree-ee-eek" and extreme alarm, reached when the birds are caught and handled, provokes a piercing, ear-shattering scream — even from newly fledged young.

DISTRIBUTION: Restricted to eastern Australia it is found from north Queensland through all of New South Wales and Victoria and most of South Australia. It does not occur in Tasmania.

Choughs are widespread and moderately common persisting tenaciously on sheeplands almost devoid of timber provided a token area of "forest" is available for nesting. They are one of the very few species which seems able to find food in the extensive exotic pine plantations. The species is largely sedentary.

HABITS: Choughs normally occur in groups of five to ten (range two to seventeen) throughout the year. They forage entirely on the ground and may cover a distance of 400 metres in half an hour. Sticks, stones, and leaves are turned over with the bill; they never rake the litter with their feet.

Choughs display by spreading the wings and tail and moving these parts up and down asynchronously. When excited for any reason the skin surrounding the eye is withdrawn exposing the "white" of the eye which rapidly becomes crimson as surface blood vessels engorge. Fighting is rare and the above display serves both as greeting and threat. When a group is attacked they rapidly form a scrum and face the attacker with spread wings and emitting a loud "hiss". This piebald mass effect is most successful in deterring attackers.

Groups of choughs are loosely territorial while breeding, occupying about fifty hectares which, because of the low density of the species, rarely needs defending. Once the young fledge they are cared for by the entire group. During autumn and winter these groups range over a larger area and may concentrate on particularly favourable food sources, such as grain stubbles, creating "clans" of up to one hundred birds. These are not flocks as they retain their group identities; apart from the coincidence of feeding sites they have no co-operative reaction, e.g., if put to flight they separate into groups.

BREEDING: Locally the breeding season is in the period September to January. The nest, shaped like a pudding basin, is made of mud and fibre and is placed on a horizontal limb of about seven centimetres in diameter and eight to twelve metres from the ground. All group members help to build and the nest takes about a week to complete and is then left for about another week to "cure". Copulation takes place on or beside the nest and eggs are laid on successive days. The clutch size is usually three to five but frequently more than one female lays in the nest so that the contents may be seven to nine eggs. The eggs are elliptical, creamy-white and strongly blotched in brown and grey. They measure 37–40 × 20–30 mm.

The eggs hatch in succession about twenty days after laying starts; with multiple clutches more than four nestlings have not been known to fledge from a nest. All eggs may hatch but frequently some don't and the size difference between the first and last hatched in a large clutch is so great that the chance of survival for the youngest is small, unless food is particularly abundant.

Nestlings remain in the nest for twenty-three to twenty-eight days and flutter to the ground before they can fly. For the next week the young run after the group, begging; when danger threatens they either scramble up sloping trunks, hop up trees, branch by branch, or else freeze motionless in the shade of a log.

Juvenile Choughs are completely dependent for several weeks after fledging. They are very slow to mature and are considerably lighter than older birds during their first winter. They have not been known to breed before they are four years old. Usually only one brood is raised per season, but if the group is very large it may fragment after the first nest has fledged, part caring for the fledglings and the remainder renesting.

FEEDING: A wide range of food is eaten, ranging in size from ants to frogs, and all is gathered from the ground. Scarab grubs are a favourite item procured from under rotting timber; several may be carried at once transversely in the bill when feeding nestlings. In winter seeds form a significant part of their diet and the species probably has benefited from the introduction of grain-cropping into their environment. Christmas beetles, grasshoppers, moths, etc. are all eaten. (I.C.R.R.)

## APOSTLE BIRD *Struthidea cinerea*

PLATE XXXIV

IDENTIFICATION: Length, 33 cm. General colour, grey with lighter tips to the feathers of the head, neck and throat; wings, brown; tail, black with a greenish gloss; bill, black; legs and feet, black; iris, dark grey with a creamy-pearl outer ring. The sexes are alike.

In juveniles the light grey tipping to the feathers of the head, neck and throat is less distinct and the iris is brown.

VOICE: In the breeding season, a variety of squeaky, animated calls are given, very often from the vicinity of a nest. Another commonly heard call, usually given in alarm by the whole group, is a loud discordant note resembling "ch-kew-ch-kew".

DISTRIBUTION: The range extends from central Northern Territory east and south throughout Queensland, excluding only the heavily timbered coastal regions, and New South Wales generally west of the Great Dividing Range. It rarely crosses the Murray River into Victoria and extends to Morgan and Adelaide in South Australia. It is included in this book on the basis of a single observation in 1948. Normally the range terminates some kilometres west of the Capital Territory in woodland country between Temora and Harden, New South Wales. The preferred habitat is lightly timbered country such as brigalow, cypress pine, belar and box on the green fringes of inland watercourses.

HABITS: Apostle Birds are sociable and live in family groups of from about four to twenty. The group consists of a dominant adult pair together with their progeny of several previous years. In the inland, congregations of several hundred birds have been seen, usually near watercourses, but these should not be regarded as true flocks as they are merely drawn together by a common food source or by water. Like many predominantly seed-eating species, Apostle Birds are closely associated with water. In hot weather they drink several times a day and also bathe frequently. They are commonly seen feeding beside the road in the inland and are often found around station homesteads where they become quite tame.

During the breeding season the group maintains a territory in which they breed and feed. These territories are defended by the whole group. They have no effective territorial song and fighting usually only occurs, as a short skirmish, between two groups if they have unwittingly been foraging on a collision course. During the non-breeding season, the area needed to maintain the group and their young increases, the boundaries of the breeding territory break down, and the birds wander over a much larger area, often feeding in close proximity to several other groups on some common food source. At this time, some interchange of juveniles occurs. However, each group maintains its identity and usually retires to a regular roost in thick foliage which may be quite close to the nesting area. Apostle Birds are quite sedentary and maintain the same territory from year to year. Only severe drought

347

would cause them to move more than a few kilometres in their lifetime.

BREEDING: The breeding season is normally from August to December and often more than one brood is raised by the same group in the one season. However, it is possible that the different clutches could be laid by separate females. The bowl-shaped nest is about fifteen centimetres in diameter and is built of mud reinforced with grass and lined with fine grass inside. It is usually fixed to a horizontal or slightly sloping branch of a shrub or tree at heights from two to fifteen metres. When building, birds prefer to use the fresh mud formed immediately after a shower of rain and the source is rarely more than fifty metres from the nest site. In dry years they will use Emu dung which forms an efficient substitute. The dung is usually used to refurbish an old nest, rather than to build a complete new structure. Several birds in a group assist in building the nest as in the case of the White-winged Chough. The clutch size varies from two to five, and four is the most common. Records of larger clutches, up to eight eggs, are rare and are the result of two females laying in the one nest. The eggs are oval in shape and measure about $29 \times 22$ mm. They are off-white in colour and are sparingly marked with blackish-brown and slate-grey spots and streaks. The incubation period is nineteen days and the young remain in the nest for about twenty-three days. The whole group co-operates in the feeding of the nestlings but the parent male and female dominate these activities. When the young ones leave the nest they are barely able to fly and remain perched in the vegetation near the nest for about a week.

FEEDING: Apostle Birds forage almost entirely on the ground, moving together in a compact group. In spring and summer, insects form a large part of the diet but in winter, when insects are scarce, they feed almost entirely on small seeds. They use their short, thick bills in a vertical motion, sparrow fashion, and in so doing, take quite a lot of grit as well. (G.S.C.)

# WOOD-SWALLOWS

The Wood-swallows are very graceful birds and, in some ways, their flight is like that of the swallows but they are not related to that group. Their nearest relatives are not known. They are sufficiently different from other birds to be placed in a family of their own. Little has been published on the group but modern thought tends to place them near to the family Cracticidae. The family is typically Australian and consists of ten species, all quite similar in appearance and belonging to a single genus, *Artamus*. Six of these occur in Australia. Four are restricted to the continent, a fifth just reaches Timor and New Guinea, while the sixth, the most widespread of all, extends as far as the Andaman and Philippine Islands. The birds are generally quietly coloured; greys, browns and whites predominating. They are very agile in flight, feed entirely on insects gathered mainly on the wing and have a characteristic wing silhouette, rather similar to that of the introduced Starling. Some species are relatively sedentary but most wood-swallows are nomadic and are adapted to move and breed rapidly in response to the irregular rainfall of the inland.

Family Artamidae — Wood-swallows
## DUSKY WOOD-SWALLOW *Artamus cyanopterus*
PLATE XXXIII

IDENTIFICATION: Length, 18 cm. Sepia-brown above and below; wings and tail, black; *when the wings are closed a narrow white line marks the edge*; tips of the tail feathers, white; iris, dark brown; bill, grey-blue with a black tip; legs, slaty-grey and very short. The sexes are alike. Juveniles have a mottled plumage.

VOICE: Both pairs and flocks keep up a persistent twittering which presumably serves to maintain contact. They also have a strident call which they utter when mobbing larger birds. Courtship is silent and although they do mimic other species they do not do so as frequently as other wood-swallows.

DISTRIBUTION: It is mainly a southern species. In Western Australia it is restricted to the south-west and seems to be decreasing in range. It extends across the continent in a narrow corridor south of the transcontinental railway and is distributed throughout Victoria and the south-western half of New South Wales. It extends up the Queensland coast in a belt of country that seldom exceeds 320 km in width, but becomes rare on Cape York. In eastern Australia it is usually found in woodland savannah. During the non-breeding season the species flocks and tends to move northwards. The Capital Territory is usually deserted by wood-swallows from April to August but in mild winters a few individuals remain. In Victoria the birds also leave in winter but it is usual for numbers to remain. Around Sydney, New South Wales, apparently the migration is not so marked as elsewhere in the south-east.

HABITS: When they arrive in the spring they are in small flocks of from ten to thirty birds. These tend to form "neighbourhoods" of breeding pairs each of which maintains a small territory containing the nest. When nesting one parent incubates at night and the other perches nearby. Foraging is mainly done outside the territory. Neighbouring pairs frequently join forces to mob intruders of larger species, e.g. birds of prey, in which activity they are quite fearless, pressing home the attack to the extent of body blows. Kookaburras, Ravens, Brown Hawks, Grey Currawongs and Nankeen Kestrels have been seen to be mobbed.

Courtship feeding occurs. Copulation is preceded by a display involving both members of the pair who perch close together and begin gently fluttering their part-open wings and at the same time rotating the half-spread tail. Particularly during the non-breeding season, they roost at night in dense clusters, sometimes up to 200 individuals, hanging onto the trunk of a tree.

BREEDING: The small nest is an open-work structure of twigs, rootlets, or pieces of grass through which it is sometimes possible to see the eggs or young. However, it is more substantial than that of the other wood-swallows. It is frequently placed in the top of a dead tree stump, or even a fence-post. Sometimes it is placed behind a part-loose piece of bark on a living tree and more rarely is built in a crotch or even in the outer foliage of a live eucalypt. Twenty-four local nests were, on an average, four metres above the ground and ranged from one to eleven metres. Either three or four eggs form the clutch, the former being more common. The eggs are elliptical and white with purplish-brown blotches, particularly at the thicker end. Ten eggs averaged $23 \times 17$ mm in size. Incubation takes sixteen days and the nestlings remain in the nest for sixteen to twenty days depending on the availability of food, the number of nestlings being fed and the weather. Both parents share incubation and care of the young. After fledging the young are dependent for about a month before the "neighbourhood" departs as a flock and forages nomadically.

In the area covered by this book the species is single-brooded and most nesting is completed by Christmas. However, pairs which fail at a first attempt may renest and this accounts for the few nests found in January. Banding results suggest that nestlings persist with the "neighbourhood" flock and that the same birds return to the same area each year to nest.

FEEDING: It is entirely insectivorous and captures most of its prey on the wing but does also make flycatcher-like sorties from favourite perches and at times takes insects on the ground. A wide variety of insects are taken, some as large as grasshoppers, but the majority are smaller. Apiarists blame the species for taking bees. (I.C.R.R.)

## WHITE-BROWED WOOD-SWALLOW *Artamus superciliosus*
PLATE XXXIII

IDENTIFICATION: Length, 19 cm. Head, throat and upper-parts, dark grey; a narrow black band reaches from the eye to the bill and above this runs the *conspicuous white eyebrow* which broadens to the rear; *under-parts, rich rufous-brown* distinguishing this species from any other wood-swallow; outer tail feathers are white-tipped; legs, grey; eye, brown; bill, blue-grey, tipped with black. The female is uniformly duller in colour and its eyestripe is less pronounced. Juveniles are mottled.

In flight the characteristic wing shape, gliding flight, and rufous under-parts are diagnostic.

VOICE: Twittering contact calls are similar to, but quite distinct from, those of the Dusky Wood-swallow. This species also has a harsh aggressive or mobbing call when warding off intruders. It is well-known for its mimicry which covers a wide range of bush birds but the function of this is unknown.

DISTRIBUTION: Both the White-browed Wood-swallow and the Masked Wood-swallow mingle in mixed-species flocks and wander extensively over the continent, wintering mainly in the tropics. Throughout much of their range the ratio in these flocks is nearly equal but the White-browed predominates in the east and the Masked in the west. Neither species reaches Tasmania and they are rare on the eastern seaboard. Mixed matings between these two species have been recorded. A few pairs breed near Canberra in most years; if there is a drought inland these numbers may rise considerably as happened in 1965 spring. The extent to which individual birds wander is at present unknown but both species are well adapted to irregular rainfall in an arid environment. They are so mobile that no particular habitat can really be ascribed to them but arid scrublands and grassland savannah are most favoured.

HABITS: Both the White-browed and the Masked Wood-swallow are highly sociable and are usually encountered in mixed flocks of up to two hundred birds. When perched both species indulge in a lot of mutual preening, and at night they roost in large clusters clinging to the trunks of trees.

BREEDING: The two species build similar, scanty nests, less substantial than that of the Dusky Wood-swallow, of rootlets, twigs, grasses or herbs, and no special lining is provided so that nests are semi-transparent and well ventilated. A wide variety of sites are used

351

ranging from bushes and small trees, to dead stumps and rotting fence-posts. Twenty-five local nests were, on average, three metres above ground. Of sixteen completed clutches, thirteen contained two eggs and three contained three. The eggs are laid early in the morning. Both sexes incubate, the female by night, and both feed the young; incubation in our climate takes sixteen days and the young fledge when fifteen days old; these times are apparently shortened when the species breeds in the warmer inland. After breeding the flock abandons the colony and resumes its nomadic existence but, sometimes, renesting pairs remain behind.

The eggs of both species are greyish or pale brownish white heavily marked with spots and smudges of brown. They are tapered oval in shape and measure about 22 × 17 mm.

In the better watered parts of the continent such as represented by this region, breeding takes place in the late spring and early summer. In more arid areas the species is adapted to respond rapidly to rainfall.

FEEDING: Like other wood-swallows, the White-browed and the Masked are entirely insectivorous, gathering most of their prey on the wing in loose flocks. They also forage extensively on the ground, especially if a strong wind is blowing and are also frequently seen feeding among blossoming *Eucalyptus*. (I.C.R.R.)

## MASKED WOOD-SWALLOW *Artamus personatus*
PLATE XXXIII

IDENTIFICATION: Length, 19 cm. Male: upper-parts, entirely medium grey except for white band at the tip of the tail; under-parts, pale grey shading to white on under-tail coverts; *face, lores, ear coverts and throat, black* and this area is separated from the grey body plumage by a *narrow, white collar*; bill, blue-grey, tipped black; legs and feet, dark grey; eye, black. The female has the same plumage pattern as the male but is browner and the separations between colours are less distinct. The juveniles are mottled.

DISTRIBUTION: It is rare in the Australian Capital Territory; see under White-browed Wood-swallow for details.

VOICE, BREEDING, HABITS: See under White-browed Wood-swallow; the eggs and nests of these two species are indistinguishable, and mixed breeding colonies are common. (I.C.R.R.)

## BLACK-FACED WOOD-SWALLOW *Artamus cinereus*
PLATE XXXIII

IDENTIFICATION: Length, 18 cm. Colour above and below, grey-brown; wings, grey; *tail, black tipped with white; a small area around the eyes and including the forehead, chin and cheeks, black*; bill, blue-grey, tipped black; legs and feet, grey; eye, brown. The absence of a white wing margin, the generally greyer colour and the black face separate this species from the Dusky Wood-swallow. The sexes are alike. The juvenile is mottled.

VOICE: A persistent twittering contact call similar to, but distinct from, other wood-swallows.

DISTRIBUTION: This resident species replaces the Dusky Wood-swallow throughout the inland of Australia and on the coast in the north, north-east and west. A rare straggler to our area it is common immediately to the west of it.

HABITS: Like the Dusky Wood-swallow this species tends to be more resident than nomadic (cf. White-browed and Masked). It is probably the most unselective of the wood-swallows with regard to nest sites, frequently nesting in bare, dead shrubs, the metal frames to radio masts, and even inside sheds.

BREEDING: The breeding season is mainly September to December. The nest is similar to that of the Dusky Wood-swallow, but less substantial. Clutch size is usually four, and the oval eggs are pinkish-white with red-brown spottings. They measure about 22 × 17 mm.

FEEDING: It is entirely insectivorous and feeds as the other wood-swallows. (I.C.R.R.)

# MAGPIES AND RAVENS

Australia has many birds that are all black or black and white and prominent among them are the two families discussed here; the family Corvidae, ravens and crows, and the family Cracticidae, magpies, currawongs and butcher-birds. Some of the members of the two families are superficially similar in appearance but they constitute quite distinct groups of birds with very different habits. They are put together here merely for convenience.

Family Cracticidae—Currawongs, Butcher-birds and Magpies
This purely Australian family includes the well-known magpies, currawongs and butcher-birds that, to some extent, occupy the niches of the jays, crows and jackdaws of other countries, members of the family Corvidae that is poorly represented in Australia. They range in length

from twenty to sixty centimetres and are solid birds with large heads and strong legs. All are omnivorous but largely insectivorous. The general coloration is black and white and their bills are characteristically dagger-like, usually hooked at the tip and massive. Their flight is strong and they are arboreal, often gregarious, and usually noisy.

The Black-backed Magpie and four species of butcher-bird occur in New Guinea but currawongs do not. Magpies have been introduced to New Zealand where no native members of the family occur. Otherwise the family is confined to Australia. Many of these birds appear to have benefited from settlement; they are frequently seen close to habitation but, apart from limited fruit damage, little conflict arises.

## PIED CURRAWONG *Strepera graculina*

PLATE XXXIV

IDENTIFICATION: Length, 49 cm. General colour, black, with *white showing clearly towards the bases of the primaries, on the rump, base and tips of the tail feathers* and on the under-tail coverts; bill and feet, black; iris, yellow. The sexes are alike. Juveniles are brownish in colour and show less white.

In flight the *white wing patches and the white base of the upper surface of the tail* are diagnostic.

VOICE: The loud ringing double call from which the genus probably takes its name may be rendered as "curra-wong". It is frequently uttered in flight and is probably the commonest bird call to be heard in Canberra during the winter months.

DISTRIBUTION: It is widespread in eastern Australia from Cape York to South Australia, but is mainly coastal in distribution. Although largely a forest species, it has adapted to settlement well and occurs on the inland plains though mainly confined to watercourses and townships. Its range overlaps that of the Grey Currawong, but is far more extensive. It breeds in forest country but in the autumn and winter is nomadic forming large flocks. This movement is largely an altitudinal shift and large flocks appear in towns on the highlands during winter. The build-up in numbers starts in April reaching a peak in July and falls off late in August. Some remain all the year round and nesting is commonly observed in Canberra suburbs.

HABITS: They are very active and noisy. In the ranges they are usually found in groups in fairly tall timber or flying high overhead. They land in the trees very noisily. In winter, when they frequent suburban gardens, they hop swiftly across lawns and fences and feed in low ornamental shrubs. The winter concentrations in Canberra have been shown to use a communal roosting place to which they fly in noisy flocks in the late afternoon.

BREEDING: The nests are not very often found as they are widely dispersed in tall forest in the ranges. They are usually placed six to twenty metres up in a eucalypt crotch. The nest is made of sticks and while usually larger than that of the magpie is smaller than that of a Raven and the sticks used are also intermediate in size. The bowl is lined with fibrous roots, dried grasses and bark. The average clutch is three and the average size of the eggs is 40 × 28 mm. The eggs are oval or elongate-oval in shape, light brown, and marked with blotches or freckles of darker brown.

FEEDING: Currawongs are omnivorous. They take young nestling birds and will feed on carrion, but are locally mainly insectivorous, although in the summer they may become a nuisance in orchards where they eat and damage fruit. The flocks seen in Canberra during the winter feed largely on berries and insect larvae, the latter frequently obtained from lawns. A study, by CSIRO Division of Entomology, of stick insects that defoliate stands of eucalypts on the southern highlands suggests that the Pied Currawong may be an important predator of these pests, particularly when the latter are at low numbers. (I.C.R.R.)

## GREY CURRAWONG *Strepera versicolor*
PLATE XXXIV

IDENTIFICATION: Length, 47 cm. Male: very similar in all dimensions to the Pied Currawong from which it differs in being grey-brown above and below. The tip of the tail, the under-tail coverts and a "window" in the wing are all white; *the rump and upper-tail coverts are grey-brown*, not white as in the Pied Currawong; bill and feet, black; iris, yellow. The female is similar but smaller.

VOICE: A ringing call of five notes often uttered in flight. The species is not so vocal as the Pied Currawong.

DISTRIBUTION: The Grey Currawong has a distribution covering the whole of southern Australia. It ranges throughout south-west Western Australia and across the extreme south of the continent to South Australia. It is distributed throughout the south-east to as far inland as the beginning of the plains and to as far north as south-east Queensland. Locally it is uncommon.

HABITS: The species is primarily a forest dweller where it is usually encountered in pairs or small family parties. Early authors described large flocks that behaved in a very similar manner to Pied Currawongs in the non-breeding season but such a sight is very rare nowadays as the species appears to have declined greatly in numbers. Some congregations occur in orchard districts as fruit ripens, but these are usually small. In winter single birds and pairs may forage in more open habitat than that in which they breed and the species appears to be much more local in its movements than the Pied Currawong although there are no banding data to support this yet.

BREEDING: Inland and in milder climates it may breed as early as July but locally eggs are generally laid in September and October. Two to three eggs form the clutch and they are light brown in colour blotched and spotted with dark brown; the average size is 48 × 30 mm. The nest is similar to that of the magpie but is slightly larger and of more open construction. The lining is generally of coarse rootlets and grass. The site chosen may be from three to fifteen metres above the ground, generally in secondary forks of eucalypts. Incubation and nestling periods are not known but the fledglings remain largely dependent on parental feeding for several months and family parties persist until autumn.

FEEDING: Besides insects, wild fruits and berries, currawongs raid the eggs and young of many other forest nesting birds and orchardists experience some trouble from them when fruit is ripening. The birds are equally at home on the ground or in the trees, probing litter, bark or foliage in search of insects and berries. (I.C.R.R.)

## PIED BUTCHER-BIRD *Cracticus nigrogularis*

IDENTIFICATION: Length, 35 cm. Head, neck, breast, most of wings and tail, *upper back and throat, black*; collar, lower breast and abdomen, white; there is a white wing bar, and the outer tail feathers are tipped with white; bill, blue-grey with black tip, and strongly hooked; legs, black; eyes, brown. The sexes are similar. Young birds are brownish instead of black and may be easily confused with the Grey Butcher-bird, especially as the young of the latter species are also brown coloured.

DISTRIBUTION: The Pied Butcher-bird is distributed throughout mainland Australia except for the far south-west and south-east but is most abundant in the tropics. It does not occur in Tasmania and is rare on the coast of New South Wales south of Sydney. Locally there are few records.

VOICE, HABITS, BREEDING: See under the Grey Butcher-bird. (I.C.R.R.)

## GREY BUTCHER-BIRD *Cracticus torquatus*

PLATE XXXIV

IDENTIFICATION: Length, 30 cm. Head, cheeks and tail, black, the last with a faint white tip; *back and wings, grey*; rump, collar, wing bar and *throat, white*; remainder of under-parts, dirty white; bill, blue-grey and black at the tip, which is strongly hooked; legs, grey-black; eyes, red-brown. The sexes are similar. Young birds have those areas that are black in the adults, brownish, making them easily confused with the young of the Pied Butcher-bird.

DISTRIBUTION: The Grey Butcher-bird ranges over southern and eastern Australia except for the extreme south-east of New South Wales and the extreme south-west of Western Australia. It is common in Tasmania. In Western Australia it reaches as far north as Wiluna and in the centre to Alice Springs, while in the east it reaches some distance north of Cairns in north Queensland. It is also found in the Northern Kimberleys, Western Australia, and the most northerly part of the Northern Territory. Over much of this area it coexists with the Pied Butcher-bird. Locally it is resident in very small numbers.

VOICE: Butcher-birds have varied rolling songs with flute-like notes, which may be sung as a duet by the pair, and are heard throughout the year. Their aggressive and alarm calls are strident by contrast. The quality of the Grey Butcher-bird's song does not quite reach that of the Pied Butcher-bird. Both species appear to have a ventriloquial component in their song which makes them extremely hard to locate. Some mimicry has been recorded, the purpose of which is not understood.

HABITS: Both species of butcher-bird are resident in a wide variety of habitats over most of inland Australia and parts of the coast, wherever open forest and scrublands occur. The two species may occur together in which case competition between them occurs and the Grey Butcher-bird, being smaller, usually comes off worse. No detailed study of this species has yet been done so the territory size is not known.

BREEDING: As might be expected for species with such a wide distribution, nest sites are very diverse depending on what is available. The nest is usually two to ten metres from the ground in the main crotch of a shrub or small tree; it is about twenty-three centimetres in diameter and consists of an outer basket of small twigs loosely inter-

357

laced and an inner lining of grasses and roots, the latter making the main part of the nest.

Three to five eggs form the clutch and the eggs are very variable in colour, but generally of a pale greenish-brown ground colour with darker specklings and occasional black spots. Average size is 31 × 23 mm compared with 33 × 24 mm for the Pied Butcher-bird.

In New South Wales most eggs are laid in September and October, but laying as early as July is reported further north. The females incubate the eggs for twenty-three days, but both birds, and sometimes last year's offspring also, feed the nestlings, which stay in the nest for about four weeks. Immature birds often stay with their parents for more than a year after leaving the nest.

FEEDING: Although largely insectivorous, these birds are efficient predators of other, smaller birds which they frequently chase and sometimes catch. Unguarded nestling birds are readily eaten, as are lizards, mice and occasionally carrion. They frequently and cheekily scavenge camp sites. Butcher-birds commonly forage from a convenient lookout post, much of their prey being captured on the ground. Quite often large insects may be battered to pieces on a stone serving as an anvil. Sometimes they cache surplus food in crevices. (I.C.R.R.)

## BLACK-BACKED MAGPIE *Gymnorhina tibicen*

PLATE XXXIV

IDENTIFICATION: Length, 44 cm. Male: black on head, back, under-parts, tail-tip and wing primaries; white on nape, rump, rest of tail, shoulder of wing and under-wings; iris, orange-brown; bill, blue-grey with black tip; legs, black. Female: similar, except that lower nape and rump are greyish and bill usually shorter. The grey on the lower nape varies, is not always easy to see in the field, and becomes completely white in a few females. The dark parts of juveniles, especially breast and abdomen, are mottled grey or buff during the first year, and vestiges of this remain in a few second-year birds; the bill is dark until the blue colour develops in the second year. Northern birds, in Queensland, are slightly smaller than southern ones.

The White-backed Magpie is similar in size, colour and habits, except that the male has a pure white back and the female and juveniles a grey one. This sub-species, and intergrades with varying amounts of black and white, or grey, on the back, occur sparingly in the area. All plumage forms interbreed and produce viable fertile offspring, while a black-backed pair can have young with grey on the back; thus they constitute a single species of two sub-species, *G. t. hypoleuca* the White-backed Magpie and *G. t. tibicen* the Black-backed Magpie. A further sub-species *G. t. dorsalis* is found in Western Australia.

VOICE: The powerful carol of these birds, singly and by social groups, serves to advertise territory and is heard throughout the year, best early in the morning during spring. There is also a harsh, aggressive call used during boundary and other fights, and a short thin note is given when a bird is disturbed or has lost contact with others of its group. The young have a loud and insistent begging call which may last for months after they leave the nest.

DISTRIBUTION: *G. tibicen* is common in suitable habitat in much of Australia. In the south-west the Western Magpie, *G. t. dorsalis*, occurs (which has a white-backed male and a black-backed female). Alice Springs has black-backed and intergrade forms of *tibicen*, which also extends to New Guinea. The region exclusively occupied by the white-backed form includes the southern end of the Great Dividing Range from 36°S (Cooma-Narooma) and a coastal belt rarely exceeding 160 kilometres through southern New South Wales, Victoria and South Australia, as well as the whole of Tasmania. The species has been introduced to New Zealand, where both *tibicen* and *hypoleuca* occur.

HABITS: Magpies are strongly territorial all the year round, and owners of good territories in open woodland with adjacent pasture remain sedentary within stable boundaries. Most territories are five to fifteen hectares, and none smaller than four hectares has supported successful breeding. Two or three adults in each territorial group is normal, but this may increase temporarily to as many as seven, with a maximum of four of either sex. The largest known group contained ten birds, including immatures. Females usually outnumber males, and a group of four adults may contain a dominant bigamous, or even trigamous, cock or consist of two more-or-less socially equal pairs.

Loose flocks of a few to several hundred magpies forage on open pasture and roost in denser woodland not suitable for territories. These consist of immature birds evicted from territories in their first or second year, older individuals that have not yet attained territorial status, and remnants of groups that disintegrate when the death of a dominant member weakens their ability to resist intruders. Social groups form in the flocks, and vacancies in the limited breeding habitat are rapidly filled by these or by individuals of the required sex. Males outnumber females in the flock, and local nomadic movements alter the location of the flock from season to season.

Magpies have readily adapted to human settlement, are common in agricultural and suburban areas with trees, are thinly distributed or

359

absent in dry country, and soon occupy clearings in woodland or new plantings in open pasture. They still suffer heavy casualties on roads, especially the juveniles. Individual as well as group aggression is highly developed, leading to peck-order within the group; in extreme cases a dominant hen may prevent a subordinate one from building, or may even destroy its eggs. Magpies commonly attack other species of birds within their territory, and in the breeding season some individuals persistently swoop at humans anywhere near the nest. A leafy branch held above the head absorbs these attacks.

BREEDING: Most females breed at two or three years old, but some are later and a few one-year-old hens in mottled plumage have bred. Males are sexually mature in their first year but have to wait several years to attain breeding status in the group or to acquire a territory of their own.

The female selects the site and builds the nest, commonly six to fifteen metres above ground in the outer canopy of a gum or other tree. Where good sites are lacking, nesting may be attempted on a telephone pole, low bush, or even on the ground. The nest is smaller than the Raven's or currawong's, the sticks are finer, wire may be used, and the lining consists of wool, hair, grass, etc. Laying is from August to October. The clutch ranges from one to six, but averages three or four. The magpie is single-brooded though some relaying occurs after failure. Eggs are 37 × 27 mm on average, and usually blue-green with many brownish spots, but the colour range is wide. The female alone incubates, but is sometimes fed on the nest by the male, and the incubation period is twenty to twenty-one days. The male may help to feed the nestlings of the brood that hatches first, but his contribution varies a lot. The young fledge in about four weeks and continue to be dependent on the parents for up to two months.

The reproductive rate is far below potential, due to non-breeding females in flocks and territories, and to high egg and chick losses. The average is one free-flying young for every two adult territorial hens, but this varies greatly according to weather and to the food-and-shelter quality and road traffic hazards of each territory.

FEEDING: The magpie feeds chiefly on surface soil invertebrates of all kinds, but is omnivorous and takes frogs, lizards, small birds on occasion, carrion, grain and even garbage. (R.C.)

### Family Corvidae — Ravens and Crows

The well known ravens and crows are related to the Northern Hemisphere jays and magpies; the Australian magpies belong to a different family. Ravens and crows are members of a large family of 103 species separated into twenty-six genera, members of which occur on every continent, with Australia and South America least well represented. Only one genus, *Corvus*, is found in Australia and this has a nearly cosmopolitan distribution and is thought by many to contain some of the most adaptable species of birds.

Australia has five species of the genus *Corvus*, two "crows" and three "ravens"; the former have white bases to the body feathers, while the latter have dirty grey bases. Four of these species are restricted to Australia; one also occurs in New Guinea. Only two ravens are known to occur in the area covered by this book. Although "crows" have been recorded in the past, these records are probably due to faulty identification since, until recently, identification of the various crows and ravens has been very confusing. The known distribution of the "crows" does not come within 300 kilometres of our area.

Unfortunately, ravens and crows are mainly scavengers and their foraging frequently brings them into conflict with man's agricultural activities; they are widely regarded as vermin and persecuted. Despite this largely erroneous view, however, they manage to thrive and are some of the commonest of birds.

## AUSTRALIAN RAVEN *Corvus coronoides*
### PLATE XXXIV

IDENTIFICATION: Length, 52 cm. *Colour all over, shining black,* with a bluish sheen when viewed in certain lights; *prominent throat hackles conspicuous when calling; extensive unfeathered area of black loose skin under the chin*; bill and legs, black as is the inside of the mouth; iris, white with a blue inner ring. Both sexes are similar but within any pair the male is the larger bird.

Nestlings have brownish-black body feathers but soon moult these after leaving the nest; the inside of the mouth and the skin under the chin is pink and this gradually changes over the next two years to black. Eye-colour also changes with age, being gun-metal in the nest and brown soon after fledging, traces of white begin to appear during the second winter and the eye reaches its adult colouring by the time the bird is about thirty months old.

Ravens have a rapid powerful flight. When perched, the tail scarcely protrudes beyond the longest primaries in profile.

VOICE: Probably one of the best known of bird calls, the territorial call of the Australian Raven is also one of the best characters for separating the two species of raven. The Australian Raven usually gives this call from a prominent position and tends to fan the long throat hackles conspicuously as it does so; it usually consists of four "cars", the last one becoming a prolonged gargle on a downwards inflection.

361

Both sexes give this and other calls in their repertoire, which include an alarm "quark", a panic or mobbing call, and a subdued chortle or rattle.

DISTRIBUTION: It extends through eastern and southern Australia, east of a line joining Brunette Downs, Northern Territory, Oodnadatta and Kingoonya, South Australia, and thence south of the transcontinental railway to Perth, Western Australia. It does not occur in Tasmania. Ravens are found throughout the region of this book except for a few areas of dense forest.

Breeding Ravens occupy territories all the year round and are therefore residents. Immatures or adults which have failed to find a mate or territory are not restrained in this way and live in nomadic flocks which may travel hundreds of kilometres. Movements from the area under discussion are random, from data obtained by banding several hundred birds. However, the forested area to the east and north of the Capital Territory appears to hinder movement in these directions. While some juveniles travel widely after leaving the parental groups, others remain locally for the rest of their lives.

HABITS: They are encountered singly, in pairs, small groups or large flocks (sometimes with Little Ravens) depending on season and food availability. Regular counts of birds seen in the area show a constant number of resident pairs, enlarging to family groups late in the spring or augmented thereafter by nomadic flocks during the summer, feeding on grasshoppers and grain stubbles, and in winter scavenging among lambing flocks of sheep and on cultivation paddocks.

BREEDING: Despite the large range occupied by the species, breeding is confined to the spring with a peak of egg-laying early in August. Pairs, once formed, persist until a partner dies, and courtship displays are therefore brief and unspectacular. They consist of aerial chases which do not reach the spectacular limits of the Northern Hemisphere Raven. Mutual preening between members of a pair is frequent in the autumn and winter and presumably helps to strengthen the pair-bond.

Nests are substantial baskets of twigs usually placed in a secondary crotch of a mature tree; few are built less than fifteen metres from the ground and some are twenty-five metres. Since savannah woodland is ideal Raven habitat and yellow box *Eucalyptus melliodora* the dominant tree in much of this community, it is the commonest nest site locally. The nests are well lined with bark and wool which is felted into a compact mat, some about two centimetres thick; rags, hair, string and even wire may also be included; it is sufficiently dense to resist charges from a shotgun.

The average clutch size is four, although as many as six and as few as two are known. The average egg dimensions are 46 × 30 mm. Incubation lasts from nineteen to twenty-one days and the young remain in the nest for forty-two to forty-five days. After fledging they become less dependent on parental feeding and by January or February join passing nomadic flocks and leave the natal territory.

FEEDING: Ravens are omnivorous birds. Despite their massive and ferocious-looking bill they are remarkably inefficient at penetrating intact animal carcasses; their bills are best adapted for probing into cracks and crevices and turning over branches, cowpats, etc. Insects make up the largest part of their diet, with grain second and carrion only third on the list. If sickly animals are discounted, and these would rarely be found until dead anyway, the number of true cases of predation of stock is extremely small. The insects eaten include grasshoppers, phasmids, Christmas beetles, pasture grubs, crickets and moth larvae. (I.C.R.R.)

## LITTLE RAVEN *Corvus mellori*

PLATE XXXIV

IDENTIFICATION: Length, 50 cm. A large black bird *very similar to the Australian Raven* from which it differs in having the *interramal area of the lower mandible well-feathered*, whereas the Australian Raven has an extensive bare area there, the skin being relatively loose. Throat hackles are shorter, less specialised and inconspicuous. The eye colour changes more rapidly and the Little Raven has fully white eyes by the time it is two years old.

VOICE: The difference in the aggressive calls of the two ravens is quite striking once recognised. Although they both last about four seconds, the Little Raven utters twice as many syllables and does not have the long, drawn out terminal gargle. Both sexes call and the repertoire includes alarm, panic, and mobbing calls, and a "conversational" subdued rattle.

DISTRIBUTION: It is confined to south-eastern Australia, and King Island in Bass Strait. Its western limit is slightly west of Ceduna, South Australia. The northern limit of the species may be taken as a line drawn from Ceduna through Port Augusta, South Australia, and Menindee, Nyngan and Narrabri, to Armidale, New South Wales. It is rare and probably only occurs as a straggler east of the Great Dividing Range in New South Wales. It is common throughout Victoria especially on the high plains and the treeless Western Districts.

HABITS: Little Ravens are more inclined to be nomadic than Australian Ravens, particularly in the drier inland areas. The majority of birds that breed above the snowline winter on the western slopes, after an intermediate sojourn in the forests feeding on phasmids. They form permanent pairs and may return to the same territory year after year to breed. Flocks are usually far larger than those of the Australian Raven (300:30) and characteristically may travel several hundred metres above ground level when changing location. Mixed assemblages do occur, the proportions of each species varying with season and district.

BREEDING: Little Ravens are far less demanding than Australian Ravens with regard to their nest tree. Nests are rarely above ten metres and are noticeably smaller. This greater tolerance enables the species to breed in places that the other species cannot, like the Western Plains, various treeless areas and the snow fields. Incubation lasts nineteen to twenty-one days. The average egg dimensions are 46 × 30 mm; eggs of the two species are indistinguishable, being pale blue-green on which are superimposed brown-olive blotches and freckles. The nestling period ranges between thirty-five to thirty-eight days; significantly shorter than for the Australian Raven.

The timing of breeding is more flexible in the Little Raven than the Australian Raven and, while the majority of birds on the tablelands and inland lay in August, laying in the Kosciusko National Park begins two months later. Young may still be found in the nest after Christmas.

FEEDING: Although omnivorous, it has a more slender bill than the Australian Raven and is adept at probing into cracks in dry soil and the like; carrion is less important and predation on stock is more myth than fact. The very large autumn flocks, numbering more than a thousand, feeding on phasmids in eucalypt forest are a feature of the area. (I.C.R.R.)

# BOWER-BIRDS

The family, containing the 43 species of birds-of-paradise and 18 bower-birds including the catbirds, is restricted to Australia, New Guinea and the Moluccas. Most species are endemic to New Guinea but Australia has four birds-of-paradise and nine bower-birds. One bower-bird is common in our area.

The bower-birds are a remarkable group, most of which build "playhouses" or bowers that are the central feature of the breeding territory and in and about which the birds court and mate. Some of these bowers are quite complex structures, decorated with coloured or shining objects. The design of the bower and the colour and arrangement of the decorations varies from species to species.

364

The complexity of the bower varies greatly. Three catbirds, *Ailuroedus*, do not build them but the fourth, the Stage-maker, *A. dentirostris* merely clears an arena on the ground and puts a few leaves and perhaps some snail shells on it. One group, the maypole-builders, select small saplings and pile twigs and sticks around them, up to three metres high. These cones often join up and form a roof or hut. Outside, the ground is decorated with moss, berries, flowers and coloured leaves; the cones of sticks are decorated also. The avenue-builders, including the Satin Bower-bird, build a dancing stage of sticks or ferns in the form of a mat, that can be more than a metre in diameter and on it some species build parallel walls of sticks rammed into the ground. The platform and the bower itself are well decorated with the particular species' preferred colours.

Bower-birds are not highly coloured as a rule but many are adorned with coloured crests or head ornaments. Several of the Australian birds, however, are brilliant. The Golden Bower-bird *Prionodura newtoniana* is a striking golden yellow, the Regent Bower-bird *Sericulus chrysocephalus* is jet black and golden yellow and the Satin Bower-bird glossy-blue.

They are all birds of the forests most being found in rainforest and a few in the denser inland scrubs. They are very active both in the air and on the ground and are mainly fruit-eaters.

Family Paradisaeidae — Birds-of-Paradise and Bower-birds
## SATIN BOWER-BIRD *Ptilonorhynchus violaceus*
PLATE XXI

IDENTIFICATION: Length, 32 cm. *Male: uniform deep lilac-blue all over*, the feathers are in fact black but have a refractive property that makes them appear blue; bill, blue with yellowish tip; legs and feet, greenish-yellow; iris, blue but varies greatly during courtship from light to very dark shades. *Female: general colour above, olive-green*, each feather prominently marked with brown; under-parts, generally lighter olive-green mottled with brown; wings, brown; tail, brown; bill, horn; legs and feet, greenish-yellow; iris, blue. Immatures of both sexes resemble the female but the feathers have light brown edges. Males begin to assume adult plumage at four years of age but may need two years before they are completely blue.

VOICE: The main call is a low, melancholy whistle "whee-ooo" but during display at the bower there are many other croaking, whirring and rattling notes.

DISTRIBUTION: It is distributed from the Atherton Tableland, north Queensland, to the Otway Ranges west of Melbourne. It is restricted to the wetter parts of the coastal strip where dense bushes or more open forests with heavy undergrowth occur. It seems to be absent or very rare in the drier parts of the coast as between Townsville and the Bunya Mountains, Queensland. Locally it is abundant in the wet sclerophyll forests and moist gullies in the ranges and in winter in the surrounding open country.

HABITS: The Satin Bower-bird can be found on the ground or in the undergrowth or in tall trees. In the summer it is restricted to the breeding territory and is seen taking short swift display flights or calling loudly from high perches. It is seldom seen at the bower without special watching from cover. In the autumn and winter it gathers into flocks of thirty or more birds that wander more widely through open forest and along scrubby creeks. These flocks always contain many more females and immatures, "green" birds, than the black adult males.

BREEDING: Males return to their breeding territories in late winter. On the New South Wales coast renovating or reconstruction of the bower begins as early as May or June but locally begins in August or September. If the bower is to be rebuilt the sticks are pulled up or broken off and removed to the new site, which is always nearby, and display objects that have retained their colour are taken along too.

The bower itself is a space sixty to ninety centimetres in diameter cleared and covered with fine, interlaced sticks to a depth of five to eight centimetres. Near the centre, two parallel walls of thin sticks, up to forty centimetres high, are built, they are about fifty centimetres long and twenty to twenty-five centimetres apart. The walls are some-times coated, "painted", with charcoal or macerated wood pulp. The platform is well decorated with coloured material; the male shows a strong preference for blue, but greenish-yellow, yellow and sometimes brown or grey are also used. The choice of material used is only limited by its colour and includes flowers, berries, feathers, an occasional coloured insect or shell as well as bits of broken glass, rag, paper or whatever can be found. If near human habitation the birds have no hesitation in removing suitable coloured objects from the vicinity of the house. Immature males build similar but less substantial bowers.

The male displays at the bower, running through the avenue, picking up display objects, "whirring", arching the neck and fanning the tail. The sound coming from the displaying male is considerable. The female is often present at the bower during display and copulation has been seen to occur within it.

The nest is built in the breeding territory, but not near the bower. It is an open cup-shaped structure, twenty-five centimetres in diameter, built of thin twigs and lined with partly dried leaves. It is built in a fork, usually less than fifteen metres from the ground. The eggs are laid in late spring but there are no precise data from this region. The clutch size is two but occasionally one or three are laid. The eggs are dark cream or buff in colour, spotted and blotched with brown and grey. They measure about $43 \times 30$ mm. The incubation period is nineteen to twenty-three days.

FEEDING: Its food is mainly fruit and, during the summer and late autumn, the nomadic flocks can do some damage to cultivated soft fruits. It also consumes insects, and locally, where there is little native fruit, doubtless these are a very important source of food, but there has been no quantitative study. (H.J.F.)

# APPENDIX

A list of the important general papers on the high-country bird life is given below:

Barrett, C.: 'Birds around a homestead' *Emu 21* (1922) pp. 257–61.

Jones, D.P.: 'List of birds of Canberra, the Federal Territory' *Emu 28* (1929) pp. 252–4.

Mathews, G.M.: *List of Birds of the Australian Capital Territory* Commonwealth Forestry Bureau Leaflet 53 (1943).

Lamm, D.W. and White, D.: 'The changing status of avifauna in the Australian Capital Territory' *Emu 49* (1950) pp. 199–204.

Lamm, D.W. and Calaby, J.H.: 'Seasonal variation of bird populations along the Murrumbidgee in the Australian Capital Territory' *Emu 50* (1950) pp. 114–22.

McKelvie, J.N.: 'Notes on birds of the Australian Capital Territory' *Emu 57* (1957) pp. 3–6

McEvey, A.: 'Zoology of the High Plains: Part II — birds and mammals' *Proceedings Royal Society of Victoria, 75* (1962) pp. 315–7.

Lamm, D.W., Wilson, S.J., and Belton, W.: 'New information or birds of the Australian Capital Territory' *Emu 63* (1963) pp. 57–65.

Lamm, D.W.: 'Seasonal counts of birds at Lake George, New South Wales' *Emu 64* (1965) pp. 114–28.

Lamm, D.W., and Wilson, S.J.: 'Seasonal fluctuations of birds in the Brindabella Range, Australian Capital Territory' *Emu 65* (1966) pp. 183–207.

*Canberra Bird Notes* No. 1 July 1968 — Vol 8, No.2 April 1983 (quarterly; continuing).

# INDEX

370

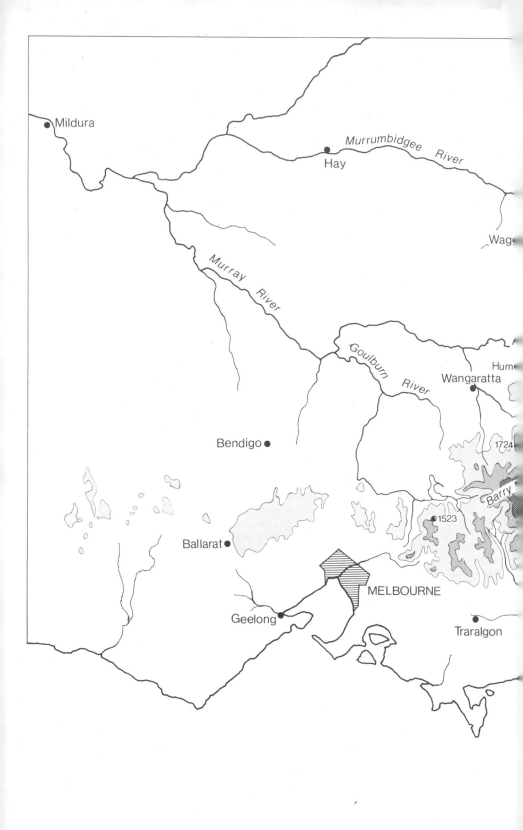

Mildura

Murrumbidgee River

Hay

Wag

Murray River

Goulburn River

Hum

Wangaratta

1724

Bendigo

Barry

Ballarat

1523

MELBOURNE

Geelong

Traralgon

15-